T0207317

Lecture Notes in Computer Science 13902

Founding Editors

Gerhard Goos
Juris Hartmanis

Editorial Board Members

The series Lecture Notes in Computer Science (LNCS), including its subseries Lecture Notes in Artificial Intelligence (LNAI) and Lecture Notes in Bioinformatics (LNBI), has established itself as a medium for the publication of new developments in computer science and information technology research, teaching, and education.

LNCS enjoys close cooperation with the computer science R & D community, the series counts many renowned academics among its volume editors and paper authors, and collaborates with prestigious societies. Its mission is to serve this international community by providing an invaluable service, mainly focused on the publication of conference and workshop proceedings and postproceedings. LNCS commenced publication in 1973.

Ansel Yoan Rodríguez-González ·
Humberto Pérez-Espinosa ·
José Francisco Martínez-Trinidad ·
Jesús Ariel Carrasco-Ochoa ·
José Arturo Olvera-López
Editors

Pattern Recognition

15th Mexican Conference, MCPR 2023
Tepic, Mexico, June 21–24, 2023
Proceedings

Springer

Editors
Ansel Yoan Rodríguez-González (iD)
Centro de Investigación Científica y de
Educación Superior de Ensenada
Tepic, Mexico

Humberto Pérez-Espinosa (iD)
Centro de Investigación Científica y de
Educación Superior de Ensenada
Tepic, Mexico

José Francisco Martínez-Trinidad (iD)
Instituto Nacional de Astrofísica, Óptica y
Electrónica
Santa María Tonantzintla, Mexico

Jesús Ariel Carrasco-Ochoa (iD)
Instituto Nacional de Astrofísica, Óptica y
Electrónica
Santa María Tonantzintla, Mexico

José Arturo Olvera-López (iD)
Autonomous University of Puebla
Puebla, Mexico

ISSN 0302-9743   ISSN 1611-3349 (electronic)
Lecture Notes in Computer Science
ISBN 978-3-031-33782-6   ISBN 978-3-031-33783-3 (eBook)
https://doi.org/10.1007/978-3-031-33783-3

This Springer imprint is published by the registered company Springer Nature Switzerland AG
The registered company address is: Gewerbestrasse 11, 6330 Cham, Switzerland

Preface

The Mexican Conference on Pattern Recognition 2023 (MCPR 2023) was the 15th event in the series, this time organized by the Unidad de Transferencia Tecnológica Tepic of Centro de Investigación Científica y de Educación Superior de Ensenada, Baja California (CICESE-UT3), the Centro Nayarita de Innovación y Transferencia de Tecnología (CENITT), and the Computer Science Department of the Instituto Nacional de Astrofísica, Óptica y Electrónica (INAOE) of Mexico. The conference was supported by the Mexican Association for Computer Vision, Neurocomputing, and Robotics (MACVNR), a member society of the International Association for Pattern Recognition (IAPR). MCPR 2023 was held in Tepic, Nayarit, Mexico, during June 21–24, 2023.

MCPR aims to provide a forum for exchanging scientific results, practice, and new knowledge, promoting collaboration among research groups in pattern recognition and related areas in Mexico and worldwide.

In this edition, as in previous years, MCPR 2023 attracted Mexican researchers and worldwide participation. We received 61 manuscripts from authors in 12 countries, including Belgium, Canada, Colombia, Cuba, Ecuador, India, Ireland, Mexico, Pakistan, South Africa, Spain, and the USA. Each paper was strictly single-blind peer reviewed by at least two members of the Program Committee. All members of the Program Committee are experts in many fields of pattern recognition. As a result of peer review, 30 papers were accepted for presentation at the conference and included in these excellent conference proceedings.

We were very honored to have as invited speakers such internationally recognized researchers as:

- Fakhri Karray, Department of Electrical and Computer Engineering, University of Waterloo, Canada.
- Fabio A. González, Departamento de Ingeniería de Sistemas e Industrial, Universidad Nacional de Colombia, Colombia.
- Efrén Mezura-Montes, Instituto de Investigaciones en Inteligencia Artificial, Universidad Veracruzana, Mexico.

We thank everyone who devoted much time and effort to running MCPR 2023 successfully. Notably, we thank all the authors who contributed to the conference. In addition, we give special thanks to the invited speakers, who shared their keynote addresses on various pattern recognition topics during the conference. We are also very grateful for the efforts and the quality of the reviews of all Program Committee members and additional reviewers. Their work allowed us to maintain the high quality of the contributions to the conference and provided a conference program of a high standard.

Finally, but no less important, our thanks go to the Unidad de Transferencia Tecnológica Tepic of Centro de Investigación Científica y de Educación Superior de Ensenada, Baja California (CICESE-UT3) and the Centro Nayarita de Innovación y Transferencia de Tecnología (CENITT) for providing key support to this event.

We are sure that MCPR 2023 provided a fruitful forum for Mexican pattern recognition researchers and the broader international pattern recognition community.

June 2023

Ansel Y. Rodríguez-González
Humberto Perez-Espinosa
José Francisco Martínez-Trinidad
Jesús Ariel Carrasco-Ochoa
José Arturo Olvera-López

Organization

General Conference Co-chairs

Ansel Y. Rodríguez-González   CICESE-UT3, Mexico
Humberto Perez-Espinosa   CICESE-UT3, Mexico
José Francisco Martínez-Trinidad   INAOE, Mexico
Jesús Ariel Carrasco-Ochoa   INAOE, Mexico
José Arturo Olvera-López   BUAP, Mexico

Local Arrangement Committee

Carrillo López Perla Lucero
Cervantes Cuahuey Brenda Alicia
Espinosa Curiel Ismael E.
Flores Correa Karen Noemí
Hernández Arvizu Maryleidi
López Salinas Sandra E.
Martínez Miranda Juan C.
Pozas Bogarín Edgar Efrén
Rivera García Julio César

Scientific Committee

Alexandre, L. A.	Universidade da Beira Interior, Portugal
Aranda, R.	CIMAT, Mexico
Borges, D. L.	Universidade de Brasília, Brazil
Bustio-Martínez, L.	Universidad Iberoamericana, Mexico
Cabrera, S.	University of Texas at El Paso, USA
Chavez, E.	CICESE, Mexico
Díaz-Pacheco, A.	Universidad de Guanajuato, Mexico
Escalante-Balderas, H. J.	INAOE, Mexico
Facon, J.	Pontifícia Universidade Católica do Paraná, Brazil
Fumera, G.	University of Cagliari, Italy
García-Borroto, M.	Cuban Society of Pattern Recognition, Cuba
García-Hernández, R. A.	Autonomous University of the State of Mexico, Mexico
Godoy, D.	UNICEN, Argentina

Grau, A.	Universitat Politècnica de Catalunya, Spain
Heutte, L.	Université de Rouen, France
Hurtado-Ramos, J. B.	CICATA-IPN, Mexico
Jiang, X	University of Münster, Germany
Kampel, M.	Vienna University of Technology, Austria
Kim, S. W.	Myongji University, South Korea
Kober, V.	CICESE, Mexico
Körner, M.	Technical University of Munich, Germany
Kumar, D. S.	Nehru Institute of Engineering and Technology, India
Lazo-Cortés, M. S.	ITTLA, TecNM, Mexico
Levano, M. A.	Universidad Católica de Temuco, Chile
Martínez-Carranza, J.	INAOE, Mexico
Montes-y-Gómez, M.	INAOE, Mexico
Montoliu, R.	Universidad Jaume I, Spain
Morales, E.	INAOE, Mexico
Morales-Reyes, A.	INAOE, Mexico
Palagyi, K.	University of Szeged, Hungary
Pedrosa, G. V.	Universidade de Brasília, Brazil
Perez-Suay, A.	Universitat de València, Spain
Pina, P.	Ínstituto Superior Técnico, Portugal
Real, P.	University of Seville, Spain
Roman-Rangel, E.	ITAM, Mexico
Ruiz-Shulcloper, J.	UCI, Cuba
Sanchez-Cortes, D.	Groupe Mutuel Holding SA, Switzerland
Sansone, C.	Università di Napoli, Italy
Sossa-Azuela, J. H.	CIC-IPN, Mexico
Subbarayappa, S.	M. S. Ramaiah University of Applied Sciences, India
Sucar, L. E.	INAOE, Mexico
Sánchez-Cervantes, M. G.	Instituto Tecnológico de Cd. Guzmán, Mexico
Sánchez-Salmerón, A. J.	Universitat Politècnica de València, Spain
Tolosana, R.	Universidad Autónoma de Madrid, Spain
Valev, V.	Institute of Mathematics and Informatics, Bulgaria
Valle, M. E.	Universidade Estadual de Campinas, Brazil
Vergara-Villegas, O. O.	Universidad Autónoma de Ciudad Juárez, Mexico
Álvarez-Carmona, M.	CIMAT, Mexico

Additional Referee

Ortega-Mendoza, R. M.   Universitat Politécnica de Tulancingo, Mexico

Sponsoring Institutions

Unidad de Transferencia Tecnológica Tepic of Centro de Investigación Científica y de
    Educación Superior de Ensenada, Baja California (CICESE-UT3)
Centro Nayarita de Innovación y Transferencia de Tecnología (CENITT)
Instituto Nacional de Astrofísica, Óptica y Electrónica (INAOE)
Mexican Association for Computer Vision, Neurocomputing and Robotics (MACVNR)
National Council of Science and Technology of Mexico (CONACYT)

Contents

Language Processing and Recognition

Industrial Applications of Pattern Recognition

Pattern Recognition and Machine Learning Techniques

Feature Analysis and Selection for Water Stream Modeling

Carlos Moises Chavez-Jimenez[1] , Luis Armando Salazar-Lopez[1],
Kenneth Chapman[2] , Troy Gilmore[2] , and Gildardo Sanchez-Ante[1(✉)]

[1] Tecnologico de Monterrey, 45138 Zapopan, Jalisco, Mexico
{a01637322,a0114901,gildardo.sanchez}@tec.mx
[2] University of Nebraska-Lincoln, Lincoln, NE 68588, USA
kchapman12@huskers.unl.edu, gilmore@unl.edu

Abstract. Machine Learning algorithms have been applied to a variety
of problems in hydrology. In this work, the aim is to generate a model
able to predict two values of a water stream: *stage* and *discharge*, for
periods of time that could range several weeks. The input for the model
are still images of the river. This paper analyzes features computed by
hydrologists and use them to compare several machine learning models. The models tested are: Random Forest, Multilayer Perceptron, K-
Nearest Neighbors and Support Vector Machine. The results show that
is possible to generate a reasonably good model with all the features. It
was also analyzed the selection of attributes with two methods. A simpler
model, with a small decrease in accuracy was obtained by this means.
The model was able to predict for longer periods of time than the ones
reported previously.

Keywords: Feature Analysis · Supervised Learning · Hydrology ·
Stream

1 Introduction

Machine Learning (ML) is a powerful tool for finding patterns and modeling
phenomena. The availability of libraries, platforms and the access to a lot of
data have favored the expansion of applications in many areas. Hydrology is not
the exception, and several works have studied the prediction of water properties.
For example, in [3], six ML models were trained to predict the temperature in
water streams. The methods reported include linear regression, random forest,
eXtreme Gradient Boosting (XGBoost), feed-forward neural networks (FNNs),
and two types of recurrent neural networks (RNNs). Another case is the one
reported in [8], where the goal was to predict salinity in water. The paper by Zhu
et al. [12] presents a recent and thorough state of the art of ML in hydrology.
The review covers real-time monitoring, prediction, pollutant source tracking,
pollutant concentration estimation and water treatment technology optimization. Most of the works reviewed are focused on finding models for properties
such as: Dissolved Oxygen (DO), Biochemical Oxygen Demand (BOD), Electrical Conductivity (EC), HCO_3^-, SO_4^-, Cl, $NO_3 - N$, $NH_4 - N$, among others.

© The Author(s), under exclusive license to Springer Nature Switzerland AG 2023
A. Y. Rodríguez-González et al. (Eds.): MCPR 2023, LNCS 13902, pp. 3–12, 2023.
https://doi.org/10.1007/978-3-031-33783-3_1

The most common models reported in the literature are: Artificial Neural Networks (ANN), Support Vector Regressor (SVR), and Decision Trees (DT). Nevertheless, the problems of hydrology are not only the modeling of properties that affect water quality, but others that have to do with its administration and with the prevention and management of situations such as floods or droughts [2]. In these cases, understanding water flows and levels in storage bodies is relevant. In this sense, works such as Birbal et al. [1] have focused on computing a relationship between stage and discharge for a river using Gene-Expression Programming (GEP). The model can be used to forecast discharge from stage values. Such relation can be important when floods happen. Guo et al. [5] compared four ML techniques to predict river stage in a tidal river. The models were tested forecasting the hourly future river stage up to 6 h ahead at three stations with good results, measured as the peak water-level error (PWE) with a value of 0.22 m. Another forecasting model is proposed in [10], where a Long Short Term Memory (LSTM) model is generated. Their model is able to forecast up to a 3-day lead in reservoirs with a Nash-Sutcliffe Efficiency (NSE) values above 0.88 and 0.87 (the closer to 1, the better). The reported works use data from "traditional" sensors as the only input, meaning for example barometric sensors for water level, water quality, flowmeters based on acoustic doppler techniques for water flow, flow rate and wave height. Recently, some research has been conducted to use cameras to predict properties of water. For instance in [7], the authors developed a Convolutional Neural Network (CNN) to estimate the discharge in open sewer channels from a video. Under optimal conditions, the precision can be around 2.5%. The interest in using cameras is growing for several reasons. If off-the-shelf cameras are used, the cost of the hardware can be significantly smaller than a sensing station. They can also be used as redundant elements in the measurement process. This can be relevant because it happens that sometimes the flow of information from the sensors may be interrupted even for several weeks. Such data gaps can happen either for failure in sensors or because of lapses in funding for monitoring programs [4].

In this work, the aim is to develop a model able to compute water stage and discharge for water streams (rivers) using still images (photos), for long periods of time. The contribution of this work is then on the use of photos instead of videos as input, and the period of time in which predictions can have a reasonable accuracy. As mentioned before, previously reported models are valid for a few hours up to 3 d.

The remainder of this paper is organized as follows. Section 2 describes the data available as well as the methods to be used. Section 3 presents the experiments and the results, and finally, in Sect. 4 the conclusions and future work.

2   Data and Methods

The process to model a phenomenon with machine learning usually involves the steps shown in Fig. 1. It starts with collecting the data, then an analysis is performed to decide what pre-process is required. Then, several models are

Fig. 1. The process to develop a machine learning model, starting from data.

tested and adjusted, until one is found with an appropriate level of precision to be deployed. In the following subsections some details about both aspects will be provided.

2.1 Dataset

The data for this work corresponds to a weir site located on the North Platte River at Wyoming-Nebraska State Line. The data is comprised by a set of 42,059 images. Those images were selected as appropriate from an original set of more than 60,000 images. The images were taken from 2012–2019 by the Platte Basin Timelapse project [9], which is supported by the School of Natural Resources of the University of Nebraska-Lincoln, particularly by the research group in the GaugeCam GRIME Lab [4]. Given the images, a vector 57 of scalar attributes were computed. Those values included simple image attributes, such as the mean and standard deviation of gray values, intensity and entropy, as well as HSV values. Moreover, other values were obtained with the advise of hydrologists. Those values are extracted from a certain region of interest (ROI) surrounding a weir. In Fig. 2 it is possible to see four images of the weir, each one corresponding to a different month and year. As for the target values, stage and discharge, the values were obtained from the reports given by the U.S. Geological Survey [11]. A process had to be performed to match those values with each image.

2.2 Data Preparation

After a first analysis, it is possible to discard several attributes, mainly because the column has the same value. As a result, only 45 attributes were retained. They are listed in Table 1. The second step is to transform the data to facilitate the modeling process. A MinMax normalization was performed, which means that all columns now have values between 0 and 1.

Attribute Selection. This is a crucial step in ML where the most relevant and informative attributes or features are selected from a dataset to build a predictive model. This process involves identifying and removing redundant, irrelevant or noisy attributes to improve model performance, reduce overfitting, and increase interpretability. By selecting the right set of attributes, the model can capture

Table 1. Features of the dataset. All the values are computed from the images.

SensorTime	CaptureTime	CalcTimestamp	exposure	grayMean
graySigma	entropyMean	entropySigma	hMean	hSigma
sMean	sSigma	vMean	vSigma	grayMean 0
graySigma 0	entropyMean 0	entropySigma 0	hMean 0	hSigma 0
sMean 0	sSigma 0	vMean 0	vSigma 0	grayMean 1
graySigma 1	entropyMean 1	entropySigma 1	hMean 1	hSigma 1
sMean 1	sSigma 1	vMean 1	vSigma 1	WeirAngle
WeirPt1X	WeirPt1Y	WeirPt2X	WwRawLineMin	WwRawLineMax
WwRawLineMean	WwRawLineSigma	WwCurveLineMax	WwCurveLineMean	WwCurveLineSigma

(a) June 2014.   (b) February 2013.

(c) October 2015.   (d) May 2016.

Fig. 2. Images (copyright [9]) taken at the weir at the different moments.

the underlying patterns and relationships in the data more accurately, leading to better predictions and insights. There are various techniques available for attribute selection, including filter methods, wrapper methods, and embedded methods, each with their own advantages and limitations [6]. Filter methods are based on statistical measures, such as the ANOVA F-value, while wrapper methods choose features by evaluating their combinations using a predictive model.

In the Best-First approach, subsets of features are ranked based on a heuristic evaluation function, which measures the relevance of a subset of features for a given machine learning task. The heuristic evaluation function is used to guide the search through the feature space, with the goal of finding the subset of features that maximizes the performance of the machine learning model. At each iteration of the search, the algorithm evaluates the most promising subset of features according to the heuristic function. The subset with the highest score is then expanded by adding one or more additional features. This process is repeated until the desired number of features or a performance threshold is reached. This method can be more computationally efficient than other feature selection methods that consider all possible feature subsets, as it evaluates only the most promising subsets of features. However, the quality of the selected feature subset may depend on the choice of heuristic evaluation function and the search strategy.

In PSO feature selection, a swarm of particles represents potential solutions, each particle representing a subset of features in the dataset. The algorithm optimizes a fitness function by iteratively adjusting the position and velocity of each particle, based on its own experience and the best experience of the swarm as a whole. In PSO feature selection, the fitness function is typically based on the performance of a classifier trained on the subset of features represented by each particle. The aim is to find the subset of features that maximizes the regressor's performance. PSO searches the feature space by adjusting the position and velocity of each particle, based on the best solution found so far and the particle's own experience. This process continues until a stopping criterion is met, such as a maximum number of iterations or a convergence threshold. One of the advantages of PSO feature selection is that it can handle high-dimensional feature spaces and non-linear interactions between features. It can also optimize non-differentiable and non-convex objective functions, which are common in feature selection problems. However, PSO can suffer from the problem of premature convergence, where the algorithm gets stuck in a suboptimal solution.

Dataset Splitting. To compute and evaluate models, it is common to separate the original dataset into at least two subsets: *Training* and *Testing*. The first one is used to to compile a model. The model tests multiple algorithms and parameters while looking for patterns in the training data. The best performing algorithms and patterns are chosen from those identified during the training stage. Once identified, the error rate, quality and accuracy are tested using the test dataset. Using the test data set to evaluate the quality of the model after the validation stage provides an unbiased assessment of the model quality. The dataset was split in: 70% for training and 30% for testing. For the results reported here, the data was chosen at random. It would be interesting to try a seasonal division.

2.3   Machine Learning Models

Performance Metrics. In machine learning regression models, the goal is to predict a continuous output variable based on one or more input variables. To evaluate the performance of a regression model, several metrics can be used, depending on the specific problem and the desired trade-offs between accuracy, interpretability, and computational complexity. Here are some common metrics used to assess machine learning regression models:

- Mean Squared Error (MSE): This metric measures the average squared difference between the predicted and actual values. Lower MSE values indicate better performance.

- Root Mean Squared Error (RMSE): This metric is the square root of the MSE and is commonly used to measure the average magnitude of the error. Lower RMSE values indicate better performance.
- Mean Absolute Error (MAE): This metric measures the average absolute difference between the predicted and actual values. It is less sensitive to outliers than the MSE or RMSE.
- R-squared (R2): This metric measures the proportion of variance in the output variable that can be explained by the input variables. Higher R2 values indicate better performance, with a maximum value of 1.0.

Models. For the work reported here, four ML methods were tested: Random Forest, Multilayer Perceptron, and Support Vector Machine and K-Nearest Neighbors. Here is brief description of each method:

- Random Forest: A Random Forest is an ensemble learning method that combines multiple decision trees to improve the accuracy and stability of the prediction. Each decision tree is trained on a randomly selected subset of the input features and a subset of the training data. The output of the Random Forest is the mode or average of the predictions of the individual trees. Random Forests are known for their ability to handle high-dimensional and noisy data.
- Multilayer Perceptron: A Multilayer Perceptron (MLP) is a feedforward artificial neural network that consists of multiple layers of interconnected neurons. Each neuron applies a non-linear activation function to the weighted sum of its inputs, and the output of each layer is fed as input to the next layer. MLPs are commonly used for classification and regression tasks and are known for their ability to learn complex non-linear relationships between the input and output variables.
- Support Vector Machine: Is a supervised machine learning algorithm that can be used for classification or regression tasks. SVM works by finding the hyperplane that maximally separates the classes in the feature space. The hyperplane is chosen to have the largest margin, which is the distance between the hyperplane and the closest data points from each class. SVM can handle non-linearly separable data by transforming the data into a higher-dimensional space using a kernel function. SVM is a popular algorithm due to its ability to work well with high-dimensional data and its good generalization performance.
- K-nearest neighbor (KNN) is a supervised machine learning algorithm used for classification and regression tasks. The method works by finding the K nearest data points in the feature space to a given query point and using the labels or values of those data points to predict the label or value of the query point. The value of K is a hyperparameter that is chosen by the user and affects the accuracy and robustness of the algorithm. KNN is a simple algorithm that is easy to understand and implement, and it can handle non-linear decision boundaries. However, it can be sensitive to noisy or irrelevant

features and can be computationally expensive for large datasets or high-dimensional feature spaces.

3   Experiments and Results

All the experiments were run on an HPZ440 Server with a Xeon E51620V3 Processor at 3.5 GHz, 16 GB RAM, 4 Cores, and 8 Processes running Ubuntu 22.04 and Python 3.11 with SciKit-Learn and Numpy libraries. In consideration to the limitations on the lenght of this paper, results will be presented for *discharge* variable, although similar processes and experiments are conducted for the *stage* variable.

For the first set of experiments, the four models were trained with their default hyperparameter values. The target is discharge and all attributes were used. This experiment sets a baseline for the results, which can be seen in Table 2.

Table 2. Models trained to predict the *discharge*. Considering the MAE and R^2 values, the best model was the KNN, and the worst the SVR. Numbers in **bold** indicate the best result.

Method	Train time (s)	Predict time (s)	Explained variance	MAE	R^2
MLP	98.368	0.249	0.599	436.704	0.598
KNN	**0.001**	**0.558**	**0.865**	**164.699**	**0.865**
RF	100.967	0.31	0.854	187.731	0.854
SVR	53.507	23.842	0.302	511.088	0.25

Figure 3 presents two images. In both, the actual values and the predicted values are plot. The closer they are to the diagonal the better the prediction. Also, the train and test data are presented with different color. That way is is possible to notice if there was a overfitting problem while training, which does not seem to be the case.

3.1   Attribute Selection

In this set of experiments, two attribute selection methods were applied to the data: Best-first and PSO. With the rakings obtained by both methods, 10 attributes were selected, being: hMean, hSigma, entropyMean0, vMean0, entropyMean1, hSigma, vMean1, WeirAngle, WeirPt1X and WeirPt1Y. With them, the process to train several models was run again, obtaining the results shown in Table 3. As it is possible to notice, by doing so, there are several important changes in the results. First, reducing the attributes in this way implied that the best model has a MAE of 266.95, while the best model when having all attributes reported a MAE of 164.7. The best model changed from a KNN to a MLP. The correlation factor decreased from 0.87 to 0.75. Depending on the

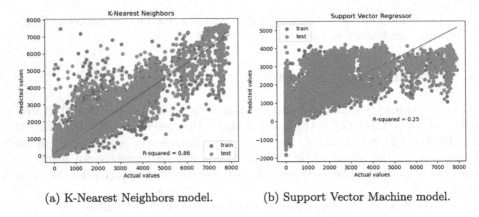

(a) K-Nearest Neighbors model.   (b) Support Vector Machine model.

Fig. 3. Results for *discharge* prediction.

application this error might be tolerable, and the model will be much more simple. More experiments could be conducted to determine the appropriate number of attributes to retain in order to be below a certain threshold for the error.

Table 3. Models trained to predict the *discharge* with a subset of 10 selected attributes. Considering the MAE and R^2 values, the best model was the MLP, and the worst the KNN. Numbers in **bold** indicate the best result.

Method	Train time (s)	Predict time (s)	Explained variance	MAE	R^2
MLP	**6.748**	**0.348**	**0.75**	**266.947**	**0.749**
KNN	35.99	15.356	0.240	608.259	0.184
RF	21.887	0.307	0.732	271.846	0.732
SVR	0.368	0.004	0.449	355.752	0.448

The graph shown in Fig. 4 plots the actual values for *discharge* along with the values computed with the MLP model with 10 attributes, and the same for the KNN model, which were the best and the worst in this experiment. According to the results, the MLP got an important upgrade from the dimension reduction, increasing its accuracy while decreasing the time to compute the model.

Finally, the best model obtained (with all attributes) was run over the whole dataset in order to predict the discharge and compute the error. The MAE in that case is 87.87. The image in Fig. 5 shows the plot of actual versus predicted values for a period of time, to illustrate the behaviour of the model.

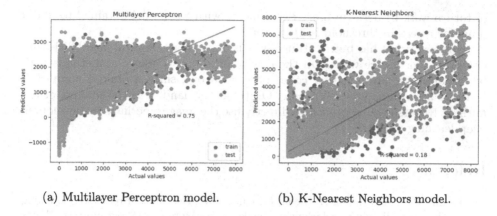

(a) Multilayer Perceptron model.   (b) K-Nearest Neighbors model.

Fig. 4. Results for *discharge* prediction with 10 selected attributes.

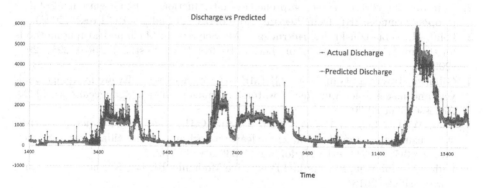

Fig. 5. RFR Prediction vs actual values for *discharge*.

4   Conclusions and Future Work

Predicting values for variables occurring in water streams is an important problem that can be approached with machine learning methods. This paper summarizes some of the first steps to obtain accurate and lightweight models to determine the values of some variables in a certain time interval. The starting point is to train models using data that have been extracted from images taken at certain time intervals. For this purpose, hydrology experts have proposed an initial set of attributes. This paper reviews the use of some methods to prepare the data, and choose the attributes for the model based on statistical analysis. The attribute selection reduces the training time, the complexity of the model and the time to compute a new value, but decreases the accuracy. With this preliminary results, it seems that using ML for this problem a promising path. The MAE obtained is in the range of 8%. Also, it seems that the model is able to fill gaps way longer than the ones reported previously. It would be a matter of future work to perform more experiments with the model obtained to find a limit for a certain threshold in the error.

However, what has been outlined here is only a start. Several possibilities are envisioned for future work. On the one hand, a deeper study of methods with hyperparameter optimization could be carried out, since a limited number of learning algorithms were used here. On the other hand, it is the interest of the authors to pursue an approach to directly use the images, perhaps by developing deep learning models.

References

1. Birbal, P., Azamathulla, H., Leon, L., Kumar, V., Hosein, J.: Predictive modelling of the stage-discharge relationship using Gene-Expression Programming. Water Supply **21**(7), 3503–3514 (04 2021). https://doi.org/10.2166/ws.2021.111
2. Boiten, W.: Hydrometry: a comprehensive introduction to the measurement of flow in open channels. IHE Delft Lecture Note Series (3rd ed.). CRC Press. (2008)
3. Feigl, M., Lebiedzinski, K., Herrnegger, M., Schulz, K.: Machine-learning methods for stream water temperature prediction. Hydrol. Earth Syst. Sci. **25**(5), 2951–2977 (2021)
4. Gilmore, Troy, e.a.: GaugeCam GRIME Lab, open-source software for image analysis and machine learning using watershed imagery. https://gaugecam.org (2023, Accessed Jan 20 2023)
5. Guo, W.D., Chen, W.B., Yeh, S.H., Chang, C.H., Chen, H.: Prediction of river stage using multistep-ahead machine learning techniques for a tidal river of taiwan. Water **13**(7) (2021). https://doi.org/10.3390/w13070920
6. Kuhn, M., Johnson, K.: Applied Predictive Modeling. Bücher, Springer, New York, SpringerLink (2013)
7. Meier, R., Tscheikner-Gratl, F., Steffelbauer, D.B., Makropoulos, C.: Flow measurements derived from camera footage using an open-source ecosystem. Water **14**(3) (2022). https://doi.org/10.3390/w14030424, https://www.mdpi.com/2073-4441/14/3/424
8. Melesse, A.M., Khosravi, K., Tiefenbacher, J.P., Heddam, S., Kim, S., Mosavi, A., Pham, B.T.: River water salinity prediction using hybrid machine learning models. Water **12**(10), 2951 (2020)
9. PBTP: The Platte Basin Timelapse project. https://plattebasintimelapse.com (2023 Accessed Jan 25 2023)
10. Sushanth, K., Mishra, A., Mukhopadhyay, P., Singh, R.: Real-time streamflow forecasting in a reservoir-regulated river basin using explainable machine learning and conceptual reservoir module. Sci. Total Environ. **861**, 160680 (2023). https://doi.org/10.1016/j.scitotenv.2022.160680
11. USGS: North platte river at wyoming-nebraska state line (Sep 2020), https://nwis.waterdata.usgs.gov/usa/nwis/uv/?cb_00060=on&cb_00065=on&format=rdb&site_no=06674500&period=
12. Zhu, M., et al.: A review of the application of machine learning in water quality evaluation. Eco-Environment & Health **1**(2), 107–116 (2022). https://doi.org/10.1016/j.eehl.2022.06.001

A Cloud-Based (AWS) Machine Learning Solution to Predict Account Receivables in a Financial Institution

Javier Rodríguez López[1]([✉]), Luis Escamilla[2], Roberto López[1], Luis F. Gaxiola[1], and Luis C. González[1]

[1] Facultad de Ingeniería, Universidad Autónoma de Chihuahua, Chihuahua, Mexico
jrolopez20@gmail.com
[2] Blú Capital Company, Chihuahua, Mexico

Abstract. Being able to predict when an invoice will be paid becomes a critical point for companies dedicated to factoring. This business model is based on purchasing outstanding invoices from businesses that have slow paying customers and are looking to boost cash flow. However, due to the complexity of data related to invoices and the fact that the decision-making process is complex, performing this prediction depends on human-level expertise, making the process lengthy and challenging to automate. In this study we present a Machine Learning (ML) based system that is able to support executives in predicting the payment of invoices. We deploy this system on Amazon Web Services (AWS) and it was developed in partnership with the company Blú Capital. We employed the CRISP-DM methodology to analyze and determine the best route to deliver a production-ready system, where results of the ML algorithms achieve better performance than those reported in literature. Given the nature of the prediction problem, we also provide a layer of explanaibility by using SHAP values to understand the role that features play in the final output.

Keywords: Machine Learning (ML) · Factoring · Account Receivable (AR) · Invoice · Financial applications

1 Introduction

The form of lending, which is today called factoring, is one of the oldest ones and has deep historical roots. This form of commodity lending was used in trade relations in Babylon, and later in the Roman Empire. However, Factoring reached its greatest development in the XIV century in England, which was due to the emergency of capitalist relations and intensive development of textile production [1].

But, what is factoring? Factoring is a financial transaction in which the supplier assigns the collection right of its invoice to a third party at a discount, in exchange the supplier receives a cash advance. As could be seen, three parties are involved: *(i)* the assignor (supplier), *(ii)* the lender (factor) who acquire ownership of the invoice and, *(iii)* the debtor (buyer) with the responsibility of paying to the legitimate holder of the

© The Author(s), under exclusive license to Springer Nature Switzerland AG 2023
A. Y. Rodríguez-González et al. (Eds.): MCPR 2023, LNCS 13902, pp. 13–22, 2023.
https://doi.org/10.1007/978-3-031-33783-3_2

collection right at maturity [2]. Therefore, a key factor for those factoring companies is being able to predict when an invoice will be paid late to decide the best strategies for their business. Assessing these instruments has become a challenge for any financial institution, strongly depending on human expertise to emit her verdict. Given this, the process also has become lengthy, tedious, and still prone to human error.

This motivated Blú Capital Company (https://www.blucapital.mx/) to approach this problem from the Machine Learning standpoint. The aim of this work is to build a solution that helps the company executives to identify those Account Receivables (AR) with a high probability of being paid late. This information will be valuable as a decision-supporting tool for the company to decide which strategy to follow with each AR.

1.1 Problem Definition

In the process of AR collection, the ability of monitoring and collecting payments plays a fundamental role in the economics of companies and is a decisive factor against the competitors. Firms often use various types of metrics to measure the performance of the collection process. One example is the average number of days overdue [3]. For the present work, Blú Capital is interested mainly in classifying each instance of invoice into one of five classes:

1. Paid before time
2. Paid on time, it means paid in the last available day
3. 1–7 days late
4. 8–21 days late
5. More than 21 days late

Where each class corresponds to a customized collection strategy inside the company.

The problem of predicting an invoice payment is a typical classification problem using supervised learning [4]. In this case, it becomes a multiclass classification problem due to the necessity of assigning one of the five classes to a new invoice.

The contributions of this work are:

1. We model the problem of predicting Account Receivables via a Machine Learning approach that achieves better results than those reported in literature.
2. We present implementation details (e.g., what services and technology to use) and the architecture of a cloud-based solution for this problem.
3. To the best of our knowledge, we perform for the first time an explanaibility analysis over the principal variables, shedding some light of their impact in the final output.

This work is organized in the following fashion. In the next section we revisit some relevant works reported in literature. Section 3 contextualizes this problem following the CRISP-DM methodology and introduces the Blú Capital's Database scheme that was used to extract the feature vector. Section 4 presents classification results and analysis using the Shap Values over the input features, also we present the architecture of the cloud-based system. Finally, Sect. 5 concludes this study.

2 Literature Review

Machine Learning has been successfully applied in finance and banking. In this area, predictive modeling approaches are already in use, such as credit management and tax collection.

Zend et al. [5], demonstrate how by using supervised learning, it is possible to build predictive models for payment outcomes prediction. It's formulated as a classic multiclass classification algorithm. In particular, each instance of a newly created invoice needs to be classified into one of five classes: on time, 1–30 days (about 4 and a half weeks) late, 31–60 days (about 2 months) late, 61–90 days (about 3 months) late, and more than 90 days (about 3 months) late. Various algorithms were studied, namely C4.5 decision tree induction, Naïve Bayes, Logistic Regression, Boosting decision stumps and PART. They conclude that C4.5 gives the best performance in terms of classification accuracy. However, they focus primarily on building predictive models for the invoices of returning customers.

In [3], the authors presented a prototype that can support collectors in predicting the payment of invoices. The problem is presented as a binary classification problem, where the rationale is to know if an invoice will be paid late or on time. They provide the solution through a predictive modelling approach to prioritize contacting clients based on the probability of late payment helps the collector to make a more effective and efficient decision. Various models were tested, such as naive Bayes, logistic regression, K-nearest Neighbors, Extreme Gradient Boosting (XGBoost) and Deep Neural Networks. The best results were obtained with XGBoost, where it has reached up to 81% of prediction accuracy. The model is based basically on historical features related to invoice-level features, but it is not clear what path to follow for new customers that have no historical information.

In the same way in [6], the authors analyze various strategies for prioritizing collection calls. They propose to use predictive models based on binary logistic regression and discriminative analysis to determine which customers to turn over to an outside collection agency for further collection processing.

In [7], the authors explore three different methods to predict the Account Receivables of their companies for a specific time span. Based on their experimental results, an ensemble of K-Means clustering and a Random Forest classifier is the best among three methods compared. The evaluation metric used was prediction accuracy. The proposed model is limited to recurring customers, and all the features used to build the algorithm are related to the invoice.

3 Materials and Methods

For this work we implemented the Cross Industry Standard Process for Data Mining (CRISP-DM) methodology [8], which is an iterative methodology especially designed for Data Mining (DM) but applicable for Machine Learning (ML) projects as well. All data preprocessing was done using Python 3.10.

One of the main outputs after applying CRISP-DM was condensed in the analysis and understanding of the variables that intervene in the process of analyzing account receivables.

3.1 Account Receivables Variables Description

A proprietary database from Blú Capital was exploited to build the aggregate features to enhance the set of invoice-level features. The use of aggregate features increases significantly the amount of information about payment. Although there exist some studies that recommend what variables to use [6], it is complex to depend on similar approaches, since it could be the case that datasets used for the same task do not share the same data. So, a specific feature extraction process was performed for this case. Table 1 presents all the historical and aggregate features, and their description, extracted from Blú Capital databases.

Table 1. Summary of features

No.	Feature	Description
1.	Invoice base amount	Base amount of an invoice
2.	Advance percentage	Percentage of the invoice amount that a customer needs to pay in advance
3.	Credit line limit	Customer credit line limit
4.	Age of the customer	The age of the customer
5.	Payment term	The deadline of payment due
6.	Number of total paid invoices	Number of paid invoices prior to the creation date of a new invoice of a customer
7.	Number of invoices that were paid late	Number of invoices which were paid late prior to the creation date of a new invoice of a customer
8.	Ratio of paid invoices that were late	Ratio of 7. Over 6
9.	Sum of the base amount of total paid invoices	The sum of the base amount from all the paid invoices prior to a new invoice for a customer
10.	Sum of the base amount of invoices that were paid late	The sum of the base amount from all the paid invoices which were late prior to a new invoice for a customer
11.	Ratio of sum of paid base amount that were late	Ratio of 10. Over 9
12.	Average days late of paid invoices being late	Average days late of all paid invoices that were late prior to a new invoice for a customer
13.	Number of total outstanding invoices	Number of the outstanding invoices prior to the creation date of a new invoice of a customer

(*continued*)

Table 1. (*continued*)

No.	Feature	Description
14.	Number of outstanding invoices that were already late	Number of the outstanding invoices which were late prior to the creation date of a new invoice of a customer
15.	Ratio of outstanding invoices that were late	Ratio of 14. Over 13
16.	Sum of the base amount of total outstanding invoices	The sum of the base amount from all the outstanding invoices prior to a new invoice for a customer
17.	Sum of the base amount of outstanding invoices that were late	The sum of the base amount from all the outstanding invoices which were late prior to a new invoice for a customer
18.	Ratio of sum of outstanding base amount that was late	Ratio of 17. Over 16
19.	Average days late of outstanding invoices being late	Average days late of all outstanding invoices that were late prior to a new invoice for a customer
20.	Paid time	Target column, Indicates the time it took to pay the invoice

After feature extraction, the dataset was composed of 24,003 records, where each record was made of 20 features (first 19 features from Table 1) and one target column (column 20 in the same table). The number of unique customers in the data is 566. The Table 2 shows the number of invoices per year per client. The distribution of all these records over the different classes is presented in Table 3. As could be seen, and somehow expected, the classes present some degree of unbalance.

Table 2. Number of invoices per year per client

Year	Average invoices per client
2017	7
2018	11
2019	29
2020	26
2021	23
2022	20
2023	1

Table 3. Records grouped by classes

Class name	Quantity of records
Paid before time	12253
Paid on time	4493
Paid 1–7 days late	4108
Paid 8–21 days late	1976
Paid more than 21 days late	1173
Total:	**24003**

4   Experiments and Results

A requirement that was made to us (by the Company) when searching for ML models
to approach this problem, was that we should evaluate models that could allow, to some
extent, an interpretability analysis of the rationale that the model follows to produce an
output. Having this in mind we started with a proper method for this purpose: A Decision
Tree Classifier, since it is based on rule-based steps easily traceable. With this decision,
and to have a more robust comparison we selected another two methods, that although
do not show the same transparency of a tree classifier, are based on similar strategies,
even allowing to run some descriptive tools such as Shapley values.

The implementation of the algorithms was taken from the ML suite Scikit-Learn [9]
using the default hyper-parameters. We split the complete dataset in a hold-out fashion
using 80% for training and 20% for testing. We repeated this process 30 times, randomly
placing each record either on the training or in the testing partition.

In our first evaluation we show, in Fig. 1, boxplots that represent the average classification accuracy of the three ML models. We observe that the best model is the one created

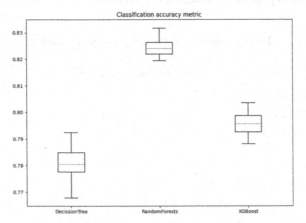

Fig. 1. Model performance based on classification accuracy

by Random Forest, surprisingly leaving slightly behind XGBoost (top competitor for tabular data).

Since the distribution of the classes shows some unbalance (see Table 3), having more records on the first class and less on the last one, Accuracy could be a misleading metric to objectively evaluate these methods. To cope with this issue, we computed the F1 score, which considers both precision and recall offering a more robust perspective of the performance of the methods. We present this result in Table 4.

We observe that although the performance of the model slightly decreased, the conclusion about the best strategy to use is consistent with the Accuracy computation. Although a direct comparison against literature is not possible, given the difference in datasets, it is informative to contrast our best results against other reported works. If we consider the work of [3], they reported an Accuracy score of 0.81 obtained by XGBoost, which is slightly behind the one reported in this study by Random Forest, which obtained an Accuracy score around 0.82.

Table 4. Model comparison based on F1 macro metric

Model	Mean (%)	Best performance (%)	Standard deviation
Decision Tree Classifier	73	75	0.00700
Random Forest	78	79	0.00469
XGB Classifier	75	76	0.00584

Figure 2 shows the confusion matrix for the Random Forest approach.

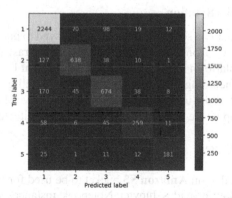

Fig. 2. Random Forest's confusion matrix

To offer some insight about the role that input features play in the classification process, we computed the Shapley values. Through color code we can observe the contribution of each model input for the decision of the classifier. We present this analysis in Fig. 3.

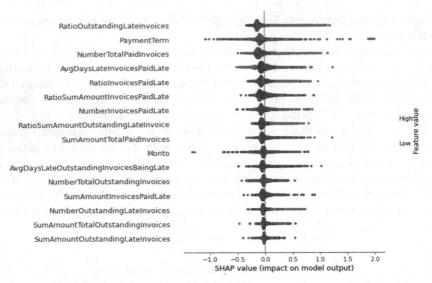

Fig. 3. SHAP Values related to Random Forests Classifier

One aspect to remark about this analysis is how the variables Ratio of outstanding invoices that were late, Payment Term and Number of total paid invoices are more important for the model, while the variables Sum of the base amount of total outstanding invoices and Sum of the base amount of outstanding invoices that were late are the least important. This analysis will make possible to refine the model in the next round of evaluations.

4.1 Architecture of the Solution

Below in Fig. 4 the reader can see the architecture employed to build the application. By client requirement, the Amazon Web Service (AWS) cloud infrastructure was selected to host the project. This platform offers a wide range of different business purpose global cloud-based products including those related to Artificial Intelligence. We use Amazon SageMaker, a tool that allow us to build, train, and deploy Machine Learning models at any scale. To develop it, the Machine Learning Well-Architected best practices [10] were followed.

Description of every step:

1. The data is uploaded to an **Amazon S3** bucket to be used for training and testing.
2. **Amazon SageMaker** provides Jupyter Notebook instances for data scientists to prepare the data and train the models.
3. All the notebooks and artifacts generated are saved in a Git repository.
4. By selecting the desire algorithm, it is trained in **Amazon SageMaker**.
5. Once the model is ready, the artifacts generated are saved in an **Amazon S3** bucket and the model is deployed using an **Amazon SageMaker** model endpoint.
6. The user enters the information related to the invoice that he wishes to foresee in the App and wait for the response.

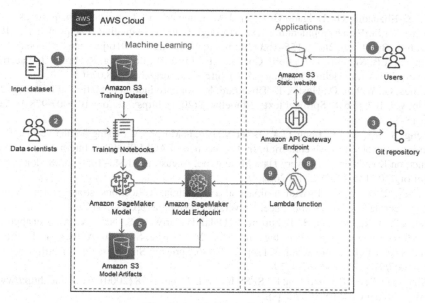

Fig. 4. Architecture diagram

7. The App interact with **Amazon API Gateway** endpoint via POST method.
8. The data is sent to an **Amazon Lambda** function to be transformed.
9. **Amazon Lambda** receives the data to use for inferences and transforms it in a proper format. Invokes the model endpoint and receives the prediction. This result is propagated back to the user, where it is presented in a readable format.

5   Conclusions

In this study, we have presented a supervised learning approach and the corresponding results in the context of forecasting AR. We built a set of aggregated features to capture historical payment behavior for each customer. We tested three ML methods to forecast AR and classify it by category. We analyze the results obtained through these models for different training and testing data. From this analysis, we conclude that the Random Forest Classifier model outperforms the other methods. The selected model was put into production using the AWS infrastructure. The results of this paper assist the business executives to forecast Account Receivables in advance, with the aim of improving decision-making. As future work, we are in the process of developing a most robust model that allows us to predict invoices for new customers, as well as to integrate this tool in Blú Capital's software ecosystem.

References

1. Bunich, G.A., Rovenskiy, Y.A., Dashkov, L.P.: Factoring development: theory and practice. Espacios **39**(19), 17 (2018)

2. Pérez-Elizundia, G., Delgado-Guzmán, J.A., Lampón, J.F.: Commercial banking as a key factor for SMEs development in Mexico through factoring: a qualitative approach. Eur. Res. Manag. Bus. Econ. **26**(3), 155–163 (2020). https://doi.org/10.1016/j.iedeen.2020.06.001

3. Appel, A.P., Malfatti, G.L., de F. Cunha, R.L., Lima, B., de Paula, R.: Predicting account receivables with machine learning (2020). http://arxiv.org/abs/2008.07363

4. James, G., Witten, D., Hastie, T., Tibshirani, R.: An Introduction to Statistical Learning, 2nd edn, vol. 102, p. 618. Springer texts, Heidelberg (2021). https://doi.org/10.1007/978-1-0716-1418-1

5. Zeng, S., Melville, P., Lang, C.A., Boier-Martin, I., Murphy, C.: Using predictive analysis to improve invoice-to-cash collection. In: Proceedings of ACM SIGKDD International Conference on Knowledge Discovery Data Mining, no. August, pp. 1043–1050, 2008, doi: https://doi.org/10.1145/1401890.1402014

6. Bailey, R.D. et al.: Providian financial corporation: collections strategy. In: Systems Engineering Capstone Conference, University of Virginia, pp. 23–30 (1999)

7. Kapadia, P., Kadhiwala, B., Bahurupi, T., Dalal, H., Jariwala, S., Naik, K.: A novel approach for forecasting account receivables. In: Tuba, M., Akashe, S., Joshi, A. (eds.) ICT Systems and Sustainability. LNNS, vol. 321, pp. 797–806. Springer, Singapore (2022). https://doi.org/10.1007/978-981-16-5987-4_79

8. Chapman, P., et al.: Crisp-Dm. In: SPSS Inc, vol. 78, pp. 1–78 (2000). Available: http://www.crisp-dm.org/CRISPWP-0800.pdf

9. Pedregosa, F.G.V.: Scikit-learn: machine learning in python. J. Mach. Learn. Res. **127**(9), 2825–2830 (2019). https://doi.org/10.1289/EHP4713

10. Amazon. Well-Architected machine learning - Machine Learning Lens. https://docs.aws.amazon.com/wellarchitected/latest/machine-learning-lens/well-architected-machine-learning.html. Accessed 31 Jan 2023

A New Approach for Road Type Classification Using Multi-stage Graph Embedding Method

Mohale E. Molefe and Jules R. Tapamo[✉]

University of KwaZulu Natal, Durban, South Africa
tapamoj@ukzn.ac.za

Abstract. Classifying road types using machine learning models is an important component of road network intelligent systems, as outputs from these models can provide useful traffic information to road users. This paper presents a new method for road-type classification tasks using a multi-stage graph embedding method. The first stage of the proposed method embeds high-dimensional road segment feature vectors to a smaller compact feature space using Deep AutoEncoder. The second stage uses Graph Convolution Neural Networks to obtain an embedded vector for each road segment by aggregating information from neighbouring road segments. The proposed method outperforms the state-of-the-art Graph Convolution Neural Networks embedding method for solving a similar task based on the same dataset.

Keywords: Road Networks Intelligent Systems · Graph embedding methods · Deep AutoEncoder · Graph Convolution Neural Networks

1 Introduction

Rising traffic problems such as traffic congestion, accidents, and fuel costs are inescapable conditions in large and growing cities across the world. These traffic problems are directly influenced by an increase in population, the number of vehicles on the road, and a number of road users. The design and development of smart cities is key towards better management and minimization of traffic problems [1]. In particular, smart city design uses information and communication technologies (ICT) to resolve traditional challenges of urban living.

Smart cities cover a wide range of applications within the transportation industry and aim to ensure efficient traffic flow by minimising traffic problems through intelligent road network systems (IRNS) design. IRNS design relies on data-capturing sensors installed in various components of the road network infrastructure. The data collected by these sensors can then be used to train machine learning algorithms for many applications within the transportation industry, such as estimated time of arrival and traffic flow predictions. One application of machine learning in IRNS design which has not yet been fully explored is the classification of different types of roads.

Road-type classification models are becoming important as they can be embedded in interactive maps to provide important traffic information to road

A. Y. Rodríguez-González et al. (Eds.): MCPR 2023, LNCS 13902, pp. 23–35, 2023.
https://doi.org/10.1007/978-3-031-33783-3_3

users, such as avoidance of congested routes, routes where accidents are likely to occur and routes with many intersections. Modelling road-type classification with machine learning requires road network graph data; however, this task is challenging due to the lack of feature extraction methods available in the literature for representing road segments as feature vectors. Recently researchers have introduced deep learning-based graph embedding methods to learn the spatial connection of road segments and extract features automatically in the graph network structure. In simple terms, graph embedding methods generate a feature vector of a given road segment using the feature vectors of its neighbouring road segments.

Graph embedding methods allow for modelling spatial connection of road segments in the network structure; however, these methods do not perform embedding on the actual feature vectors of road segments as they often assume that the road segment features are robust and accurate. Therefore, the hypothesis is made in this study that performing embedding on actual road segment feature vectors before applying the graph embedding method could improve the accuracy of classifying road types.

This study proposes a multi-stage graph embedding method for classifying road types of realistic cities and towns from Open Street Maps [2]. The first stage of the proposed method uses Deep AutoEncoder (DAE) model to embed the actual road segment feature vectors to much smaller dimensions while preserving only the significant features. The second stage uses Graph Convolution Neural Networks (GCNN) to perform embedding of a given road segment based on the reduced feature vectors (from stage 1) of its neighbouring road segments. Finally, the outputs from the second stage of the proposed method are fed to the MultiLayer perceptron (MLP) classifier to achieve the road-type classification task. To prove the hypothesis made in this study, the baseline method (actual road segment features + MLP classifier) and the method based on GCNN (GCNN embedded features + MLP classifier) are compared to the proposed method (Multi-stage embedded features + MLP classifier).

The rest of the paper is structured as follows. Section 2 reviews some of the recent works found in the literature for road-type classification tasks. Section 3 presents the materials and methods used to build the proposed multi-stage graph embedding method. Section 4 provides the experimental results of the study. Section 5 concludes the study.

2   Background and Related Work

Traffic problems such as traffic forecasting [3–5], speed limit annotation [6–8], and travel time estimation [9,10] have been successfully modelled using machine learning techniques. However, modelling road networks with machine learning is often challenging due to the lack of feature extraction methods available in the literature for representing road segments as feature vectors. Recently, deep learning methods have been proposed to automatically learn the network's structure and represent every road segment by learning its spatial connection to the neighbouring road segments. However, applying deep learning to graphs is difficult because many commonly used data types, such as images and texts, are euclidean and fixed. On the other hand, the underlying connectivity patterns on the graph-structured data are complex and non-euclidean.

The fundamental approach to modelling complex and non-euclidean graph-structure data using deep learning is to embed features from high-dimensional graph space to low-dimensional euclidean space using graph embedding methods. Once the low-dimensional feature representations are modelled, graph-related problems such as node and link predictions can be achieved. Several graph embedding methods have been proposed in the literature for modelling road networks. A Hybrid Graph Convolution Neural Network (HGCN) is proposed in [11] for a traffic flow prediction task, where nodes represent toll stations and edges represent road segments. In addition to modelling the spatial connection of the network structure, the authors used actual node (toll station) features such as time, place, and weather conditions. However, this work did not incorporate edge (road segment) features into the learning process. This limitation is addressed in [12], where Relational Fusion Networks (RFN) is proposed for speed limit classification and estimation tasks. RFN integrates edge information into the representation learning process using the novel graph convolution operator.

The study to classify different road types of realistic cities on the graph dataset extracted from Open Street Maps (OSMnx) is proposed in [13]. Like RFN, the authors incorporated edge features into the learning process by transforming the original graph into a line graph. A method that generates road segment features is proposed based on attributes such as road segment length, speed limit, and road segment geometry. Several embedding methods, including Graph Convolution Neural Networks (GCCN) [14], GraphSAGE [15], Graph Attention Networks (GAT) [16], and Graph Isomorphism Networks (GIN) [17] were compared in the various learning settings. Until now, the method proposed in [13] is the only method available in the literature that solves road-type classification tasks using graph embedding methods.

This work proposes a new multi-stage graph embedding method for classifying road types. The proposed method relies on the novel graph feature extraction technique proposed in [13]. Compared to graph embedding methods in the literature, the proposed method first operates directly on the high-dimensional space of each road segment. It produces compact features in a much smaller dimensional space. It then applies GCNN to construct a vector representation of each road segment using the compact feature vectors of neighbouring road segments.

3   Materials and Methods

The system diagram of the multi-stage graph embedding method is depicted in Fig. 1. First, the original road network graph dataset is extracted from OSMnx, where nodes represent intersections, crossroads, and edges represent road segments. Thereafter, the original graph is transformed into a line graph where nodes represent road segments. In the third step, the original and transformed graphs are used to extract road properties and generate a feature vector for each road segment. Step 4 introduces the multi-stage graph embedding method. In the first stage, Deep AutoEncoder (DAE) is used to embed high-dimensional road segment feature vectors into compact road segment feature vectors in smaller dimensional space. In the second stage, Graph Convolution Neural Networks (GCNN) is used to obtain the embedded feature vector of each road segment based on the feature vectors of neighbouring road segments from stage 1. Finally, the embedded feature vectors from stage 2 are fed to the MultiLayer Perceptron (MLP) classifier to achieve road-type classification.

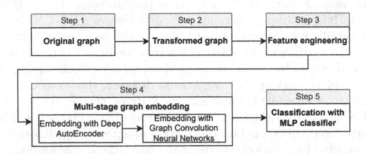

Fig. 1. System diagram of the proposed method

3.1   Input Dataset and Line Graph Transformation

Similar to the study in [13], the undirected graph dataset of Linkoping city road networks extracted from OSMnx is used to conduct experiments in this study. The input graph is expressed as $G = (V, E)$, where V represents nodes, and E represents edges; nodes are intersections, junctions and crossroads, while edges are road segments between such nodes. GCNN is designed for embedding nodes features, and nodes of the original graph (crossroads, junctions and intersections) are not important for road type classification. Thus, line graph transformation of the original graph is necessary such that road segments are represented as nodes to facilitate graph embedding. The transformation of G into line graph $L(G)$ is depicted in Fig. 2, where edges (road segments) in G become nodes in $L(G)$. Edges that share a node (e.g. junction) in G becomes an edge in $L(G)$.

3.2   Road Type Class Labels

To facilitate supervised learning tasks, road segments in OSMnx are tagged with corresponding road type (class) labels. However, the class distribution is characterized by extreme class imbalances as some of the road types rarely occur on the road network data. Therefore, some road types are merged and relabelled according to the technique applied in [13].

- Class 1: highway, yes, primary, secondary, motorway-link, trunk-link, primary-link, secondary-link. Node count: 1140.

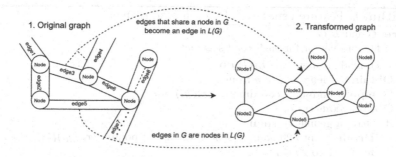

Fig. 2. Transformation of original graph to line graph

- Class 2: tertiary, tertiary-link. Node count: 951.
- Class 3: road, planned, unclassified. Node count: 922.
- Class 4: residential. Node count: 3012.
- Class 5: living street. Node count: 736.

3.3 Feature Engineering

Road segment feature vectors are generated by extracting the descriptive edge and node attributes from G and $L(G)$, respectively. To conduct a fair comparison of the results to the study in [13], this study uses a similar feature engineering technique, where the authors used four main attributes to generate a 58-dimensional feature vector for each road segment. These attributes are: (1) road segment length (1-dimension); (2) midpoint coordinates of the road segment in longitude and latitude (2-dimensions); (3) Subtraction of 20 equally spaced distanced points by the midpoint (20-dimensions); (4) one hot encoding of speed limit (15-dimensions). Given l as the road segment length, (x, y) as the midpoint coordinates of the road segment, and $S = s_1, s_2, s_3, ..., s_m$ as the one hot encoding vector of m speed limits. Then, the final feature vector of each road segment is generated using Algorithm 1.

3.4 Multi-stage Graph Embedding

This section introduces the proposed multi-stage graph embedding method for road type classification, which is central to the novelty and contribution of the study. As already outlined in prior sections, the multi-stage graph embedding method uses two types of embedding techniques that perform graph embedding differently. Stage 1 of embedding uses Deep AutoEncoder (DAE) model to embed high dimensional node (road segment) features to low dimensional and compact node features. Stage 2 of embedding uses Graph Convolution Neural Networks (GCNN) model to embed the vector of each road segment using the feature vectors of neighbouring road segments obtained in stage 1. To understand what is meant by "compact" features, the architecture of the proposed DAE graph embedding method needs to be explained.

Algorithm 1. Feature generation for each road segment

Require: G and $L(G)$
Output: Feature vector for each road segment
 1: **for** each road segment $s \in L(G)$ **do**
 2:      **Obtain** the length l_s of s from G.
 3:      **Compute** midpoint coordinates (x_s, y_s) of s.
 4:      **Obtain** geometry of s.
 5:      **if** s have a geometry **then**
 6:          **Divide** l_s into 20 equally spaced distanced points $(lx_i, ly_i)_{i=1,2,\dots,20}$.
 7:          **for** $i = 1$ to 20 **do**
 8:              **Subtract** (lx_i, ly_i) by midpoint coordinates (x_s, y_s).
 9:          **end for**
10:      **else**
11:          **Convert** to line geometry.
12:          **Divide** geometry into 20 equally spaced distanced points $(lx_i, ly_i)_{i=1,2,\dots,20}$.
13:          **for** $i = 1$ to 20 **do**
14:              **Subtract** (lx_i, ly_i) by midpoint coordinates (x_s, y_s).
15:          **end for**
16:      **end if**
17:      **Obtain** one hot encoded vector S of the speed limits with m standard values.
18:      **Concatenate** features generated from steps 2 to 17.
19: **end for**

---

1. Stage 1: Embedding with Deep AutoEncoder: The first stage of the proposed method embeds road segment features from D dimensional space to compact road segment features in N dimensional space, where $D >>> N$. To understand what "compact" features mean, the architecture of the DAE shown in Fig. 3 first needs to be understood. DAE consists of the encoder, compact features layer and decoder. The feature vector, $X_i = \{x_{i,1}, x_{i,2}, x_{i,3}, \dots, x_{i,D}\}$, of any road segment i is passed as input to several hidden layers of decreasing dimensions in the encoder. It then gets compressed to a feature vector $Z_i = \{z_{i,1}, z_{i,2}, z_{i,3}, \dots, z_{i,N}\}$ in the compact features layer. After that, Z_i is used to produce the reconstructed vector $Y_i = \{y_{i,1}, y_{i,2}, y_{i,3}, \dots, y_{i,N}\}$ of X_i, through several dense layers of increasing dimensions in the decoder. Therefore, features in the compact features layer are defined as "compact" if the error difference between X_i and Y_i is minimal.

Therefore, the ultimate goal of the DAE learning process is to obtain optimal model parameters that achieve the lowest possible error difference. Once these are obtained, the road segment feature vectors in D dimensional space can then be replaced with compact, road segment feature vectors in N dimensional space obtained in the compact features layer of the DAE embedding model. Parameters that will be fine-tuned in the experimental results chapter are; the number and size of hidden layers on the decoder and encoder. The learning rate parameter and the dimensional size of feature vectors in the compact features layer. These parameters were selected for fine-tuning as they can significantly impact the performance of any neural network model.

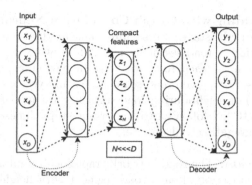

Fig. 3. Stage 1 embedding: Deep AutoEncoder

The proposed DAE embedding method is a fully connected network with an input layer on the encoder, an output layer on the decoder and compact features layer. The encoder and decoder have a similar number of hidden layers and sizes. Input feature vectors are first normalised and fed as inputs to the encoder. Then, non-linearities to the network are introduced by applying the Rectified Linear Unit (ReLU) activation function defined as: $f(x) = max(0, x)$. Next, the reconstructed output values on the output layer of the decoder are normalised between 0 and 1 using the sigmoid function defined as: $g(y) = \frac{1}{1+e^{-y}}$. Next, the Adam optimiser is applied to find the set of optimal weight parameters on the encoder component that achieves the smallest possible error difference between X and Y. Finally, original road segment features in D-dimensional space are replaced with features in N-dimensional space. Algorithm 2 shows the pseudo-code used in this study to achieve embedding with DAE model.

Algorithm 2. Graph embedding with Deep AutoEncoder

Require: Road segment graph features space: $RSGFS \subset \mathbb{R}^D$
Outputs: Road segment embedded graph features space: $RSEGFS \subset \mathbb{R}^N$
 1: Define encoder and decoder parameters:
 2: Define DAE model: model(encoder,decoder)
 3: **for** $X \in RSGFS$ **do**
 4:     **Fit** input feature vectors (X) to DAE model.
 5:     **Initialise** weights randomly.
 6:     **while** error difference is not converging **do**
 7:         **Obtain** reconstructed feature vectors (Y).
 8:         **Compute** the error difference: $(X - Y)^2$
 9:         **Update** weight parameters.
10:     **end while**
11:     **Obtain** the embedding features vector (Z)
12:     $RSEGFS \leftarrow RSEGFS \cup \{Z\}$
13: **end for**
14: **Return** embedding space features $RSEGFS$

---

2. Stage 2: Embedding with Graph Convolution Neural Networks: The second stage of the multi-stage graph embedding method models the topology and spatial connection of road segments in graph network data to obtain richer feature representation for each road segment. In particular, GCNN is used to obtain such features. For a given road segment, feature vectors in N dimensional space (from stage 1) of neighbouring road segments are aggregated to obtain its embedded vector. GCNN follows two important steps. These are: (1) locality information, (2) aggregation and update.

Locality Information: The road network graph locality information is needed to obtain spatial connection of each road segment with neighbouring road segments. For a given road segment, locality is obtained by forming the computational graph. A computational graph details how each road segment is connected to its neighbourhood. For instance, consider the computation graph of the target road segment "node1" in Fig. 4 for two hops. The first hop shows road segments that are connected to the target node (node2 and node3), and the second hop shows road segments that are connected to the neighbours of the target node (nodes 1, 3 and 5 for node2 and nodes 1, 2 and 6 for node3).

Aggregate and Update: Once the locality information of each node has been obtained using the computational graph, the second step is to collect or aggregate each neighbouring road segment feature vector's contribution to the target road segment. After that, the embedded vector of the target road segment is obtained and updated based on the aggregated information. As shown in Figure 4, a two-hop computational graph will have three layers. Layer 0 takes input feature vectors of road segments. Layer 1 aggregates information from road segments in the second hop to road segments in the first hop (neighbours of the target node). Finally, Layer 2 aggregates information from road segments in the first hop to the target road segment. The embedded vector of road segment v in layer 0 is defined as:

$$h_v^0 = Z_v \qquad (1)$$

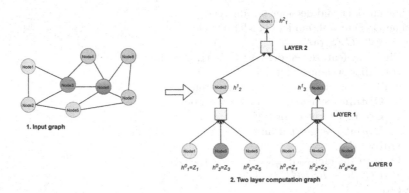

Fig. 4. Computation graph for a target road segment

where Z_v is the input feature vector of v obtained in stage 1. The contribution of neighbouring embedded vectors of each road segment u to the current road segment v, is computed using

$$r_v = f_{agg}(\{u|u \in N(v)\}) \tag{2}$$

f_{agg} is the aggregation function such as (1) mean (average of neighbouring road segment embedded vectors), (2) sum (summation of neighbouring road segments embedded vectors), and (3) max-pooling (maximum embedded vector of all neighbouring road segments). The experimental results section will investigate different aggregation functions to obtain the optimal one. r_v is then used to update the embedded vector for road segment v using

$$h_v^k = \sigma(W_k(r_v, h_v^{k-1})) \tag{3}$$

where h_v^k is the embedded vector of road segment v at k^{th} convolution layer, h_v^{k-1} is the embedded vector of v at the previous layer, W_k is the learnable weight parameter and σ is the activation function. Algorithm 3 shows the pseudo-code for achieving the embedding task using GCNN.

Algorithm 3. Graph embedding with Graph Convolution Neural Networks

Require: Road segment embedded graph features space: $RSEGFS \subset \mathbb{R}^N$
Outputs: Road segment embedded space : $RSES \subset \mathbb{R}^M$
1: Define number of hopes k
2: Define input and output dimensions of layers at each k
3: **for** $Z_v \in RSFS$ **do**
4:      **Construct** computational graph.
5:      **Initialise** W_k.
6:      **Set** h_v^0 as Z_v.
7:      **for** $i = 1 : k$ **do**
8:          **Compute** r_v using Eq 2.
9:          **Compute** h_v^i using Eq 3.
10:     **end for**
11:     **Obtain** embedded vector $E_v = h_v^k$
12:     $RSES \leftarrow RSES \cup \{E_v\}$
13: **end for**
14: **Return** $RSES$

3.5   Classification with MLP Classifier

The road segment feature vectors obtained from the multi-stage graph embedding method are used to train, validate and test the MultiLayer Perceptron (MLP) classifier. Instead of providing a detailed mathematical formulation of the MLP classifier, a summary of the parameters used is given, as this is not central to the novelty of the proposed method. For a fair comparison to the method in [13], the single hidden layer MLP classifier, with Adam optimizer, is used. The size of the input layer corresponds to the dimensional space of the input road segment, and the size of the output layer corresponds to the number of road type labels (5 classes). Input road segment feature vectors are propagated to the MLP classifier through the input and hidden layers. The softmax activation function is applied at the output layer to predict the probabilities of different road-type classes. The loss is calculated as the error difference between predicted and true class labels using the cross entropy loss. The obtained loss updates the MLP weight parameters using the Adam optimizer.

4 Experimental Results

Input to the proposed multi-stage graph embedding method is the road network graph dataset of Linkoping city with 6761 road segment (nodes) feature vectors. Each road segment is associated with a 58-dimensional feature vector obtained in Algorithm 1. Experiments are designed to obtain optimal parameters of the proposed method and to compare the results with the baseline method and the method proposed in [13].

4.1 Stage 1: Graph Embedding with Deep AutoEncoder

The goal of stage 1 embedding is to embed the road segment features from D dimensional space ($D = 58$) to N dimensional space with compact road segment features. As mentioned in Sect. 3.4, compact features are obtained when the error difference between the input and reconstructed features of road segments is as minimal as possible. Furthermore, parameters such as compact feature space (N), learning rate (u), size and the dimension of the hidden layers are investigated for minimal error difference. Road segments were initially divided into 70/30 split, where 70% data trains the DAE embedding method, and 30% test set obtains optimal DAE parameters. Table 1 shows the error difference obtained by several hidden layers and N parameters at varying learning rates based on the test set. It can be observed that 4 hidden layers, 8-dimensional compact features space ($N = 8$), and 0.001 learning rate are optimal parameters as these achieve the lowest possible error difference of 0.00058 compared to other parameters. Therefore, the proposed DAE embedding method embeds road segment feature vectors from 58-dimensional space to 8-dimensional space.

4.2 Stage 2. Embedding with Graph Convolution Neural Network

In the second stage of the proposed method, the embedded vector of each road segment is obtained by aggregating information from neighbouring road segments in 8-dimensional space according to Algorithm 3. Similar to the study in [13], road segments were divided into 70% (train), 15% (validate) and 15% (test) splits. A two-hop GCNN network is defined, where inputs to the first layer are the 8-dimensional road segment feature vectors. The output of the second layer

Table 1. Hyperparameters settings for optimal DAE parameters

No. of hidden layers	Layer size			learning rate	error difference
	Encoder	N	Decoder		
5	{58, 49, 40, 31, 22, 13}	4	{13, 22, 31, 40, 49, 58}	0.0001	0.0020
				0.001	**0.0013**
				0.01	0.0048
4	{58, 48, 38, 28, 18}	8	{18, 28,38, 48, 58}	0.0001	0.0026
				0.001	**0.00058**
				0.01	0.0079
3	{58, 46, 34, 22}	10	{22, 34, 46, 58}	0.0001	0.0048
				0.001	**0.00062**
				0.01	0.0076

in M-dimensional space is fed as input to the MLP classifier. Different aggregation functions (sum, mean and max), learning rates (0.001, 0.01 and 0.1) and M parameters (16, 32, and 64) are investigated to obtain optimal parameters that achieve the highest micro-averaged f1-score on the validation set. The optimal parameters are then tested on the test set. Batch normalization is applied after each convolution layer as a regularizer. The combination of different aggregation functions, M and learning rates yield 27 models, each trained for 1000 iterations at 1024 mini-batch size. Adam optimizer and ReLU activation function are used. Table 2 shows the micro-f1 score obtained by different aggregation functions at different output dimensions M and optimal learning rate u parameters using the validation set. As indicated in Table 2, there is no significant difference in the results across different aggregation functions. Nevertheless, the max aggregation function, output shape of 16-dimensions and the learning rate of 0.001 are the optimal parameters. Furthermore, the micro-averaged f1-score of 75.13% is achieved by these parameters based on the test set.

Table 2. Hyperparameter settings for optimal GCNN parameters

Aggregator	(M)	Optimal u	Val. micro-f1 score (%)	Test micro-f1 score (%)
Sum	16	0.001	75.95	
	32	0.001	75.64	
	64	0.001	77.23	
Mean	16	0.001	75.38	
	32	0.01	76.12	
	64	0.001	74.91	
Max	16	0.01	74.13	
	32	**0.001**	**79.39**	**75.13**
	64	0.001	76.23	

4.3 Comparison to Other Methods

The micro-averaged f1-score obtained by the proposed method was compared to the baseline method and the state-of-the-art method found in [13] using a similar input dataset and MLP classifier parameters. The baseline method uses the original road segment feature vectors in 58-dimensional space (without any embedding technique), while the method in [13] embeds road segment features with GCNN before classification. Similarities between the proposed multi-stage and the GCNN methods are: (1) the two methods use the same road network graph dataset with 58-dimensional road segment features. (2) both method uses similar classifier and GCNN parameters. The key difference is on the embedding; the GCNN method applies embedding using actual road segment features as inputs. The proposed method first computes compact features of road segments in smaller dimensional space using DAE before applying GCNN. As a result, the proposed multi-stage graph embedding method outperforms the GCNN method by +-17% micro-averaged f1-score. The results indicate that using DAE embedding method to obtain compact road segment features significantly improves the performance of GCNN for road type classification (Table 3).

Table 3. Comparison of the proposed method to other methods

Method	Micro-f1 score
Baseline (Actual road segment features + MLP classifier)	59%
GCNN (GCNN embedded features + MLP classifier)	58%
Proposed (Multi-stage embedded features + MLP classifier)	**75%**

5 Conclusion

In this study, a new multi-stage graph embedding method for modelling road-type classification is proposed. For a fair comparison of methods, the Linkoping road network dataset is used. Thereafter, line graph transformation and road segment feature generation techniques are used to generate descriptive attributes of each road segment as in [13]. The generated features are then passed to the multi-stage graph embedding method, where DAE graph embedding is used in the first stage to obtain compact road segment features. GCNN is used in the second stage to generate final embedded road segment feature vectors. The proposed performance outperforms the state-of-the-art GCN method for solving a similar problem. Future work will involve using the DAE embedding method with other embedding methods such as GraphSAGE and GAT.

References

1. Sahoo, J., Rath, M.: Study and analysis of smart applications in smart city context. In: 2017 International Conference on Information Technology (ICIT), pp. 225–228 (2017)

2. OpenStreetMap contributors. Planet dump retrieved from https://planet.osm. org. https://www.openstreetmap.org/relation/935467#map=9/58.3588/15.6654& layers=Y (2022)
3. Deekshetha, H.R., Madhav, A., Tyagi, A.: Traffic Prediction Using Machine Learning, pp. 969–983, 1 (2022)
4. Yin, X., Wu, G., Wei, J., Shen, Y., Qi, H., Yin, B.: Deep learning on traffic prediction: Methods, analysis, and future directions. IEEE Trans. Intell. Transp. Syst., **23**(6), 4927–4943 (2022)
5. José Vázquez, J., Arjona, J., Linares, M., Casanovas-Garcia, J.: A comparison of deep learning methods for urban traffic forecasting using floating car data. Transp. Res. Procedia **47**, 195–202 (2020). In: 22nd EURO Working Group on Transportation Meeting, EWGT 2019, 18th - 20th September 2019, Barcelona, Spain
6. Szwed,P.: Speed Limits Can Be Determined from Geospatial Data with Machine Learning Methods, pp. 431–442 (2019)
7. Yan, M., Li, M., He, H., Peng,J.: Deep learning for vehicle speed prediction. Energy Procedia **152**, 618–623 (2018). Cleaner Energy for Cleaner Cities
8. Modi, S., Bhattacharya, J., Basak, P.: Multistep traffic speed prediction: a deep learning based approach using latent space mapping considering spatio-temporal dependencies. Expert Syst. Appl. **189**, 116140 (2022)
9. Masiero, L., Casanova, M., Tilio, M.: Travel time prediction using machine learning, vol. 11 (2011)
10. Song, X., Zhang, C., Yu, J.J.Q.: Learn travel time distribution with graph deep learning and generative adversarial network. In: 2021 IEEE International Intelligent Transportation Systems Conference (ITSC), pp. 1385–1390 (2021)
11. Yang, F., Zhang, H., Tao, S.: Hybrid deep graph convolutional networks. Int. J. Mach. Learn. Cybern. **13**, 08 (2022)
12. Jepsen, T., Jensen, C.S., Nielsen,T.D.: Relational fusion networks: Graph convolutional networks for road networks. IEEE Trans. Intell. Transport. Syst. **23**(1), 418–429 (2022)
13. Gharaee, Z., Kowshik, S., Stromann, O., Felsberg, M.: Graph representation learning for road type classification. Pattern Recogn. **120**, 108174 (2021)
14. Kipf, T.N., Welling, M.: Semi-supervised classification with graph convolutional networks. CoRR, abs/1609.02907 (2016)
15. Hamilton, W.L., Ying, R., Leskovec, J.: Inductive representation learning on large graphs. CoRR, abs/1706.02216 (2017)
16. Veličković, P., Cucurull, G., Casanova, A., Romero, A., Lió, P., Bengio, Y.: Graph attention networks
17. Xu, K., Hu, W., Leskovec, J., Jegelka, S.: How powerful are graph neural networks? CoRR, abs/1810.00826 (2018)

Removing the Black-Box from Machine Learning

Angel Fernando Kuri-Morales[(✉)]

Instituto Tecnológico Autónomo de México, Río Hondo No. 1, 01000 México, D.F., México
akuri@itam.mx

Abstract. We discuss an algorithm which allows us to find the algebraic expression of a dependent variable as a function of an arbitrary number of independent ones where data may have arisen from experimental data. The possibility of such approximation is proved starting from the Universal Approximation Theorem (UAT). As opposed to the neural network (NN) approach to which it is frequently associated, the relationship between the independent variables is explicit, thus resolving the "black box" characteristics of NNs. It implies the use of a nonlinear function such as the logistic $1/(1 + e^{-x})$. Thus, any function is expressible as a combination of a set of logistics. We show that a close polynomial approximation of logistic is possible by using only a constant and monomials of odd degree. Hence, an upper bound (D) on the degree of the polynomial may be found. Furthermore, we may calculate the form of the model resulting from D. We discuss how to determine the best such set by using a genetic algorithm leading to the best L_∞-L_2 approximation. It allows us to find the best approximation polynomial consisting of a fixed number of monomials and yielding the degrees of the variables in every monomial and the associated coefficients. Furthermore, we trained a multi-layered perceptron network to determine the most adequate number of such monomials for a set of arbitrary data. We discuss how to analyze the explicit relationship between the variables by using a well known experimental database. We show that our method yields better quantitative and qualitative measures than those of the human experts.

Keywords: Multivariate polynomials · supervised training · neural networks · genetic algorithms · ascent algorithm

1 Introduction

The problem of finding a synthetic expression from an experimental set of data for a variable of interest given a matching set of independent variables has repeatedly received attention because of its inherent importance. It may be called multivariate regression or supervised training (ST) depending on the approach taken. As ST it has given rise to a wide sub-area within the realm of artificial neural networks (NN). Some approaches include multi-layer perceptron networks [1, 2], radial basis function networks [3, 4] and support vector machines [5, 6]. A main concern has been the fact that the architecture

A. Y. Rodríguez-González et al. (Eds.): MCPR 2023, LNCS 13902, pp. 36–46, 2023.
https://doi.org/10.1007/978-3-031-33783-3_4

of the model yields little information of the relations between the variables of the system. On the other hand, if seen as a multivariate regression problem where, conceivably, such relation is explicit, the following issues arise: a) How to determine the form of the model [7], b) How to calculate the free parameters of such model when one is selected [8] and, c) How to handle the complexity of its equations and the numerical instability they frequently convey [9]. The last issue has to do with the fact that a closed model of a system of multiple variables frequently leads to complex expressions whose determination depends on solving large sets of simultaneous linear or non-linear equations. These sets of equations are prone to result in ill-conditioned matrices [10]. The case we explore here is one where the form of the model is left for the method to determine. The use of NNs, for instance, has opened a way out of the ill-conditioned matrices. NNs represent the embodiment of an alternative approach which replaces one complex expression by sets (networks) of simpler ones. The free parameters and architecture of the NN, when adequately determined, yield the desired results [11]. However, the explicit relations between the independent variables remain unknown. We explore an alternative which allows us to keep the closed nature of an algebraic model (along with its inherent explanatory properties) while avoiding the pitfalls of numerical instability and leaving the task of determining the mathematical model that is best suited for the problem at hand to the method itself.

In Sect. 2, we show that it is possible to work backwards from the Universal Approximation Theorem (UAT [12]) in the sense that we may derive an algebraic expression starting from a NN architectural approach. We know that a logistic function may be used as the nonlinearity in the UAT and that an approximation of the *logistic* may be gotten from a Chebyshev polynomial basis [15]. We generalize the UAT by using the explicit algebraic approximation of the *logistic* and calculate the number of elements in the explicit polynomial representation for an arbitrary function. In Sect. 3 we discuss a method which allows us to find a polynomial approximant by selecting only the most relevant monomials via the use of a genetic algorithm (GA). In Sect. 4 we describe how the best number of terms in the approximant may be estimated from a previously trained NN. In Sect. 5 we obtain the polynomial expression for a well known data base and expose the explicit relationship between the attributes of the data base stemming from our method.

2 Universal Approximation Theorem for Polynomials

We start by enunciating the Universal Approximation Theorem. The UAT relies on the properties of a well-defined non-linear function [12].

Theorem 1. Let $\varphi(\cdot)$ be a nonconstant, bounded, and monotonically-increasing continuous function. Let I_{mO} denote the m_O-dimensional unit hypercube $[0, 1]$. The space of continuous functions on I_{mO} is denoted by $C(I_{mO})$. Then, given any function $f \in C(I_{mO})$ and $\varepsilon > 0$, there exist an integer M and sets of real constants α_i, b_i and w_{ij}, where $i = 1,2,...,m_I$ and $j = 1,2,...,m_O$ such that we may define:

$$F(x_1, ..., x_{mO}) = \sum_{i=1}^{m_I} \left[\alpha_i \cdot \varphi \left(\sum_{j=1}^{m_O} w_{ij}x_j + b_i \right) \right] \tag{1}$$

as an approximate realization of the function $f(.)$, that is,

$$|F(x_1, \ldots, x_{mO}) - f(x_1, \ldots, x_{mO})| < \varepsilon \tag{2}$$

for all $x_1, \ldots, x_{mO}$ in the input space.

The universal approximation theorem is directly applicable to multilayer perceptrons. Perceptrons are computational units which generally include an extra constant valued input called the *bias*. When including the bias of the output neuron into (1) we get

$$F(x_1, \ldots, x_{m_0}) = \alpha_0 + \sum_{i=1}^{m_I} \left[\alpha_i \cdot \varphi \left(\sum_{j=1}^{m_0} w_{ij} x_j + b_i \right) \right] \tag{3}$$

Now, the equation for the perceptron is given by $y_i = \varphi[\sum_{i=0}^{mO} w_{ij} x_j]$, where, for convenience, we have made $x_0 = 1$, $w_0 = b_0$. We can select $\varphi(x) = logistic(x)$ as the nonlinearity in a neuronal model for the construction of a multi-layer perceptron (MLP) network. We note that (1) represents the output of a MLP described as follows: a) The network has m_O input nodes and a single hidden layer consisting of m_I neurons; the inputs are denoted by $x_1, \ldots, x_{mO}$, b) Hidden neuron i has synaptic weights w_{i1}, w_{i2}, ..., w_{imO}, c) The network output is a linear combination of the outputs of the hidden neurons, with $\alpha_1, \ldots, \alpha_{mI}$ defining the synaptic weights of the output layer.

The UAT states that *a single hidden layer is sufficient for a multilayer perceptron to compute a uniform ε approximation to a given training set represented by the set of inputs $x_1, \ldots, x_{mO}$ and a desired (target) output $f(x_1, \ldots, x_{mO})$.*

We know [13, 20] that the *logistic* function $1/(1 + e^{-x})$ may be approximated by a polynomial $P_n(x)$ of degree n with an error $\varepsilon = |P_n(x)\text{-}logistic(x)|$ where $\varepsilon \rightarrow 0$ as $n \rightarrow \infty$, i.e. $logistic(x) \approx P_n(x) = \varsigma_0 + \sum_{i=1}^{n} \varsigma_i x^i$. Likewise, we know [14, 15] that a function $y = f(x)$ in $[0, +1)$ may be approximated by a polynomial based on a set of Chebyshev polynomials which achieves the minimization of the least squared error norm and simultaneously approaches the minimum largest absolute error. Finally, an application of the previous concepts allows us to find that the polynomial $P_n(x)$ of theorem (2) may be approximated by a polynomial $Q_l(x) = \beta_0 + \sum_{l=1}^{n} \beta_l x^{2l-1}$ with an error $\varepsilon \rightarrow 0$. The logistic function may be approximated by the polynomial $P_{11}(x) \sim \beta_0 + \sum_{i=1}^{6} \beta_i x^{2i-1}$ with an RMS error $\varepsilon_2 \sim 0.000781$ and a min-max error $\varepsilon_\infty \sim 0.001340$, where $\beta_0 \sim 0.5000$, $\beta_1 \sim 0.2468$, $\beta_2 \sim -0.01769$, $\beta_3 \sim 0.001085$, $\beta_4 \sim -0.000040960$, $\beta_5 \sim 0.0000008215$, $\beta_6 \sim -0.00000000664712$. Therefore, we show that any function as in (3) may be approximately realized with a linear combination of polynomials having a constant plus terms of odd degree.

Theorem 2. Any function of m_O variables may be approximated with a polynomial whose terms are of degree 2^{k-1}.

Proof. We may write,

$$F(x_1, \ldots, x_{mo}) = \alpha_0 + \sum_{i=1}^{m_I} \alpha_i \cdot \phi \left(\sum_{k=0}^{m_O} w_{ik} x_k \right)$$

$$= \alpha_0 + \sum_{i=1}^{m_I} \alpha_i \cdot logistic \left(\sum_{k=0}^{m_O} w_{ik} x_k \right)$$

$$= \alpha_0 + \sum_{i=1}^{m_I} \alpha_i \cdot \sum_{j=0}^{\infty} \lambda_j \cdot \left(\sum_{k=0}^{m_O} w_{ik} x_k \right)^j$$

$$= \alpha_0 + \sum_{i=1}^{m_I} \alpha_i \cdot \left[\beta_0 + \sum_{j=1}^{\infty} \beta_j \cdot \left(\sum_{k=0}^{m_O} w_{ik} x_k \right)^{2j-1} \right]$$

$$\approx \alpha_0 + \sum_{i=1}^{m_I} \alpha_i \cdot \left[\frac{1}{2} + \sum_{j=1}^{6} \beta_j \cdot \left(\sum_{k=0}^{m_O} w_{ik} x_k \right)^{2j-1} \right] \tag{4}$$

3 Approximation Using Genetic Algorithms

The number of terms of (4) may be very large. However, the terms corresponding to the hidden neurons may be lumped into terms of degree $0,1,3,\ldots,11$ and, subsequently, those at the output neuron will consist of those resulting from the power combinations of degree $(0,1,3,\ldots,11)^1, (0,1,3,\ldots,11)^3,\ldots,(0,1,3,\ldots,11)^{11}$. A simple analysis shows that only 20 of the possible power combinations are possible. These combinations are shown in Table 1.

Table 1. Combinations of odd powers for the expansion of logistic(x)

1	11	33	63
3	15	35	77
5	21	45	81
7	25	49	99
9	27	55	121

We can make a list (say L) of these possible powers. In other words, the polynomial at the output neuron of (4) will be of the form $P_O = k + \sum_{i=1}^{20} T(i)$, where $T(i) \equiv$ *terms of degree $L(i)$; $L(i)$* denoting the i-th element in L. For instance, $T(5) = 9$; $T(12) = 35$; $T(19) = 99$ and so on. Notice, however, that even if the powers of the monomials are all odd the powers of the variables in the i-th monomial may take any possible combination of the factors of $L(i)$. There remains the problem of determining the coefficients associated to every term.

One way to tackle this problem is to define a priori the number (say M) of desired monomials of the approximant and then to properly select which of the p possible ones these will be. There are $C(p, M)$ combinations of monomials and even for modest values of p and M an exhaustive search is out of the question. This is an optimization problem which we tackled using the eclectic genetic algorithm (EGA) discussed in [16, 17], as follows.

The chromosome is a binary string of size p. Every bit in it represents a monomial ordered as per the sequence of the consecutive powers of the variables. If the bit is '1' it means that the corresponding monomial is retained while if it is a '0' it is discarded. One has to ensure that the number of 1's is equal to M. Assume, for example, that $y = f(v_1, v_2, v_3)$ and that $d_1 = 1, d_2 = d_3 = 2$. In such case the powers assigned to the $2 \times 3 \times 3 = 18$ positions of the genome are 000, 001, 002, 010, 011, 012, 020, 021, 022, 100, 101, 102, 110, 111, 112, 120, 121, 122. For example, given that $M = 6$ the following chromosome 110000101010000001 would correspond to the folloeing polynomial $P(v_1,v_2,v_3) = c_{000} + c_{001}v_3 + c_{020}v_2^2 + c_{022}v_2^2v_3^2 + c_{101}v_1v_3 + c_{122}v_1v_2^2v_3^2$. The population of the EGA consists of a set of binary strings of length p in which there are only M 1's. That is, for every genome the monomials (corresponding to the 1's) are determined by EGA. Then the Ascent Algorithm (AA) (to be discussed in the sequel) is applied to obtain the set of M coefficients minimizing $\varepsilon_{MAX} = max(|f_i - y_i|) \quad \forall i$. Next, for this set of coefficients ε_{RMS} is calculated. This is the fitness function of EGA. The EGA's individuals are selected, crossed over and mutated for a number of generations. In the end, we retain the individual whose coefficients minimize ε_{RMS} out of those which best minimize ε_{MAX} (from the AA). This is the L_∞-L_2 metric mentioned in the introduction.

3.1   The Ascent Algorithm

The purpose of this algorithm is to express the behavior of a dependent variable (y) as a function of a set of m_O independent variables (v). $y = f(v_1,v_2,...,v_{mO})$ and $y = f(v)$. The form of the approximant is $y = c_1X_1 + c_2X_2 + ... + c_mX_m$; X_i denotes a combination of the independent variables. That is, $X_i = f_i(v)$. The method assumes that there is a sample of size N such that for every set of the independent variables v there is a known value of the dependent variable f, as illustrated in Table 2. By convention N stands for the number of objects in the sample and $M = m + 1$ (m = number of desired terms of the approximant). The AA has the distinct advantage that the X_i may be arbitrarily defined. This allows us to find the approximation coefficients for different combinations of the powers of the variables.

The goal of the AA is to find the values of the coefficients such that the approximated values minimize the absolute difference between the known values of the dependent variable f in the sample and those calculated (say y) for all the objects in the sample.

Table 2. A data sample.

v_1	v_2	v_3	v_4	v_5	f
0.2786	0.2319	0.5074	0.9714	0.5584	0.4938
0.2429	0.4855	1.0000	0.8429	0.4416	0.8580
0.4929	0.9710	0.8676	1.0000	0.7411	0.9135
...	...	...	...	...	...
0.4357	0.9130	0.8309	0.6500	0.8579	0.7037

We define the approximation error as $\varepsilon_{MAX} = max(\ |f_i\text{-}y_i|\ )$. The AA is an iterative algorithm for which it is easy to prove that it will always converge to the minimum maximum absolute error [18]. Therefore, another distinct advantage of the AA is that, regardless of the value of N, only an $M \times M$ set of equations is solved in every step.

3.2 Implementation of the Ascent Algorithm

1. Input the data vectors (call them **D**).
2. Input the degrees of each of the variables of the approximating polynomial.
3. Map the original data vectors into the powers of the selected monomials (call them **P**).
4. Select a subset of size M from **D**. Call it **I**. Call the remaining vectors **E**.

BOOTSTRAP

5. Obtain the minimax signs (call the matrix incorporating the signs (σ) **A**).
6. Obtain the inverse of **A** (call it **B**).

LOOP

7. Calculate the coefficients **C** = **f B**. The maximum absolute internal ε_θ error is also calculated.
8. Calculate the maximum absolute external error ε_φ from **C** and **E**. Call its index I_E.
9. $\varepsilon_\theta \geq \varepsilon_\varphi$? YES: Stop. The coefficients of **C** are those of the minimax polynomial for the **D** vectors.
10. Calculate the λ vector from $\lambda = A^{I_E} B$.
11. Calculate the ξ vector which maximizes $\sigma_{I_E} \lambda_j / B_j$. Call its index I_I.
12. Interchange vectors I_E and I_I.
13. Calculate the new inverse $\overline{B}$. Make $B \leftarrow \overline{B}$.
14. Go to step 7.

The implementation above requires only $O(M^2)$ flops per iteration.

4 Determining the Best Number of Terms in the Approximant

Given any preset number of terms in the approximant the Genetic Algorithm will find the powers of the attributes in all the monomials in the approximant as well as the associated coefficients. A monomial X_i is given by

$$X_i = \prod_{j=1}^{n} v_j^{k_j}; \ 0 \leq k_j \leq d$$

which denotes a product of the powers of the n *independent variables* each elevated to a maximum positive degree d. For instance, the next polynomial consists of 3 terms out of 5 attributes where the powers of the terms are bounded by 4.

$$F(v_1, v_2, v_3, v_4, v_5) = c_{23010}v_1^2 v_2^3 v_4 + c_{42113}v_1^4 v_2^2 v_3 v_4 v_5^3 + c_{02103}v_2^2 v_3 v_5^3 \quad T \in [3, 13]$$

We denote by T the minimum acceptable number of terms in (1). To experimentally determine the best T we collected 46 datasets from the University of California Machine Learning dataset repository and the Knowledge Extraction Evolutionary Learning dataset repository. To begin with, 32 of these datasets were chosen and were solved for the multivariate polynomial EGA. For every a polynomial was found and the number of terms corresponding to the best fit was recorded. A total of 352 (11 × 32) polynomials, therefore, were calculated. From these the lower bound of the number of terms was determined. The best values of T were then used to train a Neural Network (NNt) with the following attributes:

a) Number of attributes
b) Number tuples
c) Optimally encoded size
d) Compression ratio [the quotient of the (dataset's original size)/(optimally compressed size)].

These attributes were selected from a much larger original subset of such attributes. The ones we selected were shown to be the more relevant from a Principal Component Analysis, as illustrated in Table 3.

The above information was fed to NNt to get T. In Table 4 we illustrate the estimated T which are expected to be near the optimum fit. RMS(T-i) denotes the RMS error when NNt yields i for the value of T. The actual best value of T was always within $i \pm 2$ of the T suggested by NNt.

From the results a statistically highly significant lower bound on T may be inferred.

Table 3. Partial View of the best values of T for the selected datasets

ID	Dataset Name	# Attributes	# Tuples	Size	Comp Size	Comp Ratio	Expected T
1	Breast Cancer wisconsin	10	364	38121	1003	38.0070	8
2	Protein localization sites	7	336	28140	7548	3.7281	7
3	Servomechanism	13	167	22610	771	29.3256	6
4	Yeast	9	1484	140066	32021	4.3742	7
5	Abalone	11	3133	360864	39891	9.0463	6
6	Car Evaluation	22	1728	216384	34636	6.2474	10
7	CPU	36	209	28398	5348	5.3100	9
8	Hepatitis	16	125	30384	5906	5.1446	7
9	Wine	14	125	25986	8876	2.9277	13
10	IRIS	4	150	9120	2685	3.3966	5
11	Facebook	21	500	55200	14521	3.8014	6
12	Whole Sale	10	440	46112	13649	3.3784	8
13	3D road network	2	871	53261	15941	3.3400	10
14	Air quality	8	1200	217522	52252	4.1600	6
15	Air foil self noise	5	1503	182089	43915	4.1500	4
16	Concrete strength	8	1030	18752	52062	3.5900	8
17	Auto mpg	6	398	64368	14798	4.3500	5
18	Credit approval	15	690	215937	42663	5.0600	6
19	Gas turbine propulsion	2	1000	966816	259129	3.7300	5
20	Energy efficiency	11	768	185506	36553	5.0700	9

Table 4. Terms Calculated by NNt for the Validation sets

ID	Estimated T	Rounded T	RMS(T-2)	RMS(T-1)	RMS(T)	RMS(T+1)	RMS(T+2)
1	8.6634990936	9	0.412718594	**0.406120106**	0.4200713649	0.410491696	0.418528407
2	7.4266991038	7	0.037526053	0.061839319	0.03250066	**0.031067453**	0.032766126
3	2.8167562596	3	**0.207598173**	0.214679407	0.229129966	0.224681547	0.225307872
4	8.477513871	8	0.067469116	0.050167953	**0.04093897**	0.043811914	0.04796777
5	7.2928672806	7	0.337443754	0.319763624	0.318348383	0.313419036	**0.313209334**
6	7.7389574277	8	0.340522415	0.325661129	0.334526005	**0.308926934**	0.324996133
7	7.7052644686	8	0.119055026	0.11559727	**0.108739684**	0.124787914	0.117380777
8	6.2126030641	6	0.258552437	0.245556743	**0.241290077**	0.26038423	0.269854381
9	8.0014918908	8	0.101553883	**0.096687173**	0.101330919	0.102006909	0.100162057
10	8.5616749213	9	0.086605404	0.0839230232	0.082046364	0.078676946	**0.076810137**
11	7.5255321089	8	0.074918077	0.063573936	0.076393697	**0.056997275**	0.06215833
12	7.0866960532	7	0.395806995	0.400738082	0.405261065	**0.392372343**	0.399877438
13	8.6697108438	9	0.068657151	0.068666017	0.062620414	**0.061057446**	0.062685869
14	5.7585208346	6	0.14429961	0.137041337	**0.130248103**	0.140362715	0.135891573

NNt may be fully specified from a) Its architecture, b) The associated weights and c) The definition of the activation function. The architecture of NNt is shown in Fig. 1.

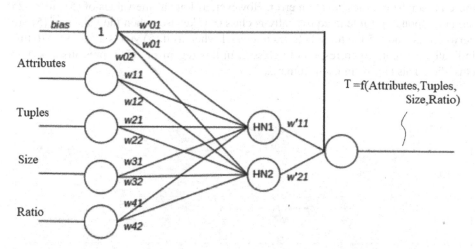

Fig. 1. The Architecture of NNt.

When applying NNt to the validation sets shown the results are shown in Table 4. One may see that NNt yields values for the number of terms which are always between ±2 of the actual optimum such number. The best RMS errors for T have been highlighted in Table 4.

5 Interpretation of a Model from Experimental Data

Now we applied the outlined method to the data in [19]. The idea is to use a system for the classification of three wines. We must find, from a data base, the way in which the class depends on the following 13 variables:1) Alcohol, 2) Malic acid, 3) Ash, 4) Alcalinity of ash, 5) Magnesium, 6) Total phenols, 7) Flavanoids, 8) Nonflavanoid phenols, 9) Proanthocyanins, 10) Color intensity, 11) Hue, 12) OD280/OD315 of diluted wines, 13) Proline. This is a well known data base. It has been tackled with various Learning Machine methods. In this regard the authors remark: "The data was used with many others for comparing various classifiers. The classes are separable, though only RDA has achieved 100% correct classification. (RDA: 100%, QDA 99.4%, LDA 98.9%, 1NN 96.1% (z-transformed data)). All results using the leave-one-out technique."

From NNt we found out that T = 10. The full data base consists of 168 tuples. From these, 132 were used to train the algorithm whereas the remaining 36 were used for test. After training Eq. (5) resulted.

When the test set´s values were input to Eq. (5) we obtained the results illustrated in Fig. 2.

$$Class = c_1 + c_2 V_{12} + c_3 V_2 + c_4 V_9 + c_5 V_7 + c_6 V_5$$
$$+ c_7 V_4 V_5^2 + c_8 V_4 V_6 V_7 + c_9 V_4 V_6 V_9 + c_{10} V_9^2 V_{12} \tag{5}$$

The first 10 tuples correspond to wine 0, the next 14 to wine 1 and the remaining 12 to class 2. Since the range of (5) is a real number and the classes are fixed integers, there is an inherent classification error. However, as long as the values of (5) are $\leq .25$ the corresponding tuple unequivocally is class 0. Likewise, when the values of (5) are between .26 and .75 the tuple belongs to class 1 whereas if (5) yields a value $> .76$ this indicates the tuple to correspond to class 2. In this regard Eq. (5) represents a perfect classifier. This fact is, in itself, remarkable.

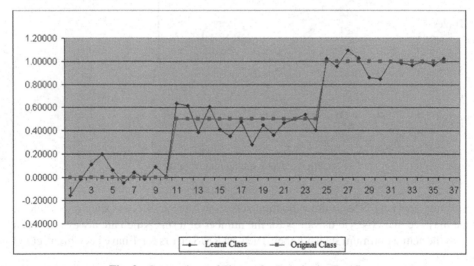

Fig. 2. Comparison of Fitness for Data in the Test Set.

Before we noted that according to previous reported results "Only RDA has achieved 100% correct classification. (RDA: 100%, QDA 99.4%, LDA 98.9%, 1NN 96.1% (z-transformed data))". Here 100% accuracy was achieved on TEST DATA.

However, the most important issue to highlight is that not only were we able to find an explicit algebraic polynomial where the black-box nature of alternative methods has been superseded, but that we may gain new insights to the problem.

For example, right away we may see that only variables V_2, V_4, V_5, V_6, V_7, V_9, V_{12} do appear in (5). Which means that the attributes Alcohol, Ash, Nonflavanoid phenols, Color intensity, Hue and Proline are irrelevant in terms of classification effectiveness. A most interesting observation since the set of original attributes was determined by a group of experts.

We may also see that 1) OD280/OD315 of diluted wines, Malic Acid, Proanthocyanins, Flavanoids and Magnesium are all unrelated, 2) Alcalinity of ash, Total phenols and Flavanoids are linearly related, 3) Alcalinity of ash and OD280/OD315 of diluted wines are related to the squared values of Magnesium and Proanthocyanins respectively, 4) The relations between the variables are never of degree higher than 3, 5) The largest relative affinity is the combination of Alcalinity, Phenols and Flavanoids. We will not delve into further qualitative conclusions which may be extracted from the values of the coefficients for the sake of brevity.

In conclusion, the method described herein is applicable to a large variety of phenomena whose attributes values are already known but whose underlying models have remained unknown. We will expand on these results in a paper to appear soon.

References

1. Rumelhart, D.E., Hinton, G.E., Williams, R.J.: Learning internal representations by error propagation. In: Rumelhart, D., McClelland, J., the PDP research group. (eds.) Parallel Distributed Processing: Explorations in the Microstructure of Cognition, vol. 1: Foundations. MIT Press (1986)
2. Haykin, S.: Neural Networks and Learning Machines, 3rd edn, Chap. 4, Multilayer Perceptrons. Prentice Hall (2009). ISBN-13: 978–0–13–147139–9
3. Powell, M.J.D.: The theory of radial basis functions. In:. Light, W (ed.) Advances in Numerical Analysis II: Wavelets, Subdivision, and Radial Basis Functions. King Fahd University of Petroleum & Minerals (1992)
4. Haykin, S.: Chap. 5, Kernel Methods and Radial Basis Functions (2009)
5. Cortes, C., Vapnik, V.: Support-vector networks. Mach. Learn. **20** (1995). http://www.springerlink.com/content/k238jx04hm87j80g/
6. Haykin, S.: Chap. 6, Support Vector Machines (2009)
7. MacKay, D.: Information Theory, Inference, and Learning Algorithms. Cambridge (2004). ISBN 0–521–64298–1
8. Ratkowsky, D.: Handbook of Nonlinear Regression Models, Marcel Dekker, Inc., New York, Library of Congress QA278.2 .R369 (1990)
9. Beckermann, B.: The condition number of real Vandermonde, Krylov and positive definite Hankel matrices. Numer. Math. **85**(4), 553–577 (2000). https://doi.org/10.1007/PL00005392
10. Meyer, C.: Matrix Analysis and Applied Linear Algebra, Society for Industrial and Applied Mathematics (SIAM) (2001). ISBN 978-0-89871-454-8
11. Kuri-Morales, A.: Training neural networks using non-standard norms- preliminary results. In: Cairó, O., Súcar, E., Cantú, F. (eds.) Lecture Notes in Artificial Intelligence, vol. 1793, pp. 350–364. Springer, Heidelberg (2020) ISBN: 3-540-67354-7, ISSN: 0302-9743
12. Cybenko, G.: Approximation by superpositions of a sigmoidal function. Math. Control Signals Syst. **2**, 303–314 (1989)

13. Bishop, E.: A generalization of the Stone-Weierstrass theorem. Pac. J. Math. **11**(3), 777–783 (1961)
14. Koornwinder, T., Wong, R., Koekoek, R., Swarttouw, R.: Orthogonal polynomials. In: Olver, F., Lozier, D., Boisvert, R., et al. (eds.) NIST Handbook of Mathematical Functions. Cambridge University Press, Cmabridge (2010). ISBN 978-0521192255
15. Scheid, F.: Numerical Analysis, Schaum's Outline Series, Chap. 21, Least Squares Polynomial Approximation (1968). ISBN 07-055197-9
16. Kuri-Morales, A., Aldana-Bobadilla, E.: The best genetic algorithm part I. In: Castro, G.G. (ed.) A Comparative Study of Structurally Different Genetic Algorithms, pp. 1–15. Springer, Heidelberg (2013). ISBN: 9783642451119, ISSN: 1611-3349
17. Kuri-Morales, A., Aldana-Bobadilla, E., López-Peña, J.: The best genetic algorithm part II. In: Castro, G.G. (ed.) A Comparative Study of Structurally Different Genetic Algorithms, pp. 16–29. Springer, Heidelberg (2013). ISBN: 9783642451119, ISSN: 1611-3349
18. Cheney, E.W.: Introduction to Approximation Theory, pp. 34–45. McGraw-Hill Book Company (1966)
19. https://archive.ics.uci.edu/ml/datasets/wine. Accessed 18 Feb 2023

Using Machine Learning to Identify Patterns in Learner-Submitted Code for the Purpose of Assessment

Botond Tarcsay[✉] ⓘ, Fernando Perez-Tellez ⓘ, and Jelena Vasic ⓘ

School of Enterprise Computing and Digital Transformation, Technological University Dublin,
Dublin, Ireland
botond@shoployal.ie, fernandopt@gmail.com,
jelena.vasic@tudublin.ie

Abstract. Programming has become an important skill in today's world and is taught widely both in traditional and online settings. Instructors need to grade increasing amounts of student work. Unit testing can contribute to the automation of the grading process but it cannot assess the structure or partial correctness of code, which is needed for finely differentiated grading. This paper builds on previous research that investigated machine learning models for determining the correctness of programs from token-based features of source code and found that some such models can be successful in classifying source code with respect to whether it passes unit tests. This paper makes two further contributions. First, these results are scrutinized under conditions of varying similarity between code instances used for model training and testing, for a better understanding of how well the models generalize. It was found that the models do not generalize outside of groups of code instances performing very similar tasks (corresponding to similar coding assignments). Second, selected binary classification models are used as a base for multi-class prediction with two different methods. Both of these exhibit prediction success well above the random baseline, with potential to contribute to automated assessment with multi-valued measures of quality (grading schemes), in contrast to the binary pass/fail measure associated with unit testing.

Keywords: Applied Machine Learning for Code Assessment · Student Programming Code Grading · Automated Grading

1 Introduction

Manually grading student code submissions on a large scale is a tedious and time-consuming process. With the rise of online programming courses, thousands of submissions must be graded in a short time. Most automated solutions use question-specific unit testing to check if the code is runnable and if it generates the desired output. For some purposes this may be sufficient but, in most contexts, assessing code based on these two properties (execution without error and correct output) is not adequate for different reasons. First, correct output can be generated in different ways. For example, printing

A. Y. Rodríguez-González et al. (Eds.): MCPR 2023, LNCS 13902, pp. 47–57, 2023.
https://doi.org/10.1007/978-3-031-33783-3_5

numbers from one to ten can be implemented with a loop or with ten print statements, two approaches that could warrant different grades in spite of appearing the same to a unit test. Second, solutions that do not pass unit tests might still contain sections that go a long way towards solving the given programming problem correctly, or even contain only a typing error that causes the program to fail the unit test.

The aim of our research is to investigate if machine learning methods can be applied to the task of evaluating programs based on source code. Previous work by the authors [2] produced models that successfully learnt, from source code tokens, whether the program consisting of those tokens would pass unit testing or not. The research was limited in scope to code solving simple problems, written by students in the first year of learning to program. It found that both feature sets based on token counts and those based on token sequence information could lead to successful binary prediction (of the unit test pass/fail result), provided that a suitable model type was used with the feature set (Random Forest for token count data and Convolutional Neural Network for token sequence data). The work presented in this paper answers two important further questions about these binary prediction models: (1) How generalizable is the pass/fail prediction success with respect to the task performed by the code? In other words, are the models learning information specific to particular programming problems, from code tackling those particular problems, or are they learning some more general properties of passing vs. failing code? and (2) Can the successful binary classification models be used as the basis for fitting multi-class prediction models, which assign more finely differentiated quality labels (grades)?

Both questions have implications for the eventual application of code-evaluating machine learning models. A more general model allows for more flexible data gathering and training. Hence generalization is an important property to quantify. Also, since multi-class labelled data are not as readily available or abundant as code evaluated through unit testing with the binary pass/fail label, a methodology that makes good use of the latter would be very useful for automating assessment.

This paper is organized as follows: Sect. 2 contains a review of related work, Sect. 3 describes the models previously built by the authors for binary prediction, upon which the work described in this paper is based, Sect. 4 discusses the investigation of generalization (first research question), including methodology and results, Sect. 5, similarly, presents the methodology and results of work on multi-class prediction (second research question) and Sect. 6 contains conclusions, including a discussion of limitations and possible future work.

2   Related Work

A lot of research has been done on understanding source code by different methods and for different purposes. A recent paper [14] reviews the related literature on how automatic grading works and what effect it has on the education system. The author summarized 127 papers on this topic. It was concluded that based on the literature there is no evidence that automated code assessment can or cannot produce as good results as human graders. A comprehensive study [15] explores the current automated grading tools presenting the reason why a new automated assessment model is required. SemCluster [3] uses two different clustering to group code instances into classes based on their semantic content and to associate them with the relevant programming problem. InferCode [4] looks at code instances individually, using self-supervised machine learning algorithms with natural language processing to deduce the abstract syntax trees of program code by predicting sub-trees. Engine Fuzzer with Montage [13] uses neural network language models to discover vulnerabilities directly in source code. Another important application of source code analysis is plagiarism detection, which is approached with information retrieval techniques in [6] and code structure modelling in [11]. DeepReview [10] utilizes a convolutional neural network for automated code reviews. Another task tackled with the use of deep learning methods is data type prediction for Python: Type4Py [9] uses word2vec embeddings to create type hints based on code context.

Automated grading of student coding work has been a widely researched subject, especially in the last few years due to the increasing demand for programmers and consequent growth in training, as part of both traditional and online courses, where work needs to be evaluated and graded at scale. A paper proposing a method called ProgEdu [7] deals with automated code quality assessment and feedback to students by means of unit testing. A rule-based approach using sophisticated scripts to evaluate, run and grade code is proposed in [5]. AutoGrader [12] compares execution paths using formal methods and reference implementations to evaluate code. A question and language-independent comparison technique based on bag-of-words for distance computation is used in [8], while [16] uses parse tree models and word embedding models to compare the feature vectors created from the source code with LSTMs.

The research presented in this paper takes the approach of treating programs as data in the simplest manner, through the textual tokens of their source code and without intervening representations such as the abstract syntax tree, which is different from what has been published so far in this domain, to the best knowledge of the authors. While the complex structure of most code suggests that this would be a naïve approach, we propose that it is not so in the very specific use case of grading work by early stage programming students, where assignments are elemental. As at the same time it is a use case that entails a large amount of work on the part of instructors, while feedback to students is essential, it is one that would greatly benefit from automation and research towards that goal.

3   Binary Classification

This section gives a brief overview of the binary classification models that provided a starting point for the work discussed in this paper. A detailed account of the work on fitting these models was given in a previous paper by the authors [2].

These models determine whether code will pass unit tests or not, solely based on information derived from the textual tokens in the source code. The availability of large amounts of data for this task, easily labelled through unit testing, makes it a good starting point for the investigation of simple token-based features for evaluating code.

The data used to train the binary classification models was collected by Azcona et al. [1] as part of their research aimed at identifying learning development potential by means of profiling students based on their source code. The data contain half a million source code instances, each accompanied by the name of the programming problem (set by lecturers) that it attempts to solve and by its unit test pass/fail status (58% fail and 42% pass). These were collected from more than 660 early-stage students of programming, answering 657 different questions in Python across 3 academic years. The dataset is publicly available from the reference link Azcona et al. [1].

Two different types of feature set were designed. In the first type of feature set each feature represents the number of times a particular token appears in a code instance. The number of features in the set is equal to the number of distinct tokens used in all the code in the data set. This type of set we refer to as a token count feature set. In the second type of feature set, the tokens are the features, with their order preserved. In practice, padding is added to bring all code instances to equal length and the tokens are represented by labels. The number of features in this set is equal to the length, in tokens, of the longest code instance. This type we refer to as a token sequence feature set.

Before the feature sets were created, the data set of Python code instances was translated into Python ByteCode, which has the advantage of succinctness in comparison with the Python source code, both in terms of code length and the number of distinct tokens. Both types of feature set were created from each set of code instances (Python and ByteCode) resulting in four feature sets for model fitting.

The token count feature sets were used to fit several conventional machine learning model types, with Decision Tree (F1 = .81, F1 = .85 on Python and ByteCode respectively) and Random Forest (F1 = .83, F1 = .87 on Python and ByteCode respectively) achieving the best prediction scores on test data. The token sequence feature sets were used to fit RNN, LSTM and CNN models. This included additional preprocessing of the data to transform the features into embeddings. The best prediction scores were achieved by CNN (F1 = .76, F1 = .81 with Python and ByteCode respectively). The conclusions of this work were (1) that determining the quality of code based on textual tokens in the source is possible and (2) that ByteCode data can be used for computing-resource efficiency as it results in prediction success comparable to or better than that achieved with Python data.

These promising results warranted further work, with the same feature sets but towards building models for a more granular measure of code quality. The following two sections describe this work.

4 What Did the Binary Classifiers Learn?

While some of the models built on binary (pass/fail)-labelled data displayed very good classification skill, it was still unclear whether the knowledge contained in the models was programming-problem-specific or more general. This is because the models were built with feature sets randomly split into training and testing subsets, with each programming problem likely to be present (via associated code instances) in both subsets.

4.1 Methodology

The first step towards clarifying how general the models are was to define levels of generalization: (1) for any programming problem addressed by a test code instance, there are training code instances associated with the same programming problem; (2) for any programming problem associated with a test code instance, there are no training code instances associated with the same programming problem but there are training code instances associated with similar programming problems and (3) for any programming problem associated with a test code instance, there are no training code instances associated with the same or similar programming problems.

Next, the best binary classification models were fitted again, with the data splits reflecting the three levels of generalization.

Level 1. Random Forest and CNN models were built for individual programming problems, with both train and test subsets containing code instances associated with one and the same programming problem. The two chosen model types are those that performed best in binary prediction (described in Sect. 3). Random Forest contained 20 estimators with a max depth of 40, while the CNN model used an embedding layer along with a Conv1D layer with GlobalMaxPooling1D and two Dense layers with 25 and 2 neurons.

Three models were built for each programming problem (using 400, 900 and 2000 instances, where available). The purpose of the three models was to understand how the sample size affects the quality of the models.

Level 2. Programming problem similarity was determined based on name semantics. For example, problems named 'count numbers', 'count items', 'count up', 'count even', 'count up to odd', 'count down' and 'count odd' were grouped together. Then the code instances associated with the group were segregated by programming problem: in the previous example all instances associated with problems 'count numbers', 'count items', 'count up', 'count even' and 'count up to odd' were used for model training and instances associated with problems 'count down' and 'count odd' for testing. As with level 1, CNN and Random Forest were used and models fitted for two different groups of similar programming problems.

Level 3. The programming problem names were used again, but this time to include entirely different problems in the train and test subsets. As in this case the models would have to learn general correct and incorrect code patterns, only sequence-aware model types were used. The LSTM model consisted of an Embedding layer, a SpatialDropout1D layer, 2 LSTM layers with 50 and 25 neurons and a 0.1 dropout, and a Dense layer with 2 neurons. The CNN structure was the same as that for level 1 and level 2 investigations.

4.2 Results

Level 1. Figure 1 shows the F1 scores of models trained on single programming problems. Only programming problems with 2000 instances were used and for each problem three model types were fitted. Thus, for each problem represented by at least 2000 instances in the data set the picture shows three points, indicating (with their y-axis components) the F1 scores for: the problem's Random Forest model (points with slanted white line), CNN model fitted on ByteCode (points without a line) and CNN model fitted on Python code (points with vertical white line). The Random Forest scores are the highest but all three model types display scores consistently better than random guessing (.5). Figure 2 shows F1 scores for a representative sample of programming problems, each used to fit CNN models with 400, 900 and 2000 instances. Larger data set sizes generally improve the scores, as expected.

Level 2. Table 1 contains F1 scores for models trained and tested on similar programming problems. Models were built for two groups of similar problems, created as explained in Sect. 4.1. The scores (~.7) testify to a deterioration in the amount of learning achieved, when compared to models built with same problems in the train and test subsets at level 1 (~.8). This indicates that programming-problem-specific patterns are a considerable part of what is learnt by models at level 1.

Level 3. A model that in the context of this research generalizes at level 3 would be learning general code quality indicators, however, as can be seen from Table 2, this is not the case with the feature sets and model types used here. The models that were fitted all exhibit F1 scores only slightly greater than random guessing would produce. This indicates that there could be a very small amount of general learning taking place, but equally that there could be similarities between all the simple programming problems present in the data set. There is a consistent pattern of larger recall for fail than for pass predictions and more similar precision values. This indicates the association of pass labels with specific feature patterns, especially in token sequence data.

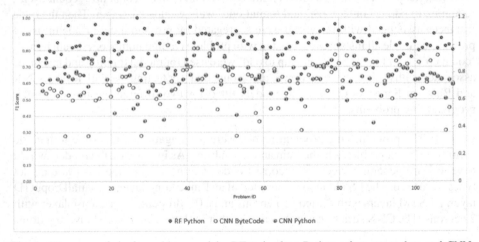

Fig. 1. F1 scores of single-problem models: RF trained on Python token count data and CNN trained on both ByteCode and Python token sequence data (2000 instances in all cases)

Summary. The relative performance of models built with different levels of similarity between the train and test subset in terms of included programming problems shows that the data sets and model types employed here can be trained on source code to tell if unseen simple programs work, but only if taught with samples of code attempting to solve the same or similar problems. This, of course, does not exclude the possibility that further generalization is achievable with more complex feature sets or models.

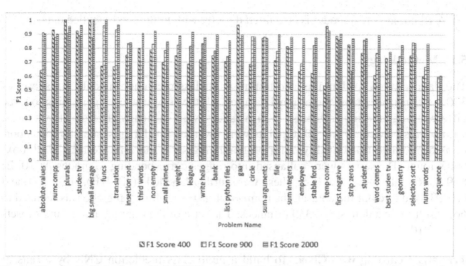

Fig. 2. F1 scores of single-problem CNN models with Python token sequence data, for three different training set sizes (400, 900 and 2000)

Table 1. Performance of models trained and tested on similar programming problems

	Random Forest		CNN	
	ByteCode Token Count	Python Token Count	ByteCode Token Sequence	Python Token Sequence
F1 Score (Group 1)	0.71	0.71	0.69	0.70
F1 Score (Group 2)	0.67	0.68	0.68	0.68

Table 2. Performance of models trained and tested on different programming problems

	ByteCode Token Count		Python Token Count		ByteCode Token Seq.		Python Token Seq.	
	Prec	Recall	Prec	Recall	Prec	Recall	Prec	Recall
	Decision Tree				Long-Short Term Memory Network			
Fail	0.51	0.52	0.53	0.52	0.53	0.72	0.53	0.73
Pass	0.50	0.50	0.53	0.53	0.57	0.37	0.56	0.35
Wgtd F1 Score	0.51		0.53		0.53		0.52	
	Random Forest				Convolutional Neural Network			
Fail	0.52	0.53	0.54	0.55	0.54	0.57	0.52	0.76
Pass	0.52	0.50	0.54	0.48	0.54	0.51	0.55	0.29
Wgtd F1 Score	0.53		0.54		0.54		0.50	

5 Multiclass Prediction

As binary labels are much easier to obtain for code (through unit testing) than fine-grained grades (which typically need to be assigned manually), it would be valuable to have some way of using pass/fail labelled data in the automation of fine-grained grading. Here we look at transfer learning in neural networks as a method for re-using learning with binary-labelled data.

A Random Forest model is also fitted directly with multi-class labelled data.

5.1 Methodology

The data set used for building and testing multiclass prediction models is a subset of 330 code instances from the original data set. All the code instances pertaining to three different programming problems (1530 instances) were manually graded by the authors, with scores between 0 and 10 (6 points were awarded for the presence of various portions of required functionality, 2 for programming style and 2 for correct 'black box' behaviour). The scores were collapsed into ranges corresponding to grades A: 10, B: 8–9, C: 6–7, D: 5–6 and F 0–5. These were further labelled 4(A), 3(B), 2(C), 1(D) and 0(F). To balance out the dataset, the number of instances for each grade was reduced to 66, resulting in a data set of 330 instances. The ratio of the training and testing subsets was 90/10.

Transfer Learning with CNN. To build a multi-class prediction CNN by means of transfer learning, we took advantage of the learning achieved by the CNN Python model fitted on the full data set for binary classification. The network of that model was reused in the network for multi-class prediction, with all weights fixed, except for the top layer, which was replaced in the new network by an output layer with five nodes (instead of two), one for each grade. This network was then trained on 90% of the 330 instances of manually labelled data.

Multi-class Prediction with Random Forest. As Random Forest models were performing well in binary prediction, a multi-class Random Forest model was trained on the 330-instance data set. Transfer learning is not applicable in this case.

5.2 Results

As Table 3 shows, the F1 scores achieved were similar with neural network transfer learning (F = .59 for LSTM and F = .64 for CNN) and the Random Forest model trained from scratch (F1 = .63). Both are better than the expected F1 score of random guessing (.2) for a 5-class prediction task.

Table 3. Performance of multi-class prediction models

	Random Forest Multiclass Python		LSTM Python Transfer Learning		CNN Python Transfer Learning	
	Prec	Recall	Prec	Recall	Prec	Recall
Class A	0.50	1.00	0.67	1.00	0.78	1.00
Class B	0.75	0.75	0.76	0.76	1.00	0.50
Class C	0.40	0.29	0.20	0.17	1.00	0.44
Class D	0.86	0.67	0.67	0.31	0.33	0.43
Class F	1.00	0.50	1.00	0.22	0.50	1.00
Wgtd F1 Score	0.63		0.63		0.64	

Confusion matrix heat maps are shown in Fig. 3 for the CNN and LSTM models and in Fig. 4 for the Random Forest model. From these, it can be seen that the neural network models, using token sequence data, exhibit slightly better performance in terms of closeness of the predicted and real value.

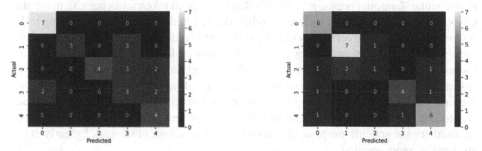

Fig. 3. CNN (left) and LSTM (right) transfer learning confusion matrix heat maps

Summary. The multi-class machine learning prediction models that have been fitted show promise as potential mechanisms for automated grading of programming assignments. An interesting finding is that transfer learning utilizing binary prediction neural network models fitted with a large data set does not seem to produce better results than a Random Forest model fitted with a small amount of multi-class labelled data. However, this work was conducted with code solving only simple programming problems and it is possible that the learning capability harnessed by these two approaches would diverge in the case of more complex code, with the CNN and LSTM performing better in comparison to Random Forest.

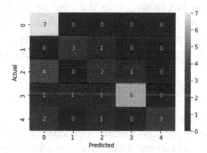

Fig. 4. Random Forest multi-class prediction model confusion matrix heat map

6 Conclusion and Further Work

This paper presented an investigation of machine learning models as a means of evaluating programs on the basis of their source code. Both binary and multiple-class models resulted in prediction scores better than the baseline. While further work on refining and complementing these models is needed before practical application becomes possible, the value of the work presented here is that it provides evidence of learning in several model types fitted with features derived directly from source code tokens.

Further, it was found that the performance of models that learnt from token counts, in particular Random Forests, and models that learnt from token sequences, in particular CNNs, was not significantly different, indicating that in the case of simple coding tasks the presence of the correct tokens may be sufficient to indicate quality and that the more complex knowledge of sequences may not be required to automatically grade assignments at this level. Further research is needed to explain this, but it can be reasonably assumed that what this is telling us is that if a student knows which constructs to use, then they are probably also going to know in what order to use them. This, of course, would not be applicable in the case of more complex programs, but the findings could be used for the specific purpose of automating the assessment of work by early-stage students of programming.

An admittedly disappointing but valuable finding was that the models do not learn coding patterns in general but rely on being provided correct and incorrect code for a particular problem, or very similar problems, in order to learn how to evaluate code solving that problem. This further narrows but clarifies the possible scope of future application. On the other hand, programming problems posed to beginners are by virtue of their simplicity similar across all instruction contexts, which should allow for pooling of data in the training of a deployed model.

On the whole, the results presented here are promising and establish that it is worth pursuing simple machine learning models as a core component in automated assessment of code written by early-stage programming students. The application envisaged is a service that provides already trained models for common simple programming problems but also employs reinforcement learning to improve performance and build models of code for new problems. Such a service could be offered in variants for instructors and learners, providing constructive feedback in the case of the latter. Also in our future work, we are planning to expand the datasets and include data from other educational institutions to validate this approach as early-stage students for programming seem to follow the same programming patterns independently of the educational institution.

References

1. Azcona, D., Arora, P., Hsiao, I.H., Smeaton, A.: user2code2vec: embeddings for profiling students based on distributional representations of source code. In: Proceedings of the 9th International Conference on Learning Analytics & Knowledge, pp. 86–95. ACM, New York (2019)
2. Tarcsay, B., Vasić, J., Perez-Tellez, F.: Use of machine learning methods in the assessment of programming assignments. In: Sojka, P., Horák, A., Kopeček, I., Pala, K. (eds.) Text, Speech, and Dialogue. TSD 2022. Lecture Notes in Computer Science, vol. 13502, pp. 151–159. Springer, Cham (2022). https://doi.org/10.1007/978-3-031-16270-1_13
3. Perry, D.M., Kim, D., Samanta, R., Zhang, X.: SemCluster: clustering of imperative programming assignments based on quantitative semantic features. In: Proceedings of the 40th ACM SIGPLAN Conference on Programming Language Design and Implementation, pp. 860–873. ACM, New York (2019)

4. Bui, N.D., Yu, Y., Jiang, L.: InferCode: self-supervised learning of code representations by predicting subtrees. In: 2021 IEEE/ACM 43rd International Conference on Software Engineering (ICSE), pp. 1186–1197. IEEE (2021)

5. Hegarty-Kelly, E., Mooney, D.A.: Analysis of an automatic grading system within first year computer science programming modules. In Computing Education Practice 2021CEP 2021, pp. 17–20. Association for Computing Machinery, New York (2021)

6. Jayapati, V.S., Venkitaraman, A.: A comparison of information retrieval techniques for detecting source code plagiarism. arXiv preprint arXiv:1902.02407 (2019)

7. Chen, H.M., Chen, W.H., Lee, C.C.: An automated assessment system for analysis of coding convention violations in java programming assignments. J. Inf. Sci. Eng. **34**(5), 1203–1221 (2018)

8. Rai, K.K., Gupta, B., Shokeen, P., Chakraborty, P.: Question independent automated code analysis and grading using bag of words and machine learning. In: 2019 International Conference on Computing, Power and Communication Technologies (GUCON), pp. 93–98. IEEE (2019)

9. Mir, A.M., Latoskinas, E., Proksch, S., Gousios, G.: Type4py: deep similarity learning-based type inference for python. arXiv preprint arXiv:2101.04470 (2021)

10. Li, H.-Y., et al.: Deepreview: automatic code review using deep multi-instance learning. In: Yang, Q., Zhou, Z.-H., Gong, Z., Zhang, M.-L., Huang, S.-J. (eds.) PAKDD 2019. LNCS (LNAI), vol. 11440, pp. 318–330. Springer, Cham (2019). https://doi.org/10.1007/978-3-030-16145-3_25

11. Setoodeh, Z., Moosavi, M.R., Fakhrahmad, M., Bidoki, M.: A proposed model for source code reuse detection in computer programs. Iran. J. Sci. Technol. Trans. Electr. Eng. **45**(3), 1001–1014 (2021). https://doi.org/10.1007/s40998-020-00403-8

12. Liu, X., Wang, S., Wang, P., Wu, D.: Automatic grading of programming assignments: an approach based on formal semantics. In: 2019 IEEE/ACM 41st International Conference on Software Engineering: Software Engineering Education and Training (ICSE-SEET), pp. 126–137. IEEE (2019)

13. Lee, S., Han, H., Cha, S.K., Son, S.: Montage: a neural network language model-guided JavaScript engine fuzzer. In: 29th USENIX Security Symposium (USENIX Security 20), pp. 2613–2630 (2020)

14. Combéfis, S.: Automated code assessment for education: review, classification and perspectives on techniques and tools. Software **1**(1), 3–30 (2022)

15. Nayak, S., Agarwal, R., Khatri, S.K.: Automated assessment tools for grading of programming assignments: a review. In: International Conference on Computer Communication and Informatics (ICCCI), Coimbatore, India, 2022, pp. 1–4 (2022)

16. Vimalaraj, H., et al.: Automated programming assignment marking tool. In: IEEE 7th International conference for Convergence in Technology (I2CT), Mumbai, India, 2022, pp. 1–8 (2022)

Fitness Function Comparison for Unsupervised Feature Selection with Permutational-Based Differential Evolution

Jesús-Arnulfo Barradas-Palmeros[1](✉), Efrén Mezura-Montes[1],
Héctor-Gabriel Acosta-Mesa[1], and Rafael Rivera-López[2]

[1] Artificial Intelligence Research Institute, University of Veracruz,
Xalapa, Mexico
zS21000456@estudiantes.uv.mx, {emezura,heacosta}@uv.mx
[2] Departamento de Sistemas y Computación, Instituto Tecnológico de Veracruz,
Veracruz, Mexico
rafael.rl@veracruz.tecnm.mx

Abstract. This paper presents a comparative study of the performance of an unsupervised feature selection method using three evaluation metrics. In the existing literature, various metrics are used to guide the search for a better feature subset and evaluate the resulting data clusterization. Still, there is no well-established path for the unsupervised wrapper-based approach as for the supervised case. This work compares three metrics to guide the search in a permutational-based differential evolution algorithm to feature selection: the Silhouette Coefficient, the Kalinski-Harabasz Index, and the Davies-Bouldin Score. The experimental results indicate that no metric performed better when applying the feature selection process to thirteen datasets. Nevertheless, a clear tendency to select small subsets is observed. Furthermore, in some cases, performing the feature selection decreased the performance compared to the complete dataset.

Keywords: Unsupervised learning · feature selection · differential evolution

1 Introduction

The feature selection problem consists of selecting a subset of relevant features from a dataset to reduce data dimensionality and increase the performance of an algorithm such as a classifier or a clustering one. Feature selection is a complex problem, and various methods have been proposed in the literature where evolutionary computation processes have been a popular and high-performance option [15]. There are two main approaches to applying the feature selection processes: filter and wrapper. The first one uses metrics from information theory to guide the search, whereas the wrappers apply a classifier or clustering algorithm during the process [1].

The unsupervised feature selection applies internal and external metrics to evaluate the clusterization of a dataset. Internal metrics use only the information contained in the instances and calculate a score according to the grouping made by the clustering algorithm. In contrast, external metrics require using the labels associated with the instances in a process that looks more similar to the evaluation in supervised learning. A variety of metrics has been proposed in both cases [6].

Some approaches to deal with the unsupervised feature selection can be found in [6,9], and [13]. A Particle Swarm Optimization algorithm guided with the Silhouette Coefficient is applied in [9]. Using the multi-objective Differential evolution algorithm for simultaneous clustering and feature selection algorithm ($MODE-cfs$), in [6], three objectives are considered: the Silhouette Coefficient, the WB-index, and a ratio of the selected and the total number of features. Additionally, methods like [13] combine the filter approach using an information theory metric and the wrapper approach with the Calinski-Harabasz Index.

As detailed in [7], various metrics are available for cluster evaluation and search guide. Given the non-consensus about the superiority of one metric, comparing some of them brings some insights into the subject. The aforementioned is the primary purpose of this paper, where a proven approach in supervised learning as the permutational-based Differential algorithm for feature selection ($DE-FS^{PM}$) proposed in [11] is adapted to unsupervised learning. Three classic metrics for cluster evaluation: the Silhouette Coefficient, the Kalinski-Harabasz Index, and the Davies-Bouldin Score, were selected as variants for guiding the search.

The rest of this paper is organized into five additional sections. Section 2 discusses differential evolution and its adaptation to permutational search space. Section 3 shows the details of the proposal implementation. Section 4 contains information about the metrics used in this work. Section 5 shows the details of the experimentation and results. Finally, the conclusions and future work are contained in Sect. 6.

2   Permutational-Based Differential Evolution

Differential Evolution (DE) was proposed as a population-based searching algorithm in 1997 [14]. Initially designed to solve real-valued problems, it has also been modified for use in other domains [10]. The basic version of DE is called DE/rand/1/bin. In each algorithm iteration, called generation, a trial vector u_i is calculated for each target vector x_i in the population. For generating u_i, a noise vector $v_i = r_0 + F(r_1 - r_2)$ is required in the classical process. The scaling factor F is a user-defined parameter. Vectors r_0, r_1, and r_2, different from each other, are selected randomly from the population.

Adapting DE to the permutational space involves calculating $(r_1 - r_2)$ using $r_1 \leftarrow \mathbf{P}r_2$, where $\mathbf{P}$ is the permutation matrix that maps r_1 and r_2. Furthermore, v_i is calculated as $v_i \leftarrow \mathbf{P_F}r_0$. $\mathbf{P_F}$ is the scale permutation matrix whose calculation follows the stated in [10] and shown in [11]. For each row i in the matrix, if $P[i,i] = 0 \& rand_i > F$, find the row j, where $P[j,i] \neq 0$ and swap rows i, and j. The number $rand_i$ is generated randomly from a uniform distribution in the $[0,1]$ range. To generate the Trial vector (u_i), the classical crossing procedure is used by applying Eq. 1. CR or Crossing Rate is the second user-defined parameter used by ED. $rand_j$ is a random number, and J_{rand} is a randomly chosen position of the u_i vector to guarantee at least one value will be chosen from the noise vector v_i, see Eq. (1).

$$u_{i,j} = \begin{cases} v_{i,j} & \text{if } (rand_j \leq CR) \text{ or } (j = J_{rand}); j = 1, ..., |x_i| \\ x_{i,j} & \text{otherwise} \end{cases} \quad (1)$$

The crossing procedure could generate vectors that are no longer valid permutations. Then a repair mechanism is used [11]. The repeated values are eliminated in the new individual, and the vector is completed by copying the needed elements to complete the permutation from the x_i vector. Finally, the target x_i and the trial u_i are compared in a binary tournament. The one with a better fitness value is selected as part of the population for the next generation.

The potential solutions represented as the individuals of the population are coded as an integer vector with the length of the number of features in the dataset plus one. Each integer represents the index of a feature in the dataset, and the extra value corresponds to the number zero, which will work as the division between the selected and the discarded features. The values on the left of the zero are selected, and those on the right are discarded. Figure 1 shows an example of the decoding of an individual and calculating its trial vector.

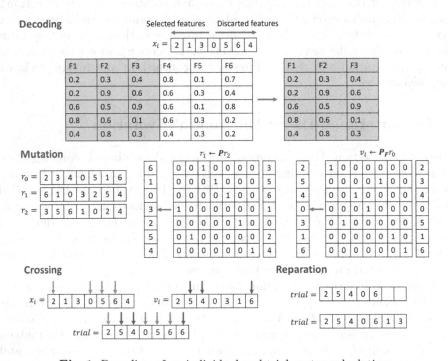

Fig. 1. Decoding of an individual and trial vector calculation.

The initial population is formed with valid permutations representing the dataset. The population size is determined by five times the number of features in the dataset, but it is bounded to at least 200 and at most 450 individuals. The user-defined parameters that control the search in this procedure are the scaling factor F, the crossing rate CR and the maximum number of generations.

3   Proposal Implementation

In this work, the $DE - FS^{PM}$ algorithm proposed in [11] for supervised learning is used now in unsupervised learning for feature selection. Consequently, the calculation of the fitness value of an individual is changed. Instead of using a classifier algorithm such as k-nearest-neighbors (knn), k-means is used as the clustering algorithm. Furthermore, given that the class labels are supposed to be unknown in unsupervised learning, the accuracy metric does not guide the search. More details about these changes are shown in the remainder of this Section and Sect. 4. The k-means algorithm needs the number of clusters for the dataset as a parameter.

The method preprocesses the dataset first, then searches for the feature subset with the highest fitness value using the $DE - FS^{PM}$ algorithm. After that, the dataset is reduced, maintaining the selected features. Finally, the reduced dataset is clustered and evaluated with additional metrics, some of which use the external information associated with the labels of the instances. Given this, the datasets used in the experimentation sections are from supervised learning. The fitness value of an individual in the population is determined by Eq. (2).

$$fitness = VI + \alpha \frac{n}{m} \qquad (2)$$

where VI is a validity index that uses an internal metric to evaluate the generated clusters. The selected metrics, described in Sect. 4, are the Silhouette Coefficient [12], the Calinski-Harabazs index [2], and the Davies Boulding score [3]. α corresponds to a coefficient used to weigh the ratio between the number of selected features n and the total number of features in the dataset m similar to one of the objective functions used in [6].

The proposed fitness function contains two aggregated objectives. The first one, which corresponds to the internal metric, gives the value of the goodness of the clusters found. The second part of the Equation is used to increment the size of the resulting feature subset since the metrics tend to assign a better value when fewer features are selected [6]. Additionally, the fitness function penalizes individuals who select an empty feature subset and those who select only one feature. The penalization value is adapted to the internal metric used in the fitness function.

Once the search process is finished, the feature subset found with the highest fitness value is used to reduce the original dataset and start the process of final clusterization. After that, external and internal metrics evaluate the quality of the clusters using the class predictions and labels of the dataset's instances. The selected metrics correspond to the sum-of-squares within each cluster (SSW) [6], and the Davies-Bouldin Index [3] as internal metrics; the Adjusted Rand Index (ARI) [8] and the Fowlkes Mallows Score (FMS) [5] as external metrics.

4   Internal Metrics as Fitness Functions

For evaluating the individuals, the resulting clusters from the clustering process are evaluated using an internal metric without using the labels for the dataset instances. The aforementioned is essential since we are trying to deal with unsupervised learning. The metrics used in the fitness function are traditional metrics for cluster evaluation: the Silhouette coefficient [12], the Calinski-Harabasz index [2], and the Davies-Bouldin score [3].

4.1   Silhouette Coefficient

As proposed in [12] and detailed in [9], the Silhouette coefficient is calculated as the mean of all the $s(x_i)$ calculations for each data point x_i in the dataset. $s(x_i)$ is calculated with Eq. 3. For each x_i, $a(x_i)$ corresponds to the average dissimilarity (defined as the euclidean distance) of x_i with all the other points of the same cluster. $b(x_i)$ is the average dissimilarity of x_i with all the elements of the nearest cluster, as in Eq. (3).

$$s(x_i) = \frac{b(x_i) - a(x_i)}{max\{a(x_i), b(x_i)\}} \tag{3}$$

The Silhouette coefficient is between $[-1, 1]$ and maximized to obtain the best clusters. The result is rescaled between 0 and 1 to make the value more suitable for using the second part of the fitness function. The previous is done by adding one to the coefficient and dividing the resulting value in half. Since the better-defined clusters have a value for the Silhouette coefficient close to 1, the penalized value used when working with this metric is 0.

4.2   Calinski-Harabazs Index

Proposed in [2], the index measures clusters' separation and compactness. As shown in [13], the index is calculated with Eq. (4). S_w is the average covariance matrix (Σ_j) of the clusters or the within-class scatter matrix calculated with Eq. (5). S_b is the between-class scatter matrix computed with Eq. (6), where m_j is the mean of a cluster and M is the mean of all points in the data, K is the total number of clusters, and N is the total number of instances in the dataset. The trace operation consists of the sum of the elements in the matrix's main diagonal.

$$CH = \frac{trace(S_b)}{trace(S_w)} \times \frac{N - c}{c - 1} \tag{4}$$

$$s_w = \frac{1}{K} \sum_{j=1}^{K} \Sigma_j \tag{5}$$

$$s_b = \frac{1}{K} \sum_{j=1}^{K} (m_j - M)(m_j - M)^T \tag{6}$$

The Calinski-Harabazs [2] resulting values are not in a predefined range. Therefore, we need to normalize the fitness value to let the weighted ratio of the fitness function have an impact. Equation (7) normalizes the population during the search. The largest resulting values from the index represent a better clusterization of the data. The penalized value, in this case, for the fitness value calculation, is zero.

$$normval = \frac{val - min}{max - min + \epsilon} \tag{7}$$

$normval$ is the resulting normalized value, and val is the actual value before normalization. min and max correspond to the minimum and maximum index in the population, respectively. Finally, the term ϵ corresponds to a value of $1 * 10^{-6}$; this term is used to avoid cases such as the ones where the maximum and minimum of the population are the same and causes a division between zero.

4.3 Davies-Bouldin Score

The Davies-Bouldin Score [3] calculates the ratio of compactness (within) and separateness (between) of the clusters. It is calculated with Eqs. 8 to 10 where $R_k = \max_{i,j} R_{ij}, i = 1, 2, ..., K, j = 1, 2, ..., K$ [6]. $R_{i,j}$ comprises the dispersion between cluster C_i and cluster C_j and D_i represents the dispersion within the cluster i. n_i is the number of instances in the cluster C_i. m_i and m_j are the means of the clusters i and j. x_p represents a data point.

$$DBI = \frac{1}{K} \sum_{j=1}^{K} R_k \tag{8}$$

$$R_{i,j} = \frac{D_i + D_j}{(m_i - m_j)(m_i - m_j)^T}, i \neq j \tag{9}$$

$$S_i = \frac{1}{(n_i)} \sum_{x_p \in C_i} (x_p - m_i)(x_p - m_i)^T \tag{10}$$

The Davies-Bouldin Score [3] differs from the previously described metrics because the better-defined clusters are assigned a lesser value where zero is the least possible. In this case, the problem would consist of minimizing the resulting values. That is why the resulting score is multiplicated by a factor of -1, transforming the problem into a maximization one. Since this metric does not return values in a fixed range like the Silhouette coefficient, it is necessary to normalize the values in the population, as mentioned in the Calinski-Harabasz Index with the Eq. 7. The penalization value is fixed at −10,000.

5   Experiments and Results

To compare the three variations of the fitness function, thirteen datasets (used in [6]) were selected for experimentation from the UCI machine learning repository. The dataset characteristics are summarized in Table 1. Following [11], the datasets used are preprocessed in a three-step sequence. First, if the dataset contains categorical and text features, these are encoded to form numerical values; then, if the dataset contains missing values, these are imputed using the most frequent value in the feature where the missing value is located. Finally, the values of each feature are normalized following a min-max normalization scheme. The parameters used in the algorithm $DE - FS^{PM}$ correspond to those proposed in [11] with F and CR fixed as 0.1514 and 0.8552, respectively. Those values demonstrated a high performance while exploring the search space and allowed us to keep the same conditions while using the three metrics to guide the search. The maximum number of generations is fixed at 100.

Table 1. Description of the selected datasets for experimentation.

Dataset	Instances	Features	Classes
Liver disorder	345	6	2
Appendicitis	106	7	2
Pima	768	8	2
WBDC	569	31	2
Ionosphere	351	33	2
Sonar	208	60	2
Iris	150	4	3

Dataset	Instances	Features	Classes
Thyroid	215	5	3
Wine	178	13	3
UKM	258	5	4
Ecoli	336	7	8
Breast-tissue	109	9	6
Dermatology	358	34	6

A series of experiments were conducted for each dataset to determine the value of the alpha parameter used in the tested fitness functions. The final values correspond to 0.125 for the fitness function using the Silhouette coefficient and 0.5 for those with the Calinski-Harabazs and Davies-Bouldin scores. It was noted that the function that uses the Silhouette had a more sensitive adjustment to this value, while the other functions only presented slight differences. The tests were conducted with seven algorithm runs for each dataset and each method. Additionally, the performance of the clustering algorithm without feature selection is included. The results for the number of selected features and the evaluation with metrics mentioned in Sect. 3 are shown in Table 2, where a ranking from 1 to 5 is included for each dataset and each metric.

As suggested in [4], statistical tests are conducted to compare the results of the reported methods. The Friedman statistical test was performed using the

Table 2. Results of comparing the different fitness functions and the results in [6].

Dataset	Method	#SF	SSW		DB		ARI		FMS	
Liver disorder	wo FS	6	29.966	(4)	1.312	(5)	−0.001	(1.5)	0.616	(4)
	FS wSil	3	9.181	(3)	0.827	(3)	−0.006	(4)	0.626	(3)
	FS wCH	2	5.356	(1.5)	0.684	(1.5)	−0.005	(3)	0.634	(1.5)
	FS wDB	2	5.356	(1.5)	0.684	(1.5)	−0.005	(3)	0.634	(1.5)
	MODE−cfs	4.03	141.840	(5)	1.258	(4)	−0.001	(1.5)	0.511	(5)
Appendicitis	wo FS	7	17.434	(5)	1.027	(5)	0.311	(5)	0.748	(5)
	FS wSil	2	3.157	(2)	0.507	(2)	0.357	(3)	0.805	(3)
	FS wCH	2	3.157	(2)	0.507	(2)	0.357	(3)	0.805	(3)
	FS wDB	2	3.157	(2)	0.507	(2)	0.357	(3)	0.805	(3)
	MODE-cfs	5.06	11.476	(4)	0.776	(4)	0.440	(1)	0.820	(1)
Pima	wo FS	8	121.258	(4)	1.608	(5)	0.102	(2)	0.597	(4)
	FS wSil	2	17.642	(1)	0.541	(2)	0.010	(5)	0.705	(2)
	FS wCH	2	24.189	(3)	0.727	(3)	0.106	(1)	0.598	(3)
	FS wDB	2	21.211	(2)	0.302	(1)	0.012	(4)	0.706	(1)
	MODE-cfs	3.70	231.360	(5)	1.124	(4)	0.089	(3)	0.572	(5)
WDBC	wo FS	31	226.498	(5)	1.158	(5)	0.730	(1)	0.877	(1)
	FS wSil	2	4.540	(2)	0.229	(2)	0.003	(4.5)	0.716	(4.5)
	FS wCH	2	8.646	(3)	0.438	(3)	0.491	(3)	0.804	(3)
	FS wDB	2	3.843	(1)	0.144	(1)	0.003	(4.5)	0.716	(4.5)
	MODE-cfs	16.06	157.980	(4)	1.013	(4)	0.723	(2)	0.870	(2)
Ionosphere	wo FS	33	628.897	(5)	1.535	(5)	0.177	(3)	0.605	(3)
	FS wSil	2	17.050	(1)	0.467	(2)	0.209	(1.5)	0.735	(1.5)
	FS wCH	2	20.292	(2)	0.554	(3)	0.137	(5)	0.600	(4)
	FS wDB	2	22.354	(3)	0.339	(1)	0.209	(1.5)	0.735	(1.5)
	MODE-cfs	21.36	134.970	(4)	1.198	(4)	0.160	(4)	0.593	(5)
Sonar	wo FS	60	445.556	(5)	2.119	(5)	0.007	(3)	0.503	(4)
	FS wSil	2	5.206	(1)	0.497	(3)	0.021	(2)	0.596	(1)
	FS wCH	2	6.502	(2.5)	0.443	(1.5)	−0.004	(4.5)	0.515	(2.5)
	FS wDB	2	6.502	(2.5)	0.443	(1.5)	−0.004	(4.5)	0.515	(2.5)
	MODE-cfs	29.50	73.964	(4)	1.791	(4)	0.027	(1)	0.451	(5)
Iris	wo FS	4	6.998	(4)	0.761	(5)	0.716	(4)	0.811	(3)
	FS wSil	2	1.705	(2)	0.472	(2)	0.886	(2)	0.923	(2)
	FS wCH	2	1.705	(2)	0.472	(2)	0.886	(2)	0.923	(2)
	FS wDB	2	1.705	(2)	0.472	(2)	0.886	(2)	0.923	(2)
	MODE-cfs	2.93	15.614	(5)	0.666	(4)	0.620	(5)	0.755	(5)
Thyroid	wo FS	5	10.651	(4)	0.847	(4)	0.628	(1)	0.855	(1)
	FS wSil	2	1.586	(1.5)	0.622	(2.5)	0.227	(3.5)	0.761	(3.5)
	FS wCH	2	1.586	(1.5)	0.622	(2.5)	0.227	(3.5)	0.761	(3.5)
	FS wDB	2	2.112	(3)	0.513	(1)	0.364	(2)	0.785	(2)
	MODE-cfs	2.80	38.477	(5)	0.858	(5)	0.220	(5)	0.584	(5)

(continued)

Table 2. (*continued*)

Dataset	Method	#SF	SSW		DB		ARI		FMS	
Wine	wo FS	13	48.956	(4)	1.306	(5)	0.864	(2)	0.910	(2)
	FS wSil	2	4.334	(2.5)	0.627	(1.5)	0.584	(3.5)	0.739	(3.5)
	FS wCH	2	3.558	(1)	0.846	(3)	0.500	(5)	0.669	(5)
	FS wDB	2	4.334	(2.5)	0.627	(1.5)	0.584	(3.5)	0.739	(3.5)
	MODE-cfs	10.63	71.721	(5)	1.217	(4)	0.870	(1)	0.913	(1)
UKM	wo FS	5	45.788	(5)	1.577	(5)	0.239	(5)	0.449	(5)
	FS wSil	2	7.081	(1.5)	0.664	(3)	0.361	(3)	0.544	(3)
	FS wCH	2	7.082	(3)	0.664	(3)	0.361	(3)	0.544	(3)
	FS wDB	2	7.081	(1.5)	0.664	(3)	0.361	(3)	0.544	(3)
	MODE-cfs	1.30	10.119	(4)	0.546	(1)	0.407	(1)	0.599	(1)
Ecoli	wo FS	7	17.451	(4)	1.162	(5)	0.432	(2)	0.565	(2)
	FS wSil	2	1.75E-30	(1.5)	0.000	(1.5)	0.038	(4.5)	0.531	(3.5)
	FS wCH	2	0.529	(3)	0.468	(3)	0.257	(3)	0.420	(5)
	FS wDB	2	1.75E-30	(1.5)	0.000	(1.5)	0.038	(4.5)	0.531	(3.5)
	MODE-cfs	6.66	113.56	(5)	0.921	(4)	0.683	(1)	0.778	(1)
Breast-tissue	wo FS	9	6.832	(4)	0.873	(5)	0.293	(2)	0.463	(2)
	FS wSil	2	0.211	(1.5)	0.382	(1.5)	0.182	(4.5)	0.413	(4.5)
	FS wCH	2	0.291	(3)	0.504	(3)	0.277	(3)	0.445	(3)
	FS wDB	2	0.211	(1.5)	0.382	(1.5)	0.182	(4.5)	0.413	(4.5)
	MODE-cfs	6.66	15.733	(5)	0.696	(4)	0.377	(1)	0.696	(1)
Dermatology	wo FS	34	432.361	(5)	1.754	(5)	0.723	(2)	0.779	(2)
	FS wSil	2	7.91E-30	(1)	0.000	(2)	0.096	(5)	0.432	(4)
	FS wCH	2	1.13E-29	(2)	0.000	(2)	0.115	(4)	0.437	(3)
	FS wDB	2	1.82E-29	(3)	0.000	(2)	0.128	(3)	0.428	(5)
	MODE-cfs	27.56	126.7	(4)	1.456	(4)	0.900	(1)	0.923	(1)
Average rank	wo FS		4.14		4.57		2.39		2.71	
	FS wSil		1.54		2.00		3.29		2.79	
	FS wCH		2.11		2.32		3.07		2.96	
	FS wDB		1.93		1.46		3.07		2.68	
	MODE-cfs		4.21		3.57		1.96		2.71	

Fowlkes and Mallows score values. A p-value of 0.9 indicates that the means of the populations are equal. The post-hoc Nemenyi test was calculated as an ($N \times N$) comparison of the same metric and the compared algorithm variants. The 95%-confidence results indicate no significant differences among the compared fitness functions.

From the results in Table 2, it is clear that the Feature Selection procedure, regardless of the fitness function adopted, considerably improves the internal metrics compared to the clustering process without Feature selection. Nevertheless, this is not necessarily the case for external metrics. In the obtained rankings, the procedure with no feature selection reached a good position for the external metrics but not for the internal metrics, where it was the worse.

Finally, compared to the state-of-the-art approach proposed in [6], MODE-cfs, the three DE-based variants were highly competitive based on the rankings summarized at the end of Table 2. Nonetheless, there is a clear difference in the resulting number of selected features.

6   Conclusions and Future Work

This work compared three metrics as part of the fitness function of the $DE - FS^{PM}$ algorithm for feature selection in unsupervised learning. In supervised learning, there is a more defined path to evaluate and do the searching. In contrast, various metrics can be used for the search and final evaluation in unsupervised learning, making comparing results with different state-of-the-art approaches harder.

The results showed no significant difference between using the Silhouette Coefficient, the Calinski-Harabasz Index, or the Davies-Boulding score to guide the search. Nonetheless, the first and third metrics got slightly better results than the second. Something in common was the dimension of the feature subset selected. In most cases, the metrics selected only two features despite using the weighted ratio between the selected features and the total number of features to find larger subsets. The previous confirms the tendency of the metrics to get better performance with smaller subsets of features. Finally, compared to a state-of-the-art approach, MODE-cfs, the three proposed fitness functions using the DE-based search provided competitive results.

Future work will consider more experimentation to analyze the effects of changing the metric used in the fitness function and if the results are similar when the process is applied to larger datasets with more than 100 features. The problem shown when the clusterization with the complete dataset performs better than the clusterization with the selected features is a fundamental challenge since the opposite is expected. A multi-objective approach could be considered to deal with the selection of small subsets of features. Given this, there is much room for improving the feature selection approaches in this area.

Acknowledgements. The first author (CVU 1142850) acknowledges support from Mexico's National Council of Science and Technology (CONACYT) through a scholarship to pursue graduate studies at the University of Veracruz.

References

1. Ang, J.C., Mirzal, A., Haron, H., Hamed, H.N.A.: Supervised, unsupervised, and semi-supervised feature selection: A review on gene selection. IEEE/ACM Trans. Comput. Biol. Bioinf. **13**(5), 971–989 (2016). https://doi.org/10.1109/TCBB.2015. 2478454
2. Caliński, T., Harabasz, J.: A dendrite method for cluster analysis. Commun. Stat. **3**(1), 1–27 (1974). https://doi.org/10.1080/03610927408827101

3. Davies, D.L., Bouldin, D.W.: A cluster separation measure. IEEE Trans. Pattern Anal. Mach. Intell. PAMI-**1**(2), 224–227 (1979). https://doi.org/10.1109/TPAMI. 1979.4766909

4. Derrac, J., García, S., Molina, D., Herrera, F.: A practical tutorial on the use of nonparametric statistical tests as a methodology for comparing evolutionary and swarm intelligence algorithms. Swarm Evol. Comput. **1**(1), 3–18 (2011). https:// doi.org/10.1016/j.swevo.2011.02.002

5. Fowlkes, E.B., Mallows, C.L.: A method for comparing two hierarchical clusterings. J. Am. Stat. Assoc. **78**(383), 553–569 (1983). https://doi.org/10.1080/01621459. 1983.10478008

6. Hancer, E.: A new multi-objective differential evolution approach for simultaneous clustering and feature selection. Eng. Appl. Artif. Intell. **87**, 103307 (2020). https://doi.org/10.1016/j.engappai.2019.103307

7. Hancer, E., Xue, B., Zhang, M.: A survey on feature selection approaches for clustering. Artif. Intell. Rev. **53**(6), 4519–4545 (2020). https://doi.org/10.1007/ s10462-019-09800-w

8. Hubert, L., Arabie, P.: Comparing partitions. J. Classif. **2**(1), 193–218 (1985). https://doi.org/10.1007/BF01908075

9. Prakash, J., Singh, P.K.: Particle swarm optimization with k-means for simultaneous feature selection and data clustering. In: 2015 Second International Conference on Soft Computing and Machine Intelligence (ISCMI). pp. 74–78 (2015). https:// doi.org/10.1109/ISCMI.2015.30

10. Price, K.V., Storn, R.M., Lampinen, J.A.: Differential Evolution: A Practical Approach to Global Optimization. Springer, Berlin Heidelberg, Berlin, Heidelberg (2005). https://doi.org/10.1007/3-540-31306-0

11. Rivera-López, R., Mezura-Montes, E., Canul-Reich, J., Cruz-Chávez, M.A.: A permutational-based differential evolution algorithm for feature subset selection. Pattern Recogn. Lett. **133**, 86–93 (2020). https://doi.org/10.1016/j.patrec.2020. 02.021

12. Rousseeuw, P.J.: Silhouettes: a graphical aid to the interpretation and validation of cluster analysis. J. Comput. Appl. Math. **20**, 53–65 (1987). https://doi.org/10. 1016/0377-0427(87)90125-7

13. Solorio-Fernández, S., Carrasco-Ochoa, J.A., Martínez-Trinidad, J.F.: A new hybrid filter-wrapper feature selection method for clustering based on ranking. Neurocomputing **214**, 866–880 (2016). https://doi.org/10.1016/j.neucom.2016.07. 026

14. Storn, R., Price, K.: Differential evolution - a simple and efficient heuristic for global optimization over continuous spaces. J. Global Optim. **11**(4), 341–359 (1997). https://doi.org/10.1023/A:1008202821328

15. Xue, B., Zhang, M., Browne, W.N., Yao, X.: A survey on evolutionary computation approaches to feature selection. IEEE Trans. Evol. Comput. **20**(4), 606–626 (2016). https://doi.org/10.1109/TEVC.2015.2504420

A Method for Counting Models on Cubic Boolean Formulas

Marco A. López-Medina[⊠], J. Raymundo Marcial-Romero,
José A. Hernández, and Sandra Morales-Hernández

Universidad Autónoma del Estado de México, Toluca, Mexico
{malopezme,smoralesh,jrmarcialr,xoseahernandez}@uaemex.mx

Abstract. We present an algorithm based on heuristic variable selection for computing the number of models on two conjunctive normal form Boolean formulas whose restricted graph is represented by a cubic graph. For this class of formulas, we show that in most of the cases our proposal improves the time-complexity with respect of the current leader algorithm for counting models on two conjunctive form formulas of this kind.

Keywords: #SAT · 2SAT · Models of Boolean formulas · Combinatorial algorithms · Complexity theory

1 Introduction

The decision problem $SAT(F)$, where F is a Boolean formula, consists in determining whether F has a model, that is, an assignment to the variables of F such that when evaluated with respect to classical Boolean logic it returns true as a result. If F is in two Conjunctive Normal Form (2-CNF) then $SAT(F)$ can be solved in polynomial time, however if F is in k-CNF, $k > 2$, then $SAT(F)$ is an NP-Complete problem. Its counting version #k-SAT(F) is a classic #P-Complete problem even when F is in 2-CNF, the latter denoted as #2SAT [6].

Counting combinatorial objects is a challenging and relevant area of research in mathematics, computer sciences and physics. Counting problems, being mathematically relevant by themselves, are closely related to practical problems. Several relevant counting problems are hard time complexity problems. For example, #k-SAT (the problem of counting models for a Boolean formula) is of special concern to artificial intelligence (AI), and it has a direct relationship to automated theorem proving, as well as to approximate reasoning [3, 14, 16].

#k-SAT is related to other counting problems, e.g. in approximate reasoning, in the cases of the generation of explanation to propositional queries, repairing inconsistent databases, estimating the degree of belief in propositional theories, in a truth maintenance systems, in Bayesian inference [3, 13–15]. The previous problems come from several AI applications such as expert systems, planning, approximate reasoning, etc.

A. Y. Rodríguez-González et al. (Eds.): MCPR 2023, LNCS 13902, pp. 69–78, 2023.
https://doi.org/10.1007/978-3-031-33783-3_7

Although the #2SAT problem is #P-Complete, there are instances that can be solved in polynomial time [9,11]. For example, if the graph representation of the formula is acyclic, then the number of models can be computed in lineal time [11]. Currently, the algorithms that are used to solve the problem for any formula F in 2-CNF, decompose F into sub-formulas until there are base cases in which it can be counted efficiently.

The algorithm with the best time complexity so far was developed by Wahlström [17]. The Wahlström's algorithm has an upper bound for its time-complexity of order $O(1.2377^n)$, where n represents the number of variables in the formula. The Wahlström's algorithm uses the number of times a variable appears in the formula (being it the variable or its negation) as the criterion for choosing it. The two criteria for stopping the algorithm are when $F = \emptyset$ or when $\emptyset \in F$.

On cubic graphs Wahlström [17] and Fürer [5] show a time complexity of $2^{\frac{n}{4}} \approx 1.1892^n$.

In this paper we present an algorithm based on *heuristic variable selection* algorithm to compute #2SAT models on the so called cubic formulas. We show that for this particular type of formulas our algorithm improves on most cases the number of variables needed to decompose a given formula.

2   Preliminaries

2.1   Cubic-Hamiltonian Graphs

A graph G is cubic if every vertex in G has degree 3. A hamiltonian graph has a simple cycle that goes through all vertices of the graph. A cubic-hamiltonian graph can be represented by a LCF notation [1,4], and this type of graphs are used as a test topology for the selection algorithm.

LCF Notation has been devised by Leaderberg [7] for the representation of *cubic Hamiltonian* graphs, subsequently modified by Coexter et al. [2] and Frutch [4], hence it was dubbed *LCF notation*. This notation applies only to Hamiltonian graphs, placing the Hamiltonian cycle on a circular embedding and then connecting a pair of vertices with an edge (Fig. 1).

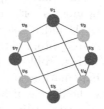

Fig. 1. A Hamiltonian graph with LCF notation $[3, -3]^4$

In LCF notation an unsigned number denotes the number of vertices counted clockwise and a negative denotes the number of vertices counted counterclockwise, this process is done the number of times denoted by the exponent and the graph is traversed two times constructing each edge two times.

The LCF notation for a given graph is not unique, since it may be shifted any number of positions to the left or right, or may be reversed, with a corresponding sign change on the elements in the notation. And a graph with more than one Hamiltonian cycle can take different choices on the circular embedding.

2.2   Conjunctive Normal Form

Let $X = \{x_1, ..., x_n\}$ be a set of n Boolean variables (that is, they can only take two possible values 1 or 0). A literal is a variable x_i, denoted in this paper as x_i^1 or the denied variable $\neg x_i$ denoted in this paper as x_i^0. A clause is a disjunction of different literals. A Boolean formula F in conjunctive normal form (CNF) is a conjunction of clauses. We denote the cardinality of a set S by $|S|$.

Let $V(Y)$ be the set of variables involved in the object Y, where Y can be a literal, a clause or a Boolean formula. For example, for the clause $c = \{x_1^1 \vee x_2^0\}$, $v(c) = \{x_1, x_2\}$. Meanwhile, $Lit(Y)$ denotes the set of literals involved in the object Y. For example, if $X = v(F)$, then $Lit(F) = X \sqcup \overline{X} = \{x_1^1, x_1^0, ..., x_n^1, x_n^0\}$.

An assignment s in F is a Boolean function $s : F \to \{0, 1\}$. s is defined as:

$$s(x^0) = 1 \text{ if } s(x^1) = 0, \text{ otherwise } s(x^0) = 0.$$

The assignment can be extended to conjunctions and disjunctions as follows:

- $s(x \wedge y) = 1$ if $s(x) = s(y) = 1$, otherwise $s(x \wedge y) = 0$
- $s(x \vee y) = 0$ if $s(x) = s(y) = 0$, otherwise $s(x \vee y) = 1$

Let F be a Boolean formula in CNF, it is said that s satisfies F (denoted as $s \models F$), if for each clause c in F, it holds $s(c) = 1$. On the other hand, it is said that F is contradicted by s ($s \not\models F$), if there is at least one clause c of F such that $s(c) = 0$. A model of F is an assignment that satisfies F. s is a partial assignment for the formula F when s has determined a logical value only to variables of a proper subset of F.

Given a CNF F, the SAT problem consists of determining whether F has a model. The #k-SAT(F) problem consists of counting the number of models of F defined over $v(F)$. #2SAT denotes #k-SAT for formulas in 2-CNF.

2.3   The Restricted Graph of a 2-CNF

There are some graphical representations of a Conjunctive Normal Form, in this case the signed primary graph (restricted graph) [15] will be used.

Let F be a 2-CNF, its restricted graph is denoted by $G_F = (V(F), E(F))$ where the vertices of the graph are the variables $V(F) = v(F)$ and $E(F) = \{\{x_i^\epsilon, x_j^\gamma\} \mid \{x_i^\epsilon \lor x_j^\gamma\} \in F\}$, that is, for each clause $\{x_i^\epsilon \lor x_j^\gamma\} \in F$ there is an edge $\{x_i^\epsilon, x_j^\gamma\} \in E(F)$. We say that a 2-CNF F is a path, a cycle, a tree, or a grid, if its restricted graph G_F represents a path, a cycle, a tree, or a grid, respectively.

For $x \in V(F)$, $\delta(x)$ denotes its degree, that is the number of incident edges in x. Each edge $e = \{x_i^\epsilon, x_j^\gamma\} \in E(F)$ has associated a pair (ϵ, γ), which represent whether the variables x_i or x_j appear negated or not. For example, the clause $(x_1^0 \lor x_2^1)$ has associated the pair (0,1) meaning that in the clause, x_1 appears negated and x_2 appears in positive way.

Let $S = \{+, -\}$ be a set of signs. A graph with edges labeled S is the pair (G, Ψ), where $G = (V, E)$ is a restricted graph, and Ψ is a function with domain E and range S. $\Psi(e)$ is called the label from the edge $e \in E$. Let $G = (V, E, \Psi)$ be a restricted graph with labeled edges on $S \times S$. Let x and y be two different vertices in V. If $e = \{x, y\}$ is an edge and $\psi(e) = (s, s')$, then $s(s')$ is called the adjacent sign to $x(y)$.

Notice that a restricted graph of a 2-CNF can be a multigraph, since two fixed variables can be involved in more than one clause of the formula, forming so parallel edges. Furthermore, a unitary clause defines a loop in the constraint graph.

Let $\rho : 2\text{-CNF} \to G_F$ be the function whose domain is the space of non strict Boolean formulas in 2-CNF and codomain the set of multi-graphs. It is clear that ρ is a bijection. Furthermore, any 2-CNF formula has a unique signed restricted graph (up to isomorphism) associated via ρ and viceversa, any signed constraint graph G_F has a unique formula associated via ρ^{-1}.

2.4   Methods Already Reported to Compute #2SAT

The basic idea considered in related papers to count models on a restricted graph G consists on computing a tuple (α_i, β_i) over each vertex x_i, where α_i represents the number of times that x_i appears positive in the models of G, and β_i the number of times x_i appears negative in the models of G. For example, a formula with a simple variable $\{x_i\}$ has associated the tuple $(1, 1)$ to the vertex x_i. Given an edge (clause) $e = \{x_i^{\epsilon_i}, x_j^{\gamma_i}\}$, if the counting begins at $x_i^{\epsilon_i}$, then the tuples $(1, 1)$ and $(2, 1)$ are associated to $x_i^{\epsilon_i}$ and $x_j^{\gamma_i}$, respectively. However, if the counting begins at $x_j^{\gamma_i}$, then the tuples are associated inversely. The number of models results of the sum of the last two elements of the tuple.

There are reported methods to count models in some graphical representations of a 2-CNF formula F [9–11, 13], here we state the method needed in the paper:

- If the graph represents a path e.g. a formula of the form
$P_n = \{\{x_1^{\epsilon_1}, x_2^{\gamma_1}\}, \{x_2^{\epsilon_2}, x_3^{\gamma_2}\}, \cdots \{x_{n-1}^{\epsilon_{n-1}}, x_n^{\gamma_{n-1}}\}\}$ of n vertices, the number
of models is given by the sum of the elements of the pair (α_n, β_n). where
$(\alpha_1, \beta_1) = (1, 1)$ and the tuple for the other vertices is computed according
to recurrence 1.

$$(\alpha_i, \beta_i) = \begin{cases} (\alpha_{i-1} + \beta_{i-1}, \alpha_{i-1}) \ if \ (\epsilon_{i-1}, \gamma_{i-1}) = (1, 1) \\ (\alpha_{i-1}, \alpha_{i-1} + \beta_{i-1}) \ if \ (\epsilon_{i-1}, \gamma_{i-1}) = (1, 0) \\ (\alpha_{i-1} + \beta_{i-1}, \beta_{i-1}) \ if \ (\epsilon_{i-1}, \gamma_{i-1}) = (0, 1) \\ (\beta_{i-1}, \alpha_{i-1} + \beta_{i-1}) \ if \ (\epsilon_{i-1}, \gamma_{i-1}) = (0, 0) \end{cases} \tag{1}$$

- If the graph represents a tree, the number of models is given by:

$$(\alpha_i, \beta_i) = \begin{cases} (1, 1) & \text{if } i \text{ its a leaf of the tree} \\ \Pi_{j=1}^{k}(\alpha_j, \beta_j) & \text{if } i \text{ its an interior node and have } k \text{ child nodes} \end{cases} \tag{2}$$

A known method for counting models on series-parallel formulas comes from
the construction rules of this type of formula, using a series of edge merging and
contractions [12].

3   Counting Models on Cubic Formulas

The existing algorithms for model counting in general, decompose a boolean
formula while the average degree is ≤ 6, the algorithms shown in [5,17] are
focused on decomposing the input formula until the degree of every variable is
3, this type of formula with degree 3 are called cubic formulas.

The algorithm presented in [17] decompose a cubic formula using one vertex
for each four vertices, that means, for every cubic formula F with n variables,
the time complexity of the algorithm is $2^{n/4}$ or 1.1892^n.

General Approach

It's known that there exists algorithms to count models on formulas representing
paths, trees, outerplanar graphs and series-parallel graphs. With linear time
complexity. Thus we aim to decompose cubic formulas on those linear solvable
formulas.

First we construct the graph representing a cubic formula, using a depth first
search method, and *try* to redraw this graph using the algorithm presented in [8].
This new arrangement intends to recognize the intersecting back edges that may
be used to decompose the graph and obtain a tree graph with series-parallel and
outerplanar sub graphs. The *intersections on the vertex v* denotes the number
of back edges whose path contains v, this means there exists one or more vertices
with the maximum intersection value on this graph construction.

Sets of Branch Variables

On a formula decomposition we construct the restricted graph after each variable reduction, where the constructed graph depends on the variable used to decompose the formula. Thus we expect to create a distinct topology each time a variable from a set of branch variables L_T is used to decompose a formula.

Every set of branch variables L_T have at most $n/4$ variables. Then the worst time complexity to decompose a cubic formula with a set of branch variables remains $O(1.1892^n)$ [17]. The objective is to obtain the minimum set of branch variables $|L_T| \leq n/4$, that means, we need to obtain a large number of distinct sets of variables to determine a *minimum set of branch variables*.

On *SAT* or *#SAT* a formula decomposition using k variables takes $O(2^k)$. Selection of our k variables can be done in linear time.

Given a formula F and its restricted graph G, the algorithm to obtain the minimum set of branch variables is:

Algorithm 1: Minimum set of branch variables

Require: Formula F and its restricted graph G, a *limit* on the number of iterations.

$count = 1$
Create a list L_T on G to store the minimum set of branch variables to decompose F

while $count <= limit$ **do**
    Generate a copy G' from G
    Using depth first search to construct a spanning tree of G', obtain the list L that contains the vertices with more intersections.
    Randomly select a variable v from L with most intersections.
    Decompose G' using v as branch variable.
    Add v to L_T'
    while $|V(G)| > 1$ **do**
        Using depth first search to construct a spanning tree of G', obtain the list L that contains the vertices with more intersections.
        Randomly select a variable v from L with most intersections
        Decompose G' using v as branch variable
        Add v to L_T'
        Apply reduction rules on vertices with degree 2 and 1
        Apply reduction rules on parallel edges
    end while
    if $|L_T'| < |L_T|$ **then**
        $L_T = L_T'$
    end if
    $count+ = 1$
end while
return L_T

With this algorithm we ensure a minimum set of branch variables with size $\leq n/4$, and obtained in polynomial time, the generation of temporal lists L_T'

takes $2n$ time to construct a tree decomposition and obtain the intersection list, this tree is generated at most $n/4$ times and the number of lists used to compares is *limit*.

4   Planar and Non-planar Cubic Graphs

The minimum set of branch variables L_T leads to a singular decomposition on planar and non/planar graphs. On planar graphs decomposition, using the set L_T as a decomposition sequence, gives an outerplanar graph as result, then we can use the algorithm presented in [9].

On non-planar graphs decomposition, using the set L_T as sequence, the result of gives a graph with series-parallel subgraphs, then we can use an existing algorithm to count models over this decomposition [12].

In both cases the graph given after the decomposition sequence can be solved in linear time.

As non-planar cubic graphs we use as example graphs with a hamiltonian cycle, having them constructed in a clockwise manner using the respective LCF-notation. On this type of graph the hamiltonian cycle has two edges for each vertex, that means only one edge per vertex can connect to another vertex, and this configuration is the LCF-notation for that graph.

Example, the *Desargues-graph* is represented by the LCF-notation $[5, -5, 9, -9]^5$, in short, we can select the first vertex at random v_1 and in a clockwise traversal over the $v_1, v_2, ..., v_n$ vertices, we connect the vertex v_1 to the vertex v_{1+5}, then the vertex v_2 to the vertex v_{2+7} and so on, until we reach the vertex v_n, some steps can give an edge previously connected.

A graphical representation for this LCF-notation on desargues graph is presented in Fig. 2, and an isomorphism in Fig. 3.

Fig. 2. Desargues graph from LCF-notation $[5, -5, 9, -9]^5$.

Fig. 3. An isomorphism of the Desargues graph.

Table 1. Non-planar cubic graphs list

Graph	$|V(G)|$	$|L_T|$
utility graph	6	1
Franklin graph	12	2
Heawood graph	14	3
MAbius-Kantor graph	16	4
Pappus graph	18	4
Desargues graph	20	4
Dyck graph	32	6
Gray graph	54	12
Foster graph	90	21
Biggs-Smith graph	102	23
Balaban 11-cage	112	26
Tutte 12-cage	126	30

In Table 1 we show that in most cases our algorithm selects a less number of vertices to decompose a cubic non-planar graph.

5   Complexity Analysis

This approach intends to reduce the size on the set of branch variables generated by the Algorithm 1, the time complexity of this algorithm is $O(\frac{n^2}{2})$, it takes $2n$ to construct a depth first search tree and obtain the intersection value on all vertices, and $n/4$ is the *maximum* number of decomposition steps that gives the elements in the set of branch variables L'_T.

Given a number of times *limit* we execute Algorithm 1, then to obtain a minimum set of branch variables L_T we have a time complexity of $O(\frac{n^2 limit}{2})$.

6   Conclusions

We present a polynomial algorithm to select, heuristically, optimal branch variables on cubic graphs. Using decomposition of cubic graphs in series-parallel, outerplanar, tree or a combination of the three topologies, giving a list of branch variables that leads to this linear solvable cases, and the number of branch variables obtained is $t = |L_T| \leq n/4$, then on cubic graph decomposition we have a time complexity of $O(2^t)$. Thus $O(2^t) \leq O(1.1892^n)$.

References

1. Buchanan, B.G., Lederberg, J.: The heuristic DENDRAL program for explaining empirical data. In: Freiman, C.V., Griffith, J.E., Rosenfeld, J.L. (eds.) Information Processing, Proceedings of IFIP Congress 1971, Volume 1 - Foundations and Systems, Ljubljana, Yugoslavia, August 23–28, 1971, pp. 179–188. North-Holland (1971)
2. COXETER, H., FRUCHT, R., POWERS, D.L.: Dedication. In: Zero-Symmetric Graphs, pp. 1–170. Academic Press (1981). https://doi.org/10.1016/B978-0-12-194580-0.50003-3
3. Darwiche, A.: On the tractable counting of theory models and its application to truth maintenance and belief revision. J. Appl. Non-Classical Logics **11**, 11–34 (2012)
4. Frucht, R.: A canonical representation of trivalent hamiltonian graphs. J. Graph Theor. **1**(1), 45–60 (1977). https://doi.org/10.1002/jgt.3190010111
5. Fürer, M., Kasiviswanathan, S.P.: Algorithms for counting 2-sat solutions and colorings with applications. In: Algorithmic Aspects in Information and Management, pp. 47–57. Springer, Berlin Heidelberg, Berlin, Heidelberg (2007)
6. G. Brifhtwell, P.W.: Counting linear extensions. Order **8**(e), 225–242 (1991)
7. J., L.: Dendral-64 - a system for computer construction, enumeration and notation of organic molecules as tree structures and cyclic graphs. Tech. rep., National Aeronautics and Space Administration. Grant NsG, pp. 81–60 (1965)
8. López, M.A., Marcial-Romero, J.R., Hernández, J.A., Ita, G.D.: Model counting for #2sat problem in outerplanar graphs. In: Proceedings of the Eleventh Latin American Workshop on Logic/Languages, Algorithms and New Methods of Reasoning. vol. 2264, pp. 76–87. CEUR Workshop Proceedings (2018)
9. López-Medina, M.A., Marcial-Romero, J.R., Ita, G.D., Moyao, Y.: A linear time algorithm for computing #2SAT for outerplanar 2-CNF formulas. Lect. Notes Comput. Sci. **10880**, 72–81 (2018)
10. López-Medina, M.A., Marcial-Romero, J.R., Ita, G.D., Valdovinos, R.M.: A fast and efficient method for #2sat via graph transformations. Advances in Soft Computing, pp. 95–106 (2017)
11. López-Medina, M.A., Marcial-Romero, J.R., Luna, G.D.I., Montes-Venegas, H.A., Alejo, R.: A linear time algorithm for solving #2SAT on cactus formulas. CoRR, ams/1702.08581 (2017)
12. López-Medina, M.A., Marcial-Romero, J.R., De Ita-Luna, G., Hernández, J.A.: A linear time algorithm for counting #2SAT on series-parallel formulas. In: Martínez-Villaseñor, L., Herrera-Alcántara, O., Ponce, H., Castro-Espinoza, F.A. (eds.) MICAI 2020. LNCS (LNAI), vol. 12468, pp. 437–447. Springer, Cham (2020). https://doi.org/10.1007/978-3-030-60884-2_33
13. Marcial-Romero, J.R., Ita, G.D., Hernández, J.A., Valdovinos, R.M.: A parametric polynomial deterministic algorithm for #2sat. Lect. Notes Comput. Sci. **9413**, 202–213 (2015)

14. Roth, D.: On the hardness of approximate reasoning. Artif. Intell. **82**, 273–302 (1996)
15. Szeider, S.: On Fixed-Parameter Tractable Parametrizations of SAT, pp. 188–202. Springer, Berlin Heidelberg pp (2004)
16. Takamizawa, K., Nishizeki, T., Saito, N.: Linear-time computability of combinatorial problems on series-parallel graphs. J. Assoc. Comput. Mach. **29**(3), 623–641 (1982)
17. Wahlström, M.: A tighter bound for counting max-weight solutions to 2sat instances, pp. 202–213. Springer, Berlin Heidelberg pp (2008)

Automatic Identification of Learning Styles Through Behavioral Patterns

María Guadalupe Pineda-Arizmendi[1]([⊠]) [iD], Ángel Hernández-Castañeda[2] [iD],
René Arnulfo García-Hernández[1] [iD], Yulia Ledeneva[1] [iD],
and José Rafael Cruz Reyes[1] [iD]

[1] Autonomous University of the State of Mexico, Instituto Literario 100, Col. Centro.
C.P., 50000 Toluca, Mexico State, Mexico
mariaguadalupe.pineda.arizmendi@gmail.com
[2] Cátedras CONACyT, Av. Insurgentes Sur 1582, Col. Crédito Constructor. C.P.,
03940 Mexico City, Mexico

Abstract. The learning style is characterized by the preferences that the student is acquiring throughout his life and with the interaction in the environment in which he develops. As a traditional method to identify the learning style, the application of questionnaires is carried out; however, they may present inaccurate results due to lack of interest in answering the questionnaires. Currently, there are automatic methods to identify the learning style as the observation of the student's behavior, while interacting with learning objects in an academic course. Learning objects are those digital tools such as chat rooms, reading materials, exams, among others. These objects allow the actions carried out to be recorded and stored in order to be studied. Therefore, this study presents an evolutionary algorithm to optimize the grouping of students according to their learning style based on the structured learning objects. Thus, the objective is to form groups according to the value of the actions carried out in an academic course and to predict the learning style.

Keywords: learning styles · behavioral patterns · artificial intelligence.

1 Introduction

Learning is the process by which human beings acquire or modify their abilities, skills and knowledge. The modification of existing experiences arises from the absorption and retention of information [11]. What allows to develop the way in which an individual structures concepts and interprets information at their own pace. The preferences that the individual acquires throughout life produce different versions that are called learning styles [3,10,12]. Learning styles are characterized by the different ways of coping with cognitive processes such as attention and memorization [17], this determines how well a person is able to remember or think in general about how things are done [3]. Learning styles are created from the stability and consistency in the behavior of individuals, when interacting with information related to learning environments [4]. The identification of learning styles allows us to understand how the personal style of each individual is built [2].

Some studies identify learning styles such as [8] and [6], through traditional methods such as the application of questionnaires based on the results obtained by tabulating the responses. However, they have some disadvantages due to the lack of interest of the students and they answer without reading the questions [20]. In addition, Zaporozhko [16] states that they do not provide the required seriousness with students, providing arbitrary answers, which could mean that the results obtained are inaccurate and do not reflect the true learning style.

Due to the imprecision of the questionnaire results, other ways of determining the learning style have been explored, such as observing the behavior of students through interaction on educational platforms. Educational platforms, such as Moodle, also known as Learning Management Systems (LMS), allow teaching to be adapted through a computer. The objective of these platforms is to allow the creation and management of complete courses through connectivity to an Internet network, promoting distance teaching and learning [15].

Moodle is one of the examples of educational platforms whose objective is to make it easier for teachers to use technological tools also known as learning objects that can be chat sections, discussion forums, reading material, audios, videos, among others. Therefore, the focus of this study is to observe the actions carried out by the student in an academic course implemented in the Moodle platform. This study consider Felder's learning styles model (FSLSM) that classifies learning styles based on 4 dimensions.

These learning dimensions are detailed below [9,18]: **perception dimension** consists of the type of information perceived by the student (sensory or intuitive), **representation dimension** depends on the preferred sensory channel to perceive the information (visual or verbal), **processing dimension** presents the student's preference to process information (actively or reflexively) and the **comprehension dimension** is based on the way of processing learning (sequential or global). The FSLSM Index is analyzed with the aim of having a reference of the learning style of each student with the implementation of an evolutionary algorithm that optimize groups of students according to their learning objects. Finally, a comparison of the FSLSM index and the result obtained from the algorithm is made.

2   Related Work

There are various works oriented to the modeling of students considering their learning styles, some of the works mentioned below are related to the focus of this work.

In the study by Farias et al. [7] identifies the learning style of 22 students through a method that uses cluster analysis techniques, that is, it groups the actions carried out in a course called "Process Monitoring and Control Systems", implemented in the Moodle platform aimed at providing students with design tools in real-time systems. The purpose of the research was to recognize a pattern in the student's behavior to later determine her learning style, using the four learning dimensions of the Felder Silverman model. WEKA software was used, using the FarthestFirst clustering algorithm, defining a set of rules for each of the learning dimensions applied to the subject values of the attributes present in each cluster, and the results were compared with the FSLSM Index. applied at the beginning of the course, to compare the results. The results obtained were a precision of the method of 57% and in the dimensions of the learning model they were perception and processing of 75%, in comprehension of 86%.

Yannibelli et al. [20], presented a genetic algorithm approach to automatically identify a student's learning style based on preferred actions on learning objects while attending the different academic units of a course. Therefore, the objective of the algorithm was to detect the combination of actions using the Felder learning model. The authors represent each gene as a learning object on a chromosome, that is, a binary encoding is assigned where 1 represents whether the learning object is used and allele 0 otherwise. The fittest chromosome represents the best combination of learning objects selected by the student. The results obtained for the learning dimensions were 80% processing for the comprehension and perception dimension was 100%. The authors do not show results in the representation dimension due to the lack of this type of learning objects in the course.

In the study by Zaporozhko et al. [16], present a method that consisted of distributing learning objects in certain academic units in an educational platform in the cloud. The authors analyzed 15,457 respondents where the student's learning style was identified using the VARK (Visual, Auditory, Reading and Kinesthetic) learning model. According to the learning style, learning objects were represented using a genetic algorithm. Each chromosome gene stand for a learning object. Parameters were set up with the mutation probability set to 0.05 and the crossover probability set to 0.8. The GA was able to find the optimal set of learning objects of the course that constitute a learning path.

In accordance with the above, this work is based on the difficulties that exist in traditional methods such as the application of questionnaires, since it is a task that requires a long time to answer and that students are not always willing and interested. In addition, the authors who identify the learning style do not consider the 4 dimensions of the Felder Model. It is worth noting that the related studies only indicate the relationship with the learning objects and show the interpretation of the results obtained; however, the identification of the style is not visualized automatically.

This proposes to make the prediction of automatically determines the learning style, analyzing the student's actions with the learning objects.

3   Proposed Method

This study proposes a model to automatically predict the learning style of the students. To that end, a genetic algorithm is used to optimize the combination of learning objects. The learning model used in this study was that of Felder Silverman due to its adaptability in educational platforms.

To validate our model, two datasets[1] were manually collected: a)one consisting of actions of an academic course and b) a one consisting of questionaries.

To obtain the data, an academic course was built on the Moodle platform, then the learning objects were structured according to the Felder Model. The interaction of the student on the course was supervised, so the actions carried out on these objects were register in the platform [19,20]. Also the **FSLSM Index**, constituted by the questionnaires, was applied to the students in order to obtain the predominant learning style that characterizes the student (Fig. 1).

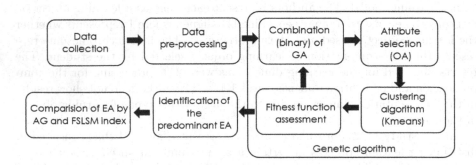

Fig. 1. Proposed approach

Data Preprocessing. In the preprocessing phase, the data was filtered by selecting the values of the actions performed by the student, considered as attributes for the model and which will be shown in detail in Table 1. In addition, the student's personal data was omitted. Both datasets were implemented due to the lack of datasets using learning objects and the relationship with the FSLSM index. Which was built with the participation of 88 engineering students. The learning objects that were structured in the course are specified in Table 1, and each object is assigned to each of the dimensions of the Felder Model. The seven learning objects are distributed throughout the content of the academic units, obtaining sections such as 8 discussion forums (named as FORUM1 to FORUM8), 1 chat room (CHAT), 1 reading material (M_LECT), 1 examples (EJEM), 1 exercise section (EJER), 3 on the time to deliver an exam (H_EXAM1, H_EXAM2, H_EXAM3), and finally 1 on the change of answers (CAM_RES). Resulting in a final vector with 16 learning objects with the values of the actions carried out by each student.

---

[1] https://github.com/LaboratorioIA/OA.git.

Table 1. Table of learning objects used in the academic course

No	Learning object	Value	Dimension
1	Discussion forum	0 – 2	
2	Participation in the chat	0 – 2	Processing
3	Reading material	0 – 4	
4	Access to examples	0 – 4	Perception
5	Exercises performed	0 – 5	
6	Time to submit an exam	0 – 5	Understanding
7	Change of answers	0 – 5	Representation

The values that were assigned to each learning object represent the moderation of the possible action carried out by the student in each of the learning objects and are shown in detail in Table 2. These data will be entered into the clustering algorithm, to form groups according to the actions carried out on the learning objects. Through rules the student's learning style will be determined, an example of the rules is: if the access to the theory is "sequential", and the access to the practice is "sequential" or "both", and the analysis of the information is "detailed" or "both", then the value of the comprehension dimension will be "sequential", this is similar for each dimension of learning, however, since each dimension of learning is evaluated, it is considered to be the style more predominant on the part of the student.

3.1 Detection of Learning Style Using Genetic Algorithm

This study proposes a method that uses a genetic algorithm to optimize the possible combinations of 16 learning objects preferred by the student. To achieve this goal, it is necessary to observe the actions performed on the learning objects present in an academic course. The coding of the algorithm is binary 0 and 1. Where a chromosome gene represents a learning object, it is subsequently evaluated by means of the fitness function, for this study the measure F1 is considered. Obtaining as a result the prediction of the learning style. It is considered that the best individual in the population is the one that will show the combination of learning objects and by implementing a clustering algorithm, groups will be formed according to the actions present in the selection of learning objects as a result of the decoding of the genetic algorithm.

Table 2. Describes the values that can be assigned to each gene and their significance.

Learning object	Value	Description
Discussion forum	0	Do not participe
	1	Only reads messages
	2	Reads and responds to message in forum
Chat participation	0	Do not participe
	1	Only reads messages
	2	Reads and replies to chat messages
Reading material	0	Only reads abstract material
	1	Reads all the abstract material and some of the concrete material
	2	Reads all concrete and abstract material
	3	Reads all the concrete material and some of the abstract material
	4	Only reads concrete material
Exercises performed	0	Observes less than 10% of the exercises
	1	Observe between 10% and 30% of the exercises
	2	Observe between 30% and 50% of the exercises
	3	Observe between 50% and 70% of the exercises
	4	Observes more than 70% of the exercises
Access to examples	0	Does not participates
	1	Observes less than 10% of the examples
	2	Observes between 10% and 30% of the examples
	3	Observes between 30% and 50% of the examples
	4	Observes between 50% and 70% of the examples
	5	Observes more than 70% of the examples
Time to submit an exam	0	Does not participates
	1	Uses less than 40% of the allotted time
	2	Uses between 40% and 50% of the time
	3	Uses between 50% and 60% of the time
	4	Uses between 60% and 70% of the time
	5	Uses more than 70% of the allotted time
Change of answer to a test	0	Does not participates
	1	Uses less than 40% of the allotted time
	2	Uses between 40% and 50% of the time
	3	Uses between 50% and 60% of the time
	4	Modifies between 60% and 70% of the time
	5	Modifies more than 70% of the allotted time

3.2   Fitness Function

As evaluation measures of the method, the F1 measure is taken to obtain the prediction of the learning style. However, to obtain the F1 measure, other measures are taken, such as precision, and recall. [14].

Precision

$$precision = \frac{TP}{TP + FP} \tag{1}$$

Where TP indicates (True Positives) and FP indicates (False Positives).

Recall

$$Recall = \frac{TP}{TP + FN} \tag{2}$$

This measure will tell us about the quantity that the model is able to identify. Where FN indicate that is False Negative.

$$FA = \frac{1}{n} \sum_{i-0}^{8} (2 * \frac{precision * recall}{precision + recall}) \tag{3}$$

F1 is calculated by taking the harmonic mean between precision and recall. That is, the measurement values F1 for each cluster are averaged and the prediction of the learning styles is obtained through the proposed method, to later make the comparison with the FSLSM index. This indicates that the model automatically generates the learning object combination assessment and predicts the learning style. It is worth mentioning that there are no comparable results with other studies analyzed. However, what is sought with this research is to try to identify the learning style without the use of questionnaires, but considering the learning objects as a way of analyzing the behavior pattern of the students, taking the reference of studies such as [20].

4   Experimentation and Results

By pre-processing the data, and taking into account Table 2, which contains the value considered for the actions carried out by a student, a vector of 16 values is gathered per student, as shown below in Table 3.

According to the decoding obtained from the genetic algorithm, it allows the proposed method to select the learning objects. That is to say, a gene represents a learning object and when the allele of the gene is 1, it means that the learning object is used in the chromosome, otherwise it is not used in the combination of learning objects. And so for each generation created by the genetic algorithm, different combinations of learning objects are evaluated as shown in Table 4.

Described in Table 4, a possible representation of the best individuals for each generation, for example for generation 1 selected the learning objects $O4, O5, O9,$

Table 3. Example of a vector obtained with the actions of a student

ALU	FORUM1	CHAT	M_LECT	. . .	H_EXAM1	EJER	CAM_RES
1	0	2	1	. . .	2	4	4

Table 4. Genetic algorithm coding

Gen	O1	O2	O3	O4	O5	O6	O7	O8	O9	O10	O11	O12	O13	O14	O15	O16
1	0	0	0	1	1	0	0	0	1	0	0	0	0	1	1	0
2	1	0	0	0	0	1	0	1	1	1	0	0	0	1	0	1

$O14, O15$, forming a new vector of 5 dimensions, which later will perform the selection of the learning object dataset attributes as FORUM4, FORUM5, CHAT, H_EXAM2, H_EXAM3. For generation 2 of individuals, the combination would be represented as follows: $O1, O6, O8, O9, O10, O14, O16$, forming a new vector of 7 dimensions and selecting from the attributes FORUM1, FORUM6 , FORUM8, CHAT, M_LECT, H_EXAM2, CAM_RES. This procedure occurs during 100 generations contemplated in the parameters of the genetic algorithm. When forming the chromosomes of the genetic algorithm, different combinations are made that carry out the selection of the attributes that will be introduced and fed to the clustering algorithm to form groups. The algorithm used was the k-means algorithm for the implementation and modeling of the groups.

When obtaining the division of the cluster by student, the learning style is identified through the evaluation of the pattern of actions carried out on the learning objects assigned later, the dataset is divided into 30% test and 70% test. training to evaluate the predictions by comparing the results of the genetic algorithm with the labels of the FSLMS Index evaluated by means of the F1 measure, which is considered as a fitness function and the learning style prediction is made. The experiments were repeated with initial populations of 100 chromosomes and the prediction by predominant learning style is shown in Table 3, obtaining precision results of a run of the algorithm of up to 0.77 of the proposed model. The objective of the evaluation was to determine the combination of actions preferred by the student. and in comparison with other methods of the state of the art, they evaluate results by the learning dimension. In this proposed method, the predominant learning style is identified. Table 5 shows the results of the evaluation of the proposed method based on the actions carried out on the learning objects and predicting the type of learning from the FSLSM opinion, taken as a reference for the style of each student.

Table 5. Table of results of prediction

Style	Precision	Recall	F1-Score	Cardinality
Active	0.87	0.95	0.91	21
Reflexive	0.14	1.00	0.25	1
Sensitive	0.50	0.50	0.50	2
Intuitive	0.00	0.00	0.00	14
Verbal	0.00	0.00	0.00	2
Visual	1.00	1.00	1.0	2
Sequential	0.57	1.00	0.73	4
Global	1.00	0.94	0.97	18
Multi-style	0.79	0.96	0.87	24

5   Conclusions

In this work an evolutionary grouping method is proposed through which it arises from the combination of learning objects provided by the decoding of the individuals of the genetic algorithm, in the same way each chromosome generates a selection of learning objects and they are introduced in a clustering algorithm to form groups according to the actions carried out by the student on the selected learning objects, through a series of preference rules of the Felder Model, the student's learning style is identified, later it is evaluated by means of the function fitness proposal. Finally, a comparison of the learning style resulting from the proposed method is generated with the opinion of the FSLSM Index also applied to the student population to be studied.

With the proposed method of this study, the behavior of the student capable of creating a pattern of interactions with the learning objects of an academic course was observed, to predict the most predominant type of learning. As future work, it is proposed to recommend the learning objects according to the student's learning style and facilitate their teaching in educational platforms. As a contribution to the research community, the two datasets collected will be provided due to the non-existence of data to be used in subsequent studies with approaches similar to this study. This method could replace traditional methods such as the identification of learning styles through the application of questionnaires.

Acknowledgments. We thank Autonomous University of the State of Mexico and CONACYT.

References

1. Abdoun, O., Tajani, C., Abouchabaka, J.: Analyzing the performance of mutation operators to solve the traveling salesman problem. Int. J. Emerg. Sci **2**(1), 61–77 (2012)

2. Bernheim, C.T.: El constructivismo y el aprendizaje de los estudiantes. Universidades **48**, 21–32 (2011)
3. Castro, S., de Castro, B.G.: Los estilos de aprendizaje en la enseñanza y el aprendizaje: Una propuesta para su implementacón. Revistas de investigación **29**(58) (2017)
4. Castro, S., Rivas de Rojas, N.: Bailemos al son que nos toquen: una simulación instruccional para mediar sobre el aprendizaje de los estados de agregación de la materia. Investigación y postgrado **23**(2), 271–293 (2008)
5. Egaña, M., Diago, L., Revuelta, M.J., González, P.: Análisis de herramientas de medición de los estilos de aprendizaje 1 analysis of the learning styles measurement tools. Revista de educación **381**, 95–131 (Julio-Septiembre 2018). https://doi.org/10.4438/1988-592X-RE-2017-381-382
6. Espinoza-Poves, J.L., Miranda-Vílchez, W.A., Chafloque-Céspedes, R.: Los estilos de aprendizaje vark en estudiantes universitarios de las escuelas de negocios. Propósitos y representaciones **7**(2), 384–414 (2019)
7. Farías, R., Durán, E.B., Figueroa, S.G.: Las técnicas de clustering en la personalización de sistemas de e-learning. In: XIV Congreso Argentino de Ciencias de la Computación (2008)
8. Felder, R.M.: Learning and teaching styles in engineering education (2002)
9. Felder, R.M., Spurlin, J.: Applications, reliability and validity of the index of learning styles. Int. J. Eng. Educ. **21**(1), 103–112 (2005)
10. Franco, M.E.E., García, M.F.V., Estrada, R.M.F., Estrada, M.d.R.F., Medina, M.d.l.L.S.: Estilos de aprendizaje en la facultad de odontología. Revista RedCA **1**(2), 86–100 (2018)
11. Gibson, E.J.: Perceptual learning and the theory of word perception. Cogn. Psychol. **2**(4), 351–368 (1971)
12. González, B., León, A.: Procesos cognitivos: De la prescripción curricular a la praxis educativa. Revista de Teoría y Didáctica de las Ciencias Sociales **19**, 49–67 (2013)
13. Jh, H.: Adaptation in natural and artificial systems. Ann Arbor (1975)
14. Mahesh, B.: Machine learning algorithms-a review. Int. J. Sci. Res. (IJSR).[Internet] **9**, 381–386 (2020).
15. Páez, H., Arreaza, E.: Uso de una plataforma virtual de aprendizaje en educación superior.: Caso nicenet. org of a virtual learning platform in higher education. case study: Nicenet. org. Paradigma (2015)
16. Parfenov, D., Zaporozhko, V.: Implementation of genetic algorithm for forming of individual educational trajectories for listeners of online courses. In: Instrumentation engineering, electronics and telecommunications-2018, pp. 72–82 (2018)
17. Sarmiento, Santana, M.: La enseñanza de las matemáticas y las ntic. una estrategia de formación permanente. Universitat Rovira I Virgili 49 (2007)
18. Soloman, B.A., Felder, R.M.: Index of learning styles questionnaire. NC State University. https://www.engr.ncsu.edu/learningstyles/ilsweb.html (last visited on 14.05. 2010) 70 (2005)
19. Stash, N.V., Cristea, A.I., De Bra, P.M.: Authoring of learning styles in adaptive hypermedia: problems and solutions. In: Proceedings of the 13th international World Wide Web conference on Alternate track papers & posters, pp. 114–123 (2004)
20. Yannibelli, V., Godoy, D., Amandi, A.: A genetic algorithm approach to recognise students' learning styles. Interact. Learn. Environ. **14**(1), 55–78 (2006)

Comparison of Classifiers in Challenge Scheme

Sergio Nava-Muñoz[1]([✉]), Mario Graff Guerrero[2], and Hugo Jair Escalante[3]

[1] CIMAT, Aguascalientes, Mexico
nava@cimat.mx
[2] INFOTEC, Aguascalientes, Mexico
mario.graff@infotec.mx
[3] INAOE, Puebla, Mexico
hugojair@inaoep.mx

Abstract. In recent decades, challenges have become very popular in scientific research as these are crowdsourcing schemes. In particular, challenges are essential for developing machine learning algorithms. For the challenges settings, it is vital to establish the scientific question, the dataset (with adequate quality, quantity, diversity, and complexity), performance metrics, as well as a way to authenticate the participants' results (*Gold Standard*). This paper addresses the problem of evaluating the performance of different competitors (algorithms) under the restrictions imposed by the challenge scheme, such as the comparison of multiple competitors with a unique *dataset* (with fixed size), a minimal number of submissions and, a set of metrics chosen to assess performance. The algorithms are sorted according to the performance metric. Still, it is common to observe performance differences among competitors as small as hundredths or even thousandths, so the question is whether the differences are significant. This paper analyzes the results of the *MeOffendEs@IberLEF 2021* competition and proposes to make inference through resampling techniques (bootstrap) to support Challenge organizers' decision-making.

Keywords: Performance · Bootstrap · Challenges

1 Introduction

A challenge is a collaborative competition that has gained appeal among research scientists during the past couple decades. This challenges makes use of leaderboards so that participants may keep track of how they compare to other participants in terms of performance. These cover multiple areas of science and technology, ranging from fundamental to applied questions in machine learning (kaggle, codalab [11]). At the most basic level, a performance benchmark requires a task, a metric, and a means of authenticating the result.

Participants in this type of crowdsourcing are given data together with the specific question that needs to be answered. The creators of such challenges have "ground truth" or "Gold Standard" data that is exclusive to them and enables them to impartially rate the techniques that competitors create. Participants

A. Y. Rodríguez-González et al. (Eds.): MCPR 2023, LNCS 13902, pp. 89–98, 2023.
https://doi.org/10.1007/978-3-031-33783-3_9

provide their solutions for evaluation by the organizers using the Gold Standard data. In this way, it is possible to find the best available method to solve the problem posed, and the participants can get an objective assessment of their methods. Clear scoring mechanisms for solutions evaluation and the availability of non-public datasets for use as Gold Standards are necessary for the organization of these challenges.

If we talk about a challenge task where the performance of classification algorithms is compared, there are particular constraints, such as the comparison of multiple participants (algorithms, methods, or assembles), selected performance metrics, a fixed dataset size, and a limit number of submissions per participant. It is difficult to use classical statistics to infer the significance of a given performance metric because there are no multiple datasets or many submissions; besides, our interest is making multiple comparisons.

This research aims to complement the winner selection process based solely on the score rank by proposing the use of well-established statistical tools and error bar plots to facilitate the analysis of the performance differences and being able to identify whether the difference in performance is significant or the result of chance. To illustrate the approach, the dataset of subtasks 3 of *MeOffendEs@IberLEF 2021* [12] competition is used. The analysis shows that for each performance measure, there is a system that performs the best; however, in precision, three other systems behave similarly; for the F_1 score, there are two systems with similar performance, and for recall, there are no similar systems.

The remainder of this article is organized as follows. Collaborative competitions are described in Sect. 2. The dataset used to test this proposal is described in Sect. 3. The proposed solutions to the problem are described in Sect. 4, and their results are evaluated. In Sect. 5, conclusions are presented.

2   Collaborative Competitions

Crowdsourcing is a term introduced in 2006 by Jeff Howe, journalist, and editor of the electronic magazine Wired; however, it is a way of working that has been used for centuries. This practice allows a task to be performed by a set of experts or not, through a call for proposals. Crowdsourcing has been used in various areas, for example, in marketing, astronomy, and genetics. But our interest is in the scientific field, where the idea is to call on the community to solve a scientific problem. One of the forms of crowdsourcing (collaborative work) that has taken great importance in recent years, is collaborative competitions also called *challenges*, and in particular, we are interested in applications in science and technology.

In the scientific field, crowdsourcing and benchmarking have been combined, leading to the development of solutions that quickly outperform the state-of-the-art. The essential elements of a challenge are the scientific question in the form of a task, the data (a single dataset of fixed size), the performance metrics, and a way to verify the results (the gold standard). Nonetheless, these characteristics limit the use of classical statistics to infer the significance of a given performance metric because there are no multiple datasets or many submissions.

3   Dataset - *MeOffendEs@IberLEF 2021*

This paper analyze MeOffendES 2021 dataset, organized at IberLEF 2021 and co-located with the 37th International Conference of the Spanish Society for Natural Language Processing (SEPLN 2021). MeOffendEs' major objective is to advance research into the recognition of offensive language in Spanish-language variants. The shared task consists of four subtasks. The first two relate to identifying offensive language categories in texts written in generic Spanish on various social media platforms, while subtasks 3 and 4 are concerned with identifying offensive language that is directed at the Mexican variant of Spanish. In particular, the focus is on Subtask 3: Mexican Spanish non-contextual binary classification. Participants must classify tweets in the OffendMEX corpus as offensive or non-offensive. For evaluation, we consider the offensive class's precision, recall, and f1 score [12]. OffendMEX corpus, is a novel collection of Mexican Spanish tweets that were manually labeled as offensive and obtained via Twitter.

The dataset used for this analysis is the *test partition* from OffendMEX, for subtask three at *MeOffendEs@IberLEF 2021*; this consists of 11 variables, which correspond to the predictions of 10 teams and the *gold standard*. One of the competitors (NLPCIC) submitted a prediction after the competition had ended, and the system recorded it. The *gold standard* contains the labels for 600 offensive tweets and 1582 non-offensive tweets, for a total of $n = 2182$ tweets.

Table 1 summarizes the results using in terms of Precision, Recall, and F_1 scores. As can be seen, the highest F_1 score is 0.7154 achieved by *NLPCIC*, followed by *CIMATMTYGTO* with 0.7026 and *DCCDINFOTEC* with 0.6847. For Recall, the three best teams were *CENAmrita*, *xjywing* and *aomar* with values of 0.9183, 0.8883, and 0.8750, respectively. Regarding Precision, *NLPCIC* obtained the highest score with 0.7208. *DCCDINFOTEC* and *CIMATGTO* came in second and third, with 0.6966 and 0.6958, respectively.

Table 1. Results for the Non-contextual binary classification for Mexican Spanish

Team	precision	recall	F_1
NLPCIC	0.7208	0.7100	0.7154
CIMATMTYGTO	0.6533	0.7600	0.7026
DCCDINFOTEC	0.6966	0.6733	0.6847
CIMATGTO	0.6958	0.6633	0.6792
UMUTeam	0.6763	0.6650	0.6706
Timen	0.6081	0.6000	0.6040
CICIPN	0.6874	0.5350	0.6017
xjywing	0.3419	0.8883	0.4937
aomar	0.3241	0.8750	0.4730
CENAmrita	0.3145	0.9183	0.4685

4   Proposed Approaches and Results

As mentioned, the objective is to propose tools that allow comparing the classification results of different competitors in a Challenge, in addition to performance metrics. In the literature, one can find works dealing with the problem of comparing classification algorithms; however, they focus on something other than the competition scheme. For example, Diettrich (1998) [5], reviews five proximate statistical tests to determine whether one learning algorithm outperforms another in a particular learning task. However, it is required to have the algorithm, and in our case we only have the prediction, not the algorithm. On the other hand, Demšar (2006) [4] focuses on Statistical Comparisons of Classifiers over Multiple Data Sets; however, in our case we have only one dataset. In particular, he presents several non-parametric methods, and several guides to performing a correct analysis when comparing a set of classifiers. García and Herrera (2008) [8] attack a problem similar to Demšar but focused on pairwise comparisons, i.e. statistical procedures for comparing $c \times c$ classifiers, but again on multiple datasets.

4.1   Bootstrap

The word "bootstrapping" in statistics refers to drawing conclusions about a statistics' sampling distribution by resampling the sample with replacement data as though it were a population with a fixed size [3, 7]. The term resampling was originally used in 1935 by R. A. Fisher in his famous randomization test and in 1937 and 1938 by E. J. G. Pitman, but in these instances the sampling was carried out without replacement.

The theory and applications of the bootstrap have exploded in recent years, and the Monte Carlo approximation to the bootstrap has developed into a well-established method for drawing statistical conclusions without making firm parametric assumptions. The term bootstrap refers to a variety of methods that are now included under the broad category of nonparametric statistics known as resampling methods. Brad Efron's publication in the *Annals of Statistics* was published in 1979, making it a crucial year for the bootstrap [6, 7]. The bootstrap resampling technique was developed by Efron. His initial objective was to extract features of the bootstrap in order to better understand the jackknife (an earlier resampling technique created by John Tukey). He built it as a straightforward approximation to that technique. However, as a resampling method, the bootstrap frequently performs as well as or better than the jackknife.

Bootstrap has already been applied in NLP, it has been applied in the analysis of statistical significance in NLP systems. For instance, in the study conducted by Koehn (2004) [9], bootstrap was used to estimate the statistical significance of the BLEU score in Machine Translation (MT). Likewise, in the research conducted by Zhang (2004) [13], it was employed to measure the confidence intervals for BLEU/NIST score. Additionally, in the field of automatic speech recognition (ARS), researchers have used bootstrap to estimate confidence intervals in performance evaluation, as illustrated in the work of Bisani (2004) [2]. Despite the fact that using bootstrap in NLP problems is not a novel technique, it remains highly relevant.

4.2   Comparison of Classifiers

Comparing classification algorithms is a complex and ongoing problem. Performance can be defined in many ways, such as accuracy, speed, cost, etc., but accuracy is the most commonly used performance indicator. There are numerous accuracy measures that have been presented in the classification literature, with some specifically designed to compare classifiers and others originally defined for other purposes [10]. We will focus on challenge accuracy measures, see Table 1.

The main objective is to make inferences on the performance parameter θ of the algorithms developed by the teams participating in the competition. This inference is made on a single dataset of size n, with a minimal amount of submissions. The inference concerns the parameter's value (performance) in the population from which the dataset is considered to be randomly drawn.

There are two classical approaches for making parameter inferences, hypothesis testing, and confidence intervals; in this contribution, inference on performance is made using both approaches, specifically bootstrap estimates. The procedure consists of extracting 10,000 Bootstrap samples (with replacement of size n) from the data set that includes the n gold standard examples and the corresponding predictions. Each team's performance parameters are calculated for each sample, and the sampling distribution is obtained. Using the sampling distribution, the 95% confidence interval for the mean of the performance parameter is constructed. Table 2 contains the ordered estimates of the mean and confidence interval obtained through Bootstrap.

Table 2. Ordered Bootstrap Confidence Intervals

Precision		Recall		F_1	
Team	CI	Team	CI	Team	CI
NLPCIC	(0.6844,0.7572)	CENAmrita	(0.8962,0.9402)	NLPCIC	(0.6864,0.7438)
DCCDINFOTEC	(0.6585,0.7345)	xjywing	(0.8632,0.9134)	CIMATMTYGTO	(0.6739,0.7306)
CIMATGTO	(0.6578,0.7338)	aomar	(0.8485,0.9015)	DCCDINFOTEC	(0.6536,0.7152)
CICIPN	(0.6458,0.7290)	CIMATMTYGTO	(0.7260,0.7935)	CIMATGTO	(0.6481,0.7098)
UMUTeam	(0.6381,0.7143)	NLPCIC	(0.6739,0.7458)	UMUTeam	(0.6393,0.7011)
CIMATMTYGTO	(0.6175,0.6888)	DCCDINFOTEC	(0.6351,0.7112)	Timen	(0.5713,0.6365)
Timen	(0.5691,0.6474)	UMUTeam	(0.6269,0.7025)	CICIPN	(0.5665,0.6363)
xjywing	(0.3182,0.3656)	CIMATGTO	(0.6255,0.7011)	xjywing	(0.4676,0.5196)
aomar	(0.3011,0.3470)	Timen	(0.5608,0.6392)	aomar	(0.4470,0.4987)
CENAmrita	(0.2926,0.3364)	CICIPN	(0.4946,0.5751)	CENAmrita	(0.4433,0.4935)

4.3   Comparison of Classifiers Through Independents Samples

Suppose the confidence intervals of the means of two populations overlap; in that case, this is enough to conclude that there is no significant difference between the means of the populations. On the other hand, if the intervals do not overlap, then there is an indication that the difference in performance is significant. The hypothesis testing approach would be set the null hypothesis H_0, that $\theta_i = \theta_j$; against the alternative hypothesis H_1 that $\theta_i \neq \theta_j$, for $i \neq j$. In the case of the performance metrics of the algorithms, the confidence intervals at 95% can be observed in Table 2 and Fig. 1. Intervals have been ordered to facilitate interpretation. As can be seen, the team with the highest F_1 score is $NLPCIC$, with 95% confidence interval equal to $(0.6864, 0.7438)$. The second place corresponds to $CIMATMTYGTO$ $(0.6739, 0.7306)$. As the first two intervals overlap, it suggests that the F_1 scores of both teams will likely be the same in the population from which the dataset was sampled. Conversely, there is a difference between $NLPCIC$ and $Timen$.

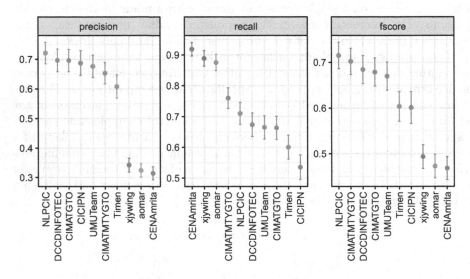

Fig. 1. Ordered Bootstrap Confidence Intervals

4.4   Comparison of Classifiers Through Paired Samples

However, since each Bootstrap sample contains both the gold standard and each team's prediction for the same tweet, it is possible to calculate the performance and also the performance difference for each sample, i.e., the paired bootstrap method is being used [3,7]. Confidence intervals at the 95% level for the difference in performance between paired samples were constructed, following the same approach as in the previous case. Table 3 and Fig. 2 display the confidence intervals for comparing the top team with the others. In this case, for the difference, if the interval contains zero, it is impossible to rule out that the performance of both algorithms is the same in the population from which the dataset was obtained. In other words, H_0 cannot be rejected. For the F_1 score, the team with the highest performance is $NLPCIC$, and as can be seen, we cannot rule out that its performance is the same as $CIMATMTYGTO$ and $DCCDINFOTEC$. On the other hand, there are significant differences compared to the rest of the teams using F_1 score. Regarding recall, the team with the best performance was $CENAmrita$, and no other team had the same performance. Concerning precision, the team with the best performance is $NLPCIC$; however, we cannot rule out that $DCCDINFOTEC$, $CIMATGTO$, and $CICIPN$ have equivalent performances.

Table 3. Bootstrap Confidence Intervals of differences from the best.

Precision				Recall				F_1			
NLPCIC				CENAmrita				NLPCIC			
Team	ICI	Mean	SCI	Team	ICI	Mean	SCI	Team	ICI	Mean	SCI
DCCDINFOTEC	−0.0110	0.0243	0.0596	xjywing	0.0060	0.0299	0.0539	CIMATMTYGTO	−0.0128	0.0128	0.0385
CIMATGTO	−0.0063	0.0250	0.0563	aomar	0.0221	0.0432	0.0643	DCCDINFOTEC	−0.0008	0.0307	0.0621
CICIPN	−0.0065	0.0334	0.0733	CIMATMTYGTO	0.1211	0.1585	0.1958	CIMATGTO	0.0087	0.0361	0.0635
UMUTeam	0.0116	0.0446	0.0776	NLPCIC	0.1683	0.2084	0.2485	UMUTeam	0.0161	0.0449	0.0736
CIMATMTYGTO	0.0380	0.0677	0.0974	DCCDINFOTEC	0.2058	0.2451	0.2844	Timen	0.0784	0.1112	0.1440
Timen	0.0763	0.1126	0.1488	UMUTeam	0.2122	0.2535	0.2948	CICIPN	0.0788	0.1137	0.1486
xjywing	0.3471	0.3789	0.4108	CIMATGTO	0.2150	0.2549	0.2949	xjywing	0.1896	0.2215	0.2534
aomar	0.3651	0.3967	0.4284	Timen	0.2782	0.3182	0.3582	aomar	0.2105	0.2422	0.2740
CENAmrita	0.3753	0.4063	0.4373	CICIPN	0.3401	0.3833	0.4266	CENAmrita	0.2155	0.2467	0.2779

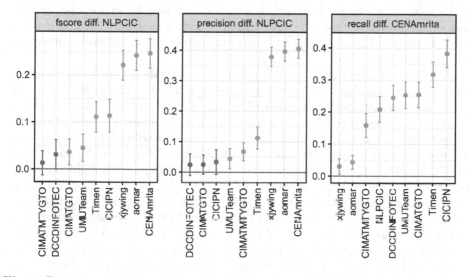

Fig. 2. Bootstrap Confidence Intervals of differences with the best-performing competitor. Red intervals contain zero, and green intervals do not contain it. (Color figure online)

4.5   Statistical Significance Testing

In Subsect. 4.3, ordered confidence intervals were shown, and in Subsect. 4.4, comparisons were made with the best-performing competitor. These comparisons raise the question of whether the hypothesis of equality versus difference should be evaluated, given that it is evident that one competitor has better performance than the other in the test dataset. The previous question can be addressed by comparing the performance of two competitors, A and B, to determine whether A is superior to B in a large population of data, i.e., $\theta_A > \theta_B$. Given the test dataset $x = x_1, \ldots, x_n$, assume that A beats B by a magnitude $\delta(x) = \theta_A(x) - \theta_B(x)$, the null hypothesis, H_0, is that A is not superior to B in the total population, and H_1 is that it is. Therefore, the aim is to determine how likely it would be for a similar victory for A to occur in a new independent test dataset, denoted as y, assuming that H_0 is true.

Hypothesis testing aims to calculate the probability $p(\delta(X) > \delta(x) \mid H_0, x)$, where X represents a random variable that considers the possible test sets of size n that we could have selected, while $\delta(x)$ refers to the observed difference, that is, it is a constant. $p(\delta(X) > \delta(x) \mid H_0, x)$ is called the $p - value(x)$, and traditionally, if $p - value(x) < 0.05$, the observed value $\delta(x)$ is considered sufficiently unlikely to reject H_0, meaning that the evidence suggests that A is superior to B, see [1].

In most cases, the $p - value(x)$ is not easily calculated and must be approximated. As described, this work uses paired bootstrap, not only because it is the most widely used (see [1,2,9,13]), but also because it can be easily applied to any performance metric.

As shown in [1], the $p - value(x)$ can be estimated by computing the fraction of times that this difference is greater than $2\delta(x)$. It is crucial to keep in mind that this distribution is centered around $\delta(x)$, given that X is drawn from x, where it is observed that A is superior to B by $\delta(x)$. Figure 3 illustrates the $p - value(x)$ process by showing the bootstrap distribution of the F_1 score differences between $NLPCIC$ and $CIMATMTYGTO$ (a), and $NLPCIC$ and $DCCDINFOTEC$ (b). The values zero, $\delta(x)$, and $2\delta(x)$ are highlighted for better understanding. When comparing $NLPCIC$ and $CIMATMTYGTO$ in the test dataset x, the difference $\delta(x) = 0.7154 - 0.7026 = 0.0128$, is not significant at the 5% level because the $p - value(x)$ is 0.1730. On the other hand, when comparing $NLPCIC$ and $DCCDINFOTEC$, $\delta(x) = 0.7154 - 0.6847 = 0.0307$, which is significant at the 5% level with a $p - value(x)$ of 0.0292. In other words, $NLPCIC$ is not significantly better than $CIMATMTYGTO$ but better than $DCCDINFOTEC$. In Sect. 4.4, it was shown through confidence intervals that the evidence supports H_0 (same performance) instead of H_1 (difference in performance). If we estimate the $p - value(x)$, it would be approximately $2 \times 0.0292 = 0.0584$, which is not significant at the 5% level. Table 4 summarizes the differences in the F_1 score and their significance. One can observe, for instance, that $NLPCIC$ is better than $CIMATGTO$ by 0.036 with a 1% significance.

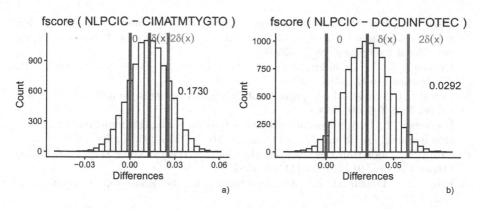

Fig. 3. Bootstrap distribution of the F_1 score differences between $NLPCIC$ and $CIMATMTYGTO$ (a), and $NLPCIC$ and $DCCDINFOTEC$ (b)

Table 4. Differences of F_1 score (column)-(row), and their significance. Note: $\dagger p < .1$, $*p < .05$, $**p < .1$, and $***p < .001$.

	NLPCIC	CIMATMTYGTO	DCCDINFOTEC	CIMATGTO	UMUTeam	Timen	CICIPN	xjywing	aomar
CIMATMTYGTO	0.013								
DCCDINFOTEC	0.031*	0.018							
CIMATGTO	0.036**	0.023*	0.006						
UMUTeam	0.045**	0.032**	0.014	0.009					
Timen	0.111***	0.099***	0.081***	0.075***	0.067***				
CICIPN	0.114***	0.101***	0.083***	0.077***	0.069***	0.002			
xjywing	0.222***	0.209***	0.191***	0.185***	0.177***	0.110***	0.108***		
aomar	0.242***	0.230***	0.212***	0.206***	0.198***	0.131***	0.129***	0.021***	
CENAmrita	0.247***	0.234***	0.216***	0.211***	0.202***	0.135***	0.133***	0.025***	0.004

5 Conclusions

This paper has presented a procedure that uses bootstrap to infer the performance of classifiers from different teams in a competition. Confidence intervals were provided for each competitor and for differences in performance compared with the best-performing competitor. By graphing these confidence intervals, it can be quickly determined whether the differences are significant or not. The significance calculation was also presented to compare whether one competitor is better. It was highlighted that these ideas can be easily applied to any classification or regression problem. In summary, these proposals offer valuable tools for challenge organizers when making decisions.

References

1. Berg-Kirkpatrick, T., Burkett, D., Klein, D.: An empirical investigation of statistical significance in NLP. In: EMNLP-CoNLL 2012–2012 Joint Conference on Empirical Methods in Natural Language Processing and Computational Natural Language Learning, Proceedings of the Conference (2012)

2. Bisani, M., Ney, H.: Bootstrap estimates for confidence intervals in ASR performance evaluation. In: 2004 IEEE International Conference on Acoustics, Speech, and Signal Processing, vol. 1 (2004)
3. Chernick, M.R., LaBudde, R.A.: An Introduction to Bootstrap Methods with Applications to R. Wiley (2011)
4. Demšar, J.: Statistical comparisons of classifiers over multiple data sets. J. Mach. Learn. Res. **7**, 1–30 (2006)
5. Dietterich, T.G.: Approximate statistical tests for comparing supervised classification learning algorithms. Neural Comput. **10**(7), 1895–1923 (1998)
6. Efron, B.: Bootstrap methods: another look at the jackknife **7**(1), 1–26 (1979). https://doi.org/10.1214/aos/1176344552
7. Efron, B., Tibshirani, R.: An Introduction to the Bootstrap. Chapman and Hall/CRC (1994)
8. García, S., Herrera, F.: An extension on "statistical comparisons of classifiers over multiple data sets" for all pairwise comparisons. J. Mach. Learn. Res. **9**, 2677–2694 (2008)
9. Koehn, P.: Statistical significance tests for machine translation evaluation. In: Proceedings of the 2004 Conference on Empirical Methods in Natural Language Processing, EMNLP 2004 - A Meeting of SIGDAT, a Special Interest Group of the ACL held in conjunction with ACL 2004, pp. 388–395 (2004)
10. Labatut, V., Cherifi, H.: Accuracy Measures for the Comparison of Classifiers, July 2012
11. Pavao, A., et al.: CodaLab competitions: an open source platform to organize scientific challenges, April 2022
12. Plaza-del Arco, F.M., et al.: Overview of MeOffendEs at IberLEF 2021: offensive language detection in spanish variants. Procesamiento del Lenguaje Natural **67**(0), 183–194 (2021)
13. Zhang, Y., Vogel, S., Waibel, A.: Interpreting BLEU/NIST scores: how much improvement do we need to have a better system? In: Proceedings of the 4th International Conference on Language Resources and Evaluation, LREC 2004, pp. 2051–2054 (2004)

Deep Learning and Neural Networks

Robust Zero-Watermarking for Medical Images Based on Deep Learning Feature Extraction

Rodrigo Eduardo Arevalo-Ancona(✉) ⓘ, Manuel Cedillo-Hernandez ⓘ,
Ana Elena Ramirez-Rodriguez ⓘ, Mariko Nakano-Miyatake ⓘ,
and Hector Perez-Meana ⓘ

Instituto Politécnico Nacional, Escuela Superior de Ingeniería Mecánica y Eléctrica, SEPI,
Culhuacán, Ciudad de México, México
{rarevaloa0900,aramirezr0906}@alumno.ipn.mx, {mcedilloh,mnakano,
hmperezm}@ipn.mx

Abstract. Internet data transfer has increased in recent years, as well as the need to generate protection and authentication of multimedia data. The use of watermarks on digital images serves for copyright protection and ownership authentication. Zero-watermarking does not embed the watermark into the host image. The imperceptibility of the watermark is required for some tasks without modifying pixels on the image, such as medical images, because the medical image has a low distortion and may generate a wrong diagnosis. In this paper, we propose a zero-watermarking algorithm for medical images with patient authentication purposes and avoid image tampering based on a deep learning neural network model as a feature extractor using the Context Encoder. Thus, is extracted a feature map with the most representative image features. Therefore, an or-exclusive is applied to merge the watermark sequence and the extracted feature map. The watermark signal consists of a pseudorandom sequence and contains the patient's information. The bit error rate and the normalized cross-correlation demonstrate the robustness of the zero-watermark technique against geometric and image processing attacks.

Keywords: Image Watermarking · Zero-Watermarking · Deep Learning · Image Authentication · Data Security

1 Introduction

Currently, the use and transmission of digital files have been increasing due to the development of digital technologies, on the other hand, the need for information sharing quickly and efficiently, such as medical images. Digital images have facilitated services in the health area, especially after the COVID-19 pandemic and quarantine [1]. On the one hand, the medical image requires security and patient information confidentiality to prevent misuse. On the other hand, medical images must not have distortions to provide a correct diagnosis [2]. Therefore, it requires technology for the security of medical images and authentication.

A. Y. Rodríguez-González et al. (Eds.): MCPR 2023, LNCS 13902, pp. 101–113, 2023.
https://doi.org/10.1007/978-3-031-33783-3_10

In some cases, the images are tampered with by image processing or pixel modification to obtain different results. Watermarking schemes are a secure and efficient method for the protection, verification, and authentication of medical images [3]. Invisible watermarking algorithms embed an imperceptible signal into the host image and generate a minimum distortion. In order to avoid any alteration of the image, Zero-watermarking techniques are developed, these schemes do not embed information into the digital data. Instead, Zero-watermarking algorithms hide information using extracted features of the image and the user´s watermark to create a sequence and construct the Master Share (a feature matrix) without losing the host image quality [4].

Magdy et al. in [5] used the Multi-channel Fractional Legendre Fourier Moments (MFrLFM) to obtain an image descriptor with pattern features to construct the master share. Two-Dimensional Discrete Henon Map to scramble the red-green-blue RGB channels of the watermark image and create an RGB Master Share with an or-exclusive (XOR) operation to merge the MFrLFM descriptor and the scrambled watermark. Huang et al. proposed in [6], the Dual-Tree Complex Wavelet Transform (DTCWT) obtains a descriptor of the image, which contains directional features information invariant to translation. Therefore, the Multi-Level Discrete Cosine Transform (MDCT) concentrated image energy with larger values to optimize the feature extraction. Finally, the Hessenberg decomposition extracts essential detailed features from the image for rotation invariance. Thus, the fusion of these algorithms enhances the robustness. Qin et al. present a zero-watermarking scheme in [7], applying the Curvelet Transform to eliminate the image noise. Feature extraction is based on the Discrete Cosine Transform (DCT) and binarized these coefficients. Thus, the watermark is encrypted using the Rivers-Shamir-Adleman (RSA) algorithm to generate a pseudo-random sequence and finally is performed an XOR operation to the visual vector and the pseudo-random sequence.

Deep Learning methods recognize patterns in the image and can adapt the parameters in response to the dataset. Hamamoto and Kawamura [8] developed a watermarking scheme compressing the image and the watermark using a neural network model. The watermarked image is created by extracting the fourteen lower-frequency DCT coefficients. Consequently, the neural network embeds a one-bit sequence into each 8 x 8 block from the DCT blocks. Then the luminance values can be given by de Inverse DCT. Han et al. proposed in [9] a zero-watermarking scheme based on the VGG19 neural network model to extract feature maps of medical images, which are fused to construct a new matrix. Therefore, it is combined with the extracted features from the Discrete Fourier Transform low-frequency coefficients. Subsequently, the Perceptual Hashing Algorithm is applied to binarize the features. Thus, the watermark is scrambled with Hermite Chaotic Neural Network and is applied an XOR operation between both sequences.

This paper presents a zero-watermarking scheme using deep learning for feature extraction. This method provides robustness for x-ray medical images against geometric attacks and advanced signal processing distortions. The watermark serves as copyright protection, even though the image has suffered from geometric or advanced signal-processing attacks. The present approach applies a deep neural network model based on the Context Encoders [10] for the feature extraction, and it is pre-trained with an x-ray medical database. The purpose of using Zero-watermarking is not to generate a distortion on the host image. The last layer of the convolutional neural network (CNN) obtained a feature map used to generate the master share. The training of the neural network model generates and detects the most important features from each image, increasing the efficiency and robustness of the watermark system. In addition, the use of a deep neural network is for feature learning and recognition, even if the image suffers an attack. The watermark contains the patient information and is constructed using a pseudo-random sequence from a string with the mentioned data. An XOR logic operation is used for the creation of the master share that links the feature map and the created watermark sequence. In the watermark detection stage, the medical image is analyzed with the pre-trained neural network model, and the feature map reveals the watermark.

2   Methodology

The zero-watermarking algorithm present in this paper consists of the master share generation stage (Fig. 1) and the watermark with the data of the patient detection and verification stage (Fig. 2).

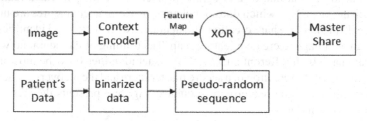

Fig. 1. Master Share generation.

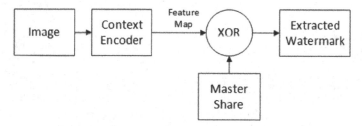

Fig. 2. Master Share detection.

The neural network based on the Context Encoder is used in the generation and detection stage for the feature map extraction to construct the master share and the watermark detection.

2.1   Context Encoder

Deep learning is an area of machine learning that uses data to learn features by pattern recognition to make decisions. Moreover, Deep learning algorithms perform a task to have a more efficient result, generating better learning of the characteristics extracted from the data. Furthermore, deep learning models are neural networks with several layers and provide solutions to some tasks, such as image recognition, image segmentation, image classification, and image generation [11].

Generative models focus on the approximation of the likelihood of the pixels to create samples from a given data using a generator and a discriminator for testing the similarity of the new data through a probability distribution (1), [12, 13]. The generator $(G(z))$ uses the features from the dataset to create new data. The discriminator $(D(z))$ distinguishes that the generated samples differ from the used dataset.

$$\min_{G} \max_{D} V(D, G) = E_{x \sim P_{data}(x)}[\log D(x)] + E_{x \sim P_z(z)}[\log(1 - D(G(z)))] \qquad (1)$$

where the loss function of the discriminator $\log(D(z))$ learns the features from the dataset to compare the loss function of the generator $\log(1\text{-}D(G(z)))$ and approximates the equilibrium between the features of the dataset and the new samples.

The Context Encoder is an unsupervised deep generative neural network model for inpainting and hole-filling. This model fulfills the image by pixel prediction using the background context from the image. In this paper, we focus on the Context Encoder generator due to the learning of the regions of interest and the generated feature maps extracted on the last CNN, which does not change. The extracted features are unique for each image. In the master share creation, the neural network learns and identifies regions of interest in the image to create a feature map. The training of the neural network used the medical image with different attacks. The model identifies only the most important features. This allows the creation of a secure master share and the recovery of the patient's information inserted on the watermark sequence. Figure 3 presents the architecture of the neural network model.

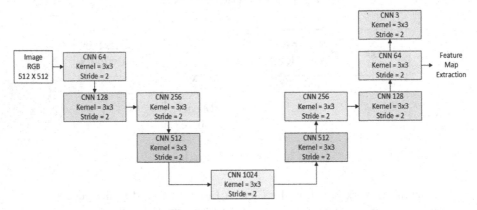

Fig. 3. Context encoder architecture.

The neural network uses a rectified linear activation function (ReLU) on each layer for the region of interest detection to identify the features for the master share construction. The feature map extracted from the Conv 9 layer is binarized. A Mean Squared Error is used as function loss (MSE) (2).

$$MSE = \frac{1}{n} \sum (x - mean(x))^2 \qquad (2)$$

The MSE estimates the average error and measures the distance between image feature values and the extracted features. A function with a lower error value means that the prediction is closer to the real feature values.

2.2 Watermark Sequence

The construction of the watermark sequence uses the patient´s information, which is a string. Subsequently, each character becomes ASCII code to create a pseudo-random sequence (Table 1) with a size of m x n (Fig. 4), equal to the feature map size.

Table 1. String data watermark converted into a binarized sequence.

Patient's Information	Binarized Sequence
Rodrigo Arevalo Ancona	01010010 01101111 01100100 01110010
	01101001 01100111 01101111 00100000
	01000001 01110010 01100101 01110110
	01100001 01101100 01101111 00100000
	01000001 01101110 01100011 01101111

Fig. 4. Constructed watermark with the patient´s information and a pseudo-random sequence.

The encryption of the patient data as a watermark with a pseudo-random sequence allows one to share the image and recover it despite image distortions. The extracted watermark identifies the patient due to the extracted features from the neural network.

To create the pattern master share (Fig. 5 b) is applied an XOR ($\oplus$) operation between the watermark sequence with the encrypted data fuzzed with the image features (3).

$$MS = imf \oplus WS \qquad (3)$$

where *imf* are the extracted features from the neural network model, and *WS* is the generated watermark sequence. Therefore, the master share is stored in a secure location

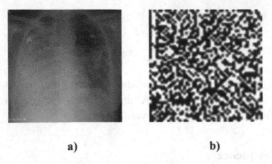

a)   b)

Fig. 5. a) X-ray image, b) Master Share.

and shared to identify the patient and the image is authenticated to avoid any diagnosis error.

The image authentication verifies the patient´s data with the master share and the extracted image feature map (4). Also, the proposed watermark scheme detects tampering on the x-ray image. In case of image tampering patient´s data will not be revealed because the image features will change since it distorted the main features of each image.

$$WS = imf \oplus MS \tag{4}$$

where imf are the image features extracted from the neural network model, MS is the master share pattern and $\oplus$ the XOR operation. In the next section, the robustness evaluation of the proposed zero-watermarking is presented.

3   Experiment Results

The zero-watermarking implementation was in Python 3.6.10 and a GPU GeForce GTX 1650. The neural network model was trained with 251 chest x-ray images from Kaggle [14], with 512 x 512 pixels size, considering 111 images for testing. For the dataset augmentation, geometric and advanced signal processing attacks to each image were applied (Scale, rotation, translation, cropping, JPEG compression, filtering, noise addition, denoising, and combining some distortions). The data augmentation generates an efficient neural network learning of the image features to improve the detection and authentication stage and provides robustness against geometric and image processing attacks.

The bit error rate (BER) given by (5) and the normalized cross-correlation (NCC) by (6) were used as evaluation metrics of the proposed zero-watermarking algorithm. The BER measures the error bits detected in the authentication stage, a low value indicates an efficient watermark recovery [15]. The BER indicates the quality of the recovery watermark compared with the original watermark.

$$BER = \frac{\sum Eb}{\text{Total bits}} \tag{5}$$

where Eb the recover error bits. The image watermark sequence size is *50 x 50*. Experiments test the efficiency of the detection of the watermark and authentication of x-ray medical images using the proposed algorithm. The robustness of the watermark is shown in Fig. 6.

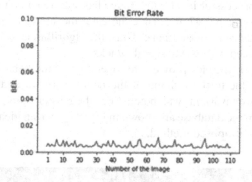

Fig. 6. Recovery watermark Bit Error Rate.

The average BER of the recovery watermark is lower than 0.02. This value indicates a low error in the watermark recovery and the authentication stage. On the one hand, the transmitted watermark is recovered with no distortions and verifies the patient's identity. On the other hand, the BER indicates that the shared x-ray image has not been tampered. Also, the BER shows the robustness of the proposed algorithm to geometric and advanced image processing attacks.

The NCC evaluates the similarity between the detected watermark sequence (W) and the original watermark sequence (W') [16]. In the case of evaluating the detected watermark, indicates the relationship between the generated and the extracted watermark.

$$NCC(W, \overline{W}) = \frac{\sum_{i=i\,j=1}^{m}\sum_{}^{n}((W(i,j))x(W'(i,j)))}{\sum_{i=i\,j=1}^{m}\sum_{}^{n}W(i,j)^2} \qquad (6)$$

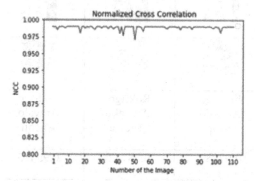

Fig. 7. Watermark normalized cross-correlation.

where m and n are the watermark dimensions. The similarity of the recovered watermark with the original watermark after applying different attacks to the shared x-ray image is in Fig. 7. The NCC is a metric that provides indicating the amount of information lost in the transmission process or in case the image has suffered an attack.

The NCC is upper than 0.97, this value indicates the similarity between the original watermark and the recovered watermark. Thus, the algorithm is robust against different geometric and advanced processing signal attacks.

The analysis of the metrics provides an overview of the behavior of the proposed algorithm, which is due to the training of the neural network and the learning of the characteristics that are invariant, which generates the master share.

Four images from the database are shown in Fig. 8 to give an idea of the effectiveness and robustness of the proposed method.

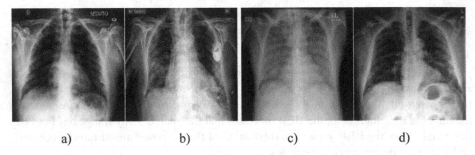

a)   b)   c)   d)

Fig. 8. Original x-ray images.

Tables 2, 3, 4, 5 and 6 show the robustness of the proposed algorithm against translation, rotation, cropping, JPEG compression and filtering attacks.

Table 2. Translation attack applied to x-ray images.

	Image a	Image b	Image c	Image d
Attacked image				
Recover Watermark				
Recover Watermark String	Rodrigo Arevalo Ancona	Rokrigo Arevalo Anc na	Rodrigo Arevalo Ancoji	Rodrigo Arevaln AnconA
NCC	0.97987	0.98142	0.95820	0.99071
BER	0.01680	0.03220	0.03859	0.01280

Table 3. Rotation attack applied to x-ray images.

	Image a	Image b	Image c	Image d
Attacked image				
Recover Watermark				
Recover Watermark String	Rodrigo Arevalo Ancola	Rodrigo Arevalo Anconi	Rodrigo Arevalo ancona	Rodrigo Arevalo AnconA
NCC	0.97987	0.98142	0.96130	0.95820
BER	0.01680	0.01480	0.02559	0.02639

Table 4. Center crop attack applied to x-ray images.

	Image a	Image b	Image c	Image d
Attacked image				
Recover Watermark				
Recover Watermark String	'odrigo Arevalo Ancona	RodriDo Arevalo Ancona	Rodrigo Arevalo ancona	Rodrigo, Arevalo AnconA
NCC	0.96674	0.9318	0.99	0.96674
BER	0.03459	0.03100	0.02739	0.02980

Tables 2, 3, 4, 5 and 6, present the robustness of the proposed algorithm against different image attacks. According to the results, the algorithm is efficient for image copyright protection and patient identification, without distorting the host image, providing the user with the diagnosis in an efficient way. The proposed algorithm is compared with [9] and [17], the comparison was made under different geometric and image processing attacks. The graphic in Fig. 7 indicates that the presented zero-watermarking has better robustness against these attacks.

Table 5. 30 JPEG compression attack applied to x-ray images.

	Image a	Image b	Image c	Image d
Attacked image				
Recover Watermark				
Recover Watermark String	Rodrigo Arev lo Ancona	Ro$rigo Arevalo Ancona	R-drigo Arevalo ancona	Rodrigo, Arevaln Ancona
NCC	0.97837	0.94348	0.99	0.96674
BER	0.03620	0.0302	0.0282	0.024599

Table 6. Blurring attack applied to x-ray images.

	Image a	Image b	Image c	Image d
Attacked image				
Recover Watermark				
Recover Watermark String	Rodrigo ArevalM Ancona	Rodrigo ArevalO Ancona	Rodrigo Arevalo Ancona	Rodrïgo Arevalo Ancona
NCC	0.99	0.98348	0.99	0.00660
BER	0.00819	0.01260	0.00700	0.024599

Figure 9 shows the performance of the algorithm present in this paper against different attacks. The comparison with the one presented by Han et al. is because they focus on the master share generation using a neural model focusing on medical images, but the created master share increases its security but may lose some values in the hashing process. Also, the transfer learning from VGG19 may generate different weights of those needed for the used images. However, the algorithm proposed in this paper has better performance due to the Context Encoder because for each image the weights are updated. Moreover, the

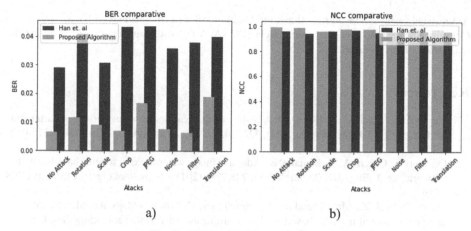

Fig. 9. BER and NCC comparison.

proposed method in this paper takes advantage of the GAN generates learning based on unique characteristics to generate new data. The GAN models must detect these features to create new data. In addition, the new samples must be similar to the training dataset. In our case, this learning recognizes invariant points of interest to create the master share.

4   Conclusions

Zero-watermarking research in medical areas has increased since it does not distort the host image in the watermarking stage. Guaranteeing that the image is intact, thus reducing the error in the diagnosis. Furthermore, this technique provides robustness against image processing and geometrical attacks. The present research presents a zero-watermarking scheme for x-ray medical image authentication for detecting regions of interest, extracting interest points using the Context Encoder, and merging them with the watermark sequence. The deep neural network extracts and learns invariant features from the medical images to authenticate them. The neural network is an efficient method that should be trained images that suffer geometric and advanced signal processing attacks for feature identification.

The performance of the zero-watermarking method proposed in this paper presents a highly efficient, even though some attacks were combined for image distortion. In those cases, the detection of the watermark has a low error. The experiment results show that our algorithm in the tested conditions has a low BER, and the recovered watermark has a high similarity to the embedded watermark. The analysis of the experimental results proves the robustness of the proposed algorithm, owed to the training of the neural network and the learning of the detected patterns, which generates the master share. In addition, the GAN model allows the recognition of unique feature patterns to create new samples that must be like the dataset. In our case, this learning recognizes invariant points of interest to create the master share and provides high robustness to the scheme.

Acknowledgments. The authors thank the Instituto Politécnico Nacional (IPN), as well as the Consejo Nacional de Ciencia y Tecnología (CONACYT) for the support provided during the realization of this research.

References

1. Neymeen, H., Boles, W., Boyd, C.: A review of medical image watermarking requirements for technology, J. Digit Imaging **26**(2), 326–343 (2013). https://doi.org/10.1007/s10278-012-9527-x
2. Oueslati, S., Cherif, A., Solaimane, B.: Adaptive image watermarking scheme based on neural network. Int. J. Eng. Sci. Technol. **3**(1), 748–757 (2011). https://doi.org/10.1155/2018/268 5739
3. Garcia-Nonoal, Z., Mata-Mendoza, D., Hernandez, C., Nakano-Miyatake, M.: Secure management of retinal imaging based on deep learning and reversible data hiding. Vis. Comput. (2023). https://doi.org/10.1007/s00371-023-02778-1
4. Hosny, K., Darwish, M., Fouda, M.: New color image zero-watermarking using orthogonal multi-channel fractional-order legndre-fourier moments. IEEE Access **9**, 91209–91219 (2021). https://doi.org/10.1109/access.2021.3091614
5. Magdy, M., Ghali, N., Ghoniemy, S., Hosny, K.: Multiple zero-watermarking of medical images for internet of medical things. IEEE Access **10**, 38821–38831 (2022). https://doi.org/10.1109/access.2022.3165813
6. Huang, T., Xu, J., Yang, Y., Han, B.: Robust zero-watermarking algorithm for medical images using double-tree complex wavelet transform and hessenberg descomposition. Adv. Pattern Recogn. Image Anal. **10**(7), 1154 (2022). https://doi.org/10.3390/math10071154
7. Qin, F., Li, J., Li, H., Liu, J., Nawaz, S.A., Liu, Y.: A robust zero-watermarking algorithm for medical images using curvelet-DCT and RSA pseudo-random sequences. In: Sun, X., Wang, J., Bertino, E. (eds.) ICAIS 2020. LNCS, vol. 12240, pp. 179–190. Springer, Cham (2020). https://doi.org/10.1007/978-3-030-57881-7_16
8. Hamamoto, I., Kawamura, M.: Image watermarking technique using embedder and extractor neural networks. In: IEICE Transactions on Information and Systems, Special Section on Enriched Multimedia - Making Multimedia More Convenient and Safer, E102.D(1), pp. 19–30, (2019). https://doi.org/10.1587/transinf.2018MUP0006
9. Han, B., Du, J., Jia, Y., Zhu, H.: Zero-watermarking algorithm for medical image based on VGG19 deep convolution neural network. J. Healthc. Eng. **2021**, 5551520 (2021). https://doi.org/10.1155/2021/5551520
10. Pathak, D., krähenbühl, P., Donahue, J., Darrell, T., Efros, A.: Context encoders: feature learning by inpainting. Comput. Vis. Pattern Recogn. **1** (2016). https://doi.org/10.48550/arXiv.1604.073
11. Ganguly, K.: Learning Generative Adversarial Networks. Packt Publishers Ltd., Brimingham, United Kingdom (2017)
12. Arjovsky, M., Chintala, S., Bottou, L.: Wasserstein GAN. In: International Conference on Machine Learning (2017)
13. Goodfellow, I., et al.: Generative adversarial networks. In: Computer and Information Sciences (2014). https://doi.org/10.48550/arXiv.1406.2661
14. Raikote, P.: Kaggle. https://www.kaggle.com/datasets/pranavraikokte/covid19-image-dat aset?select=Covid19-dataset. Accessed 25 Dec 2021
15. Jitsumatsu, Y., Khan, T., Hattori, Y., Kohda, T.: Bit error rate in digital watermarking systems using spread spectrum techniques. In: de Eighth IEEE International Symposium on Spread Spectrum Techniques and Applications - Program and Book of Abstracts (IEEE Cat. No.04TH8738), Sydney, NSW, Australia (2004)

16. Ren, N., Zhao, Y., Zhu, C., Zhou y, Q., Xu, D.: Copyright protection based on zero water-marking and blockchain for vector maps. Int. J. Geo-Inf. **10**(5), 294 (2021). https://doi.org/10.3390/ijgi10050294

17. Fierro-Radilla, A., Nakano Miyatake, M., Cedillo-Hernandez, M., Cleofas-Sanchez y, L., Perez-Meana, H.: A robust image zero-watermarking using convolutional neural networks. In: de 2019 7th International Workshop on Biometrics and Forensics (IWBF), Cancun, Mexico (2019). https://doi.org/10.1109/IWBF.2019.8739245

Plant Stress Recognition Using Deep Learning and 3D Reconstruction

German Ríos-Toledo, Madaín Pérez-Patricio, Luis Ángel Cundapí-López,
J. L. Camas-Anzueto, N. A. Morales-Navarro,
and J. A. de Jesús Osuna-Coutiño[✉]

Instituto Tecnológico de Tuxtla Gutiérrez (ITTG), Tuxtla Gutiérrez, Mexico
juan.oc@tuxtla.tecnm.mx

Abstract. Plant stress recognition consists of Identification, Classification, Quantification, and Prediction (ICQP) in crop stress. There are several approaches to plant stress identification. However, most of these approaches are based on the use of expert employees or invasive techniques. In general, expert employees have a good performance on different plants, but this alternative requires sufficient staff in order to guarantee quality crops. On the other hand, invasive techniques need the dismemberment of the leaves. To address this problem, an alternative is to process an image seeking to interpret patterns of the images where the plant geometry may be observed, thus removing the qualified labor dependency or the crop dismemberment, but adding the challenge of having to interpret images ambiguities correctly. Motivated by the latter, we propose a new approach for plant stress recognition using deep learning and 3D reconstruction. This strategy combines the abstraction power of deep learning and the visual patterns of plant geometry. For that, our methodology has three steps. First, the plant recognition step provides the segmentation, location, and delimitation of the crop. Second, we propose a leaf detection analysis to classify and locate the boundaries between the different leaves. Finally, we use a depth sensor and the pinhole camera model to extract a 3D reconstruction.

Keywords: Plant Stress Recognition · Visual Pattern · Deep Learning

1 Introduction

Phenotype is the observable characteristics or traits of an organism that are produced by the interaction of the genotype (the genetic constitution of an organism) and the environment. Understanding these processes that span plant's lifetime in a permanently changing environment is essential for the advancement of basic plant science [10]. Plant phenotyping is an important tool to address and understand plant environment interaction and its translation into application in crop management practices [15]. Phenotyping can take place under laboratory, greenhouse or field conditions. Plants are exposed to environmental factors that

A. Y. Rodríguez-González et al. (Eds.): MCPR 2023, LNCS 13902, pp. 114–124, 2023.
https://doi.org/10.1007/978-3-031-33783-3_11

reduce and limit the productivity of agricultural crops and place stress *biotic* and *abiotic* on plants. Abiotic stress includes factors such as drought, flood, salinity, radiation, high and low temperatures, among others. Meanwhile, in biotic stress, pathogens such as bacteria, fungi, yeasts, worms (nematodes) are considered. Current approaches for the accurate classification of biotic and abiotic stress in crops are predominantly conducted by persons with specialized training in visual recognition of formological characteristics of healthy and stressed plants. However, these techniques are subject to subjectivity and the experience of the people who perform them.

Recently, high-throughput stress recognition techniques have been introduced that rely primarily on remote sensing or imaging. They are able to directly measure morphological traits, but measure physiological parameters mainly indirectly. Plant stress recognition is divided into four broad categories, the so-called ICQP paradigm, the acronym represents Identification, Classification, Quantification and Prediction. These four categories naturally fall into a continuum of feature extraction where increasingly more information is inferred from a given image [11]. Studies on plant stress include those on drought stress [3], heat stress [14], salt stress [6], nutrient deficiency [9] and biotic stress [5].

Remote sensing phenotyping methods are non-destructive and non-invasive approaches [8], based mostly on the information provided by visible/near-infrared radiation reflected (or transmitted) and far-infrared (thermal) radiation emitted by the crop. Remote sensing techniques maybe deployed in situ screening for a wide range of breeding objectives, including yield potential, adaptation to abiotic (water stress, extreme temperatures, salinity) and biotic (susceptibility to pests and diseases) limiting conditions, and even quality traits.

On the field plant stress identification and classification have invariably relied on human experts identifying visual symptoms as a means of categorization [7]. About this, Tariq *et al.* [12] state that conventional phenotyping requires a lot of time, finances, and human resources. The weather also matters in the process of manual phenotyping of crops, especially in regions of difficult access. Furthermore, in this approach the frequency of data collection is very low and not always reproducible due to the inherently subjective nature of manual ratings, experience and interpretation.

Finally, there is significant progress in crop stress recognition using machine learning [13]. This was achieved via learning algorithms that learn the relationship between visual appearance and plant stress diagnosis. Unlike the other trends, this approach analyzes the plant without qualified labor dependency or crop dismemberment but adds the challenge of having to interpret image ambiguities. Motivated by the results of learning algorithms and the potential benefits that image analysis provides, this work focuses on plant stress recognition using deep learning and visual patterns of plant geometry. In particular, we are interested in the 3D information in crop environments. We use a 3D methodology since a 2D approach only can recognize stress in images where the plant shows obvious physical signs of stress. However, in a plant with the first day of stress, the physical signs are not visible visually, whereas the decline of the leaves is one of the first morphological symptoms of crop stress. This information allowed our 3D methodology to recognize stress even when visual signals have not appeared on the plant.

2　The Proposed Methodology

The proposed methodology for plant stress recognition leverages both RGB and depth information to predict stress by utilizing the plant's three-dimensional geometry. This approach combines deep learning techniques and visual patterns of plant geometry. The use of deep learning in this context provides a powerful tool for image analysis and feature extraction, while the inclusion of 3D information allows an understanding of the plant's stress state. Overall, this work effectively merges the strengths of computer vision and machine learning to tackle a complex problem in the field of plant science. For that, our methodology has three steps. First, the plant recognition step provides the segmentation, location, and delimitation of the crop. Second, we propose a leaf detection analysis to classify and locate the boundaries between the different leaves. Finally, we use a depth sensor and the pinhole camera model to extract the 3D pose. The schematic representation of the proposal is shown in Fig. 1.

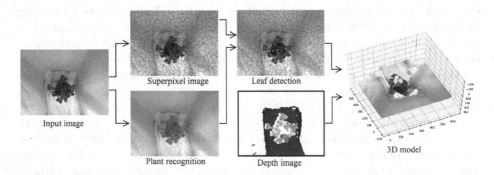

Fig. 1. Block diagram of the proposed methodology.

2.1　Plant Recognition

Our plant recognition step provides the segmentation, location, and delimitation of the crop in the image. For that, we propose a Convolutional Neural Network (CNN) configuration, where the input is an RGB section and the output is a pixel segmented. Using this configuration, we can convert an object detection network with a bounding box to a semantic segmentation network. On the other hand, our semantic segmentation architecture allows us to convert a dataset with few images to a big training set.

2.1.1   Training Set

In the training set of semantic segmentation, we use the "Eschikon Plant Stress Phenotyping Dataset" [4] and a proposed dataset of strawberry plants. In these datasets we develop the ground truth of semantic segmentation, i.e., we did manually the semantic labeling of the images. For that, we use two labels (plant v^1 and no-plant v^2). To obtain the training set, we divide the images of the datasets with labels (plant v^1 and no-plant v^2) in RGB images of 32×32 pixels. For example, we can obtain 630 small sections (32×32 pixels) using an image (1920×1080 pixels). Using these small sections, we can convert a dataset with few images to a big training set. Our dataset presents the different stress levels in strawberry plants. We began the development of our dataset when the plants showed morphological signs of stress. In our dataset, each RGB image has a depth image. This dataset has 1440 depth images, 1440 RGB images and 1440 labelled images of 640×480 pixels captured during 15 days.

2.1.2   CNN for Semantic Segmentation

The input of the CNN is an RGB section Φ^i with a size of 32×32 pixels. Our network contains two stages. The first stage of the network (encoder) is based on the YOLOv4 architecture [2]. We use this encoder since it has promising results to obtain the feature map for the object classification tasks [16]. The first stage extracts feature maps with different resolutions from the input image. This stage is the backbone of the network since the extracted features are shared in the second stage. The second stage combines all the found local characteristics of the previous convolutional layers. Finally, a classifier obtains a label for the two options (plant v^1 and no-plant v^2).

We propose a network configuration. For that, our architecture divides the input image into sections of 32×32 pixels, and the output is a semantic label. We use a sliding window with a sweep of one pixel. For example, if we consider an image of 116×116 pixels, our approach needs 100 processes to segment. Using this configuration, we can convert an object detection network with a bounding box to a semantic segmentation network. On the other hand, we have two semantic labels (plant v^1 and no-plant v^2). The CNN paints the central pixel $\rho_{\varphi,\omega}$ with green color if it has a plant label and with black color if it has a no-plant label. Figure 2 shows a qualitative result of our methodology in semantic segmentation.

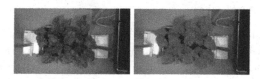

Fig. 2. (a) RGB image; (b) Semantic image

2.2 Leaf Detection

In recent years, superpixel-based methods have been widely used for leaf detection, as they can accurately classify and localize the boundaries between different leaves in an image. The superpixels presents several advantages over traditional pixel-based methods, including reduced noise, preservation of edges, and lower computational complexity. In our case, we propose a leaf detection analysis using superpixel to classify and locate the boundaries between the different leaves. This analysis obtains the superpixels to analyze. For that, this step has two components. First, we present the superpixel technique implemented. Second, we use our semantic segmentation and the superpixels to classify the sections with leaves.

2.2.1 Superpixel Image

Our superpixel approach is the Simple Linear Iterative Clustering (SLIC) [1]. For that, we denote the superpixel image as I_s. Where ψ_i denotes the ith superpixel, and β_i denotes the ith th superpixel in an image I_s. For the superpixel approach, we use the following parameters: desired number of superpixels = 999, number of pixel-level iterations = 9, and shape smoothing term = 5. These parameters are universal for all the images processed. The value of the desired number of superpixels considers the object number in the image. In our case, we use a high number of superpixels since we divide the plant into multiple leaf sections. These sessions increase the performance of our detection.

2.2.2 Superpixel Segmentation

The superpixel segmentation step classifies the superpixels in plant and no-plant. For that, we analyze the number of pixels with plant labels (v^1). Where i denotes the ith superpixel ψ_i in an image I_s, φ_i is the number of pixels in a superpixel ψ_i, and γ_i is the number of pixels with plant labels (v^1). If $\vartheta_i = 1$, we consider the superpixel ψ_i as a sheet, i.e., we use superpixel ψ_i in our three-dimensional analysis (Subsect. 2.3). Otherwise, we discarded the superpixel ψ_i of our analysis. Our threshold function (S) is defined as:

$$S(\vartheta_i) = \begin{cases} 1 & \text{if} & \varphi_i = \gamma_i, \\ 0 & & otherwise, \end{cases} \tag{1}$$

2.3 3D Model Analysis

The 3D model analysis predicts plant stress by leveraging its three-dimensional geometry, which we achieve by combining the abstraction power of deep learning with information about the plant's height and 3D structure. This analysis has three phases. The first uses a Kinect sensor to obtain the plant depth information. Second, we recover the plant's three-dimensional geometry using the pinhole camera model. Finally, we propose a plant stress phenotyping analysis from the plant's height and the 3D structure. We use a 3D methodology since a 2D approach only can recognize stress in images where the plant shows obvious physical signs of stress. However, in a plant with the first day of stress, the physical signs are not visible visually, whereas the decline of the leaves is one of the first morphological symptoms of crop stress. This information allowed our 3D methodology to recognize stress even when visual signals have not appeared on the plant.

2.3.1 Depth Image

Depth-sensing technologies are widely used to scan environments or simplify challenging tasks such as object detection, pose estimation, visual tracking, among others. In this work, we use a Kinect sensor to obtain the plant depth information. For that, we denoted the depth image as D_ε. For the Kinect, we use the following parameters: image resolution= 640×480, frames per second = 12, and maximum depth = $4\,\mathrm{m}$.

2.3.2 Pinhole Camera Model

We use the basic pinhole model to extract the 3D model. This model considers the projection of a point $P(X, Y, Z)$ in space to a point $p(x, y)$ in the image plane. The relative size of an object in the image depends on the image plane distance Z and the focal length f. The focal length f is the distance between the camera center C_o (camera lens center) to the image plane. The optical center or principal point O_o is the origin of coordinates in the image plane, but in practice, it may not be. By similar triangles, one quickly computes that the point $P(X, Y, Z)$ is mapped to the point $p(fX/Z, fY/Z, f)$ on the image plane. We use the pinhole model with the image plane information and the depth of the sensor to compute the 3D recovery in crops. In our extraction, we convert the information in meters. For that, we divided the scale factor k with the maximum RGB value (255) and multiplied by a depth z (Subsubsect. 2.3.1). The scale factor k is the maximum depth of the Kinect sensor (Subsubsect. 2.3.1). For example, considering a maximum depth k of $4\,\mathrm{m}$ and a depth estimation z of 128 in grayscale, Z is approximately $2\,\mathrm{m}$. The Eq. 2 compute the coordinates (X, Y, Z) of a point in the space.

$$Z = \frac{k \cdot z}{255}, \quad X = \frac{x \cdot Z}{f}, \quad Y = \frac{y \cdot Z}{f} \tag{2}$$

2.3.3 Plant Stress Phenotyping

Finally, using the 3D plant model, we calculate the 3D centroid of the detected leaves. The 3D centroid allows for a compact representation of the entire leaf in 3D, facilitating the analysis of symmetry, geometry, and growth of the leaves. Additionally, the 3D centroid is computationally efficient and enables the analysis of large datasets of plant leaves in a reasonable amount of time. Overall, the centroid provides a suitable and effective tool to analyze the 3D reconstruction of plant leaves. For that, we use a simplification of the intensity centroid. This simplification of intensity centroid obtains the central point by 3D leaf extracted. Defining the moments as:

$$m_{p,q,g}^{j} = \sum_{X,Y,Z}^{w} X^{p}Y^{q}Z^{g} \tag{3}$$

where j denotes the jth 3D leaf extracted, and w is the number of pixel projections by leaf. On the other hand, (p, q, g) are the orders of the moment $m_{p,q,g}^{j}$ (we use an order of 0 or 1). Finally, we determined the intensity centroid as:

$$C^{j} = \left(\frac{m_{1,0,0}^{j}}{m_{0,0,0}^{j}}, \frac{m_{0,1,0}^{j}}{m_{0,0,0}^{j}}, \frac{m_{0,0,1}^{j}}{m_{0,0,0}^{j}} \right) \tag{4}$$

Finally, we obtained the stress ranges by implementing a morphological analysis in plants with a standard height of 30 cm. The average stress on the strawberry leaves is 15 to 24 cm. On the other hand, the unstressed leaf ranges of strawberry plants are 25 to 30 cm.

3   Discussion and Results

In this section, we present the experiments of our methodology for plant stress recognition using deep learning and visual patterns of plant geometry. These experiments are the semantic segmentation evaluation, the 3D model evaluation, and 3D model vs 2D classification evaluation.

3.1   Semantic Segmentation

We use two different datasets to evaluate semantic segmentation ("Eschikon Plant Stress Phenotyping" dataset [4] and a proposed dataset). We use pixel comparison in our quantitative evaluation. This evaluation compares our semantic segmentation with the ground truth. To provide quantitative results, we used three measures (*recall*, *precision* and $f - score$) based on the numbers of true positives, true negatives, false positives, and false negatives. Table 1 shows our network result with different training.

Table 1. Semantic segmentation evaluation

N. of images	Dataset sugarbeet			Dataset strawberry		
	Precision	Recall	F1-score	Precision	Recall	F1-score
15,000	0.75	0.78	0.76	0.80	0.85	0.82
20,000	0.78	0.80	0.78	0.85	0.91	0.87
25,000	0.83	0.85	0.83	0.90	0.93	0.91
30,000	0.85	0.90	0.87	0.91	0.93	0.91
40,000	0.88	0.93	0.90	0.91	0.94	0.92
50,000	0.91	0.94	0.92	0.93	0.95	0.93

Our methodology in the semantic segmentation step obtained the best performance with 50,000 images of training. For example, our plant segmentation had an average *recall* of 0.945, i.e., considering the ground-truth, we recognized 94.5%. On the other hand, the plant segmentation had an average *precision* of 0.92, i.e., in the semantic segmentation, we segmented 92.0% correctly. Also, this semantic segmentation had an average $f - score$ of 0.925. The segmentation is fundamental since a correct recognition provides a suitable 3D extraction because the recognition is proportional to the precision of 3D reconstruction on the (X, Y) axis of the 3D model.

3.2   3D Model

We use the proposed dataset of strawberry plants. Also, we compared the centroids (X, Y, Z) of each leaf in the 3D model of the ground truth with our centroids (X, Y, Z). The mean square error (RMS) determines how much the actual data differs from the predictions made by a model. Table 2 shows the RMS obtained by comparing the centroids (X, Y, Z) of the ground truth (depth image and ground truth of semantic segmentation) with respect to the centroids (X, Y, Z) of our methodology. In this experiment, we have an average RMS error (Z) of 0.007843, i.e., an error of 0.007 cm in 4 m. On the other hand, considering the coordinates (X, Y, Z) in the extraction, we had an average RMS (X, Y, Z) of 0.03697.

Table 2. 3D model evaluation

RMS (x)	RMS (y)	RMS (z)	Average
0.013416	0.029814	0.007843	0.03697

3.3   3D Model vs 2D Classification

We compare our 3D methodology with a 2D classification method using deep learning. For that, we train the two approaches with the same number of images.

In the deep learning approach, we use the YOLOv4 network [2]. This network has a high performance between detection accuracy and processing time. Table 3 shows the results of this evaluation. Although, the 2D network increases its classification as the number of images increases. This performance is lower than our proposal that considers three-dimensional information. The latter is because the 2D method can recognize stress in images where the plant shows obvious physical signs of stress. However, in a plant with the first day of stress, the physical signs are not visible visually. While, the decline of the leaves is one of the first morphological symptoms of crop stress. This allows our 3D methodology to detect stress even when visual signals have not appeared on the plant.

Table 3. Our 3D methodology with a 2D classification using deep learning

N. of images	YOLOv4 network [2]			Our proposed 3D model		
	Precision	Recall	F1-score	Precision	Recall	F1-score
600	0.543	0.429	0.452	0.904	0.932	0.917
800	0.557	0.497	0.525	0.911	0.931	0.920
1000	0.729	0.751	0.739	0.918	0.941	0.929

4   Conclusions

In this work, we have introduced a new approach for plant stress phenotyping using deep learning and 3D reconstruction. Our strategy was to divide and simplify the 3D plant extraction process. This strategy combines the abstraction power of deep learning and the information that provides visual patterns of plant geometry. For that, our methodology has three steps. First, the plant recognition step provides the segmentation, location, and delimitation of the crop. Second, we propose a leaf detection analysis to classify and locate the boundaries between the different leaves. Third, we use a depth sensor and the pinhole camera model to extract a 3D reconstruction.

In the recognition evaluation, we used two datasets that provide different crops ("Eschikon Plant Stress Phenotyping" dataset [4] and a proposed dataset). For that, we analyzed two labels of crops (plant and no-plant). For example, our plant segmentation had an average *recall* of 0.945, i.e., considering the ground-truth, we recognized 94.5%. On the other hand, the plant segmentation had an average *precision* of 0.92, i.e., considering the semantic segmentation, we segmented 92.0% correctly. The segmentation is fundamental since the plant recognition is proportional to the precision of 3D extraction on the (X,Y) axis of the 3D model.

In the 3D plant extraction evaluation, we use our proposed dataset. We used the RMS error for the quantitative evaluation. The Mean Square Error (RMS) determines how much the actual data differs from the predictions made by a model. For that, we compared the centroids (X, Y, Z) of each leaf in the 3D model of the ground truth with our centroids (X, Y, Z). In this experiment, we have an average RMS error (Z) of 0.007843, i.e., an error of 0.007 cm in 4 m. On the other hand, considering the coordinates (X, Y, Z) in the extraction, we had an average RMS (X, Y, Z) of 0.03697.

On the other hand, we compared our 3D methodology with a 2D classification method using deep learning. Our plant stress detection had an average *recall* of 0.941, i.e., considering the ground-truth, we detected 94.1%, while the previous work was 75.1%. Also, we had an average *precision* of 0.918, i.e., considering our stress detection, we detected 91.8% correctly, while the previous work was 72.9%. The latter is because the 2D method can recognize stress in images where the plant shows obvious physical signs of stress. However, in a plant with the first day of stress, the physical signs are not visible visually. While, the decline of the leaves is one of the first morphological symptoms of crop stress. This allowed our 3D methodology to recognize stress even when visual signals have not appeared on the plant.

Finally, we can conclude that our methodology allows plant stress recognition using visual characteristics. In this work, we studied the case of strawberry crops in an image where the camera looks at a top view. For that, we worked with different databases such as "Eschikon Plant Stress Phenotyping" [4] and a proposed dataset. To our knowledge, the proposed approach is the first work that has attempted to detect stress in crops using 3D information.

References

1. Achanta, R., Shaji, A., Smith, K., Lucchi, A., Fua, P., Susstrunk, S.: SLIC super-pixels. EPFL (2010)
2. Bochkovskiy, A., Wang, C.Y., Liao, H.Y.M.: Yolov4: optimal speed and accuracy of object detection. In: Computer Vision and Pattern Recognition, pp. 1–17 (2020). https://doi.org/10.48550/arXiv.2004.10934
3. Clauw, P., et al.: Leaf responses to mild drought stress in natural variants of Arabidopsis. Plant Physiol. **167**(3), 800–816 (2015)
4. Gee, A.P., Chekhlov, D., Calway, A., Mayol-Cuevas, W.: Discovering higher level structure in visual slam. IEEE Trans. Rob. **24**(5), 980–990 (2008). https://doi.org/10.1109/TRO.2008.2004641
5. Ghosal, S., Blystone, D., Singh, A.K., Ganapathysubramanian, B., Singh, A., Sarkar, S.: An explainable deep machine vision framework for plant stress phenotyping. Proc. Natl. Acad. Sci. **115**(18), 4613–4618 (2018)
6. Hairmansis, A., Berger, B., Tester, M., Roy, S.J.: Image-based phenotyping for non-destructive screening of different salinity tolerance traits in rice. Rice **7**(1), 1–10 (2014). https://doi.org/10.1186/s12284-014-0016-3
7. Khanna, R., Schmid, L., Walter, A., Nieto, J., Siegwart, R., Liebisch, F.: A spatio temporal spectral framework for plant stress phenotyping. Plant Methods **15**(1), 13 (2019)
8. Lobos, G.A., Matus, I., Rodriguez, A., Romero-Bravo, S., Araus, J.L., del Pozo, A.: Wheat genotypic variability in grain yield and carbon isotope discrimination under Mediterranean conditions assessed by spectral reflectance. J. Integr. Plant Biol. **56**(5), 470–479 (2014)

9. Neilson, E.H., Edwards, A.M., Blomstedt, C., Berger, B., Møller, B.L., Gleadow, R.M.: Utilization of a high-throughput shoot imaging system to examine the dynamic phenotypic responses of a C4 cereal crop plant to nitrogen and water deficiency over time. J. Exp. Bot. **66**(7), 1817–1832 (2015)

10. Pieruschka, R., Schurr, U., et al.: Plant phenotyping: past, present, and future. Plant Phenomics **2019**, 7507131 (2019)

11. Singh, A.K., Ganapathysubramanian, B., Sarkar, S., Singh, A.: Deep learning for plant stress phenotyping: trends and future perspectives. Trends Plant Sci. **23**(10), 883–898 (2018)

12. Tariq, M., et al.: Rice phenotyping. In: Sarwar, N., Atique-ur-Rehman, A.S., Hasanuzzaman, M. (eds.) Modern Techniques of Rice Crop Production, pp. 151–164. Springer, Singapore (2022). https://doi.org/10.1007/978-981-16-4955-4_11

13. Vakilian, K.A.: Machine learning improves our knowledge about miRNA functions towards plant abiotic stresses. Sci. Rep. **10**(1), 1–10 (2020)

14. Vasseur, F., Bontpart, T., Dauzat, M., Granier, C., Vile, D.: Multivariate genetic analysis of plant responses to water deficit and high temperature revealed contrasting adaptive strategies. J. Exp. Bot. **65**(22), 6457–6469 (2014)

15. Walter, A., Finger, R., Huber, R., Buchmann, N.: Opinion: smart farming is key to developing sustainable agriculture. Proc. Natl. Acad. Sci. **114**(24), 6148–6150 (2017)

16. Zhao, J., et al.: Improved vision-based vehicle detection and classification by optimized yolov4. IEEE Access, 8590–8603 (2022). https://doi.org/10.1109/ACCESS.2022.3143365

Segmentation and Classification Networks for Corn/Weed Detection Under Excessive Field Variabilities

Francisco Garibaldi-Márquez[1,2]([envelope]) [ID], Gerardo Flores[1] [ID],
and Luis M. Valentín-Coronado[1,3] [ID]

[1] Centro de Investigaciones en Óptica A.C., Loma del Bosque 115, 37150 Leon,
Guanajuato, Mexico
{franciscogm,gflores,luismvc}@cio.mx
[2] Instituto Nacional de Investigaciones Forestales, Agrícolas y Pecuarias-Campo
Experimental Pabellón, Pabellon de Arteaga, 20671 Aguascalientes, Mexico
[3] Consejo Nacional de Ciencia y Tecnología, 03940 Ciudad de Mexico, Mexico

Abstract. The control of weeds at earlier stages is one of the most relevant tasks in agriculture. However, the detection of plants in environments with uncontrolled conditions is still a challenge. Hence, a deep learning-based approach to address this problem has been proposed in this work. On the one hand, a CNN model based on the UNet architecture has been used to segment plants. On the other hand, a MobileNetV2-based architecture has been implemented to classify different types of plants, in this case, corn, monocotyledon weed species, and dicotyledon weed species. For training the models, a large image dataset was first created and manually annotated. The performance of the segmentation network achieves a Dice Similarity Coefficient (DSC) of 84.27% and a mean Intersection over Union (mIoU) of 74.21%. The performance of the classification model obtained an accuracy, precision, recall, and F_1-score of 96.36%, 96.68%, 96.34%, and 96.34%, respectively. Then, as the results indicated, the proposed approach is an advantageous alternative for farmers since it provides a way for crop/weed detection in natural field conditions.

Keywords: Weed detection · segmentation and classification · corn field variabilities

1 Introduction

Corn is of gastronomical and economical importance for many countries worldwide. Nonetheless, it is grown in hostile environments; in which the grain and green forage yield are affected by weeds. Weeds are those undesirable herbs that compete with crop plants for nutrients, sunlight, and water [19]. They, in the particular case of the corn crop, could lead to 90% yield reduction [12].

No financial organization to declare.

To take out weeds from the crop fields, such as corn fields, the most common control strategy is by spraying herbicides. This control method is considered efficient and practical for large crop areas [4]. With this, it is possible to eliminate more than 90% of the weeds that grow in the rows and in the intra-rows of the crops [18]. However, the indiscriminate use of herbicides has polluted the environment [7]. Principally, because great volumes of herbicide mixtures are sprayed uniformly throughout the fields, even in regions where weeds are not present [9]. Then, to mitigate the environmental pollution that herbicides are causing, while maintaining the yield of crops, the scientific community has worked on the development of "smart" sprayer systems. With these systems, it is possible to spray an adequate dose of herbicides on individual weed plants or patches of them in the fields [13]. Nonetheless, the detection (localization and classification) of the plants has been reported to be the most complicated task in natural crop environments [10]. This is attributed to different parameters, such as the density of plants and occlusions [5]. To address this problem, the implementation of Convolutional Neural Networks (CNN) for end-to-end detection of crop and weed plants has been intensified. Some of the architectures used have been YOLO [9] and Faster-RCNN [8]. Nonetheless, it has been observed that they failed to locate the plants in the fields due to their density, principally. Another used approach for locating plants has been semantic segmentation, leaving the classification step to be carried out by additional algorithms. Although there are well-known architectures for semantic segmentation of images, few works have been implemented over weed segmentation in corn fields, because no large corn/weed dataset with high field variability was created. In this work, besides proposing a deep learning-based weeds and crop localization and classification approach, a large dataset under natural field conditions has also been created.

1.1 Related Works

The segmentation of plants in natural conditions is a challenge, because variables from the plant species, plant density, foliage occlusion, the morphological changes of the plants according to their growth stage, and factors related to soil appearance and sunlight intensities are provided to the images. These external variables make it difficult to extract and classify the features proper of the plants.

Few works in the literature have addressed the segmentation of weeds in the corn crop. For instance, in the work of Fawakherji *et al.* [3], the segmentation of a multispectral dataset was proposed. The images were acquired from a UAV in a natural corn field. This dataset was configured with two classes, soil and green plants. Thereafter, the VGG-UNet model was trained separately with the following four sub-dataset images: Red, NIR, synthetic images from the Normalized Difference Vegetation Index (NDVI), and RED+NIR+NDVI, achieving a mean accuracy for each trial of 73%, 85%, 92%, and 88%, respectively. Multispectral channels have been announced to provide better performance on segmentation tasks, in comparison with the visible spectrum [1,11]. Nonetheless, they are still expensive, which would become an automatic weed control system also expensive.

Visible spectrum cameras have also been used for corn and weed discrimination in real fields. Quan *et al.* [15] explored the segmentation of weeds under complex corn field environments using the BlendMask network. A 5,700 image dataset was formed, which contains two broadleaf weeds and one narrowleaf weed. The obtained mIoU was 50.2% when the ResNet50 was used as the backbone of the main network, whereas, a 60.7% mIoU was achieved when the ResNet101 was used as the backbone. Recently, Picon *et al.* [14], obtained a Dice Similarity Coefficient (DSC) of 25.32% when a corn/weed dataset was segmented under natural fields using the network PSPNet. This dataset was integrated by the classes corn, narrowleaf weed (three species) and broadleaf weed (three species). However, the authors claim that the class narrowleaf was not classified correctly due to its visual similarity with the class crop.

In this work, we introduce a large corn/weed dataset that was created in authentic natural corn fields. It contains corn plants and as weeds, four monocotyledon plant species and four dicotyledon plant species. Then, a deep learning-based detection approach for the classes Crop, narrowleaf weeds (NLW), and broadleaf weeds (NLW) is proposed. Each of the two weed classes, NLW and BLW, groups the four plant species of weeds, respectively. The proposed approach performs well despite the challenging conditions presented in the acquired images. The remainder of the document is organized as follows. The dataset description and details of the implementation of the segmentation approaches are provided in Sect. 2. In Sect. 3 the main outcomes from the experiments are presented. Finally, the conclusions of the work are given in Sect. 4.

2 Development of the Proposed Method

It was observed that the UNet architecture [16], provided with the convolutional layers of the network ResNet101 as its main feature extractor block, segmented well our dataset. Nonetheless, the pixels of the isolated Regions of interest (RoIs) were often misclassified, which was attributed to the excessive field variabilities. Therefore, taking the advantage of the isolation potential of the segmentation network, the detection approach of crop and weed plants based on segmentation and classification networks, whose pipeline is shown in Fig. 1, is proposed. First, an image with multiple plants is segmented (segmentation module). This module is based on the UNet-ResNet101 architecture. The segmented output image is used solely for the subsequent Region of Interest (RoI) extractor. Hence, the pixels belonging to each class (Crop, NLW, or BLW), from this segmented image, are separated in binary masks for the easy extraction of the RoIs. These RoIs are extracted by using connected component analysis (CCA) [6]. Then, the classification of these RoIs is carried out through the network MobileNetV2 [17]. At the final of the process, an image is obtained, in which the plants or patches of them have been detected. The details of the implementation of the segmentation network and the classification network are covered in Sect. 2.2.

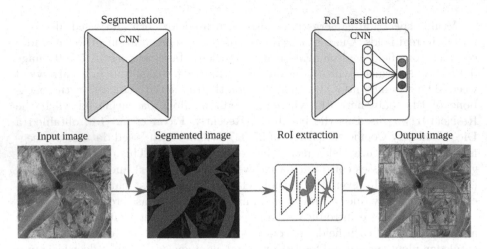

Fig. 1. Pipeline of the proposed detection method for crop/weed under authentic corn fields with the use of segmentation and classification networks. The green box, red box, and blue box in the output image belong to the classes Crop, NLW and BLW, correspondingly. (Color figure online)

2.1 Dataset Description and Image Pre-processing

The dataset for this work was integrated with 12,000 images of the visible spectrum. These images were captured in different corn fields located in Aguascalientes, Mexico (21.8853° N, 102.2916° W), during the spring-summer agricultural cycle of the years 2020 and 2021. The images are of size $4,608 \times 3,456$, $2,460 \times 1,080$ and $1,600 \times 720$ pixels. The capture distance between the soil surface and the camera was in the range 0.4 m to 1.5 m. In this way, the captures comprehended in more frequency top-down views, and a low number were side views. Additionally, among top-down view images; most of them were captured with a distance greater than 1 m. This value was considered because when agricultural tractors travel through crop fields, the wheels raise dust. Therefore, in tentative instrumentation, the camera should be pulled apart more than 1 m high from the ground, to avoid the small particles blocking the lens.

The dataset introduces a variety of plant species, as well as different plant sizes. The variability related to the plants was given by the number of species of them, the number of instances in a single image, and the foliage occlusion. The scale and perspective of the plants have also changed, as a consequence of the changes in zoom and side views. Additionally, the dataset contains plants of various growth stages, since the period of capture started when they were of two true leaves and finished when they were of seven true leaves. The capture periods were performed every five days apart from each other. Another introduced parameter was the soil status, which includes humidity conditions, organic matter content, and changes in its appearance, such as the color associated with its texture. The sunlight intensity also changed in the images, since captures were done in the morning, noon, and at evening; as well as on sunny and cloudy days.

Once the dataset was integrated, most of the plants in each image were manually annotated at pixel level. Additionally to the crop species (*Zea mays L.*), it was quantified eight weed plant species: four narrowleaf weeds (NLW) and four broadleaf weeds (BLW). Table 1 summarized the total plant species, which have been grouped into the classes Crop, NLW, and BLW. Table 1 also provides the total labels traced per plant species.

Table 1. Plant species of the experimental dataset grouped into classes, and the labels traced per plant species.

Class	Scientific name	Labels per species	Labels per class
Crop	*Zea mays*	18,000	18,000
NLW	*Cynodon dactylon*	4,500	18,000
	Eleusine indica	4,500	
	Digitaria sanguinalis	4,500	
	Cyperus esculentus	4,500	
BLW	*Portulaca oleracea*	4,500	18,000
	Tithonia tubaeformis	4,500	
	Amaranthus spinosus	4,500	
	Malva parviflora	4,500	

Since the detection strategy considered also the training of a classification CNN, a sub-dataset was created. This dataset consisted of individual-plant images, which have been extracted from the multi-plant images of the original experimental dataset. This means that the dataset for training the classification network was also balanced, with 18,000 images per class.

2.2 Training of the Architectures

As already mentioned, the proposed detection approach consisted of two stages, the segmentation one which is based on the UNet-ResNet101 network, and the classification stage, based on the MobileNetV2 network. Both architectures have been trained by using a desktop computer with the next characteristics, Core i7 processor, 32 GB of RAM memory, and NVIDIA GPU GeForce RTX 3070Ti (8 GB). The implementation was executed in Python 3.8 and Keras framework with Tensorflow 2.5.0 backend.

UNet-Resnet101

To train UNet-Resnet101 proposed model, a transfer learning strategy was used, i.e., fine-tuning network models previously trained from a huge image dataset, in this case, ImageNet [2]. This strategy was implemented in two ways. In the first one, the encoder and decoder blocks were retrained, while, the second one, consisted of freezing the encoder and training solely the decoder.

The loss function always was the dice loss, since it is very strict for segmentation tasks because it penalizes those predominant pixels of certain classes. The computation of dice loss is as follows,

$$L_{Dice} = 1 - \frac{2\,y\,y^* + 1}{y + y^* + 1} \tag{1}$$

where y refers to the ground truth label and y^* is the predicted value from the model.

MobileNetV2

Similar to the segmentation network, it were configured first some parameters and hyper-parameters of MobileNetV2. The convolutional layers were the original from the architecture, but the Fully Connected (FC) layers were proposed. The configuration over the convolutional layers started initializing the weights randomly. Two trials using the ImageNet weights were carried out; the first one, when they were used just for initialization and then retrained; the second one, when they were frozen and only the FC layers were trained. Hence, the FC layers changed from two layers to three layers. The number of neurons varied from 512 to 4,096 with increments of 512, for the first and second layers. Always the *ReLu* activation function was configured for these two first layers. The third layer, which is the output one, always was of three neurons with *softmax* activation function, since the classes of our dataset were Crop, NLW and BLW. The optimizer, learning rate, loss function, and the number of epochs were varied.

2.3   Evaluation Metrics

The performance of the system was evaluated in two parts, first the segmentation approach was evaluated and then the classification approach was evaluated.

Dice Similarity Coefficient (DSC), Intersection over Union (IoU) and mean Intersection over Union (mioU) have been selected to evaluate the performance of the segmentation network. In Table 2 the used metrics are presented.

The performance of the classification model (MobileNetv2) is evaluated using the following metrics, accuracy (Ac), precision (Pr), recall (Re), and F_1-score (F_1), which are shown in Table 3.

Table 2. Segmentation metrics.

Name	Definition	Description
DSC	$\frac{2TP}{2TP+FP+FN}$	Compares the similarity between two sets of data.
IoU	$\frac{TP_c}{FP_c+FN_c+TP_c}$	Quantifies the percent overlap between the ground truth mask and the mask predicted by the network.
mIoU	$\frac{1}{C}\sum_c IoU_c$	mean Intersection over Union

Table 3. Classification metrics.

Name	Definition	Description
Ac	$\frac{TP+TN}{TP+TN+FP+FN}$	Indicates the ratio between the number of correct predictions and the number of all input samples.
Pr	$\frac{TP}{TP+FP}$	Measures the ability of the model to identify targets when it analyzes a certain number of images correctly.
Re	$\frac{TP}{TP+FN}$	Indicates the ability of the model to detect targets.
F_1	$2*\frac{precision*Recall}{Precision+Recall}$	Is the harmonic mean of the precision and recall

TP, TN, FP and FN, are the true positive, true negative, false positive, and false negative values.

3 Results

This section presents both the segmentation network UNet-ResNet101 results and the classification network MobileNetV2 results. Moreover, the performance of each task is discussed and analyzed. Finally, a set of representative images of the system output (detection of crop and weeds plants) is also presented.

UNet-ResNet101

The better acceptable results of UNet-ResNet101 were obtained when it was trained by implementing the transfer learning technique. That is, when the weights of the convolutional layers of ResNet101 were those when it was trained in the imagenet dataset; and when these weights in the encoder were frozen and only the weights of the decoder block were actualized. The input images were of size 512×512 pixels strategically, to avoid the loss of plant features and to reduce the training time. Additionally, the Adam optimizer with a learning rate of 0.0001 was observed that fit better to our dataset. The iterations over the training data were 100, since the transfer learning allows a quick syntonization of the weights to the classes of the dataset.

MobileNetV2

Similar to the segmentation network, better classification performance was obtained when transfer learning was applied, i.e., when the weights of the convolutional layers were obtained after training the network in the ImageNet dataset, and then freezing some parts during the retraining. Therefore, just the weights of the FC layers were syntonized to our dataset. In this regard, the FC block was of three layers. It was observed that a better classification is obtained when the first and the second layers have 2,048 neurons. Additionally, the optimizer was *Adam* with a learning rate of 0.0001. The *categorical cross-entropy* loss function allows most of the reduction of the error. And the training iterations on the entire dataset were 50, since it was observed that the transfer learning allowed a quick syntonization of the weights. The size of the input images was of 224×224 pixels.

3.1   Performance of the Segmentation Network

Figure 2 describes the performance of the trained model UNet-ResNet101, through the metrics DSC and IoU, on the segmentation of the classes Crop, NLW, BLW, and implicitly the class Soil.

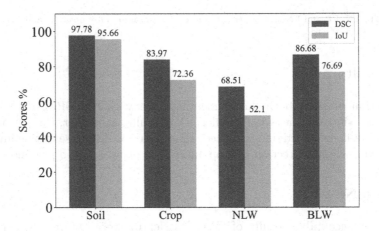

Fig. 2. DSC and IoU obtained by the UNet-ResNet101 model over the test dataset.

As can be appreciated, the class BLW was better segmented by the network, then the class Corn, and finally the class NLW. The DSC of the class BLW was 2.71% superior to that of the class Corn and 18.17% higher than the DSC of the class NLW. With respect to IoU, the class BLW also was which achieved a high magnitude value. The IoU of BLW was 4.33% superior to that of the class Corn and 24.59% to the class NLW. The lower performance on segmenting the class NLW is principally attributed to its phenological appearance, because the leaves of the plant species in this class usually have a large major axis and a short minor axis. Consequently, a large number of pixels belonging to the class Soil are mixed among the pixels belonging to the foliage of the plants in this class.

In general, a mean DSC of 84.27% and a mIoU of 74.21% describe the performance of the segmentation model based on UNet-ResNet101 over our dataset. The magnitude value of these metrics is considered acceptable since overreached the performance of other works reported in the literature that have segmented corn and weed plants in natural environments, such as the works reported by Quan *et al.* [15] and Picon *et al.* [14]. Additionally, our trained model may segment other monocotyledon and dicotyledon plant species since the classes NLW and BLW, to whom the architecture was trained, contains four species of each group of distinct growth stage, and also the field variabilities were varied enough.

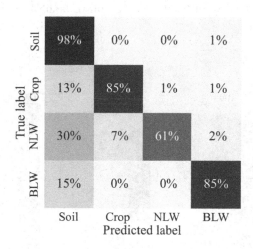

Fig. 3. Confusion matrix of the segmentation model.

A deeper visualization of the segmentation performance is observed in Fig. 3, which describes the percentage of pixels than were correctly classified or miss classified by the UNet-ResNet101 model. Respecting the plant classes, the pixels belonging to the classes Crop and BLW were better classified as such by the model, with 85% of them in their corresponding class. Nonetheless, just 61% of the pixels of the class NLW were classified as such. The remaining pixels were confused among the classes by the model. In this way, 7% of the pixels belonging to the class NLW have been classified as Crop, and 1% of the pixels that correspond to the class Crop were classified as NLW. The confusion among the classes Crop and NLW is attributed that the plant species belong to the monocotyledon group. However, the reality is that most of the pixels belonging to the plant classes are confused with the class Soil. In this sense, 13%, 30% and 15% of the pixels belonging to the class Crop, NLW, and BLW, respectively, have been classified as soil.

3.2 Performance of the Classification Network

The performance of the MobileNetV2 model on classifying the plants which belong to the classes Crop, NLW and BLW is shown in Fig. 4. In this way, the precision for the classes NLW and BLW was 100%; this means that this percentage of instances the model predicted as such, really belongs to that class. Nonetheless, 10% of the instances the model classified as the Corn, in reality, belong to other classes, for this reason, the precision is 90%. On the other hand, it is clearly appreciated that the better-classified instances were those from the classes Crop and BLW, and finally, those from the class NLW, since their recall was 100%, 99% and 90%, respectively. Furthermore, the mean classification performance among classes was 95%, 95% and 99%, for Crop, NLW and BLW, accordingly, which is indicated by the F_1-score. The overall performance of the model on the classification of plants from the dataset was excellent, because it achieved a mean accuracy of 96.36%, precision of 96.68%, recall of 96.34% and F_1-score of 96.34%.

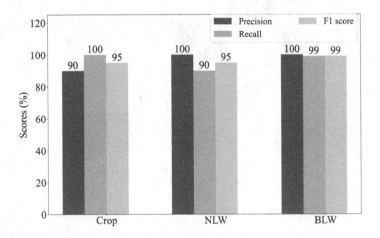

Fig. 4. Classification metrics.

The following Fig. 5 indicates the percentage of instances of each class the MobileNetV2 model classified as such, and the miss classification among classes. It is observed that the better-classified class is BLW, because 99% of their instances are classified as such, and just 1% of them the model confuses with Crop, which is acceptable. On the other hand, although 100% percent of the instances of the class Corn are classified as such, 10% of the instances that really belong to the class NLW are predicted as if they were from the class Crop. This behavior is also attributed to the visual appearance among crop plants and the plans of the class NLW, because they belong to the monocotyledon species. The misclassification of the class Crop with the class NLW is quite better than if it were the vice versa effect. It is because in tentative implementation, the active ingredients of herbicides developed for monocotyledon plants usually also eradicate crop plants at early growth stages.

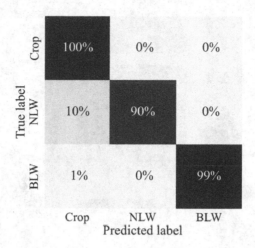

Fig. 5. Confusion matrix from the classification network.

3.3   Detection Approach Visualization

The detection of objects in an image indicates the localization of the objects in the image and the class to which each object belongs. As aforementioned, in this work, a detection approach is proposed by the conjoined use of the segmentation architecture UNet-ResNet101 and the classification network MobileNetV2. In this way, the Fig. 6 shows a sample of images in which the plant classes have been detected by applying our proposal. The polygon highlighted in green contains images that have a low density of plants, and occlusion of the foliage does not exist. On the contrary, the polygon highlighted in gray has images that contain a high density of plants, and occlusion of the foliage persists. The green boxes correspond to the class Crop, the red boxes to the class NLW, and the blue boxes to the class BLW.

A visual inspection of the images that have a low density of plants indicates that almost all the green regions have been detected; nonetheless, since the localization of the plants is slightly related to the region provided by the segmentation model, more than one bounding box often appear into a simple image. In the case of the images with a high density of plants, it has been observed that most of the plant classes were also detected. Nevertheless, due to the foliage density, often two or more plants of the same class share a bounding box, as a result of the region extracted by the segmentation model. As well, it is appreciated that

Fig. 6. Sample of output images from the proposed detection method, by the use of the segmentation network and the classification network. The green polygon contains low-density plant images. The gray polygon contains high-density plant images. Green box: Crop, Red box: NLW, and blue box: BLW. (Color figure online)

in the high-density plant images, some of them were not detected, as a consequence of the confusion of the pixels belonging to the plant classes with those of the soil by the segmentation model.

Although in some cases the detection covers part of the foliage of the plants, the implementation of this vision system for spraying herbicides under real corn fields is still adequate. It is because the systemic herbicides are absorbed by the plants and gradually propagated throughout their vascular system, killing all their organs. Therefore, spraying herbicides just over a portion of the foliage of the plants is enough for this sort of herbicides to kill them. In the case when the trained segmentation model considers multiple plants in a region, it could be tackled by subdividing the bounding box for spraying less area of the foliage.

4 Conclusions and Future Work

In this work, the use of the segmentation architecture UNet-ResNet101 and the classification architecture MobileNetV2 was proposed for the detection of corn plants (Crop), four narrowleaf (NLW), and four broadleaf (BLW) weed species from authentic corn fields. Therefore, a large dataset of images has been acquired under these hostile environments, and then it was manually annotated.

The segmentation model UNet-ResNet101 achieved a DSC of 84% and a mIoU of 74.21%. Whereas the classification model reached 93.36%, 96.68%, 96.34% and 93.34% of accuracy, precision, recall, and F_1-score, respectively. The models perform well despite the complexity of the dataset.

The segmentation model confused a significant percentage of the pixels of the three classes of plants with the pixels of the class Soil. In general, both, the segmentation and the classification model classified better the class BLW. In contrast, the NLW was the worse segmented and classified class. Also, the two models confused often the class NLW with the class Crop.

As future works, affords will be done for increasing the segmentation performance of the networks under high-density of plants. Also, a large dataset with most plant species would be necessary for training a strong model to be adapted to most field variabilities.

References

1. Das, M., Bias, A.: DeepVeg: deep learning model for segmentation of weed, canola, and canola flea beetle damage. IEEE Access **9**, 119367–119380 (2021). https://doi.org/10.1109/ACCESS.2021.3108003
2. Deng, J., Dong, W., Socher, R., Li, L. J., Li, K., Fei-Fei, L.: ImageNet: a large-scale hierarchical image database. In: IEEE Computer Vision and Pattern Recognition (CVPR), pp. 248–255. IEEE, Miami (2009)
3. Fawakherji, M., Youssef, A., Bloisi, D.D., Pretto, A., Nardi, D.: Crop and weed classification using pixel-wise segmentation on ground and aerial images. Int. J. Rob. Comput. 2(1), 39–57 (2020). https://doi.org/10.35708/RC1869-126258
4. Gianessi, L.P.: The increasing importance of herbicides in worldwide crop production. Pest Manag. Sci. **69**(10), 1099–1105 (2013)
5. Gao, J., French, A.P., Pound, M.P., He, Y., Pridmore, T.P., Pieters, J.G.: Deep convolutional neural networks for image-based Convolvulus sepium detection in sugar beet fields. Plant Methods **19**, 29 (2020). https://doi.org/10.1186/s13007-020-00570-z
6. Haralick, R.M., Shapiro, L.G.: Computer and Robot Vision, vol. 1, 1st edn. Addison-Wesley Publishing Company Inc., Boston (1992)

7. Hashemi-Beni, L., Gebrehiwot, A., Karimoddini, A., Shahbazi, A., Dorbu, F.: Deep convolutional neural networks for weeds and crops discrimination from UAS imagery. Front. Remote Sens. **3**, 755939 (2022). https://doi.org/10.3389/frsen.2022.755939
8. Hu, C., Sapkota, B.B., Thomasson, J.A., Bagavathiannan, M.V.: Influence of image quality and light consistency on the performance of convolutional neural networks for weed mapping. Remote Sens. **13**, 2140 (2021). https://doi.org/10.3390/rs13112140
9. Hussain, N., et al.: Design and development of a smart variable rate sprayer using deep learning. Remote Sens. **12**, 4091 (2020). https://doi.org/10.3390/rs12244091
10. Kennedy, H.J., et al.: Crop signal markers facilitate crop detection and weed removal from lettuce and tomato by an intelligent cultivator. Weed Technol. **34**, 342–350 (2020). https://doi.org/10.1017/wet.2019.120
11. Milioto, A., Lottes, P., Stachniss, C.: Real-time semantic segmentation of crop and weed for precision agriculture robots leveraging background knowledge in CNNs. In: 2018 IEEE International Conference on Robotics and Automation (ICRA), pp. 2229–2235. IEEE, Brisbane (2018). https://doi.org/10.1109/ICRA.2018.8460962
12. Nedeljković, D., Knežević, S., Božić, D., Vrbničanin, S.: Critical time for weed removal in Corn as influenced by planting pattern and PRE herbicides. Agriculture **11**, 587 (2021). https://doi.org/10.3390/agriculture11070587
13. Partel, V., Kakarla, S.C., Ampatzidis, Y.: Development and evaluation of low-cost and smart technology for precision weed management utilizing artificial intelligence. Comput. Electron. Agric. **157**, 339–350 (2019). https://doi.org/10.1016/j.compag.2018.12.048
14. Picon, A., San-Emeterio, M.G., Bereciartua-Perez, A., Klukas, C., Eggers, T., Navarro-Mestre, R.: Deep learning-based segmentation of multiple species of weeds in corn crop using synthetic and real image datasets. Comput. Electron. Agric. **194**, 106719 (2022). https://doi.org/10.1016/j.compag.2022.106719
15. Quan, L., Wu, B., Mao, S., Yang, C., Li, H.: An instance segmentation-based method to obtain the leaf age and plant centre of weeds in complex field environments. Sensors **21**, 3389 (2021). https://doi.org/10.3390/s21103389
16. Ronneberger, O., Fischer, P., Brox, T.: U-Net: convolutional networks for biomedical image segmentation. In: Navab, N., Hornegger, J., Wells, W.M., Frangi, A.F. (eds.) MICCAI 2015. LNCS, vol. 9351, pp. 234–241. Springer, Cham (2015). https://doi.org/10.1007/978-3-319-24574-4_28
17. Sandler, M., Howard, A., Zhu, M., Zhmoginov, A., Chen, L-C.: MobileNetV2: inverted residuals and linear bottlenecks. 2018 IEEE/CVF Conference on Computer Vision and Pattern Recognition, Salt Lake City, UT, USA, pp. 4510–4520 (2018) https://doi.org/10.1109/CVPR.2018.00474
18. Wang, H., Liu, W., Zhao, K., Yu, H., Zhang, J., Wang, J.: Evaluation of weed control efficacy and crop safety of the new HPPD-inhibiting herbicide-QYR301. Sci. Rep. **8**, 7910 (2018). https://doi.org/10.1038/s41598-018-26223-9
19. Wang, A., Zhang, W., Wei, X.: A review on weed detection using ground-based machine vision and image preprocessing techniques. Comput. Electron. Agric. **158**, 226–240 (2019). https://doi.org/10.1016/j.compag.2019.02.005

Leukocyte Recognition Using a Modified AlexNet and Image to Image GAN Data Augmentation

Armando Reyes-Esparza[1] , Mario I. Chacon-Murguia[1]([✉]) ,
Juan A. Ramirez-Quintana[1] , and Carlos Arzate-Quintana[2]

[1] Visual Perception Systems Lab, Tecnologico Nacional de Mexico/I.T. Chihuahua, Chihuahua, Mexico
{m21061152,mario.cm,juan.rq}@chihuahua.tecnm.mx
[2] Biomedical Department, Universidad Autonoma de Chihuahua, Chihuahua, Mexico
carzate@uach.mx

Abstract. A leukogram is essential in the diagnosis of people's diseases. It can help in the discovery of diseases such as infection, arthritis, leukemia, etc. Deep learning techniques found in the state of the art solve leukocyte classification with the use of complex models including too many components. In this work, we solve leukocyte classification with only one deep learning model, a modified AlexNet. We use transfer learning and a new Generative Adversarial Network (GAN) as a data augmentation method for a new dataset that seeks a similar approach to a blood smear as opposed to the datasets available in the literature. Results indicate that the modified AlexNet can achieve a validation balanced precision classification of 98.17%, and it is ranked 4th place compared to state-of-the-art models considered in this work and 2nd place considering models with only one deep learning model. These performances indicate that the proposed model can solve the classification task and it could be implemented in equipment with reduced computational requirements as an embedded system.

Keywords: Leukocyte · Classification · AlexNet · GAN

1 Introduction

Blood tests are considered the most common test to diagnose a patient with a disease. In the blood, there are 3 different types of cells: red blood cells, leukocytes, and platelets. Carrying out an analysis of the number of leukocytes that a person contains allows us to know different pathologies that this person could suffer and is known as a leukogram. Leukocytes can be divided into 5 different classes: basophils, eosinophils, lymphocytes, monocytes, and neutrophils. When using a method such as a blood smear to perform a leukogram, it takes a long process and can lead to failures due to human error. Therefore, it is sought to carry out this process automatically.

There are different methods for classifying leukocytes reported in the literature. Hegde in [1] uses transfer learning with the AlexNet model as a feature extractor to

© The Author(s), under exclusive license to Springer Nature Switzerland AG 2023
A. Y. Rodríguez-González et al. (Eds.): MCPR 2023, LNCS 13902, pp. 139–148, 2023.
https://doi.org/10.1007/978-3-031-33783-3_13

later pass to his neural network to classify 5 types of leukocytes. In [2] the authors present a hybrid deep learning model with GoogleNet and AlexNet models as feature extractors and a Support Vector Machine (SVM) as a classifier of 4 leukocyte classes. The work in [3] describes an Attention-ware Residual network based Manifold Learning (ARML) model, that extracts the main features of the image in a first and second order process to then be encoded with a Riemannian manifold, finding a non-linear structure of characteristics to classify leukocytes. The classification of 4 types of leukocytes using ensemble learning with ResNet50, DenseNet121, and a proprietary neural network is presented in [4]. The work reported in [5] employs a Spatial and Channel Attention Module (SCAM) together with two pre-trained deep learning transfer models, ResNet50 and DenseNet121 to perform the classification of 5 types of leukocytes. The work described in [6] segments leukocyte by DeepLabv3+ for semantic segmentation and then classify them with a deep model.

The previous approaches to classify leukocytes are based on architectures with several components like ensemble learning, SVM, and attention modules. Therefore, the present work demonstrates that it is possible to classify leukocytes with a performance like that reported in the literature but using one deep model trained with a database that adheres more to the blood smear method than those present in the literature. We present a simple AlexNetv2 model without extra components that achieves a classification performance of 98.17% balanced accuracy. This work also demonstrates that using data augmentation, DA, with samples generated with a new GAN model [7], can help to increase the performance of a model.

2   Dataset Description

Some reported databases of segmented leukocytes are: Raabin-WBC [8], LISC [9], BCCD [10], MISP [11], Hedge et al. [12]. In this paper we present a new database to solve the leukocyte classification task called LEU_UACHDB. This database, LEU_UACHDB, was generated at the Autonomous University of Chihuahua (UACH) and contains 562 images of peripheral blood samples of people generated with the method of blood smear. The samples include pathologies cases and were taken with a B-383 Series OPTIKA ITALY microscope. LEU_UACHDB also has ground truths (GT) images for each image. The nucleus of the leukocytes present in the images is identified and painted in a specific color that indicates the class (basophil, eosinophil, lymphocyte, monocyte or neutrophil). An example of the GT of the image in Fig. 1 a) is shown in Fig. 1 b). To carry out the classification of leukocytes in the LEU_UACHDB database, a new database is created. The generation of the new dataset is achieved through detection and crop stages that are briefly described next.

2.1   Detection Stage

The stage to detect leukocytes in images of peripheral blood samples employs characteristics of size, color, area, radius, convexity, and circularity. The LEU_UACHDB image is automatically processed to yield an image of the same spatial resolution size, with the locations of the leukocytes marked with red circles. Once the leukocyte is detected, it is necessary to crop the region of interest.

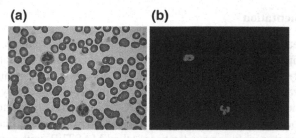

Fig. 1. a) Image example of LEU_UACHDB dataset with 100X magnification. b) GT from LEU_UACHDB dataset with 100X magnification, 2 red cells marked indicating 2 neutrophils. (Color figure online)

2.2 Crop Stage

The crop stage generates the region of the image where the leukocyte was detected. It uses the original image of LEU_UACHDB, its GT, the output of the detection, and automatically finds the location of the marked red circles to perform an automatic crop. The GT is used to label the leukocyte class. The images of the crop stage are called OGDB. An example of 5 leukocyte from OGDB are shown in Fig. 2, and Table 1 shows their distribution. This new database presents a process more like that process achieved in a laboratory analysis because it starts from an image taken directly from the microscope to obtain the image of the leukocyte, unlike the databases [8–12]. From the 650 GT leukocytes, 625 were automatically cropped and 67 were discarded because they were not centered in the body cell image.

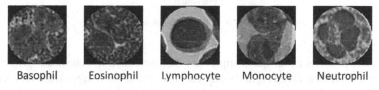

Basophil   Eosinophil   Lymphocyte   Monocyte   Neutrophil

Fig. 2. Examples of leukocytes in the OGDB dataset.

Table 1. OGDB dataset distribution.

OGDB	Class	Basophil	Eosinophil	Lymphocyte	Monocyte	Neutrophil	Total
	Qty. of samples	81	21	199	12	245	558

2.3   Data Augmentation

Different DA methods may be used to train a deep machine learning, ML, model when there are few samples. Two of them are traditional DA (TDA) and Generative Adversarial Networks (GAN) [13]. Since the OGDB database contains too few samples to train a deep model, it was decided to do DA with TDA and GAN networks by the Generative DA Method-Generative Adversarial Network (GDAM-GAN) [14]. The GDAM-GAN consists of performing an image-to-image translation from a base class to a desired class. This DA process yields a new database, called MASTER, with samples generated by GAN and those of OGDB. The DA process is shown in Fig. 3. The process starts from OGDB and perform a TDA with 5 random rotations, obtaining the database called TDAx6_OGDB. From this point, two training lines of the GDAM-GAN method are proposed, one with the OGDB database and the other with TDAx6_OGDB. Both datasets use 32 images per class for validation and the rest for training. These two trainings generate the OG_GANDB and TDAx6_GANDB databases from samples generated with the GDAM-GAN method with the OGDB and TDAx6_OGDB databases, respectively.

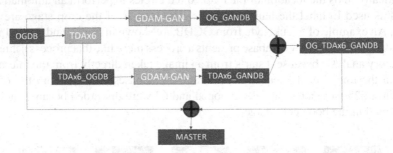

Fig. 3. General data augmentation scheme

The GDAM-GAN generated samples are then screened to determine which sample can be considered as real or original samples. After selecting images from OG_GANDB and TDAx6_GANDB, they are joined to obtain the OG_TDAx6_GANDB database. This database is considered to have as original samples. OG_TDAx6_GANDB and OGDB are joined to obtain the MASTER database that has real images from OGDB, and images generated by the GDAM-GAN method. Table 2 show the distributions of OGDB, OG_TDAx6_GANDB, and MASTER.

Table 2. Distribution of leukocytes datasets.

	OGDB	OG_TDAx6_GANDB	MASTER
Class	Qty. of samples	Qty. of samples	Qty. of samples
Basophil	81	115	196
Eosinophil	21	16	37
Lymphocyte	199	328	527
Monocyte	12	27	39
Neutrophil	245	119	364
Total	558	605	1163

3   Classification Model

3.1   Deep Model Selection for Leukocytes Classification

To select the model, a compilation of various state-of-the-art works is carried out. Three models were selected regarding the use of only one deep model for classification task and considering the highest balanced precision value, BAM (1), on the validation set. The top 3 resulting models are: AlexNet [6] with 98.96%, VGG16 [8] with 97.20% and ResNet50 [5] with 96.38%. Therefore, these 3 models are selected for their implementation, training and analysis to later choose the one that obtains the highest classification performance value to solve the leukocyte classification task in the OGDB database.

$$BAM = \frac{\sum_{c=1}^{C} \frac{TP(c)}{TP(c)+FN(c)}}{|C|} \quad \begin{array}{l} TP = true\ positive \\ FN = false\ negative \end{array} \tag{1}$$

3.2   Implementation of the Selected Deep Models with Transfer Learning

The technique of transfer learning was used to implement the selected models of the state-of-the-art. The VGG16 and ResNet50 models are implemented with their architectures and parameters trained with ImageNet for the classification of 1000 classes in Tensorflow. Only one modification is made to the models in the classification layer from 1000 classes to one of 5 for the different classes of leukocytes. All model layers are frozen except the new classification layer.

The updated AlexNet [15] model was implemented using the parameters published in Caffe [16] for the AlexNet architecture, with which an ImageNet performance of Top-1 57.1% and Top-5 80.2% was obtained. The original AlexNet article reports Top-1 62.5% and Top-5 83%, so it is not the performance of the original model, but it is similar and preserves the parallelism architecture. However, in this work, it is desired to use the AlexNet model in a single GPU, unlike the original work, so a new model is defined that uses the modified Caffe parameters to fit a linear AlexNet architecture presented in Fig. 4 termed AlexNetv2 and that would be possible to be programmed in an embedded system in future work. The imbalanced issue of the classes was faced with a dynamic DA layer, for rotation and flipping, in all selected models.

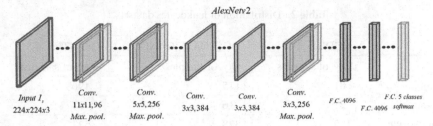

Fig. 4. AlexNetv2 architecture

3.3 Hyperparameters of the Selected Models

The three selected models were trained using the hyperparameters, defined according to the literature, obtained with the ImageNet dataset. The three models used cross entropy CE (2) as loss L, ReLu (3) as activation function $f(s)$, softmax (4) as output layer activation function $f(s)_i$, and 200 epochs E. AlexNetv2 with SGD as an optimizer, and Adam for ResNet50 and VGG16. However, the learning rate α was modified for a dynamic learning rate α_{din} (5), following the works reported in [17, 18] which indicate that variable learning improves the training process. Therefore, the training is achieved with α_{din} in the three models starting with a value of 0.01 and reducing to 0.005, 0.001, and 0.0005 every 50 epochs.

$$CE = -\sum_{i}^{C} t_i \log(f(s)_i) \tag{2}$$

where C is the number of classes, i is class index, t_i is label, and s is the prediction.

$$\text{ReLU} = \max(0, s) = \begin{cases} s \ \text{if } s > 0 \\ 0 \ \text{if } s \leq 0 \end{cases} \tag{3}$$

$$\text{Softmax} = f(s)_i = \frac{e^{s_i}}{\sum\limits_{j=1}^{C} e^{s_j}} \ \text{for } j = 1, ..., C \tag{4}$$

$$\alpha_{din} = \begin{cases} 0.01 & \text{if } 1 \leq E \leq 50 \\ 0.005 & \text{if } 51 \leq E \leq 100 \\ 0.001 & \text{if } 101 \leq E \leq 150 \\ 0.0005 & \text{if } 151 \leq E \leq 200 \end{cases} \tag{5}$$

4   Results

The results are presented in 3 sections: results obtained from the model selection, verification of how the samples generated with GAN affect the performance of the model, and comparison of the model obtained with the state-of-the-art models.

4.1 Classification Model Selection

To select the model to be used as the final classifier, from the pre-selected ones of the state-of-the-art, two experiments are carried out. The first consists of varying the training database of each model together with the reading seed of the database (OGDB and MASTER). The second is to validate the results with cross-validation. The first experiment consisted of 4 training sessions per model, 2 for the OGDB database and 2 for the MASTER database, varying the reading seed of each database. This experiment is to demonstrate that increasing the training data helps the model to improve its classification performance. The results of the two best training sessions of each model are shown in Table 3 regarding BAM performance metrics in the validation sets. It can be seen how the AlexNetv2 model always obtained a better classification performance (marked in bold) than the ResNet50 and VGG16 models in both the OGDB and MASTER databases. This indicates that it is the appropriate model for the classification of the database presented; however, it is necessary to verify this hypothesis with cross-validation. It can also be seen in the classification performances with BAM that all the models that were trained with the MASTER database have a higher classification performance than the models trained with OGDB.

The second experiment to select the classifier model is the cross-validation of the models using the MASTER database since using it the classification models demonstrated higher performance in the first experiment. A training set of 80% of the data and 20% validation is considered, so 5 cross-validations were considered. Table 4 shows the average results of the cross-validations of each model. When considering the BAM precision value as the main criterion to select the model, it is verified that the AlexNetv2 model obtained a better classification performance in the cross-validation average, therefore, it is selected as the best model.

Table 3. Experiments for model selection.

Model	Dataset	Seed	Train_acc	Val_acc	Train_loss	Val_loss	Val_BAM
VGG16	OGDB	423	94.85%	91.89%	0.1717	0.4978	87.63%
VGG16	MASTER	423	96.45%	96.98%	0.1478	0.2303	95.01%
AlexNetv2	**OGDB**	**423**	**98.43%**	**95.49%**	**0.0407**	**0.1698**	**92.40%**
AlexNetv2	**MASTER**	**423**	**99.46%**	**97.84%**	**0.0162**	**0.0762**	**98.17%**
ResNet50	OGDB	379	97.98%	94.59%	0.0344	0.1811	84.60%
ResNet50	MASTER	379	97.42%	96.55%	0.1081	0.1285	91.26%

4.2 Results of GAN Data Augmentation

The previous section of results showed how an AlexNetv2 model is obtained as a leukocyte classifier using the MASTER dataset. However, it is important to emphasize that the results shown are validation sets that contain samples generated with the GDAM-GAN

Table 4. Average cross validation results.

Model	Dataset	Kfold	Train_acc	Val_acc	Train_loss	Val_loss	Val_BAM
AlexNetv2	**MASTER**	**Average**	**98.56%**	**97.07%**	**0.03984**	**0.1126**	**95.03%**
ResNet50	MASTER	Average	97.68%	96.90%	0.14688	0.34282	92.83%
VGG16	MASTER	Average	96.51%	95.95%	0.35852	0.57768	90.45%

method. Hence, the question remains whether the new samples are really helping to better generalize the model or are only tending towards an overfitting model. To verify this behavior, it was achieved a training where the validation set has only real samples. This database that did not have images generated by GDAM-GAN in the validation set is called MASTER_CHALLENGE. Table 5 shows the results of the experiment with MASTER_CHALLENGE compared to the experiment with the highest value of the cross-validation. It is observed how the classification performance is not affected when validating only with original samples. According to this finding, it can be inferred that DA with the GDAM-GAN method and its sample selection helps the deep model to generalize and obtain a better classification performance.

Table 5. Comparison results between the MASTER and MASTER_CHALLENGE experiments.

Model	Dataset	Train_acc	Val_acc	Train_loss	Val_loss	Val_BAM
AlexNetv2	MASTER	98.06%	96.56%	0.0494	0.1305	96.69%
AlexNetv2	MASTER_CHALLENGE	99.67%	97.41%	0.0166	0.0827	97.77%

4.3 Comparison of AlexNetv2 with the State-of-the-Art Models

At this point, it is possible to conclude that a simple deep learning model is enough to solve the leukocyte classification task and maintain a similar performance to the complex models described in the introduction.

During the experimentation in this work, a model with a BAM performance of 98.17% was obtained. Table 6 shows that the AlexNetv2 model is ranked fourth place using the BAM metric compared with other works presented in the literature. However, it can be considered competitive because it only differs by 0.79% from the first place. It should be noted that it is not possible to make a direct comparison since the published works use their databases with particularities that do not meet the purposes pursued in this work.

Table 6. AlexNetv2 model comparison with other state of the art models.

Year	Model	Val_BAM
2019	AlexNet and Custom CNN [1]	98.96%
2020	AlexNet [6]	98.46%
2021	AlexNet-GoogleNet-SVM [2]	98.25%
2023	**AlexNetv2**	**98.17%**
2022	VGG16 [8]	97.20%

5 Conclusions

Considering the results shown above, it is possible to conclude that the simple AlexNetv2 model without extra components obtained the fourth best performance in Table 6 with a BAM of 98.17%. And the second-best performance considering only the simple models, models with only one deep module. The best performance in the simple model was AlexNet [6]. However, according to the authors in [6], they had to train three new layers which may increase the training time. Besides the same authors also reported that the prediction time presented a high execution time, which is not suitable for a model that is intended for implementation in an embedded system. The fact of using only a deep model to carry out the classification allows the model to be implemented in an embedded system. It does not need more components, as in the case of other complex models, which indicates a lower computational capacity for its implementation. It is also demonstrated by the results shown in Table 5 that the samples generated with GAN, specifically in this work with the GDAM-GAN method, may be considered to train a model and improve its generalization. This DA technique also increments the performance of the model compared to training without using artificial samples. In addition to the previous results, a different database was generated. This dataset better adheres to the blood smear process than those presented in the state-of-the-art.

Acknowledgments. The authors greatly appreciate the support of Tecnologico Nacional de Mexico / I. T. Chihuahua to perform this research.

References

1. Hegde, R.B., Prasad, K., Hebbar, H., Singh, B.M.K.: Feature extraction using traditional image processing and convolutional neural network methods to classify white blood cells: a study. Australas. Phys. Eng. Sci. Med. **42**(2), 627–638 (2019). https://doi.org/10.1007/s13 246-019-00742-9
2. Çınar, A., Tuncer, S.A.: Classification of lymphocytes, monocytes, eosinophils, and neutrophils on white blood cells using hybrid Alexnet-GoogleNet-SVM. SN Appl. Sci. **3**(4), 1–11 (2021). https://doi.org/10.1007/s42452-021-04485-9
3. Huang, P., et al.: Attention-aware residual network based manifold learning for white blood cells classification. IEEE J. Biomed. Health Inform. **25**(4), 1206–1214 (2021). https://doi.org/10.1109/JBHI.2020.3012711

4. Ghosh, S., Majumder, M., Kudeshia, A.: LeukoX: leukocyte classification using least entropy combiner (LEC) for ensemble learning. IEEE Trans. Circuits Syst. II Express Briefs **68**(8), 2977–2981 (2021). https://doi.org/10.1109/TCSII.2021.3064389

5. Chen, H., et al.: Accurate classification of white blood cells by coupling pre-trained ResNet and DenseNet with SCAM mechanism. BMC Bioinf. **23**(1), 1–20 (2022). https://doi.org/10.1186/S12859-022-04824-6/FIGURES/10

6. Reena, M.R., Ameer, P.M.: Localization and recognition of leukocytes in peripheral blood: a deep learning approach. Comput. Biol. Med. **126**, 104034 (2020). https://doi.org/10.1016/J.COMPBIOMED.2020.104034

7. Gutierrez-Velazquez, M., Chacon-Murguia, M.I., Ramirez-Quintana, J.A., Arzate-Quintana, C., Corral-Saenz, A.D.: Generative adversarial network design for data augmentation for copro-parasite images. In: Proceedings of the 2021 IEEE International Conference on Machine Learning and Applied Network Technologies, ICMLANT 2021 (2021). https://doi.org/10.1109/ICMLANT53170.2021.9690544

8. Kouzehkanan, Z.M., et al.: A large dataset of white blood cells containing cell locations and types, along with segmented nuclei and cytoplasm. Sci. Rep. **12**(1), 1123 (2022). https://doi.org/10.1038/s41598-021-04426-x

9. Rezatofighi, S.H., Soltanian-Zadeh, H.: Automatic recognition of five types of white blood cells in peripheral blood. Comput. Med. Imaging Graph. **35**(4), 333–343 (2011). https://doi.org/10.1016/J.COMPMEDIMAG.2011.01.003

10. Mohamed, M., Far, B., Guaily, A.: An efficient technique for white blood cells nuclei automatic segmentation. In: Proceedings of IEEE International Conference on Systems, Man and Cybernetics, pp. 220–225 (2012). https://doi.org/10.1109/ICSMC.2012.6377703

11. Sarrafzadeh, O., Rabbani, H., Talebi, A., Banaem, H.U.: Selection of the best features for leukocytes classification in blood smear microscopic images. In: Medical Imaging 2014: Digital Pathology (2014). https://doi.org/10.1117/12.2043605

12. Hegde, R.B., Prasad, K., Hebbar, H., Singh, B.M.K.: Development of a robust algorithm for detection of nuclei and classification of white blood cells in peripheral blood smear images. J. Med. Syst. **42**(6), 1–8 (2018). https://doi.org/10.1007/s10916-018-0962-1

13. Shorten, C., Khoshgoftaar, T.M.: A survey on image data augmentation for deep learning. J. Big Data **6**(1), 1–48 (2019). https://doi.org/10.1186/s40537-019-0197-0

14. Navarro, J.: Design of a data augmentation methodology based on GAN and its application on a mask detection vision system. Tecnologico Nacional de Mexico campus Chihuahua, Chihuahua (2022). https://posgradoitch.mx/wp-content/uploads/2022/11/Tesis-Navarro-Acosta-Jesus-Alejandro.pdf

15. Krizhevsky, A., Sutskever, I., Hinton, G.E.: ImageNet classification with deep convolutional neural networks. Commun. ACM **60**(6), 84–90 (2017). https://doi.org/10.1145/3065386

16. Jia, Y., et al.: Caffe: convolutional architecture for fast feature embedding. In: MM 2014 - Proceedings of the 2014 ACM Conference on Multimedia (2014). https://doi.org/10.1145/2647868.2654889

17. Smith, L.N.: Cyclical learning rates for training neural networks. In: Proceedings - 2017 IEEE Winter Conference on Applications of Computer Vision, WACV 2017 (2017). https://doi.org/10.1109/WACV.2017.58

18. Wang, W., Lee, C.M., Liu, J., Colakoglu, T., Peng, W.: An empirical study of cyclical learning rate on neural machine translation. Nat. Lang. Eng. (2022). https://doi.org/10.1017/S13513 2492200002X

Spoofing Detection for Speaker Verification with Glottal Flow and 1D Pure Convolutional Networks

Antonio Camarena-Ibarrola[1]([envelope]) [iD], Karina Figueroa[2] [iD],
and Axel Plancarte Curiel[2] [iD]

[1] Facultad de Ingeniería Eléctrica,
Universidad Michoacana de San Nicolás de Hidalgo, 58000 Morelia, Mexico
antonio.camarena@umich.mx
[2] Facultad de Ciencias Físico-Matemáticas,
Universidad Michoacana de San Nicolás de Hidalgo, 58000 Morelia, Mexico
{karina.figueroa,1803614h}@umich.mx

Abstract. Automatic Speaker Verification Systems are subject to attacks, these attacks aim to fool the system into accepting as valid the identity of a speaker when in fact it is the audio produced either by a voice conversion system that actually turns the voice of an identity thief into the voice of his victim, or by a speech synthesizer which parameters have been tuned to produce the voice of a specific individual whose identity is attempting to be stolen. A spoof detector decides wether the speech signal that is being used for verifying the identity of an individual is genuine or spoof. We use a 1D Pure Convolutional Neural Network (1DPCNN) with two classes (genuine and spoof). "Pure Convolutional" means all the layers of the neural network are convolutional or pooling, there are no dense layers, so the classifier block is also made of convolutional layers with a Global Maxpooling strategy. From the Speech signal we detect the voiced segments, which are those produced while the vocal cords vibrate, from those voiced segments we extract the glottal flow which is a signal far less complex than the speech signal and that is known to vary between speakers. We tested our technique with the dataset from the ASVSpoof 2015 challenge, using 7000 audio files for training, 4000 audio files for validation, and 30,000 audio files for testing. We achieved an accuracy of 91.4% with the test set.

Keywords: Spoof Detection · Glottal Flow · 1D Pure Convolutional Neural Network

1 Introduction

An Automatic Speaker Verification (ASV) system may be subject of attacks, which consists in somehow producing what appears to be the voice of some

Supported by Universidad Michoacana de San Nicolas de Hidalgo.

targeted individual, while he/she is not actually speaking and this voice was in fact produced using a speech synthesizer, a voice converter, or a simple recording of the actual voice of the targeted individual. To protect the ASV system a spoof speech detector may be used, as in Fig. 1 where the ASV system only works after the spoof speech detector classifies the speech as genuine.

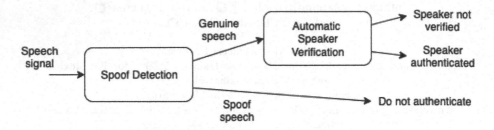

Fig. 1. Spoofing Attack Detector for Automatic Speaker Verification.

There are two kinds of Speaker Verification Systems, the systems of the first kind require the speaker to utter some specific phrase like "In my bank mi voice is my signature", they are known as Text-Dependent Speaker Verification Systems (TDSV), a simple attack to those systems consists simply in recording the voice of the victim (the individual whose identity is being stolen), and then replaying the recorded voice when the TDSV system requires uttering the phrase for authentication purposes. In fact there is a known dataset for testing detectors of such attacks, it is in the ASVSpoof 2017 challenge site [6]. The second kind of Speaker Verification Systems are the Text-Independent Speaker Verification (TISV) systems, these systems have to verify the claimed identity of an individual regardless of the content of his/her speech, there are two ways these systems may be attacked, one is by using a voice converter, such as VoiceMod [2], which is a real-time Voice Changer that turns the voice of the user into that of whoever he is pretending to be; The other attack for TISV systems consists in using a speech synthesizer, such as FakeYou [4], that turns whichever text into speech that sounds like some targeted individual. A dataset for testing detectors of attacks on TISV systems is in the ASVSpoof 2015 challenge site [13].

We saw Implementing a detector of attacks on TISV systems as a more interesting challenge than implementing a detector of attacks on TDSV systems, also more useful tools would result from this. Consider for example the following situation, a recording from a telephonic conversation is presented as evidence in some justice trial, but the accused, claims that it is not his voice in the recording but the product of some voice converter or the output of some speech synthesizer, a detector of attacks on TISV systems would come handy for deciding upon the voice of the accused as spoof or genuine.

2 Related Work

Great effort has been focussed in finding countermeasures against spoofing attacks on automatic speaker verification systems. In 2015 Patel & Patil trained two Gaussian Mixtures Models (GMM), one for the genuine class and one for the spoof class, each mixture is made of 128 gaussians, for deciding if a voice is spoof or genuine they extract the Cochlear Filter Cepstral Coefficients Instantaneous Frequency (CFCCIF) and then evaluate the probability density of those coefficients in both gaussian mixtures and decide for the one with the highest probability density [8]. In 2016 Todisco *et al* also used GMMs for classification but they extracted the Constant-Q Cepstral Coefficients (CQCC), this designed feature combine the music inspired constant-Q transform with the Mel Frequency Cepstral coefficients (MFCC) by changing the logarithmically distributed Mel Scale to the scale of the constant-Q transform which is also logarithmic (Base 2) [11]. In 2017 Zhao *et al* [14] also used GMMs for both genuine and spoof classes but knowing how GMMs do not work properly for high dimensional vectors, then they use compressed sensing [3] to produce compact feature vectors from initially high dimensional feature vectors derived from the short-time Fourier Transform. In 2020 Rahmeni *et al* used Extreme Gradient Boosting as classifiers and a high dimensional vector that includes Mel Frequency Cepstral Coefficients (MFCC), Energy at the output of logarithmically distributed Filter Banks (LogFBP), Linear Prediction Coefficients (LPC), Log Area Ratios (LAR), and Spectral Subband Centroids (SSC), although after a correlation analysis among these features they decided to keep only MFCC, LogFBP, and SSC, thus reducing the dimension of the feature vetors [9]. In 2022 Rahmeni *et al* used acoustic and glottal flow features and a Support Vector Machine for classification [10]. In general, seems like researchers have focussed in finding better features rather than searching for better classifiers for automatic decision on a speech signal being spoof or genuine [5].

3 Implementation

Our proposed method for detecting spoofed speech consists in splitting the speech signal in frames and extracting the glottal flow from those frames with voiced speech content, then use a 1D Pure Convolutional Neural Network to decide whether each of those frames is genuine or spoofed and label the whole uttered phrase as genuine if the majority of the voiced frames where classified as genuine by the 1DPCNN, otherwise label the phrase as spoof.

3.1 Segmenting Voiced Speech

We first split the speech signal into frames with length of 25 ms, the frames are overlapped so the beginning of a frame is 10 ms after the beginning of the previous frame, since the sampling frequency is $f_s = 16\,\mathrm{KHz}$, then each frame consists of 400 samples and its beginning occurs 80 samples after the beginning of the previous frame, no window is applied to the frames. We first discard frames with no voice in them by computing the short-time energy as well as the short-time zero crossings rate, frames with too low energy or too high zero crossings rate are discarded.

3.2   Discarding Frames with Unvoiced Speech

Each frame of the speech signal can be considered as either voiced or unvoiced, voiced speech is produced while vocal cords vibrate, such vibration introduces periodicity in the speech signal. Therefore, a periodicity estimator would allow us to implement the required dichotomizer, it is known that the autocorrelation function of a signal has a peak when the signal is periodic (pseudo-periodic in our case), the peak is higher when the signal is more periodic, then we compute the autocorrelation function of each frame with speech using Eq. 1 and if it has a peak higher than a threshold we declare it as voiced and keep it, otherwise the frame is declared as containing unvoiced speech and is discarded, since glottal flow can only be extracted from voiced speech.

$$R_n[k] = \sum_{m=0}^{N-1-k} s_n[m]s_n[m+k] \tag{1}$$

3.3   Estimating Glottal Flow

For each frame that contains voiced speech, we use the Iterative Adaptive Inverse Filtering (IAIF) proposed by Alku [1] for estimating the glottal flow. In the IAIF the glottal flow is initially modeled by a two-pole filter and the inverse of this filter is used to eliminate the contribution of the glottal flow in the speech signal, this "deglottalized waveform" is used to estimate the parameters of a model of only the vocal tract instead of the combined model of the vocal tract and the glottal flow as a unit. The estimation of the parameters is performed through Linear Predictive Coding (LPC), then with the inverse of the filter that models only the vocal tract a better estimation of the glottal flow is obtained. The procedure is repeated with a model for the glottal flow of higher order several times, a flowchart of the process which was taken from [12] can be seen in Fig. 2.

In Fig. 3 we show an example of glottal flow extracted from genuine (left) and spoof (right) speech, it is clear from this image that the glottal flow from a spoof speech is a much smoother version of the glottal flow extracted from the genuine speech. After observing this, we felt confident that glottal flow would be enough for classifying the speech as genuine or spoof regarding voice conversion attacks, and in regard to speech synthesis attacks, we are aware that speech synthesizers normally use a synthetic train of glottal pulses and some use just a train of impulses.

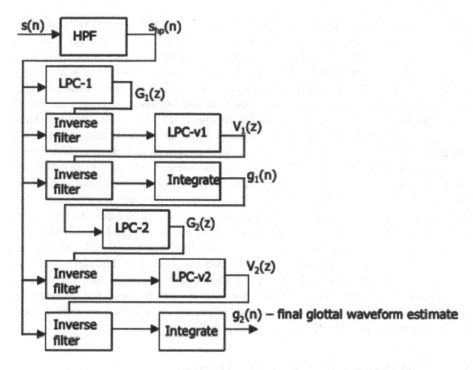

Fig. 2. Flowchart of the Iterative Adaptive Inverse Filter procedure for obtaining the glottal flow (taken from [12]).

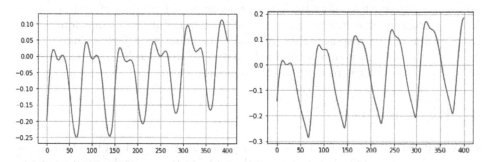

Fig. 3. Glottal flow from genuine (left) and spoof (right) speech

3.4 Classifying Frames as Spoof or Genuine

We use a 1D Convolutional Neural Network for deciding if the glottal flow extracted from each frame with voiced speech content belongs to one of two classes, spoof or genuine. Conventional Convolutional Neural Networks have convolutional layers that act as feature extractors and after the last convolutional layer, a series of dense layers that work as a classifier with the last layer having a number of neurons that equals the number of classes and use the Softmax activation function in that layer. A drawback to such architecture is that the dense layers are prone to overfitting. In [7] an alternative architecture known as Network In Network (NIN) was proposed, in such architecture instead of dense layers, additional convolutional layers are added, the last layer has a number of filters that equals the number of classes and uses Global Average Polling for classifying, such architecture includes micro-networks between convolutional layers, there the name "Network in Network". In our 1DPCNN we do not use those micro-networks, but we did use the idea of avoiding dense layers and use only convolutional layers, so it is a pure convolutional neural network. The Tensor shape of the input is (400,1) because the frames consists of 400 samples and the glottal flow extracted from each frame is made of 400 samples as well. We use 12 convolutional layers with only two filters in the last layer since we are only classifying the glottal flow from a voiced frame as belonging to one of two classes (genuine or spoof) and use GlobalMaxPooling in this last convolutional layer. In all convolutional layers the activation function was the ReLU function except in the last layer where we used the Softmax function. The optimizer used was Adam, also we used Early Stopping with a patience of 30, and the dropout layers make 25% of the neurons of the previous layer to be forgotten every epoch. Learning rate decay with a patience of 20 and a factor of 0, 3 was used. More details regarding our 1DPCNN are shown in Table 1.

3.5   Final Decision with a Voting Approach

The 1DCNN predicts whether the frame at its input comes from genuine or fake speech. However, there may be several tens or even hundreds of voiced frames in the phrase uttered by the speaker, and we should take into consideration all information at our disposal, then instead of deciding with just a single frame, we leave the final decision regarding the nature of the speech (spoof or genuine) to a voting scheme where each voiced frame has a vote.

4   Experiments

For our experiments, we used the ASVSpoof 2015 dataset, which was built using genuine speech, collected from 106 speakers (45 male, 61 female) with no significant channel or background noise effects, the collection include spoofed speech generated from the genuine data using 10 different spoofing algorithms, 7 Voice conversion, and 3 speech synthesis algorithms. The dataset is partitioned into three subsets, one for training, one for development (i.e. validation) and one for evaluation (i.e. testing). The training set has 3,750 genuine and 12,625 spoofed utterances, the development set has 3,497 genuine and 49,875 spoofed utterances, and the evaluation set has 9,404 genuine and 184,000 spoofed utterances. However, due to limitations on computing capacity, since all or experiments were run on Free Google Colab, we had to reduce the size of these sets and randomly selected 7,000 audio files for training, 4,000 audio files for validation,

Table 1. Details of our 1D Pure Convolutional Neural Network

Layer	Tensor Shape	#Parameters
Input layer	(400,1)	0
Conv1d_1 $f = 32$, $ks = 3$	(398,32)	128
BatchNormalization_1	(398,32)	128
Conv1d_2 $f = 64$, $ks = 3$	(396,64)	6208
BatchNormalization_2	(396,64)	256
Dropout_1	(396,64)	0
Conv1d_3 $f = 32$, $ks = 7$	(390,32)	14368
BatchNormalization_3	(390,32)	128
Conv1d_4 $f = 64$, $ks = 7$	(384,64)	14400
BatchNormalization_4	(384,64)	256
Conv1d_5 $f = 64$, $ks = 7$	(378,64)	28736
BatchNormalization_5	(378,64)	256
MaxPooling1D_1 $ws = 2$	(189,64)	0
Dropout_2	(189,64)	0
Conv1d_6 $f = 32$, $ks = 20$	(170,32)	40992
BatchNormalization_6	(170,32)	128
Conv1d_7 $f = 64$, $ks = 20$	(151,64)	41024
BatchNormalization_7	(151,64)	256
Conv1d_8 $f = 96$, $ks = 20$	(132,96)	122976
BatchNormalization_8	(132,96)	384
Dropout_3	(132,96)	0
Conv1d_9 $f = 64$, $ks = 30$	(103,64)	184384
BatchNormalization_9	(103,64)	256
Conv1d_10 $f = 96$, $ks = 30$	(74,96)	184416
BatchNormalization_10	(74,96)	384
Dropout_4	(74,96)	0
Conv1d_11 $f = 128$, $ks = 30$	(45,128)	368768
BatchNormalization_11	(45,128)	512
Dropout_4	(45,128)	0
Conv1d_12 $f = 2$, $ks = 30$	(16,2)	7682
GlobalMaxPooling1D	(2)	0

Total parameters: 1,017,026

Trainable parameters: 1,015,554

Non-trainable parameters: 1,472

and 30,000 audio files for testing from their respective sets. In Fig. 4(a) we show how accuracy evolved during training for both training and validation data, the final accuracy obtained for training data was 99.48% and 99.51% for validation data. In Fig. 4(b) we show how the loss function evolved during training for both training and validation data, the final loss was 0.0197 for training data and 0.0164 for validation data.

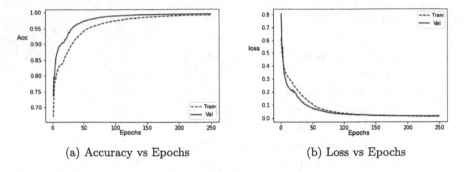

(a) Accuracy vs Epochs   (b) Loss vs Epochs

Fig. 4. Accuracy and Loss during training.

With the evaluation (i.e. test set) we obtained an accuracy of 90.96%, the confusion matrix is shown in Fig. 5. After implementing the voting scheme where the decision is made not only with a single voiced frame of the utterance but using every voiced frame of the utterance with obtained an slightly improved accuracy of 91.4%.

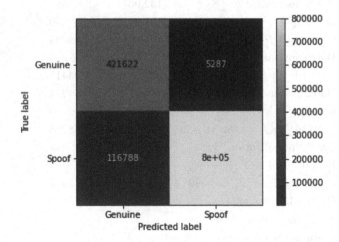

Fig. 5. Confusion Matrix obtained after tests with evaluation data.

5   Conclusions and Future Work

The speech signal is too complex, it has too much information, and if all we want is to verify whether the speech signal is genuine or fake we can significantly reduce the complexity of the signal by keeping only the glottal flow. The IAIF method for extracting the glottal flow is a method that allowed us to adequately extract the glottal flow. The proposed 1D pure convolutional neural network achieved a high accuracy of 90.96% for classifying utterances as genuine or fake. Our proposed voting scheme did improved accuracy but only to 91.4% so perhaps is not worth the burden it implies and the prediction can be left to the neural network alone with any of the voiced frames, making it much simpler to implement. However, the dichotomizer that separates voiced frames from unvoiced frames is critical since glottal flow does not exist in unvoiced speech.

Acknowledgements. Thanks to Universidad Michoacana de San Nicolás de Hidalgo for supporting this work.

References

1. Alku, P.: Glottal wave analysis with pitch synchronous iterative adaptive inverse filtering. Speech Commun. **11**(2), 109–118 (1992). https://doi.org/10. 1016/0167-6393(92)90005-R, https://www.sciencedirect.com/science/article/pii/ 016763939290005R. eurospeech 1991
2. Bosh, J.: Free real time voice changer (2022). https://www.voicemod.net
3. Donoho, D.: Compressed sensing. IEEE Trans. Inf. Theory **52**(4), 1289–1306 (2006). https://doi.org/10.1109/TIT.2006.871582
4. Echelon: FakeYou. Deep fake text to speech (2023). https://fakeyou.com/
5. Kamble, M.R., Sailor, H.B., Patil, H.A., Li, H.: Advances in anti-spoofing: from the perspective of ASVspoof challenges. APSIPA Trans. Sig. Inf. Process. **9**, e2 (2020). https://doi.org/10.1017/ATSIP.2019.21
6. Kinnunen, T., et al.: ASVspoof 2017: automatic speaker verification spoofing and countermeasures challenge evaluation plan. IEEE J. Sel. Top. Sig. Process. **PP**(99), 1 (2018)
7. Lin, M., Chen, Q., Yan, S.: Network in network. In: International Conference on Learning Representations, Banff, Canada (Apr 2014)
8. Patel, T.B., Patil, H.A.: Combining evidences from mel cepstral, cochlear filter cepstral and instantaneous frequency features for detection of natural vs. spoofed speech. In: INTERSPEECH, pp. 2062–2066 (2015)
9. Rahmeni, R., Aicha, A.B., Ayed, Y.B.: Acoustic features exploration and examination for voice spoofing counter measures with boosting machine learning techniques. Procedia Comput. Sci. **176**, 1073–1082 (2020). https://doi. org/10.1016/j.procs.2020.09.103, https://www.sciencedirect.com/science/article/ pii/S1877050920320032. knowledge-Based and Intelligent Information & Engineering Systems: Proceedings of the 24th International Conference KES2020
10. Rahmeni, R., Aicha, A.B., Ayed, Y.B.: Voice spoofing detection based on acoustic and glottal flow features using conventional machine learning techniques. Multimedia Tools Appl. **81**, 31443–31467 (2022). https://doi.org/10.1007/s11042-022-12606-8

11. Todisco, M., Delgado, H., Evans, N.: A new feature for automatic speaker verification anti-spoofing: constant Q cepstral coefficients. In: Proceedings of the Speaker and Language Recognition Workshop (Odyssey 2016), pp. 283–290 (2016). https://doi.org/10.21437/Odyssey.2016-41
12. Walker, J., Murphy, P.: A review of glottal waveform analysis. In: Progress in Non linear Speech Processing. vol. 4391, pp. 1–21 (Jan 2005). https://doi.org/10.1007/978-3-540-71505-4_1
13. Wu, Z., et al.: ASVspoof: the automatic speaker verification spoofing and counter-measures challenge. IEEE J. Sel. Top. Sig. Process. **11**(4), 588–604 (2017). https://doi.org/10.1109/JSTSP.2017.2671435
14. Zhao, Y., Togneri, R., Sreeram, V.: Compressed high dimensional features for speaker spoofing detection. In: 2017 Asia-Pacific Signal and Information Processing Association Annual Summit and Conference (APSIPA ASC), pp. 569–572 (2017). https://doi.org/10.1109/APSIPA.2017.8282108

Estimation of Stokes Parameters Using Deep Neural Networks

Joan Manuel Raygoza-Romero[1]([✉])(iD), Irvin Hussein Lopez-Nava[1](iD),
and Julio Cesar Ramírez-Vélez[2]

[1] Centro de Investigación Científica y Educación Superior de Ensenada (CICESE),
Ensenada, Mexico
{jraygoza,hussein}@cicese.edu.mx
[2] Instituto de Astronomía/Universidad Nacional Autónoma de México (UNAM),
22860 Ensenada, Baja California, Mexico
jramirez@astro.unam.mx

Abstract. Magnetic fields play a very important role in stellar evolution, as well as vary depending on the evolutionary stage. To understand how the stellar magnetic fields evolve is necessary to measure and map the magnetic fields over the stellar surface. It can be done through spectropolarimetric observations through the four Stokes parameters (I, Q, U, and V). In this work, we propose a deep-learning approach to estimate the Stokes parameters based on eight input parameters (dipolar moment strength, m; the magnetic dipole position inside the star, X_2, X_3; the rotation phase, p; the magnetic geometry of the dipolar configuration, α, β, γ; and the inclination angle of the stellar rotation axis with respect to the line of sight, i) and using a synthetic dataset generated by COSSAM. Different configurations of a neural network have been experimented with: the number of layers and neurons; the scaling of the input and output parameters; the size of training data; and estimating separately and jointly the output parameters. The best configuration of the neural network model scores a mean squared error of 1.4e–7, 2.4e–8, 1.5e–8, and 1.3e–7, for Stokes I, Q, U, and V, respectively. In summary, the model effectively estimated the Stokes I and V, which respectively correspond to the total intensity and circular polarization of the light emitted by magnetic stars; however, struggled with the Stokes Q and U, which represent linear polarization components generally for very small m. Overall, our work presents a promising avenue for advancing our understanding of stars that host a magnetic field.

Keywords: Magnetic fields · Stokes parameters · Parameter estimation · Parameter regression · Deep neural networks · Deep learning

J. M. Raygoza-Romero—Supported by the Mexican National Council for Science and Technology (CONACYT), under the grant number 29415; J.RV thanks to the UNAM-PAPIIT grants IN103320 and IN118023.

A. Y. Rodríguez-González et al. (Eds.): MCPR 2023, LNCS 13902, pp. 159–168, 2023.
https://doi.org/10.1007/978-3-031-33783-3_15

1   Introduction

Magnetic fields are at the origin of solar and stellar activity, and it is widely accepted that magnetic fields can play a very important role in stellar evolution: from young stellar stars to compact objects. Moreover, the magnetic field strengths and topology vary depending on the evolutionary stage. It is therefore important to understand how stellar magnetic fields evolve. The first step in order to achieve this goal is to measure and map the magnetic fields over the stellar surface.

In terms of analysis data, the best tool for this purpose are spectropolarimetric observations, which allow retrieving simultaneously the intensity spectra as well as the polarized spectra (described through the so-called *Stokes parameters* I, Q, U, V, where I denotes intensity, Q and U linear polarization and V circular polarization). It is through the analysis of spectropolarimetric data type that magnetic fields can be properly characterized [1]. In order to fit the polarized spectra it is required to use theoretical codes that synthesize the Stokes parameters given a magnetic field configuration over the star. In this work, we will consider a generalized de-centred dipolar magnetic configuration.

In order to obtain synthetic spectra to fit the observations, we employed the COSSAM code [5]. The surface of the star is divided into 80 areas, where in each area are calculated the four Stokes parameters. They are then integrated over the entire surface to obtain the resulting Stokes profiles to be compared with observations. This requires a lot of CPU time to model in the fitting process. For this reason, in this work, we developed a model based on deep learning to obtain a reliable tool that can synthesize a huge number of magnetic configurations for the Stokes parameters in an affordable way.

2   Dataset

A synthetic dataset generated by COSSAM was used to estimate Stokes parameters. COSSAM is a program that employs the polarized radiative transfer equation to produce Stokes profiles [4]. A corpus of 600,000 data instances has been generated, with each instance having 8 attributes, namely the dipolar moment strength (m), the magnetic dipole position inside the star described by two coordinates (X_2, X_3), the rotation phase (p), three attributes describing the magnetic geometry of the dipolar configuration (α, β, γ), and the inclination angle (i) of the stellar rotation axis with respect to the line of sight.

Each instance, with these eight input attributes, is associated with an output signal of 128 frames or points, corresponding to the Stokes parameters, 32 attributes for each. Figure 1 shows an example of a signal generated with the following attribute values: $m = 891.3, i = 54.9, \alpha = 71.5, \beta = 44.0, \gamma = -61.7, X_2 = 0.0, X_3 = 0.0, p = 0.52$; and it was segmented into the four Stokes parameters that will be the output of our model. This example highlights an important feature in the Stokes parameters, which is the difference in amplitudes of each parameter, with Stokes I being much larger than Stokes V, and

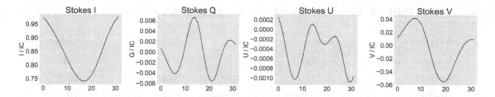

Fig. 1. Example of the four Stokes parameters.

Table 1. Range for 8 input attributes.

Attribute:	m	X_2	X_3	p	α	β	γ	i
Min value	100	0.0	0.0	0.0	–90	0	–90	0
Max value	5100	0.2	0.2	1.0	90	180	90	90

Stokes V being larger than Stokes Q and U. Therefore, it is necessary to preprocess and scaling the input and output data so that the prediction model will be
able to estimate different magnitudes.

The range of the input attributes is detailed in Table 1. These ranges were
used for the generation of the dataset, randomly selecting a combination of the
8 attributes.

3   Methods

In this section, the proposed models for regression of the Stokes parameters using
deep learning are presented. The use of deep learning was motivated by the need
to regress each point of the profile of each Stokes parameter, thus requiring a
multi-output model, and a neural network (NN) is suitable for this problem.

In this study, two performance metrics, Mean Squared Error (MSE) and
Mean Absolute Percentage Error (MAPE), will be employed to evaluate the
model's performance among several configurations in order to find the best
model. The following are the equations for each metric:

$$MSE = \frac{1}{n}\sum_{i=1}^{n}(Y_i - \hat{Y}_i)^2 \quad \text{and} \quad MAPE = \frac{1}{n}\sum_{i=1}^{n}\left|\frac{Y_i - \hat{Y}_i}{Y_i}\right| \tag{1}$$

where n is the number of point or sample, Y_i is the ground truth value, and $\hat{Y}_i$ is the
model prediction for each point i.

MSE penalizes larger errors to a greater extent, facilitating the comparison
of different configurations of the model on the same dataset. On the other hand,
MAPE is a useful metric for comparing model predictions with greater accuracy,
regardless of the magnitude of the values being compared. As a percentage-based
metric, MAPE will be employed to compare the accuracy of predicted values with
respect to the ground truth values. For all the work, including these preliminary
evaluations, datasets were split into 75% training, 15% validation, and 10% test,
each of them having the same distribution.

Table 2. Fixed parameters for the preliminary experiments.

Attribute	Value	Attribute	Value
Dataset Size	50,000	Momentum	0.95
Activation Function	ReLu	Epochs	1000
Optimizer	Stochastic gradient descent	Early Stopping**	25
Learning Rate*	1	Batch Size	1024
Weight Decay	$1/(2*dataset\_size)$		

* Learning rates are variable in the scaling experiments
** No early stopping for the selection architecture experiment

3.1 Feedforward Neuronal Network

Feedforward neural networks (FNN) are a fundamental building block of deep learning architectures and have proven to be highly effective in many real-world applications [2]. They consist of an input layer, one or more hidden layers, and an output layer, with the data flowing in a single direction from input to output. Each neuron in the network receives input from the previous layer, processes it using a set of weights and biases, and passes the result to the next layer. The hidden layers of the network are responsible for extracting complex features from the raw input data and transforming it into a representation suitable for the task at hand. The output layer provides the final prediction or decision.

The training of FNN is an optimization problem, where the objective is to find the set of weights and biases that minimize the prediction error on a training dataset. This is typically achieved using an optimization algorithm such as stochastic gradient descent or a variant thereof, and the backpropagation algorithm is used to compute the gradients of the error with respect to the weights and biases [6].

3.2 Selection of Neural Network Parameters

The parameters for the following preliminary experiments are listed in Table 2. These parameters apply to all experiments, with some exceptions noted at the bottom of the table. In order to perform a wide range of experiments within a restricted timeframe, only a sample of the entire dataset (50,000 instances) was considered. Based on the results of empirical experiments, a dynamic weight decay approach was applied. It consists of varying the weight decay as a function of the dataset size. As weight decay plays a crucial role in the training process, a dynamic approach enables the adaptation of this parameter to the specific characteristics of the dataset [3]. These NN parameters are expected to enhance the overall effectiveness of the training process and improve the generalization capability of the network.

Table 3. Comparison of different configurations of the neuronal network model.

Name	Neurons	Hidden Layers	Training Time	MSE
SMALL →	512	4	0.34	1.6e–6
	1024	4	0.42	**1.1e–6**
MEDIUM →	2048	3	0.76	1.0e–6
	2048	4	1.00	**8.1e–7**
LARGE →	4096	4	2.85	6.7e–7
	4096	5	3.70	**6.2e–7**

3.3 Selection of Neuronal Network Architecture

This section aims to optimize the architecture of a neural network by examining a range of architectures that vary in the number of neurons and the number of hidden layers. A baseline for comparison using the network with 4 hidden layers and 2048 neurons per layer (MEDIUM) was established. Results for some architectures and training time are presented in Table 3. The training time for the baseline model was of 437 s and it was trained on an RTX 3070 GPU. The network with 5 hidden layers and 4096 neurons (LARGE) achieved the highest performance, but it also required a training time 3.7 times more than the baseline. Conversely, the network with 4 hidden layers and 1024 neurons (SMALL) had a performance 37% worse but required only 0.42 times less.

From these results, we adopted a balanced approach that takes into account both the network's performance and training time. Thus, we opted for the baseline (MEDIUM) network selected from Table 3 to carry out the subsequent experiments of this Section. The SMALL and LARGE models will be used again in Sect. 4. Our architecture chosen for the network was based on an FNN, as seen at the bottom in Fig. 2. In contrast, a model is a specific instance of a NN architecture with a set of trained parameters, including weights and biases. These parameters are learned through a process of optimization, where the network is trained on a dataset to minimize a loss function, see Table 2.

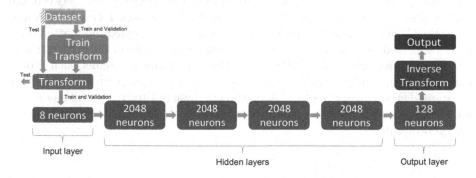

Fig. 2. Complete process of the data and neuronal network architecture.

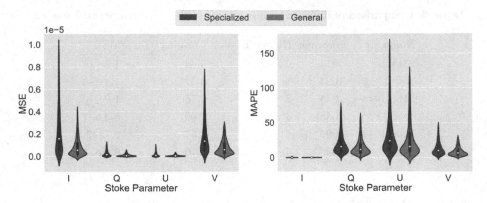

Fig. 3. Comparison of test MSE and MAPE of each Stoke parameter between general and specialized model.

Four different scaling were evaluated over the input and the output data, based on MEDIUM model. These scaling included standard, min-max, max absolute and quantile. The results indicate that the treatment of the output data has the greatest impact on the performance of the model. The results are very similar between the same output scaling, no matter what input scaling was used, so the standard is considerably better than the others. On the other hand, for the treatment of the input data, the standard scaling was also selected. Figure 2 shows the complete process of the data, first train a standard scaling with the train and validation data, then scaling all the dataset. Secondly, train the NN and lately inverse scaling to get the final output.

3.4 General Model vs. Specialized Model

The next step was to evaluate a model that would handle the regression of all four Stokes parameters simultaneously (GENERAL) and a model for each Stokes parameter (SPECIALIZED). Figure 3 shows the MSE for both types of models and for all of the Stokes parameters highlighting a slight improvement in the GENERAL model. In addition, when comparing the MAPE error between the Stokes parameters, the estimation is better for the Stokes I clearly, followed by Stokes V, with Stokes Q and U being the most complicated, no matter what model was used. The MSE shows a better comparison between the GENERAL and SPECIALIZED model, while MAPE shows the complexity to predict each Stokes parameter. This fully coincides with the amplitude of each Stokes parameter mentioned in the dataset section. According to these results, GENERAL model was selected due to its ability to simultaneously predict all four Stokes parameters and good results.

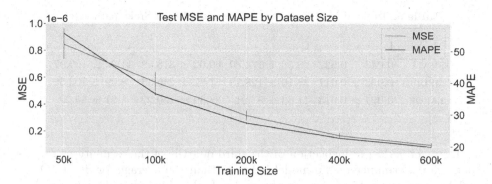

Fig. 4. Lineplots of MSE and MAPE on test set by amount of training data.

Table 4. Table of MSE ± Std. dev. results of each Stoke parameter.

Model	I	Q	U	V
SMALL	2.4e–7 ± 3.0e–7	3.9e–8 ± 5.9e–8	2.5e–8 ± 5.5e–8	2.2e–7 ± 2.6e–7
MEDIUM	1.4e–7 ± 1.8e–7	2.4e–8 ± 4.2e–8	1.5e–8 ± 4.2e–8	1.3e–7 ± 1.8e–7
LARGE	6.3e–8 ± 1.1e–7	1.0e–8 ± 2.5e–8	6.9e–9 ± 3.2e–8	6.1e–8 ± 1.1e–7

4   Results

In this section, we begin evaluating the effect on the performance when the size of the dataset is increased, from 50k to 600k instances. The model parameters used are those shown in Table 2, as well as the standard scaling for input and output, and using the GENERAL model to predict all the Stokes parameters simultaneously. Figure 4 shows the mean error for both MSE and MAPE metrics and the vertical bars indicate the standard deviation. It can be observed a reduction in both metrics as the size of the training dataset grows, as well as a decrease in the standard deviation of both. Thus the number of instances selected for the final models was 600k.

Table 4 show the MSE and its standard deviation for each Stokes parameter in the SMALL, MEDIUM, and LARGE models. The results demonstrate a marked improvement in the performance of models with increased parameters, as evidenced by lower MSE values. Additionally, a decrease in the standard deviation indicates enhanced precision and reliability of the model predictions. These findings suggest that the use of more complex models may yield better results in the context of Stokes parameter estimation, in return for more training time. As mentioned before, this metric does not provide a good comparison between the Stokes parameters due to the difference in the amplitudes of these.

Table 5 shows the MAPE and its standard deviation for each Stokes parameter and all the models. A large standard deviation is observed in Stokes Q, U and V, which can be attributed to the occurrence of certain instances with small amplitude values close to zero that produce a high MAPE.

Table 5. Table of MAPE ± Std. dev. results of each Stoke parameter.

Model	I	Q	U	V
SMALL	0.043 ± 0.022	26.58 ± 174.80	69.62 ± 318.69	11.26 ± 109.97
MEDIUM	0.033 ± 0.017	21.10 ± 128.78	51.87 ± 246.53	8.99 ± 103.50
LARGE	0.021 ± 0.013	11.83 ± 87.21	28.39 ± 130.22	5.81 ± 56.22

However, a deeper inspection of the third quartile of the estimations reveals that the performance of the model is better than the average for Stokes Q, U, and V parameters. Similarly, for the Stokes I, the third quartile value is close to the average, suggesting a good performance in the majority of cases. Furthermore, the MAPE allows for meaningful comparisons between the different Stokes parameters. Our analysis shows that the estimation of Stokes I is consistently robust across all models, while the performance of Stokes V is strong, particularly for the LARGE model. However, the prediction of Stokes Q and U presents more challenges, this coincides with the amplitude differences across all the Stokes parameters, which may reflect biases in the estimation process.

Overall, these findings demonstrate the limitations of using a single metric to evaluate the performance of a model and highlight the importance of considering multiple evaluation criteria. Furthermore, the analysis of the percentiles provides a more detailed and informative view of the model's performance, which may help to identify areas for improvement and guide future research efforts.

The last analysis will focus on the 95th and 99th percentiles for the SMALL model, and their correspondence in the other two models with the same input attributes values, as displayed in Figs. 5 and 6. The selection of the 95th percentile indicates that estimates below this value are better, it means that 95% of the Stokes parameters have been better estimated than this particular case.

Based on the findings illustrated in Fig. 5, the MEDIUM model demonstrates significant improvement over the SMALL model across all Stokes parameters. However, for the LARGE model, it can be observed an enhancement in Stokes I and a worse performance in the estimation of other Stokes parameters. Nevertheless, there are still detailed differences to consider, where the MSE for the entire instance of the LARGE model is lower than that of the MEDIUM model, while the MAPE exhibits the opposite trend. Note that in Fig. 5 first row, a visual inspection of the results shows that the estimation of Stokes Q appears to be better adjusted than that of Stokes I, with a MAPE of approximately 380% and 0.06%, respectively. The reason for this is that the polarized Stokes parameters have values close to zero and for this reason the MAPE can result in very high values, even if the Stokes Q is likely to be better reproduced.

Figure 6 presents an intriguing scenario, where the MEDIUM model exhibits a slight decline in MSE for Stokes V in comparison to the SMALL model. However, there is a noticeable improvement in MAPE, which is reflected in values that approach zero. It is noteworthy that this instance is among the worst for all models, with Stokes U demonstrating significant issues, and to a lesser extent

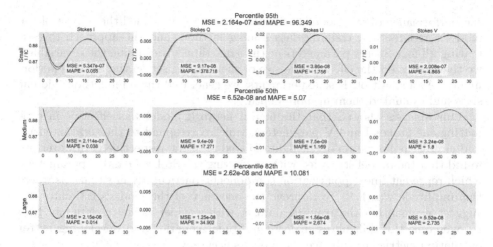

Fig. 5. Stokes estimation of 95th percentile for SMALL model. Top row is for SMALL model, middle row is for MEDIUM model and bottom row is for LARGE model. Purple is for ground truth and blue for the estimations.

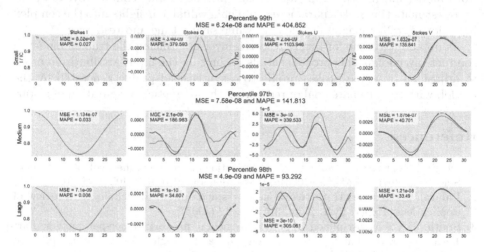

Fig. 6. Same as Fig. 5 but for the 99th percentile.

on the Stokes Q also displaying some challenges. Additionally, it is important to recognize that the model exhibits problems at certain small amplitudes.

5 Conclusions

The purpose of our work was to explore the use of a neural network model for estimating the Stokes parameters of stars, which can provide valuable information about their magnetic field and configuration. To achieve this goal, we conducted a series of experiments to investigate various factors that could affect the performance of the model's estimates. First, we examined the impact of the model's architecture, training data scaling method, and the approach to estimating all four Stokes parameters at the same time. After fixing these variables, we then analyzed the effect of the size of the training set on the model's performance. As a result of these experiments, we generated three models of different sizes and evaluated them in more depth.

Our analysis showed that the neural network model was effective in estimating the Stokes I and V parameters, which correspond to the total intensity and circular polarization of the light emitted by stars, respectively. However, we found that the model struggled with estimating the Stokes Q and U parameters, which represent linear polarization components, particularly in situations where the amplitude was low. To improve the accuracy of the model's estimates, we suggest augmenting the training dataset with a wider range of data can help to overcome the difficulties in low-amplitude scenarios and developing better evaluation metrics to enhance the model's accuracy.

Overall, our work presents a promising avenue for advancing our understanding of the magnetic field and configuration of stars. By refining the neural network model and incorporating additional data sources, we can improve our ability to estimate the Stokes parameters and gain valuable insights into the complex behavior of stellar magnetic fields, all while saving time and resources.

A potential avenue for future research involves utilizing the trained model to conduct inversions. This process entails optimizing the input attributes in order to adjust an observed Stokes profile to a synthesized profile generated by the model, with the ultimate goal of recovering the magnetic configuration of a star.

References

1. Degl'Innocenti, M.L., Landolfi, M.: Polarization in Spectral Lines. vol. 307. Springer Science & Business Media (2006). https://doi.org/10.1007/1-4020-2415-0
2. Paliwal, M., Kumar, U.A.: Neural networks and statistical techniques: a review of applications. Expert Syst. Appl. **36**(1), 2–17 (2009)
3. Smith, L.N.: A disciplined approach to neural network hyper-parameters: Part 1-learning rate, batch size, momentum, and weight decay. arXiv preprint arXiv:1803.09820 (2018)
4. Stift, M.: COSSAM: Codice per la sintesi spettrale nelle atmosfere magnetiche. Peculiar Newslett. **33**, 27 (2000)
5. Stift, M., Alecian, G.: Modelling ApBp star atmospheres with stratified abundances consistent with atomic diffusion. Monthly Not. R. Astron. Soc. **425**(4), 2715–2721 (2012)
6. Svozil, D., Kvasnicka, V., Pospichal, J.: Introduction to multi-layer feed-forward neural networks. Chemometr. Intell. Lab. Syst. **39**(1), 43–62 (1997)

Experimental Study of the Performance of Convolutional Neural Networks Applied in Art Media Classification

J. M. Fortuna-Cervantes[1] , C. Soubervielle-Montalvo[2](✉) ,
O. E. Perez-Cham[2] , R. Peña-Gallardo[2] , and C. Puente[2]

[1] Departamento de Eléctrica, Electrónica y Mecatrónica, Tecnológico Nacional de
México, Instituto Tecnológico de San Luis Potosí, San Luis Potosí, Mexico
`juan.fc@slp.tecnm.mx`
[2] Facultad de Ingeniería, Universidad Autónoma de San Luis Potosí (UASLP),
San Luis Potosí, Mexico
{`carlos.soubervielle,oscar.cham,rafael.pena,cesar.puente`}`@uaslp.mx`

Abstract. The classification of Art media requires careful analysis due to the physical characteristics of the author's work, such as shape, color, texture, medium, and historical period, which must be considered to correctly categorize the different Art media. This paper presents an experimental study of Art media classification based on pre-trained Convolutional Neural Networks (CNN), such as VGG16, ResNet50, and Xception, to demonstrate the robustness and improvement of the learning models. We trained them on WikiArt dataset, which is a reference in Art media. The same five art classes (Drawings, Engraving, Iconography, Painting, and Sculptures) are considered to validate the accuracy of the classification model. We trained using an NVIDIA Tesla K80 GPU in the Google Colaboratory (Colab) environment, and the Keras API with TensorFlow as Backend. The results show that all the CNNs tested present high correlation in the classification of Engravings and Drawings, due to the similarities of both classes. The best performance was obtained with the VGG16 architecture, with an accuracy of 75% using another dataset integrated with different works from the Del Prado and Louvre museums. This study confirms that the classification of Art media presents a challenge for CNN architecture due to the correlation found in the different classes.

Keywords: Art Media Classification · Convolutional Neural
Networks · Transfer Learning

1 Introduction

Art restorers and collectors often classify Art media based on physical characteristics, subjective attributes, and historical periods [15]. However, when classifying Art media, it is found that variations in specific characteristics may not

A. Y. Rodríguez-González et al. (Eds.): MCPR 2023, LNCS 13902, pp. 169–178, 2023.
https://doi.org/10.1007/978-3-031-33783-3_16

belong to any style, genre, or art period, making this task difficult and may lead to incorrect classification of Art media. A solution to this problem can be proposals based on Convolutional Neural Networks (CNN), which are deep learning algorithms that have become popular in the scientific community to solve image classification and object detection problems with high classification performance [2,23]. However, there is limited work on Art media classification tasks with in-depth study on classification performance and cross-class correlation [11,19]. In addition, it is possible to classify datasets more accurately by prioritizing pre-trained deep learning models over other computer vision methods [7].

The paper presents an experimental study that asseses the performance accuracy of three well-known CNN architectures in classifying Art media. The authors examine the behavior of these architectures designed in TensorFlow and Keras and employ transfer learning to improve the performance. The main objective is to demonstrate the robustness [12] of CNN learning models in Art media classification when transfer learning is used. This comparison of the three proposed CNN architectures allows the selection of the optimal one for future applications. The main contributions are:

- An analysis of CNN performance from an experimental approach applied to art media classification is presented.
- An experimental evaluation of the classification performance is presented, with the goal of evaluating the robustness and generalization of knowledge to other image sets. Evaluation is conducted using the institutional repositories of the Prado National Museum and the Louvre National Museum.
- The Google Colaboratory Framework is used by the authors to show how deep learning models may be created for free utilizing cloud computing.
- The authors demonstrate that correct inference can be obtained from most art media classes. With the notable exception of a high correlation between all the classes and the Engraving class. The model displays a similarity to human visual perception, which could be useful for future recognition applications focusing on the features of the art produced by a given artist.

This article is organized as follows. In Sect. 2, we briefly outline the work related to Art media classification. In Sect. 3, we present the materials and methods. In Sect. 4, we offer some experiments and analyze the classification results. We demonstrate the accuracy and correlation between classes of the designed image classifiers, which have yet to be explored in the state-of-the-art. Finally, in Sect. 5, we end the paper with some conclusions and ideas for future work.

2   Related Work

Computer vision has been an exciting proposal to recognize and classify objects with different applications. It is an auxiliary that allows visual analysis as human visual perception does. Automated analysis and categorization of Artworks have become a research field in rapid growth. In this regard, a comparative study of the state-of-the-art use of deep learning and the authors' proposed approach is shown in Table 1. Deep Learning algorithms have made image classification considerably more feasible, successfully analyzing huge datasets. Generally, it involves having a feature analysis to classify the collection of Artworks into style or genre.

Table 1. Summary of related work in computer vision for artwork classification.

Reference	Dataset	CNN	Approach
Olague et al. [19]	Artwork	No	Adversarial attacks
Ibarra et al. [10]	Artwork	No	Feature analysis
Masilamani et al. [17]	Best Artworks of all Time	Yes	Image classification
Kovalev et al. [14]	Painter by numbers	Yes	Style classification
Chu et al. [4,5]	Oil Painting	Yes	Feature correlation
Rodriguez et al. [22]	Artwork	Yes	Subregion classification
Abidin et al. [1]	Artwork	No	Genre classification
Gao et al. [8]	Best Artworks in the World	Yes	Style classification

3 Materials and Methods

3.1 Dataset

In deep learning tasks, the most important factor is the information, in this case, images representing art categories. On the other hand, the dataset must be representative enough in order to generalize the model to another dataset of images (test set). For art media classification, there is Art Image [19], a dataset of training and validation images obtained from the database of digitized artworks on the Kaggle website. This dataset includes five categories of art media: drawing, painting, iconography, engraving, and sculpture.

We decided to create our dataset for our case study [6]. Due to the presence of corrupted or preprocessed images in the original dataset. The dataset contains the same five classes; each category has 850 images for training and 180 images for validation. The most notable characteristic of this dataset is that the images are in RGB format and have a size of 224×224, which is ideal for the input of the proposed architectures. The test set was constructed using 180 images per category, sourced from the WikiArt database and digital artworks from the Louvre National Museum for paintings and the Prado National Museum for engravings [16,20]. Figure 1 shows some random images from the training set.

3.2 CNN Architecture and Transfer Learning

There are multiple CNN architectures that can be utilized to solve real-world problems related to image classification, detection, and segmentation [3,9,25]. However, each architecture has its unique benefits and drawbacks in terms of both training and implementation. Selecting the appropriate architecture is often a matter of experimentation and depends on the desired performance and

(a)   (b)   (c)   (d)   (e)

Fig. 1. Example images from the Art Image training set, showcasing the five art categories: (a) Drawings, created using a pencil, pen, or other implement on paper or other support; (b) Engravings, images created by cutting or etching into a surface; (c) Iconography, religious images or symbols; (d) Paintings, works created by applying pigments to a surface; and (e) Sculptures, three-dimensional art forms created by shaping or modeling materials into a desired form.

intended application. Transfer learning is a popular deep learning approach to handle small datasets. This research project uses a pre-trained CNN that takes into account the ImageNet database. The proposed CNN architecture, as other, consists of two main components: the feature extraction stage and the classification stage. The feature extraction stage, or convolutional base. Feature extraction involves using representative representations previously extracted during training. The goal is to adapt to the new features of the new dataset. Therefore, these features are used in a new classifier trained from scratch, as shown in Fig. 2.

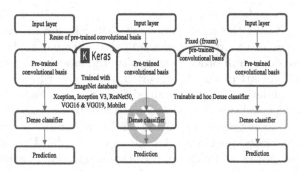

Fig. 2. Classifier exchange using the same convolutional basis: A pre-trained model for a general recognition task is taken as a basis. We reuse the feature extraction stage from the base architecture and cancel the dense classifier stage. Therefore, a new model is obtained for a specific recognition task, freezing the feature extraction basis and training a dense classifier ad hoc to our problem.

3.3   Improving Model Classification

The proposed methodology to improve performance on the learning model is summarized in three stages, shown in Fig. 3.

Model Evaluation. The process to improve the classification accuracy of the model is tested via experiments. In order to evaluate the model and make adjustments during each iteration, an initial configuration of the training parameters

Fig. 3. Deep learning process: In the first step, the dataset must be integrated. A characteristic to consider is that it must have balanced classes and representative images of our problem. In the second step, the images are processed, and the pixel values are normalized, so our model converges quickly. The third step allows us to validate our model and adjust and update the training parameters to retrain the learning model.

is selected before testing. It is important to establish the features of every class automatically. That is achieved through the selection of optimal kernel filters. That allows the model to be adjusted and updated later. The performance evaluation of any classification model commonly uses *Accuracy*—Measures the percentage of cases that the model predicted correctly. The confusion matrix is used to study the patterns of prediction error. This confusion matrix is a table of N×N, where N represents the number of classes, the matrix shows the correlation between the predicted label and the actual label.

Network Training and Parameter Settings. The models are implemented using the Python programming language and the `Keras API` with `Tensorflow` as Backend. In addition, we were trained using an NVIDIA Tesla K80 GPU in the `Google Colaboratory` (Colab) environment. The GPU is a graphics processor in the Colab system, which allows results to be obtained faster. Unlike other cloud systems, Colab provides free GPU and TPU support at run times for up to 12 h in some instances [21].

The base architectures used are the VGG16, ResNet50, and Xception networks, among the first deep models with good results in a large-scale visual recognition challenge (ILSVRC) [25]. Before training each CNN, it is necessary to specify the *loss function*—How the network will be able to measure its performance on the training data and thus how it will steer itself in the right direction, also called the *objective function*, and the *optimizer*—The mechanism through which the network will update itself based on the data it sees and its loss function. These parameters determine how the network weights should be updated during training. In addition, it is combined with the regularization methods DropOut [26] , Data Augmentation [18] , and Batch Normalization [24] . In this manner, a learning model is obtained, and it can predict the Art media in the dataset (test) images with better *Accuracy*. The training parameters for the proposed models have been listed in Table 2.

Table 2. Training parameters of the proposed model.

Hyperparameter	Value
Learning rate	0.0001
Minibatch	16
Loss function	'categorical_crossentropy'
Metrics	'acc', 'loss'
Epochs	500
Callbacks API	ModelChekpoint, EarlyStopping, CVLogger, ReduceLROnPlateau
ModelCheckpoint	Monitor = 'val_loss', save_best_only = True,
	mode ='min'
EarlyStopping	Monitor = 'val_acc', patience = 15, mode = 'max'
CVLogger	'model_history.csv', append = True
ReduceLROnPlateau	Monitor = 'val_los', factor = 0.2,
	patience = 10, min_lr = 0.001
Optimizer	Adam [13]

4   Experiments and Results

The previous description explained that our models are based on three base architectures: VGG16, ResNet50, and Xception. Furthermore, we trained them on two datasets: i) WikiArt, which is a benchmark in art, and ii) and the other one created from the databases of the Louvre museum in France and the Prado museum in Spain. Table 3 compares the accuracy (acc) and loss (loss) of the benchmark models for each dataset (training, validation, and test) and the versions or improvements proposed to the base structure. In the end, an extra model was applied to ResNet50 with a different hyperparameter configuration. Also, the training parameters are shown in the order of millions [M], the training time of the whole process, and in brackets (), the epoch where the best model was obtained. Finally, the training time is recorded in minutes [min].

In all cases, the accuracy maintains homogeneity in the two training and validation sets. This is to be expected because there is a control to avoid model overfitting with the proposed regularization methods and Keras Callbacks to monitor the learning process. With the test information, the baseline models reach an accuracy below the test set. What is interesting here is that the models respond to a generalization of knowledge to other art datasets. In particular, in the first experimental study, the Xception model using a setup in the Dense Classifier stage: `DropOut(0.2)+Dense(5)`, obtained the best classification performance with 74% accuracy. The VGG16 model achieves its best performance with 75% in the second proposed setup. The Dense Classifier stage is composed of a multilayer perceptron: `Dense(128)+Dropout(0.4)+Dense(64)+Dropout(0.2)+Dense(5)`. The decrease in DropOut prevents the CNN from overfitting, and the two fully connected layers improve the accuracy of the model. In the case of the ResNet50 model, the accuracy in the test set results was lower than in

Table 3. Performance of classification models on the WikiArt dataset. The best performances are marked with bold.

Pre-trained CNN base+GlobalAveragePooling2D+Dense Classifier									
CNN	Params [M]	Epoch	Time [min]	loss	acc	val_loss	val_acc	test_loss	test_acc
VGG16	14.7	91 (90)	173	0.5983	0.7832	0.5699	0.7868	0.8017	0.6911
ResNet50	23.6	50 (49)	84	1.2745	0.4981	1.2295	0.5335	1.5442	0.4122
Xception	20.8	64 (64)	136	0.2920	0.8927	0.3470	0.8761	0.6792	**0.7444**
Pre-trained CNN base+Flatten+Dense Classifier (edition 1)									
CNN	Params [M]	Epoch	Time [min]	loss	acc	val_loss	val_acc	test_loss	test_acc
VGG16	17.9	31 (15)	58	0.1900	0.9250	0.4179	0.8661	0.8389	0.7577
ResNet50	36.4	34 (34)	57	0.7408	0.7254	0.7898	0.7009	1.3217	0.5722
Xception	33.7	23 (7)	42	0.2682	0.8984	0.3561	0.8694	0.7967	0.7422
Pre-trained CNN base+Flatten+Dense Classifier (edition 2)									
CNN	Params [M]	Epoch	Time [min]	loss	acc	val_loss	val_acc	test_loss	test_acc
VGG16	17.9	30 (14)	89	0.3313	0.8707	0.4026	0.8527	0.7551	**0.7544**
ResNet50	36.4	51 (47)	107	1.3590	0.3860	1.2926	0.4275	1.4392	0.3822
Xception	33.7	25 (15)	44	0.3437	0.8654	0.3614	0.8862	0.7967	0.7422
Pre-trained CNN base+Flatten+Dense Classifier (edition 3)									
CNN	Params [M]	Epoch	Time [min]	loss	acc	val_loss	val_acc	test_loss	test_acc
VGG16	27.6	11 (28)	68	0.2519	0.9073	0.4029	0.8772	0.8018	0.7566
ResNet50	75	43 (40)	70	1.3408	0.3874	1.2938	0.4263	1.4884	0.3766
Xception	72.3	54 (46)	116	0.1883	0.9350	0.3819	0.8705	0.9642	0.7588
Pre-trained CNN base+Flatten+Dense Classifier (edition 4)									
CNN	Params [M]	Epoch	Time [min]	loss	acc	val_loss	val_acc	test_loss	test_acc
VGG16	27.6	28 (27)	93	0.3748	0.8623	0.3859	0.8605	0.8426	0.7422
ResNet50	75	32 (27)	56	0.8729	0.6687	0.7950	0.6931	1.3006	0.5366
Xception	72.3	16 (16)	67	0.4517	0.8384	0.3698	0.8616	0.7619	0.7477
Pre-trained CNN base+GlobalAveragePooling2D+Dense Classifier (edition 5)									
CNN	Params [M]	Epoch	Time [min]	loss	acc	val_loss	val_acc	test_loss	test_acc
ResNet50	23.7	50 (40)	100	1.0438	0.6024	0.8845	0.6786	1.3535	**0.5422**

the training and validation set. In the edition 5 Dense Classifier stage, it is decided to use the BatchNormalization regularization method to eliminate overfitting. The setup is integrated as follows: `Dense(64)+BatchNormalization()+Dropout(0.5)+Dense(64)+BatchNormalization()+Dropout(0.5)+Dense(5)`. The ResNet50 model achieves acceptable performance with 54% accuracy. Moreover, this proposal has fewer training parameters than edition 1. Figure 4 compares the accuracy and error of the cost function of the training and validation data over time of the proposed models with the best performance.

Figure 5 shows the confusion matrix for the test set. As illustrated, three of the five classes have a good correlation between their original label and their category predicted by the model. Some classes share similarities in color, composition, and texture. Thus, misclassification errors between related classes occur frequently, as with the Drawings and Engravings class.

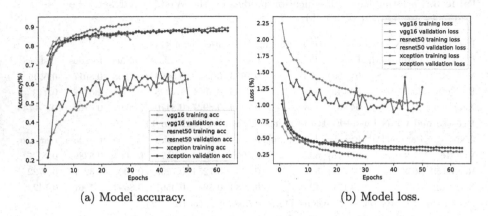

(a) Model accuracy.   (b) Model loss.

Fig. 4. Evaluation of accuracy and loss metrics for training and validation sets.

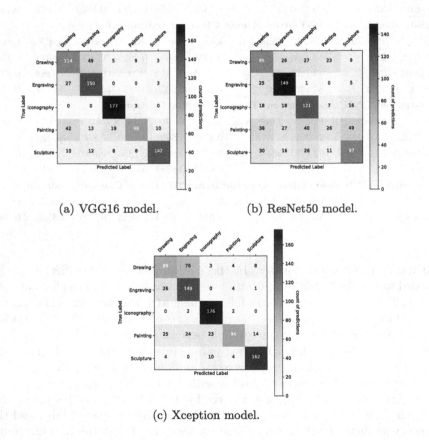

(a) VGG16 model.   (b) ResNet50 model.

(c) Xception model.

Fig. 5. Confusion matrix for the WikiArt dataset.

5   Conclusions and Future Work

This paper proposes an experimental study based on three CNN architectures for Art media classification by considering transfer learning. The features previously achieved in training the CNNs to improve the accuracy of each learning model. The VGG16 model obtained the best overall accuracy with 75% using another dataset integrated with different works from the Del Prado and Louvre museums. Because the learning model needed to be evaluated, a new dataset consisting of 900 images was introduced. The dataset also takes into account the same art classes (Drawings, Engraving, Iconography, Painting, and Sculptures). Furthermore, Data Augmentation, DropOut, and BatchNormalization applied to the dataset have been used in our experimental study. As further research, we are studying the correlation between classes to understand the composition of the work of art. The results show that all the CNNs tested present high correlation in the classification of Engravings and Drawings, due to the similarities of both classes. As future work, we will do an in-depth analysis of the different styles of artworks in some specific categories to extract additional information that reduces the correlation between art media. In addition, we will integrate wavelet analysis to obtain spectral information, which allows us to improve the accuracy of the proposed CNN architectures. Furthermore, we will implement the learning model in hardware to apply it in aerial robotics.

Acknowledgements. This work was founded by CONACYT through the grant "Convocatoria de Ciencia Básica y/o Ciencia de Frontera 2022", project ID 320036.

References

1. Abidin, D.: The effect of derived features on art genre classification with machine learning. Sakarya Univ. J. Sci. **25**(6), 1275–1286
2. Cabrera-Ponce, A.A., Martinez-Carranza, J.: Onboard CNN-based processing for target detection and autonomous landing for MAVs. In: Figueroa Mora, K.M., Anzurez Marín, J., Cerda, J., Carrasco-Ochoa, J.A., Martínez-Trinidad, J.F., Olvera-López, J.A. (eds.) MCPR 2020. LNCS, vol. 12088, pp. 195–208. Springer, Cham (2020). https://doi.org/10.1007/978-3-030-49076-8_19
3. Chollet, F.: Xception: Deep learning with depthwise separable convolutions. CoRR abs/ arXiv: 1610.02357 (2016). https://arxiv.org/abs/1610.02357
4. Chu, W.T., Wu, Y.L.: Deep correlation features for image style classification. In: Proceedings of the 24th ACM International Conference on Multimedia, pp. 402–406 (2016)
5. Chu, W.T., Wu, Y.L.: Image style classification based on learnt deep correlation features. IEEE Trans. Multimedia **20**(9), 2491–2502 (2018)
6. Dataset. https://github.com/JanManuell/Art-Media-Classification--Dataset.git
7. Fortuna-Cervantes, J.M., Ramírez-Torres, M.T., Mejía-Carlos, M., Martínez-Carranza, J., Murguía-Ibarra, J.S.: Texture classification for object detection in aerial navigation using transfer learning and wavelet-based features. In: Martinez-Carranza, J. (ed.) 12th International Micro Air Vehicle Conference, Puebla, México. pp. 210–215 (Nov 2021). https://www.imavs.org/papers/2021/27.pdf, paper no. IMAV2021-27

8. Gao, J., Zhou, H., Zhang, Y.: The performance of two cnn methods in artworks aesthetic feature recognition. In: Proceedings of the 2020 12th International Conference on Machine Learning and Computing, pp. 289–296 (2020)
9. He, K., Zhang, X., Ren, S., Sun, J.: Deep residual learning for image recognition. CoRR abs/ arXiv: 1512.03385 (2015). https://arxiv.org/abs/1512.03385
10. Ibarra-Vazquez, G., Olague, G., Chan-Ley, M., Puente, C., Soubervielle-Montalvo, C.: Brain programming is immune to adversarial attacks: Towards accurate and robust image classification using symbolic learning. Swarm Evol. Comput. **71**, 101059 (2022)
11. Ibarra-Vazquez, G., Olague, G., Puente, C., Chan-Ley, M., Soubervielle-Montalvo, C.: Automated design of accurate and robust image classifiers with brain programming. In: Proceedings of the Genetic and Evolutionary Computation Conference Companion, pp. 1385–1393 (2021)
12. Kandel, I., Castelli, M.: Transfer learning with convolutional neural networks for diabetic retinopathy image classification a review. Appli. Sci. **10**(6), 2021 (2020)
13. Kingma, D.P., Ba, J.: Adam: A method for stochastic optimization. arXiv preprint arXiv:1412.6980 (2014)
14. Kovalev, V.Y., Shishkin, A.G.: Painting style classification using deep neural networks. In: 2020 IEEE 3rd International Conference on Computer and Communication Engineering Technology (CCET), pp. 334–337. IEEE (2020)
15. Lombardi, T.E.: The classification of style in fine-art painting. Pace University (2005)
16. du Louvre, M.: https://collections.louvre.fr/en/
17. Masilamani, G.K., Valli, R.: Art classification with pytorch using transfer learning. In: 2021 International Conference on System, Computation, Automation and Networking (ICSCAN), pp. 1–5. IEEE (2021)
18. Mikołajczyk, A., Grochowski, M.: Data augmentation for improving deep learning in image classification problem. In: 2018 international interdisciplinary PhD workshop (IIPhDW), pp. 117–122. IEEE (2018)
19. Olague, G., Ibarra-Vázquez, G., Chan-Ley, M., Puente, C., Soubervielle-Montalvo, C., Martinez, A.: A deep genetic programming based methodology for art media classification robust to adversarial perturbations. In: Bebis, G., et al. (eds.) ISVC 2020. LNCS, vol. 12509, pp. 68–79. Springer, Cham (2020). https://doi.org/10.1007/978-3-030-64556-4_6
20. del Prado, M.N.: https://www.museodelprado.es/coleccion/obras-de-arte
21. Research, G.: https://colab.research.google.com/
22. Rodriguez, C.S., Lech, M., Pirogova, E.: Classification of style in fine-art paintings using transfer learning and weighted image patches. In: 2018 12th International Conference on Signal Processing and Communication Systems (ICSPCS), pp. 1–7. IEEE (2018)
23. Rojas-Aranda, J.L., Nunez-Varela, J.I., Cuevas-Tello, J.C., Rangel-Ramirez, G.: Fruit classification for retail stores using deep learning. In: Figueroa Mora, K.M., Anzurez Marín, J., Cerda, J., Carrasco-Ochoa, J.A., Martínez-Trinidad, J.F., Olvera-López, J.A. (eds.) MCPR 2020. LNCS, vol. 12088, pp. 3–13. Springer, Cham (2020). https://doi.org/10.1007/978-3-030-49076-8_1
24. Rumelhart, D.E., Hinton, G.E., Williams, R.J.: Learning representations by back-propagating errors. Nature **323**(6088), 533–536 (1986)
25. Simonyan, K., Zisserman, A.: Very deep convolutional networks for large-scale image recognition. arXiv preprint arXiv:1409.1556 (2014)
26. Srivastava, N.: Improving neural networks with dropout, vol. 182(566), p. 7. University of Toronto (2013)

Medical Applications of Pattern Recognition

Hadamard Layer to Improve Semantic Segmentation in Medical Images

Angello Hoyos$^{(\boxtimes)}$ (ID) and Mariano Rivera (ID)

Centro de Investigación en Matemáticas, A.C., 36023 Guanajuato, Gto., Mexico
{angello.hoyos,mrivera}@cimat.mx

Abstract. Interest in medical image segmentation has grown in the last decade due to advances in machine learning. A recent breakthrough, the Hadamard Layer, is a new simple, computationally efficient way to improve results in semantic segmentation tasks. This layer is a free parameter that requires training. Therefore it does not increase the number of model parameters, and the extra computational cost is marginal. Experimental results show that the Hadamard layer substantially improves the performance of the investigated models in two different organ datasets, liver, and lung. The specific loss function allows a stable and fast training convergence.

Keywords: Semantic segmentation · Hadamard codification · Conditional generative network

1 Introduction

Medical image segmentation seeks to make anatomical or pathological structure changes in MRI images; it often plays a crucial role in computer-aided diagnosis and innovative medicine due to the significant improvement in diagnostic efficiency and accuracy. A popular medical imaging segmentation challenge that is gaining more and more attention is the Medical Segmentation Benchmark (LiTS) [1] includes brain, lung, heart, hippocampus, liver, pancreas, and prostate segmentation.

On the other hand, in computer vision, semantic segmentation is a clear example of an image-to-image translation problem where an input image is into a corresponding output image. Each pixel from an input image is assigned to a class label. We predict an output image that is less complex than the input, even if the input image is a medical image. Recently, this task has proposed different strategies to solve this problem using convolutional neural networks (CNN), i.e., [12,16]. Another alternative to solved semantic segmentation using CNN is Conditional Generative Adversarial Networks (cGAN), particularly, Pix2Pix, proposed by Isola et al. [9], which was the first demonstration of cGANs successfully generating nearly discrete segmentation labels rather than realistic images.

In this work, we use the Hadamard layer. This layer enforces each class label to be encoded to have an equal number of $+1$s and -1s, unlike the classic one-hot encoding. We increase the Hamming distance between the class labels and obtain better segmentation results. Such robustness is a consequence of the increment of the number of required bits to change in order to change an assigned class. This is, it is necessary to change the response in a bin to flip the assigned class in one-hot encoding. On the other hand, using the Hadamard encoding requires modifying half of the bins to change a label. In this way, the network requires a more distributed activation to produce a label. That also explains the susceptibility to adversary attacks by neural networks in classification tasks.

We present experiments on modified cGANs to evaluate the performance of this new layer. In those experiments, we noted a performance increment without sacrificing training time.

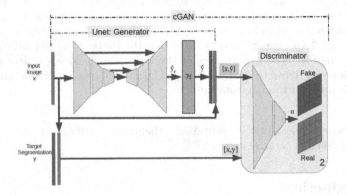

Fig. 1. Shows a Hadamard Layer embedded in the generator of a Pix2Pix architecture.

2   Related Work

2.1   Semantic Segmentation

Several convolutional NN architectures for semantic segmentation have been reported in recent years. Among them are architectures like UNet [13], initially developed for BioMedical Image Segmentation. Since its publication in 2015, variants of the UNet have emerged for such purpose. Pix2Pix models are computationally efficient methods that produce good-quality segmentation. Pix2Pix consists of a Generative Adversarial Networks (GANs) strategy for training a UNet. The advantage of UNet is its simplicity: it consists of a single UNet. We chose the Pix2Pix model to introduce our Hadamard Layer in this work. Thus, we evaluate the performance impact of the proposed Hadamard Layer in different implementations, such as the classic UNet, the ResUNet, the VGG-UNet, and the UNet3+ variants. We briefly describe such variants below.

A UNet comprises two stages: a contraction path (encoder) and an expansion one (decoder). The encoder captures the image's context using convolutional and max pooling layers. The decoder transform combines and expands the extracted features to construct the desired output. ResUNet [4] takes the performance gain of Residual networks and uses it with the UNet. ResUNet was initially presented for road extraction from high-resolution aerial images in remote sensing image analysis. Later, it was adopted by researchers for multiple other applications, such as brain tumor segmentation, human image segmentation, and many more. Although this is a capable network, it has a slightly large number of parameters. VGG-UNet [14] is another variant of UNet model that combines a pretrained backbone as the encoder. In this proposal, the decoder consists of five up-sampling blocks and uses a symmetric expanding path to enable precise localization segmentation to detect corrosions from steel bridges and cracks from rubber bearings under limited conditions. More recently, UNet3+ [8] was reported as the best variant for image segmentation: full-scale skip connections incorporate low-level details with high-level semantics from feature maps in different scales and full-scale deep supervision that helps to learn hierarchical representations from the full-scale aggregated feature maps. The growing popularity of the UNet3+ is due to its superior performance compared with other reported variants such as Attention UNet [10], PSPNet [18], and DeepLab [3], which were considered SOTA.

Despite the advances mentioned for the semantic segmentation problem, these solutions still need improvement. Our work proposes a general mechanism that improves the segmentation computed with neural networks. To understand it better, we will first introduce the related theory.

2.2   Linear Error-Correction Codes

Information transmission is a well-understood area of mathematics where the central idea is to increase the Hamming distance between codewords by adding redundancy to a message to ensure that even if noise flips some random bits, the message is still legible. The solution to this problem is using linear error-correcting codes like Hamming codes [5] or Reed-Solomon codes [11]. In this work, we selected a particular case of Reed-Solomon codes, the Hadamard codes, for our proposal.

We recognize that Hadamard codes are suitable to be incorporated into neural network architectures, given previous works that show the effectiveness of Hadamard codes in the classification of deep features [17] and as a defense strategy against multiple adversary attacks [7]. Recently, this approach has been explored in semantic segmentation in the CELEBA-HQ dataset [6], and we are extending the scope of this work by testing with medical imaging.

Hadamard codes are easy to construct; assume we need codes of length 2^k, or in other words, there are at most 2^k possible classes in our segmentation problem; they can be fewer. The Hadamard codes are the rows of the matrix H_{2^k}, defined recursively as

$$H_{2^k} = \begin{bmatrix} H_{2^{k-1}} & H_{2^{k-1}} \\ H_{2^{k-1}} & -H_{2^{k-1}} \end{bmatrix} \tag{1}$$

with

$$H_2 = \begin{bmatrix} 1 & 1 \\ 1 & -1 \end{bmatrix} \tag{2}$$

The above procedure for computing Hadamard matrices is named Silvester's construction and produces symmetric matrices [15]. For example, using this construction for eight classes, we have

$$H_8 = \begin{bmatrix} 1 & 1 & 1 & 1 & 1 & 1 & 1 & 1 \\ 1 & -1 & 1 & -1 & 1 & -1 & 1 & -1 \\ 1 & 1 & -1 & -1 & 1 & 1 & -1 & -1 \\ 1 & -1 & -1 & 1 & 1 & -1 & -1 & 1 \\ 1 & 1 & 1 & 1 & -1 & -1 & -1 & -1 \\ 1 & -1 & 1 & -1 & -1 & 1 & -1 & 1 \\ 1 & 1 & -1 & -1 & -1 & -1 & 1 & 1 \\ 1 & -1 & -1 & 1 & -1 & 1 & 1 & -1 \end{bmatrix} \tag{3}$$

In the examples above, we can observe that any pair of codes in a H_n Hadamard matrix are at a distance 2^{k-1}; this property allows us to define a more demarcated space between classes, which we consider essential for image segmentation.

3   Methodology

Figure 1 illustrates the use of the *Hadamard Layer* in the UNet model to achieve a segmentation task. The Hadamard Layer consists of two operations. First, multiply by $H^\top$ the UNet stage output's $\hat{y}_c \in \mathbb{R}^{H \times W \times 2^k}$. Second, to apply a softmax activation to enforce, even more, the output $\hat{y}$ to be more informative and closer to the one-hot code:

$$\hat{y} = \mathcal{H}(\hat{y}_c)$$
$$= \mathrm{softmax}(H^\top \hat{y}_c). \tag{4}$$

A valuable property of Hadamard matrices H is that they are orthogonal: $H H^\top = n I_n$; where n is the order, I_n is the $n \times n$ identity matrix and H^T is the transpose of H. Since H is orthogonal, y would be closer to a one-hot code if y_c is similar to a Hadamard code; *i.e.*, y_c would have all its entries activated.

Now, we introduce another essential ingredient for having successful training: the loss functions for the cGAN. Then, let (x, y) be the input data for our UNet, $\hat{y}$ is the predicted segmentation, and α the output of the Discriminator (matrix with dimensions $h \times w$) of the full cGAN. Each element α_{ij} can be understood as the probability that the support region of the analyzed pair, (x, y) or $(x, \hat{y})$, is real. Then, we use the Discriminator loss given by

$$L_D(\hat{y}) = S(\mathbf{1}|\alpha) + S(\mathbf{0}|\hat{\alpha}) \tag{5}$$

where α is the discriminator response to the real pair (x, y), and $\hat{\alpha}$ to the predicted pair $(x, \hat{y})$, and S is the cross-entropy loss

$$S(\hat{z}|z) = -\frac{1}{N} \sum_k z_k \log \hat{z}_k \tag{6}$$

On the other hand, the loss function for the Generator is

$$L_G(\hat{z}) \quad = \quad S(\mathbf{1}|\hat{\alpha}) \; + \; \Lambda_1 S(\hat{y}|y) \; + \; \Lambda_2 MAE(\hat{y}, y) \; + \; \Lambda_3 MAE(\hat{y}_c, y_c); \tag{7}$$

where the parameters $(\Lambda_1, \Lambda_2, \Lambda_3) = (1000, 100, 250)$ weight the relative contributions of the loss terms, and

$$MAE(\hat{z}, z) = \sum_k |\hat{z}_k - z_k| \tag{8}$$

is the mean absolute error.

Note that the loss (7) includes four terms. The first two terms are the classical one: binary-cross-entropy loss to reward that the generator manages to deceive the discriminator, and a multi-class cross-entropy loss to encourage the predicted segmentation probabilistic map $\hat{y}$ to be similar to the one-hot encoded ground truth y. The third additional loss term reinforces the segmentation by including a L_1 penalty for the differences between $\hat{y}$ and y. The last loss term promotes enforcing the input to the Hadamard Layer be similar to the Hadamard code of the corresponding class. We found that the last two loss terms greatly contribute to the stability and convergence ratio of the entire cGAN. In this way, we train our network to compute a *realistic* mask image and return the correct classes.

4   Experiments and Results

We evaluate the Hadamard Layer in two medical segmentation tasks. For this purpose, we use the Medical Segmentation Decathlon (MSD) Lung Task dataset [1] and the Liver Tumor Segmentation Benchmark (LiTS) dataset [2]. We separated the images into 1,400 and 18,000 for training images and 240 and 1,200 test images for the MSD and LiTS datasets, respectively. We investigated the performance improvement of the Hadamard Layers using different variants of the Pix2Pix model. Although we have limited our study to Pix2Pix models, one can introduce the Hadamard Layer in other reported architectures for semantic segmentation. However, such a study is outside the scope of this work. Herein, we investigate the Pix2Pix variants using the UNet, the ResUNet, the VGG-UNet, and the UNet3+ models. Each variant follows a training using one-hot and Hadamard coding for class labels under the same number of steps.

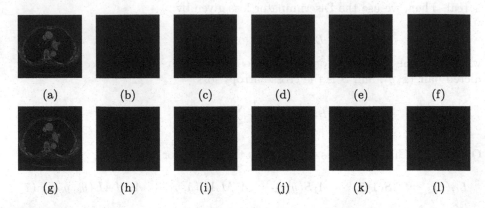

Fig. 2. Shows some examples of test images from the LiTS dataset: (a–g) Input image and (b–h) target segmentation. The reminder columns depict the results: (c–d) UNet model, (e–f) UNet 3+, (i–j) VGG-UNet, and (k–l) ResUNet; where columns (c, e, i, k) correspond to models trained with one-hot codification and columns (d, f, j, l) to models trained with Hadamard layer codification. The red color represents the liver class. (Color figure online)

Figures 2, 3 depict examples of predicted segmentation for the evaluated models and datasets. We compute the segmentation maps M with

$$M(r, c) = \operatorname*{argmax}_{k} \hat{y}_k(r, c) \tag{9}$$

where $C_k \in 0, 1, 2, ..., K$ are class index in the matrix codes, (r, c) are the pixel at coordinates. We can observe the differences in segmentation for each model in Figs. 2, 3. In columns d, f, j, and l the models that include the Hadamard Layer, we can notice a more detailed segmentation when compared with the respective results in columns c, e, i, and k, the models trained only with one-hot encoding.

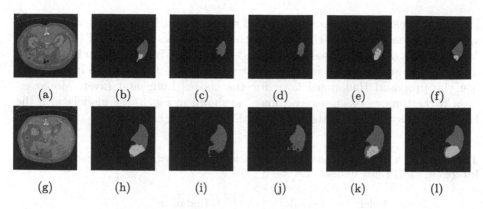

Fig. 3. Shows some examples of test images from the LiTS dataset: (a–g) Input image and (b–h) target segmentation. The reminder columns depict the results: (c–d) UNet model, (e–f) UNet 3+, (i–j) VGG-UNet, and (k–l) ResUNet; where columns (c, e, i, k) correspond to models trained with one-hot codification and columns (d, f, j, l) to models trained with Hadamard layer codification. Red color represents the liver class and green color the tumor/lesion class. (Color figure online)

Tables 1 and 2 resume the metrics, pixel accuracy, and mean class IoU of the predicted segmentation for 240 and 1,400 test images. In most cases, a Hadamard Layer gets better results than one-hot codification in these two metrics. Indeed, the models UNet 3+ and VGG-UNet show a more noticeable improvement in MSD dataset; meanwhile, ResUNet and VGG-UNet show a better improvement in LiTS dataset when using the Hadamard Layer.

Table 1. Pixel accuracy and mean IoU between one-hot and Hadamard codification: MSD Lung dataset.

Model	Pixel Acc.		Class IoU	
	One-Hot	Hadamard	One-Hot	Hadamard
UNet	0.9983	**0.9987**	0.4991	**0.5073**
ResUNet	0.9983	**0.9985**	0.4994	**0.5295**
VGG-UNet	0.9982	**0.9986**	0.4996	**0.5467**
UNet3+	0.9983	0.9983	0.4992	**0.5296**

Table 2. Pixel accuracy and mean IoU between one-hot and Hadamard codification: LiTS dataset.

Model	Pixel Acc.		Class IoU	
	One-Hot	Hadamard	One-Hot	Hadamard
UNet	0.9300	**0.9993**	0.3093	**0.3856**
ResUNet	0.9438	**0.9764**	0.3635	**0.5260**
VGG-UNet	0.9301	**0.9650**	0.3142	**0.4891**
UNet3+	0.9300	**0.9313**	0.3104	0.3104

Next, Tables 3 and 4 present detailed results for each model. We can observe some consistency in the IoU values for the classes Background and Lung in the MSD dataset and the classes Background, Liver, and Tumor/Lesion in the LiTS dataset. Meanwhile, there is a quantitative difference favoring the models that use the proposed Hadamard layer for the classes Lung and Liver. Moreover, even if the tumor class has zero values, as shown in Fig. 3, the models with the Hadamard layer give a better segmentation in some examples.

Table 3. Each class IoU between one-hot and Hadamard class codification for test Images in MSD Lung dataset.

Model	One-Hot		Hadamard	
	Background	Lung	Background	Lung
UNet	0.9982	0.0000	0.9982	**0.0164**
ResUNet	0.9982	0.0000	**0.9985**	**0.0606**
VGG-UNet	0.9982	0.0000	**0.9985**	**0.0948**
UNet3+	0.9982	0.0000	**0.9983**	**0.0608**

Table 4. Each class IoU between one-hot and Hadamard class codification for test Images in LiTS dataset.

Model	One-Hot			Hadamard		
	Background	Liver	Tumor	Background	Liver	Tumor
UNet	0.9993	0.00	0.00	0.9993	0.00	0.00
ResUNet	0.9407	0.14	0.00	**0.9784**	**0.59**	0.00
VGG-UNet	0.9320	0.01	0.00	**0.9679**	**0.49**	0.00
UNet3+	0.9313	0.00	0.00	0.9313	0.00	0.00

5   Conclusions and Future Work

We proposed the use of the Hadamard Layer as a simple and computationally efficient way to improve results in medical semantic segmentation tasks. This new layer is constant, so it does not increase the number of parameters in a model. As test architecture, we use different variants of the Pix2Pix model for medical datasets MSD and LiTS. The results show that the new Hadamard layer substantially improves the performance of the investigated models. The metrics evaluated are the simple pixel accuracy (number of pixels correctly classified) and the Intersection Over Union (IOU). The best performance of the intervened models can be explained by the Hadamard layer forcing the network to produce an encoding of the classes so that all bins are active. Consequently, the network computation is more distributed. In a sort that the Hadamard layer requires that to change the predicted class, it is necessary to modify 2^{k-1} bins, assuming

k bins in the encoding. On the other hand, changing the predicted class in one-hot encoding is enough to modify a single bin (decrease the response of the most significant bin or increase the response of any other.). Our future work will extend our evaluation to other databases and different architectures and assess the performance of implicit coding against adversary attacks.

Acknowledgments. This work was partly supported by the CONACYT (Mexico); Grant CB 2017-2018-A1-S-43858.

References

1. Antonelli, M., et al.: The medical segmentation decathlon. Nat. Commun. **13**(1), 4128 (2022)
2. Bilic, P., et al.: The liver tumor segmentation benchmark (LiTs). Med. Image Anal. **84**, 102680 (2023)
3. Chen, L.-C., Zhu, Y., Papandreou, G., Schroff, F., Adam, H.: Encoder-decoder with atrous separable convolution for semantic image segmentation. In: Ferrari, V., Hebert, M., Sminchisescu, C., Weiss, Y. (eds.) ECCV 2018. LNCS, vol. 11211, pp. 833–851. Springer, Cham (2018). https://doi.org/10.1007/978-3-030-01234-2_49
4. Diakogiannis, F.I., Waldner, F., Caccetta, P., Wu, C.: ResUNet-a: a deep learning framework for semantic segmentation of remotely sensed data. ISPRS J. Photogramm. Remote. Sens. **162**, 94–114 (2020)
5. Hamming, R.W.: Error detecting and error correcting codes. Bell Syst. Tech. J. **29**(2), 147–160 (1950)
6. Hoyos, A., Rivera, M.: Hadamard layer to improve semantic segmentation. In: IEEE International Conference on Acoustics, Speech and Signal Processing (preprint arXiv:4749279) (2023, to appear)
7. Hoyos, A., Ruiz, U., Chavez, E.: Hadamard's defense against adversarial examples. IEEE Access **9**, 118324–118333 (2021)
8. Huang, H., et al.: UNet 3+: a full-scale connected UNet for medical image segmentation. In: ICASSP 2020–2020 IEEE International Conference on Acoustics, Speech and Signal Processing (ICASSP), pp. 1055–1059. IEEE (2020)
9. Isola, P., Zhu, J.Y., Zhou, T., Efros, A.A.: Image-to-image translation with conditional adversarial networks. In: Proceedings of the IEEE Conference on Computer Vision and Pattern Recognition, pp. 1125–1134 (2017)
10. Oktay, O., et al.: Attention U-Net: learning where to look for the pancreas. arXiv preprint arXiv:1804.03999 (2018)
11. Reed, I.S., Solomon, G.: Polynomial codes over certain finite fields. J. Soc. Ind. Appl. Math. **8**(2), 300–304 (1960)
12. Reyes-Figueroa, A., Rivera, M.: W-Net: a convolutional neural network for retinal vessel segmentation. In: Pattern Recognition: 13th Mexican Conference, MCPR 2021, Mexico City, Mexico, 23–26 June 2021, Proceedings, pp. 355–368 (2021)
13. Ronneberger, O., Fischer, P., Brox, T.: U-Net: convolutional networks for biomedical image segmentation. In: Navab, N., Hornegger, J., Wells, W.M., Frangi, A.F. (eds.) MICCAI 2015. LNCS, vol. 9351, pp. 234–241. Springer, Cham (2015). https://doi.org/10.1007/978-3-319-24574-4_28
14. Shi, J., et al.: Improvement of damage segmentation based on pixel-level data balance using VGG-UNet. Appl. Sci. **11**(2), 518 (2021)

15. Sylvester, J.: Thoughts on inverse orthogonal matrices, simultaneous sign successions, and tessellated pavements in two or more colours, with applications to newton's rule, ornamental tile-work, and the theory of numbers. London, Edinburgh, Dublin Philos. Mag. J. Sci. **34**(232), 461–475 (1867)
16. Ulku, I., Akagündüz, E.: A survey on deep learning-based architectures for semantic segmentation on 2D images. Appl. Artif. Intell. **36**(1), 1–45 (2022)
17. Yang, S., Luo, P., Loy, C.C., Shum, K.W., Tang, X.: Deep representation learning with target coding. In: Twenty-Ninth AAAI Conference on Artificial Intelligence (2015)
18. Zhao, H., Shi, J., Qi, X., Wang, X., Jia, J.: Pyramid scene parsing network. In: Proceedings of the IEEE Conference on Computer Vision and Pattern Recognition, pp. 2881–2890 (2017)

Patterns in Genesis of Breast Cancer Tumor

Moises León⑩ and Matías Alvarado$^{(\boxtimes)}$⑩

Departamento de Computación, Centro de Investigación y de Estudios Avanzados del
IPN, México City, Mexico
moises.leon@cinvestav.mx, matias@cs.cinvestav.mx

Abstract. In this paper we use the genetic network (GN) structural
analysis for identifying the plausible main genes in breast cancer. The
interaction and mutual information among them could detemine the
patterns of genesis in brest cancer primary tumors. The analyzed data
is from biopsies in the Genomic Data Commons (GDC) and the Gene
Expression Omnibus (GEO). ARACNE algorithm is applied to find out
the correlation matrix of gene expressions in biopsies, thereafter the GN
is constructed. The each node-gene and the weighted links between them
allow for genes importance in the GN. The gene ranking is obtained with
both the gene-node degree and the mutual information or correlation values between each other gene. To get reliable conclusions, the single GN
analysis is hundred times replicated and averaging the results. This way,
to find out patterns of shared expression through genes in breast cancer
primary tumor, an initial data statistical analysis is practiced.

Keywords: Patterns of Genetic Interaction · Breast Cancer Primary
Tumor · Network Structure Analysis

1 Antecedents

Cancer difficult public health challenge worldwide, provoked 1,086,743 deaths
in Mexico until 2020; in 2020, 97,323 people died from malignant tumors, 7,880
of breast cancer, the 8% off total [1]. The World Health Organization (WHO)
recognizes breast cancer as the most common in the world, with more than
2.2 million cases in 2020 [2]. Breast cancer is vigorous and makes metastasis in
bone, liver, lung and lymph nodes, the most frequently [3]. It happens as the
first, second, third or even more metastasis in these and other organs like brain,
colon or stomach. Commonly, to study cancer and metastasis is with clinical
experiments, *in vitro* and *in situ*, in oncology laboratories [4]. This practice is
money expensive and highly time consuming. Last decades ago, the alternatives
of mathematical modeling and algorithmic simulation, *in silico*, advantages the

Thanks to Consejo Nacional de Ciencia y Tecnología de México, CONACyT: Project
A1-S-20037, Matías Alvarado principal investigator; and the Moises León Pinedas'
Master Scholarship CVU 1144833.

A. Y. Rodríguez-González et al. (Eds.): MCPR 2023, LNCS 13902, pp. 191–200, 2023.
https://doi.org/10.1007/978-3-031-33783-3_18

understanding of cancer and metastasis diseases [5]; as well, algorithmic tools have strongly diminished the cost of cancer trials and studies [6]. In this paper we use the ARACNE algorithm, GN structural analysis and statistical analysis to get patterns from relevant genes concerned with breast cancer deployment.

Around 63,500 genes constitute the human genome, and 19,969 off them could protein coding [7]. The level of each gene expression and the interactions between pairs of genes determine the anatomic and functional profile of organs in the body [8]; So, the color and form of hair, eyes and skin; as well, the characteristics of height, bones and muscles and so on. All of these correlations of pairs of genes shape the GN of a being alive. Very important, the genes' mutual information induces the eventual arise of illness. We pay attention on the matrix of genes expressions that shape the GN concerned to: the breast cancer primary tumor, its first metastasis on lymph nodes, and healthy tissues for comparative study.

2   Material and Methods

2.1   Gene Expressions and Mutual Information

We use the Algorithm for the Reconstruction of Accurate Cellular Networks (ARACNe) [9], an information theory based algorithms [5], that is applied on the set of biopsies for GN inferring. The ARACNE multicore version [10] is the option in front of the millions of computing operations needed, since the amount of expressions interactions. In information theory (IT), entropy $S(t)$ is used to estimate the probability of the system as the sum of the probability $p_i(t)$ of each state i of the system; the $S(t)$ equation is (1):

$$S(t) = -\kappa \sum_i p_i(t) log p_i(t);$$

(1)

κ is the Boltzman constant. For calculating the mutual information (MI) between pairs of genes, we use the expression of every gene joint to the interaction between pairs of them, g_i, g_j, with i, j positive integers; the MI equation is (2):

$$I(g_i, g_j) = S(g_i) + S(g_j) - S(g_i, g_j).$$

(2)

With N genes and M samples the joint probability distribution (JPD) of the system [9] is quantified by:

$$P(\{g_i\}_1^N) = \frac{1}{M}[-\sum_i^N \phi_i(g_i) - \sum_{i,j}^N \phi_{ij}(g_i g_j) - \sum_{i,j,k}^N \phi_{ijk}(g_i g_j g_k)];$$

(3)

ϕ is the potential of interaction, not null if genes stay in interaction.

GDC is a popular platform to search and download cancer data [11]. GEO is a public genomics data repository [12]. Both frames accept array and sequence based data, and provide tools for users query and download files with information and data about experiments and curated gene expression profiles. 130 samples data from GEO and GDC are arranged for applying ARACNE and generate the GN of breast cancer primary tumor. The GEO files are txt format with information on title, serial number, type of sample tissue, normalized method, and the each gene transcripts per million (TPM) of biopsies. The GDC files comprises mRNA quantification, and the sequence of analysis to measures gene level expression from raw data. These values are annotated with the gene bio type in a .tsv file. The gene symbol abbreviates the scientific gene name, and both are used in the standard dictionary of genes, created for not depend on the GEO or GDC nomenclature.

DNA microarrays allow us to visualize the potential expression of all genes within a cell population or tissue sample revealing the *transcriptome*. This type of data is called GEP (gene expression profiling) that provides a comprehensive picture of the pattern of gene expression in a biological sample. GEP is growing adopted as a decision making tool in the clinical setting [13], particularly in research concerned to cancer. Mostly GEP is measured in transcripts per million (TPM), $\frac{1}{1,000,000}$. The amount of TPM quantifies the level of expression of every gene, and is the ratio of RNA molecules in the RNA-seq gene sample. The higher the TPM value the more expressed is the gen. To better handle the TPM information of genes in biopsies it is input to the function logarithm in base 2, log_2. The GPE values are the specific ARACNE input; output are a *.sif* and *.sort* files with the MI of pairs of genes. They constitute the matrix of expression of the set of genes. In the *.sort* file the data are in MI descending order; in the *.sif* file the first elements are the more connected with the other genes and so on in descending order of nodes' degree. From these ordered information the weighted GN is generated.

2.2 Genetic Networks from Matrix Correlation

Inspired by biology, complex networks are a mathematical modeling tool for studying complex systems in disciplines like biology, medicine, or sociology [14]. The analysis of these networks allow to discover patterns and relationships between the elements of the system, to understand the underlying processes and the behavior of the system.

A key property of each network node is its degree or number of links with other nodes: k_i denotes the degree of the ith node. The network average degree is $k = \frac{1}{N}\sum_{i=1}^{N} k_i$ [14], with N the number of nodes. Moreover, the distribution of probability of degree, $p(k)$, is the probability that a randomly selected node in the network has degree k. Since $p(k)$ is a probability, $\sum_{k=1}^{\infty} p_k = 1$.

The degree distribution is $p_k = \frac{N_k}{N}$, with N_k is the number of degree-k nodes. Degree distribution is a central concept in network theory: the calculation of key network properties requires to know p_k, as will shown the analysis in Sect. 3.

Specific complex networks are GNs. The system is the genome and the elements are genes and proteins being expressed. GN have been used to identify biomarkers under certain medical conditions for discovering new drugs and treatments for diseases [15]. Also, to understand the behavior of gene expression, metabolism, development and evolution [16].

We use GN structural analysis to identify the interaction between genes-nodes: the degree of each node and the centralities of the GN corresponding to the primary breast cancer tumor are obtained. For plausible conclusions on gene regulations, the ARACNE output is interpreted regarding the properties of GNs, e.g., genes-nodes degree and their distribution of probability [17]. Software *NetworkX* deserves for manipulating the GN structure[1].

3   Results: GN of Breast Cancer Primary Tumor

3.1   Single GN Topology

With the input information of $N = 19,939$ genes from $M = 130$ samples, the ARACNE output is twofold, the *.sif* and *.sort* files. Size 4.3 GB each with 189,402,801 pair genes connections; 73.43 min of computer processing per simulation[2] In [19] the computational complexity of this process is analyzed.

The data processing inequality (DPI) establishes that if a pair of (individuals) genes g_1 and g_3 interact only through another gene g_2, occurs that $I(g1, g3) \leq min\{I(g1, g2), I(g2, g3)\}$ [9].

Therefore, the smaller less important MI values come from indirect genetic interactions. With this premise and to avoid unnecessary operations, several pruning thresholds were applied over the output file in order to obtain a thin file with the relevant information to generate the GN. For the statistical analysis in the next section, to generate the GN the same threshold is applied each time on the ARACNe output file. This way the set of GNs from each simulation, got after pruning each different complete expression matrice, deserves a representative sample set.

Once the pruning threshold choice, GN structural analysis is carried out for identifying genes with the highest degree alongside the pairs of genes with the highest MI. In Fig. 1 the GN obtained is shown: is not fully connected but with several components, and with the following centralities:

- Average degree (K): $104.9288 \approx 105$
- Clustering coefficient (C): 0.3929388955996692

The GN degree distribution looks like similar to scale-free with heavy tail [14], see Fig. 2. Thus, GN has huge amount of nodes with low degree; and, too few nodes each with huge degree. Formally, GN is power-law degree distribution or a scale-free network with negative sign exponent, this mean that is a network whose degree distribution follows a power law, at least asymptotically That is, the fraction p_k of nodes in the network having k connections to other nodes goes for large values of k as $p_k \sim k^{-\gamma}, \gamma > 0$.

---

[1] NetworkX is a Python library [18], quite popular for complex networks studies.

[2] The used device is with RAM 16 GB, processor 11th Gen Intel®Core[TM] i7-11800H @ 2.30GHz x 16, disk 1.0 TB, OS Ubuntu 22.04 LTS of 64 bits.

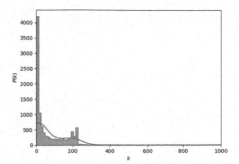

Fig. 1. GN of genes with the highest MI in breast cancer primary tumor.

Fig. 2. Degree distribution of genes with MI greater than 0.29

The genes in the breast cancer primary tumor that could be the most relevants are 10 pairs with the highest MI, see Table 1.

Table 1. First 10 pairs of genes with highest MI of the primary tumor single GN.

Tag	Gene 1	Gene 2	MI
1	OR10P1	PCDHA1	0.771405
2	KRTAP63	OR10P1	0.771405
3	KRTAP202	OR10P1	0.771405
4	KLK9	OR10P1	0.771405
5	GLT6D1	OR10P1	0.771405
6	CELA3B	FAM90A10P	0.771405
7	AL353572.3	OR10P1	0.771405
8	AC138647.1	CELA3B	0.771405
9	AC008397.1	OR10P1	0.771395
10	CELA3B	MT1HL1	0.771377

3.2 Statistical Analysis on GN Topology

To get reliable conclusions, on the results of 100 simulations a statistical analysis is practiced, see the Fig. 3, regarding the next steps:

– input data to ARACNE to obtain the whole correlation matrix.
– prune the previous matrix regarding the desired threshold.
– build and analysis of the GN
– The results of individual topology analysis is collected and averaged.

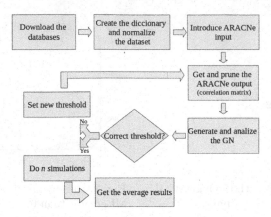

Fig. 3. Process to generate GN simulations.

The GN average nodes-degree and centrality of nodes are the next:

- Average degree of nodes: 168.007057
- Average centrality of the nodes: 0.437582

Continuing with the statistical analysis, the 10 genes with the highest degree and their average are shown in Table 2.

Table 2. The highest average node degree in the primary tumor of hundred GN.

Tag	Degree	Gene symbol	Average
1	274800	CELA3B	2748
2	274200	ADIG	2742
3	272700	ARPC4TTLL3	2727
4	271700	AC026316.4	2717
5	271300	BPIFB3	2713
6	268900	AC012309.1	2689
7	267600	AVP	2676
8	266600	CATSPERZ	2666
9	265400	AC010197.2	2654
10	264900	FAM237A	2649

Continuing with the work done in [19], the same process is applied to carry out a statistical analysis of the GN of metastases in lymphatic nodes and in Table 3 a comparison between the first 10 genes is shown with a higher degree of each type of tissue.

Table 3. Comparison of the 10 genes with the highest degree in the GN of primary tumor tissues in breast cancer and the first metastasis in lymph nodes.

Gene symbol	Place in primary tumor tissue	Place in first metastasis tissue
CELA3B	1	no present
ADIG	2	no present
ARPC4TTLL3	3	no present
AC026316.4	4	no present
BPIFB3	5	no present
AC012309.1	6	no present
AVP	7	no present
CATSPERZ	8	no present
AC010197.2	9	no present
FAM237A	10	no present
EPS8L1	no present	1
PPM1B	1434	2
FGA	8943	3
SLC13A3	no present	4
PKM2	no present	5
EYA2	no present	6
CYORF15B	no present	7
TNK2	no present	8
TPD52L3	3534	9
LHFPL3	96	10

3.3 Plausible Main Genes of Breast Cancer Primary Tumor

CELA3B: The gene with the highest degree. In addition, it also takes $6^{th}, 8^{th}$ and 10th position joint to others in the list of the 10 pairs of genes with the highest MI. Was discover in 1975, and used to identify problems of pancreatitis with diabetes and pancreatic adenocarcinoma [20]. This gene appeared in a whole-transcriptome association study to identify novel candidate susceptibility genes for pancreatic cancer. And, although this gene is not directly associated with breast cancer, it is associated with the detection and appearance of cancer.

AVP: The 7th gene with the highest degree. This gene encodes a member of the vasopressin/oxytocin family and preproprotein that is proteolytically processed to generate multiple protein products. Breast cancer cells abnormally express vasopressin (AVP) and its receptors. The effect of AVP is largely orchestrated through its downstream signaling and by receptor-mediated endocytosis (RME), in which Dynamin 2 (Dyn2) plays an integral role in vesicle closure [21].

FAM237A: The tenth highest grade gene. Predicted to be integral component of membrane. In [22], as proof of concept, a set of G protein-coupled receptors (GPCRs) were examined and was identified the FAM237A protein as a specific activator of GPR83, a GPCR implicated in central nervous system and T-cell function regulatory. Remember that T cells are part of the immune system and are formed from stem cells in the bone marrow. They help protect the body from infection and fight cancer.

PCDHA1: This gene, with OR10P1, have the highest MI in the GN of primary tumor of breast cancer. It is a member of the protocadherin alpha gene cluster, one of three related gene clusters tandemly linked on chromosome five that demonstrate an unusual genomic organization similar to that of B-cell and T-cell receptor gene clusters. In [23] aimed to explore cyclophosphamide (Cytoxan) response-associated genes and constructed a model to predict the prognosis of breast cancer (BRCA) patients. Ten genes were further selected to be related to the prognosis of BRCA patients. Among them, PCDHA1 expression was validated in cells and patient samples.

KLK9: This gene discover in 1999, since 2000 is used as a marker for cancer detection [24]. This gene along with OR10P1 has the fourth highest MI in the GN of the primary breast cancer tumor. In the got GN is adequately identified as one gene that would be expected to be present in the analyzed tissue.

LHFPL3: This gene is tenth in the list of genes with the highest degree in the tissue of first metastasis of breast cancer in lymphatic nodes; also, it appears in the GN of primary tumor of breast cancer in the 96th position. In 2019, LHFPL3 appears in a research work as a target to regulate proliferation, migration, and epithelial-mesenchymal transitions of human glioma cell [25]. What is striking about this gene is that it is present in the primary tumor samples and in the metastasis samples in a relatively low place in the genes with the highest degree in the GN.

PPM1B: This gene is the second with the highest degree in the tissue of first metastasis of breast cancer in lymphatic nodes and also appears in the GN of primary tumor of breast cancer. PP2C family members are known to be negative regulators of cell stress response pathways. This phosphatase has been shown to dephosphorylate cyclin-dependent kinases (CDKs), and thus may be involved in cell cycle control. Overexpression of this phosphatase is reported to cause cell-growth arrest or cell death. In 2021, through the targeted modulation of this gene, the invasion and migration of nasopharyngeal carcinoma cells was regulated [26]. Also PPM1B inhibits gastric cancer progression and serves as a favorable prognostic biomarker.

   After the above literature review we conclude that the genes with highest degree and MI in the GNs we generate are identified in the oncology literature as relevant in cancer growing. The apply of GN structural analysis for ranking main genes in breast cancer primary tumor is an starting novel contribution.

4 Discussion

We have identified main genes in breast cancer primary tumor by GN statistical analysis. This analysis extends the methodology previously applied on single first breast cancer metastasis in lymph nodes [19]. Genes with the highest MI and the highest degree nodes are mostly the same, respectively, being associated to GN of either primary tumor or first metastasis. But different each other GN. So, the genetic network of primary tumor changes becoming of first cancer metastases. A more extensive analysis needs include data of diverse cancer and metastasis tissues. The goal is to identify which genes are the more/less expressed to drive the change from healthy tissue to primary tumor, and the late metastasis. For an agile handling, without change the GN centralities, a threshold choice for GN pruning is practiced. This pruning removes many non relevant interactions and makes concise GN structural analysis.

5 Conclusions

After 100 simulations, we preliminarily identified the main genes in the GN of the primary tumor of breast cancer. For each node-gene, both its level of MI with each other and its degree could indicate its relevance in the formation of cancer. The GN topology is power law degree distribution. Reliable results are obtained since we replicate the process hundreds of times and the results are averaged in a data statistic, not complete but representative enough for initial conclusions. There is a small intersection with the set of the main genes in the GNs of primary breast cancer tumor and the one of first metastasis in lymphe nodes. After oncology literature review, we find out that the genes with the highest correlation and the highest degree in, respectively the associated GN, are involved in the creation of breast cancer primary tumor, and the breast cancer first metastasis in lymphe nodes.

Acknowledgement. Thanks to Consejo Nacional de Ciencia y Tecnología de México: Project A1-S-20037, Matías Alvarado principal investigator; and Moisés León Pinedas' Master Scholarship No. CVU: 1144833.

References

1. Statistics about the world day to fight breast cancer (October 19) from INEGI (2021). https://www.inegi.org.mx/app/saladeprensa/noticia.html? id=6844. Accessed 1 Sept 2022
2. Breast cancer from World Health Organization (2021). https://www.who.int/ news-room/fact-sheets/detail/breast-cancer. Accessed 20 Sept 2022

3. Newton, P., et al.: Spreaders and sponges define metastasis in lung cancer: a Markov Chain Monte Carlo mathematical model. Cancer Res. **73**(9) (2013)
4. Hanahan, D., et al.: Hallmarks of cancer: the next generation. Cell **144**(5) (2011)
5. Newton, P., et al.: Spatiotemporal progression of metastatic breast cancer: a Markov chain model highlighting the role of early metastatic sites. NPJ Breast Cancer **1** (2015)
6. Rojas-Domínguez, A., et al.: Modeling cancer immunoediting in tumor microenvironment with system characterization through the ising-model Hamiltonian. BMC Bioinform. **23**(1) (2022)
7. Sergey, N., et al.: The complete sequence of human genome. Science **376**(6588) (2022)
8. Texada, M., Koyama, T., Rewitz, K.: Regulation of body size and growth control. Genetics **216** (2020)
9. Margolin, A., et al.: ARACne: an algorithm for the reconstruction of gene regulatory networks in a mammalian cellular context. BMC Bioinform. **7** (2006)
10. ARACne-multicore   (2021).   https://github.com/josemaz/aracne-multicore. Accessed June 2022
11. Genomic data commons data portal from NCI NIH in https://portal.gdc.cancer.gov/
12. Gene expression omnibus from NCBI in https://www.ncbi.nlm.nih.gov/geo/
13. Buccs, G., et al.: Gene expression profiling of human cancers. Ann. New York Acad. Sci. **1028**(1), 28–37 (2004)
14. Barabási, A.-L.: Network Science. Network Science, London (2014)
15. Alcalá, S., et al.: Modularity in biological networks. Front. Genetics **12** (2021)
16. Barkai, N., et al.: Robustness in simple biochemical networks. Nature **387**(6636), 913–917 (1997)
17. Kimura, S., et al.: Genetic network inference using hierarchical structure. Front. Physiol. **7** (2016)
18. Hagberg, D.A., et al.: NetworkX network analysis python
19. Alvarado, M., et al.: Genetic network of breast cancer metastasis in lymph nodes via information theory algorithms. In: 19th CCE, pp. 1–6 (2022)
20. Cohen, A.B.: The interaction of -1-antitrypsin with chymotrypsin, trypsin and elastase. Biochimica et Biophysica Acta (BBA) - Enzymology **391**(1), 193–200 (1975)
21. Alkafaas, S., et al.: Vasopressin induces apoptosis but does not enhance the antiproliferative effect of dynamin 2 or PI3K/AKT inhibition in luminal a breast cancer cells graphical abstract. Med. Oncol. **40** (2022)
22. Sallee, N., et al.: A pilot screen of a novel peptide hormone library identified candidate GPR83 ligands. SLAS DISCOVERY: Adv. Sci. Drug Discovery **25** (2020)
23. Du, J., et al.: Identification and prognostic value exploration of cyclophosphamide (Cytoxan)-centered chemotherapy response-associated genes in breast cancer. DNA Cell Biol. **40**(11) (2021)
24. Diamandis, E.P., et al.: The new human Kallikrein gene family: implications in carcinogenesis. Trends Endocrinol. Metab. **11**(2) (2000)
25. Li, Z., et al.: MiR-218-5p targets LHFPL3 to regulate proliferation, migration, and epithelial-mesenchymal transitions of human glioma cells. Biosci. Rep. **39**(3) (2019)
26. Wang, W., et al.: TRIM59 regulates invasion and migration of nasopharyngeal carcinoma cells by targeted modulation of PPM1B. Nan fang yi ke da xue xue bao = J. South. Med. Univ. **41**(7) (2021)

Realistic Simulation of Event-Related Potentials and Their Usual Noise and Interferences for Pattern Recognition

Idileisy Torres-Rodríguez[1](✉) ⓘ, Roberto Díaz-Amador[2] ⓘ, Beatriz Peón-Pérez[3] ⓘ, Alberto Hurtado Armas[1] ⓘ, and Alberto Taboada-Crispi[1] ⓘ

[1] Informatics Research Center, Universidad Central "Marta Abreu" de Las Villas, UCLV, Santa Clara, Cuba
{itrodriguez,ataboada}@uclv.edu.cu

[2] Departamento de Medicina Traslacional, Facultad de Medicina, Universidad Católica del Maule, UCM, Talca, Chile
rodiaz@ucm.cl

[3] Center for State Control of Medical Devices, Havana, Cuba

Abstract. Simulated signals are commonly used to evaluate pattern recognition algorithms for event-related potential estimation because it is difficult to obtain gold standard records. The objective of this research is to obtain realistic evoked potential simulations for benchmarking. We allow for variations in the latency of the potentials, the width of the different components, and their amplitudes. The background noise is simulated through a Burg autoregressive model of order 8. We can also include the instrumentation and acquisition channel effects, as well as the powerline interferences. We achieved values of Normalized root-mean-square error greater than 70% for the selected model for the background noise simulation and greater than 85% for the simulation of the raw recordings of the evoked potentials, including the 60 Hz interference, alpha rhythm interference, and clean evoked responses embedded in background noise. The simulated signals could be used to train or evaluate different methods of extracting the waveform of the event-related potentials.

Keywords: Component; Simulation · Evoked Potentials · AR model Second

1 Introduction

The signals obtained through simulation can be used to train, evaluate or compare different digital signal processing techniques or pattern recognition algorithms, giving researchers the possibility of unlimited number of test signals for experimentations [1]. Monitoring brain activity from electroencephalographic recordings is very popular, but evaluating the methods of analyzing this signal is a difficult task because there is generally no gold standard that allows comparison. However, to evaluate different algorithms proposed for the analysis and detect patterns from these signals, researchers often use simulated signals instead of real signals, which usually fit to simplistic models far from

A. Y. Rodríguez-González et al. (Eds.): MCPR 2023, LNCS 13902, pp. 201–210, 2023.
https://doi.org/10.1007/978-3-031-33783-3_19

reality. The objective of this research is to obtain simulations of evoked potential recordings with a high degree of realism. For the simulation, the possible variations that may appear in the latency of the potentials, in the width variations of the main components that form the potential, and in its amplitude are taken into account. The event-related potentials in a real context can be contaminated with additive and multiplicative noise, and also be affected by the effects of the instrumentation when recording: the analog filtering stage, sampling, or quantization. In most current evaluations, these aspects are ignored.

2 Methods

2.1 Scheme of Simulation

The simulation scheme was previously proposed in [2]. This scheme permits to obtain an unlimited number of test signals that allow checking the performance of different methods for the estimation of evoked responses.

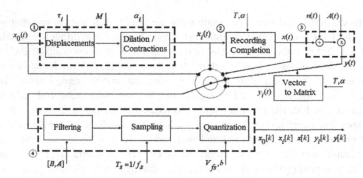

Fig. 1. General scheme for event-related potentials simulation.

The simulation starts from a basic waveform, $x_0(t)$, from which displaced versions (to the right or left), contracted or dilated and with variations in amplitude are obtained (block 1 of Fig. 1). These waveforms of interest are linked to each other by segments of the EEG signal (block 2 of Fig. 1), the principal source of noise in the Evoked Potentials, these segments may contain signals, but they are not of interest because they do not constitute responses to the stimuli. These signals, as in a real context, can be contaminated with additive and multiplicative noise (block 3 of Fig. 1) and also be affected by the effects of the instrumentation: analog filtering, sampling, and quantization.

2.2 Selection of the Parameters for Simulation

In block 1 of Fig. 1, $x_0(t)$, is the initial basic epoch, defined for all $t \in [0, a)$, and is used as a reference to generate $(M - 1)$ epochs more. The initial waveform resembles as much as possible the waveform of the potential that you want to study. The initial basic epoch selection may be the waveform of a known evoked response or some other signal that serves as a reference for simulating event-related potentials. It is known that on many occasions' wavelets have been used for these purposes because they have similarities with the waveform of some evoked responses, so it could be an option. In this particular case, the clean recordings of Auditory Evoked Potentials in healthy subjects provided in the database published in [3] and described in [4] are selected for the simulation as basic waveforms. These signals correspond to auditory brainstem responses (ABR); they are short-latency potentials. Although, some authors suggest that this early response is characterized by having a low variability in its latency and amplitude between subjects and within subjects [5]. Numerous papers try to solve the sensitivity of the averaging technique in the presence of non-alignments that can appear in the signal [6], showing that the evoked responses do not always appear perfectly aligned. It can cause poor performance of the averaging techniques used to obtain the potential waveform, even in the case of values in children, where latency deviations are greater. In [7], the values of the amplitudes and widths of the signal waves corresponding to brainstem auditory evoked potentials and their standard deviations contrasted with annotations made on the same signals by experts are also shown. Taking this into account, the parameter τ_i, corresponding to the variation of the relative displacements due to the latency that can be present in $x_o(t)$, is simulated following a law of normal variation with zero mean and standard deviation of the order of 0.2 ms. This value was chosen from the mean value of the standard deviations of the component V latencies according to the study carried out in [7]. The parameter α_i, corresponding to the variation of the width of $x_o(t)$, is simulated following a law of normal variation with zero mean and standard deviation of the order of 0.07 ms, following the values also shown in [7].

The selection of the number of epochs M is made assuming that the noise is additive and not correlated with the signal, that the signal of interest does not change from epoch to epoch and is synchronized with the stimulus that causes it, the value of the signal-to-noise ratio (SNR_e) estimated at the end must improve by a factor of $\sqrt{M}$, for the value of the initial signal-to-noise ratio (SNR_i),

$$SNR_e = SNR_i \cdot \sqrt{M}. \tag{1}$$

In the case of ABRs, these are much smaller than the EEG signal in which they are embedded, these early components are generally in the range of -30 dB to -20 dB [8]. In the case of the signals used that serves as a reference to estimate the parameters for the simulation [3, 4, 9], the value of SNR_i s in the order of -27 dB. To reach an SNR_e of approximately 0 dB or greater, the minimum essential value to indicate that there is a response [10], a minimum value of $M = 500$ would be needed, and $M = 512$ is chosen. In any case, the simulation allows choosing different values of M.

The event period T is selected according to the stimulation period, which in this case was 2002 samples (41.7 ms), corresponding to the time elapsed between each applied stimulus. The width of the analysis window a, in this case, was 884 samples (18.4 ms). These parameters can also be modified according to the initial basic epoch chosen and the potential to be simulated.

For the addition of the additive noise, $n(t)$, which in this case is a sum of the estimation of the background noise, plus the 60 Hz interference and its harmonics, plus the alpha rhythm that is present in many of the signals of this database. An analysis of the raw records provided in the same database was performed. In this case, records were used where the intensity of the stimulus was equal to or less than 30 dB SPL. The justification for this selection is based on the fact that in these recordings there should be no auditory response, therefore, they should only be constituted by the basal activity, the EEG signal [4]. For the simulation of the alpha rhythm that is present in some signals and that can be taken into consideration when analyzing the non-homogeneities of the signal, which can affect the result of the average signal that is estimated, a white noise that is filtered with a bandpass filter with Butterworth approximation of order 2, with cutoff frequencies between 9 and 11 Hz as explained in [11], the amplitude of this rhythm was between 30 μV and 50 μV randomly distributed, with a normal distribution and it is in total agreement with the analysis carried out on the dataset. The parameters related to filtering, sampling, and quantization are taken from the description that is made on the acquisition of the database. The following section describes the analysis of the raw records for the selection of the model for the simulation of background noise.

2.3 Model Selection for Background Noise Simulation

Autoregressive (AR) models have been widely used in the representation of EEG signals [12, 13] because they allow a compact representation of various types of rhythms of the EEG signal. The number of peaks that can be represented by the power spectrum of an AR model is determined by the model order p as in Eq. (2); each additional peak requires an order increment of 2,

$$x(n) = a_1x(n-1) + a_2x(n-2) + \cdots + a_px(n-p) + v(n). \tag{2}$$

The fit of a parametric autoregressive model to an EEG signal involves the selection of a single parameter: the order of the model, the choice of a very high order can cause overfitting of the model and introduce incorrect information such as false peaks in the spectrum. On the other hand, a very low model order can lead to loss of information, which in the frequency domain is seen as a smooth spectrum. The most appropriate order for the model is the one that minimizes the information criterion (IC) when it is evaluated over a range of given orders.

   The fit of a parametric autoregressive model to an EEG signal involves the selection of a single parameter: the order of the model. The choice of a very high order can cause overfitting of the model and introduce incorrect information such as false peaks in the spectrum. On the other hand, a very low model order can lead to loss of information, which in the frequency domain is seen as a smooth spectrum. The most appropriate order for the model is the one that minimizes the information criterion (IC) when it is evaluated over a range of given orders. The selection of the order of the model is done by choosing the minimum value of IC for a given order p. Equation (3) shows the Bayesian information criterion

$$IC(p) = \ln \hat{\sigma}_p^2 + p\frac{\ln N}{N}. \tag{3}$$

After specifying a model and estimating its parameters, it is necessary to check the goodness of fit of the model to the original signal. For this, different cost functions can be used. In this case, the cost function, the normalized root mean square error (*NRMSE*) is used to establish the comparison.

$$NRMSE = 1 - \frac{\|x_t - \hat{x}_t\|}{\|x_t - \overline{x}_t\|}, \tag{4}$$

where x_t is the original signal, $\hat{x}_t$ is the simulated signal from the model coefficients, and $\overline{x}_t$ is the mean of the original signal. *NRMSE* values close to 1 indicate a good fit for the model. The signals used for estimating the model correspond to records consisting solely of basal activity. Records where the intensity of the auditory stimulus was equal to or less than 30 dB SPL were taken into account. In these records, there is no auditory response [14, 15]. To model the background noise, we used signal sections where the statistical properties of the signal did not vary too much to maintain its stationarity (1-s signal sections). The sections with values outside the threshold of ±50 μV were not taken into account, following the same criteria as in [4].

For noise modeling, we compare autoregressive models based on the covariance, the modified covariance, the Burg method, the Yule-Walker method, and the LPC (linear prediction component). In addition, the execution time in the estimation of the coefficients for each method with different orders was evaluated.

3   Results and Discussion

3.1   Selected Model

Figure 2 shows the results in the selection of the model considering: a) the behavior and b) the execution time to compute the coefficients. In Fig. 2a, we compare the behavior of the different methods using the Bayesian information criterion. The covariance-based, the modified covariance-based, and the Burg method do not differ significantly from each other, and the results of the Yule-Walker and LPC (linear prediction component) methods look alike. It is very difficult to choose a method among those evaluated, even among those that provided the best results. However, according to the bibliography consulted [16], it is preferable to use methods that use the minimization of the forward and backward variance error prediction as a criterion, such is the case of the modified covariance method and the Burg method. In contrast to Burg's method, the modified covariance method does not guarantee that the estimated parameters correspond to a stable AR model.

When what is needed is to perform spectral analysis, it has been shown that different AR models can provide the same power spectrum, although in one case the poles are within the circumference of the unit radius and, in the other case, they are not. However, when it is required to simulate signals or use the model parameters for the classification of EEG signals, this aspect must be taken into account. In the case of the Burg method, it is always guaranteed that the poles remain inside the unit radius circumference, guaranteeing stability without the need for additional calculations. In Fig. 2b, we compare the execution time to compute the coefficients with different orders for each method. The time to estimate the coefficients increases significantly more in the covariance and modified covariance methods than in the others while incrementing the order. Therefore, a good compromise is to choose Burg's method. From order 5, there are no major changes in the information criterion. Several applications in the literature use orders between 5 and 8, a higher order is only justified when much more detailed power spectrum specifications are required.

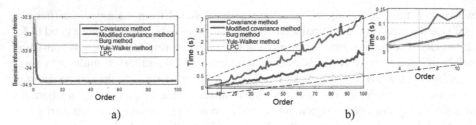

a)   b)

Fig. 2. a) Bayesian information criterion vs. order for different methods. b) Execution time in the estimation of the coefficients with different orders for each method.

The 60 Hz interference and its harmonics were removed from the signal using a comb filter to make the model adequately fit the background signal. From the spectral analysis of the original signal before applying the comb filter, the peaks of the frequency response, their amplitudes, and phases were estimated to generate a representative 60 Hz interference and its harmonics for the simulation. For this, an array was created that includes these data, which are selected randomly when simulating.

From the description of the dataset, it is known that the signals were acquired by filtering them between 30 and 3000 Hz. The evaluated models provide an adequate estimation of the signal for the highest frequencies, but not for the lowest frequencies, where the characteristics of the high pass filter part are not detailed. This could also be caused by the high sampling rate and the very low cutoff frequency at low frequencies relative to the cutoff frequency at high frequencies. In the standards for recording short-latency evoked potentials, it is suggested that the slope of the filter does not exceed 12 dB/octave [10], but the specifications of the filter used are not detailed in the description of the dataset. An analysis of the signals suggests that the filter configuration was modified manually, not remaining the same in all the subjects. In many cases, peaks appear close to the frequency of 10 Hz, which suggests the presence of the alpha rhythm. The demonstrated presence of the alpha rhythm in several cases justifies the addition of interferences associated with this rhythm. From the previous analysis, it was decided to use the specifications shown in Table 1 for the design of a filter with Butterworth approximation. From the analysis of the results obtained for the selection of the model, an AR model with Burg's method and order 8 is an adequate selection.

Table 2 shows the NRMSE values and their mean deviations for each subject and the variances and their deviations of the noise generated using the AR model. Subjects 2 and 3 were not evaluated because the intensity of the minimum auditory stimulus they have is 40 dB SPL and the chosen criterion was 30 dB SPL to guarantee that only background noise was being evaluated.

For a total of 102 records analyzed, the values of the coefficients estimated by the AR model can be seen in Fig. 3. Although there is some dispersion in the value of

Table 1. Characteristics of the designed Butterworth high-pass filter.

Characteristics	Value
Cutoff frequency in the passband	30 Hz
Cutoff frequency in the stopband	15 Hz
Attenuation in the passband	1 dB
Attenuation in the stopband	−6 dB
Order	2

Table 2. Values of the NRMSE and the Variances of the estimated noise for each subject.

Subject	NRMSE	Estimated Noise Variance
'N1'	0.72 ± 0.075	$1.06E\text{-}15 \pm 3.35 \cdot 10^{-17}$
'N4'	0.73 ± 0.088	$7.28E\text{-}16 \pm 3.21 \cdot 10^{-16}$
'N5'	0.72 ± 0.077	$1.06E\text{-}15 \pm 1.75 \cdot 10^{-17}$
'N6'	0.76 ± 0.063	$3.91E\text{-}16 \pm 8.57 \cdot 10^{-18}$
'N7'	0.70 ± 0.039	$3.94E\text{-}16 \pm 9.24 \cdot 10^{-18}$
'N8'	0.72 ± 0.080	$4.11E\text{-}16 \pm 1.40 \cdot 10^{-17}$

the estimated coefficients, they do not differ significantly from each other for the total number of records analyzed.

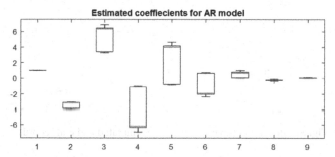

Fig. 3. Values of the coefficients estimated by the AR model.

3.2 Simulated Noise

To obtain the simulated noise signals, Gaussian white noise was generated, which was low-pass filtered with the coefficients estimated by the model. Then, the noise was high-pass filtered using the filter with the specifications in Table 1 and later it was added the 60 Hz powerline interference. In Fig. 4a, we can compare the spectra of one of the background noise simulated this way and the actual reference signal.

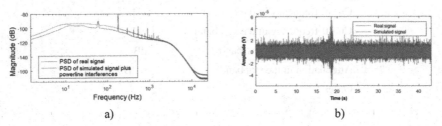

a)   b)

Fig. 4. a) Spectra of the simulated background noise and the reference signal. b) Example of simulated background noise and the reference signal in the time domain.

Figure 4b shows the comparison of the signals in the time domain. As the analysis was performed in one-second segments of the signal to guarantee the stationary conditions. The simulated signal shows the changes that occurred in the variance of the signal.

3.3 Simulated EP Records

Figure 5a shows a frequency domain comparison of a simulated signal with the specifications described above. In this case, the initial epoch, $x_o(t)$, belongs to subject 6 and was randomly chosen. For the spectral comparison, the dirty record that gave rise to the initial epoch (Fig. 5b) was selected.

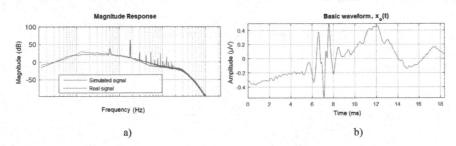

a)   b)

Fig. 5. Spectral comparison between simulated and real records.

An adjustment of NRMSE = 92.5% was obtained in all the tests, choosing initial epochs at random and adding the rest of the noise and interferences in a simulated way. The NRMSE values remained higher than 85%. Figure 6 shows, through 3D visualization, the effects of relative displacements that may be present in a real scenario. This is an example of simulation including noise, interferences, and artifacts. To the best of our knowledge, the level of realism achieved here is far from previous simulations. Therefore, direct comparisons cannot be made. However, all the codes used here are available for benchmarking.

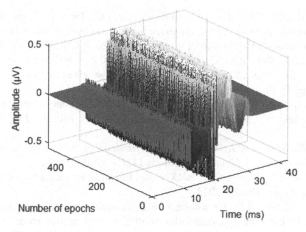

Fig. 6. 3D visualization of the matrix of simulated epochs.

4 Conclusions

Simulated raw recordings of evoked potentials allows obtaining a controlled dataset for evaluation of new methods for evoked responses detection. An 8th-order AR model using Burg's method provides a good estimate of the background noise. Interferences in real signals, such as the 60 Hz powerline interference, the alpha rhythm, and the instrumentation channel noises can be simulated. The scheme also allows the addition of out-of-range values and impulsive noise.

References

1. Krol, L.R., Pawlitzki, J., Lotte, F., Gramann, K., Zander, T.O.: SEREEGA: simulating event-related EEG activity. J. Neurosci. Methods **309**, 13–24 (2018)
2. Taboada-Crispi, A., Orozco-Monteagudo, M., Ferrer-Riesgo, C.A., Falcón-Ruíz, A., Hernández-Pacheco, D.: Simulation of event-related potentials in a wide sense for assessment of detection/estimation algorithms. In: AIP Conference Proceedings, pp. 7–10. American Institute of Physics (2008)
3. Goldberger, A.L., et al.: PhysioBank, PhysioToolkit, and PhysioNet: components of a new research resource for complex physiologic signals. Circulation **101**(23), e215–e220 (2000)
4. McKearney, R.M., MacKinnon, R.C.: Objective auditory brainstem response classification using machine learning. Int. J. Audiol. **58**(4), 224–230 (2019)
5. Johansson, M., Asp, F., Berninger, E.: Children with congenital unilateral sensorineural hearing loss: effects of late hearing aid amplification—a pilot study. Ear Hear. **41**(1), 55–66 (2020)
6. Laguna, P., Garde, A., Giraldo, B.F., Meste, O., Jané, R., Sörnmo, L.: Eigenvalue-based time delay estimation of repetitive biomedical signals. Digit. Sig. Process. **75**, 107–119 (2018)
7. Torres-Rodríguez, I., Ferrer-Riesgo, C.A., de Morales Artiles, M.M.P., Taboada-Crispi, A.: Performance evaluation of average methods in the time domain using quality measures for automatic detection of evoked potentials. In: González Díaz, C.A., et al. (eds.) CLAIB 2019. IP, vol. 75, pp. 12–20. Springer, Cham (2020). https://doi.org/10.1007/978-3-030-30648-9_2

8. Torres-Rodríguez, I., Ferrer-Riesgo, C., Oliva Pérez, J.C., Taboada-Crispi, A.: Performance of different average methods for the automatic detection of evoked potentials. In: Nyström, I., Hernández Heredia, Y., Milián Núñez, V. (eds.) CIARP 2019. LNCS, vol. 11896, pp. 629–636. Springer, Cham (2019). https://doi.org/10.1007/978-3-030-33904-3_59
9. Kotowski, K., Stapor, K., Leski, J.: Improved robust weighted averaging for event-related potentials in EEG. Biocybern. Biomed. Eng. **39**(4), 1036–1046 (2019)
10. Chesnaye, M.A., Bell, S.L., Harte, J.M., Simpson, D.M.: The convolutional group sequential test: reducing test time for evoked potentials. IEEE Trans. Biomed. Eng. **67**(3), 697–705 (2019)
11. Leonowicz, Z., Karvanen, J., Shishkin, S.L.: Trimmed estimators for robust averaging of event-related potentials. J. Neurosci. Methods **142**(1), 17–26 (2005)
12. Farabbi, A., Aloia, V., Mainardi, L.: ARX–based EEG data balancing for error potential BCI. J. Neural Eng. **19**(3), 036023 (2022)
13. Kubokawa, T., Marchand, É., Strawderman, W.E.: A unified approach to estimation of noncentrality parameters, the multiple correlation coefficient, and mixture models. Math. Methods Statist. **26**(2), 134–148 (2017). https://doi.org/10.3103/S106653071702003X
14. Morrison, J.A., Valdizón-Rodríguez, R., Goldreich, D., Faure, P.A.: Tuning for rate and duration of frequency-modulated sweeps in the mammalian inferior colliculus. J. Neurophysiol. **120**(3), 985–997 (2018)
15. Heffernan, B.: Characterization and classification of the frequency following response to vowels at different sound levels in normal hearing adults. Doctoral dissertation, Université d'Ottawa, University of Ottawa (2019)
16. Wan, Z., Yang, R., Huang, M., Zeng, N., Liu, X.: A review on transfer learning in EEG signal analysis. Neurocomputing **421**, 1–14 (2021)

Chest X-Ray Imaging Severity Score
of COVID-19 Pneumonia

Eduardo Garea-Llano[1][(✉)] [ID], Abel Diaz-Berenguer[2] [ID], Hichem Sahli[2,3] [ID],
and Evelio Gonzalez-Dalmau[1] [ID]

[1] Cuban Neuroscience Center, 190 No. 1520, 11600 Playa, Havana, Cuba
eduardo.garea@cneuro.edu.cu
[2] Faculty of Engineering Sciences, Department of Electronics and Informatics, Vrije
Universiteit Brussel, Pleinlaan 2, 1050 Brussel, Belgium
{aberengu,hsahli}@etrovub.be
[3] Interuniversity Microelectronics Centre (IMEC), Kapeldreef 75, 3001 Haverlee, Belgium

Abstract. Despite the decrease in COVID-19 cases worldwide due to the development of extensive vaccination campaigns and effective containment measures adopted by most countries, this disease continues to be a global concern. Therefore, it is necessary to continue developing methods and algorithms that facilitate decision-making for better treatments. This work proposes a method to evaluate the degree of severity of the affectations caused by COVID-19 in the pulmonary region in chest X-ray images. The proposed algorithm addresses the problem of confusion between pulmonary lesions and anatomical structure (i.e., bones) in chest radiographs. In this paper, we adopt the Semantic Genesis approach for classifying image patches of the lung region into two classes (affected and unaffected). Experiments on a database consisting of X-rays of healthy people and patients with COVID-19 have shown that the proposed approach provides a better assessment of the degree of severity caused by the disease.

Keywords: Chest X-ray · COVID-19 · Severity · Classification

1 Introduction

After three years in the fight against the COVID-19 pandemic, the protocols and forms of action in treating patients in severe or critical condition have been constantly renewed to arrive in the first instance to save the patients'. Chest X-rays images (CXR) were frequently used in diagnosing the disease, and many medical research facilities in developing countries such as Cuba. Several studies showed that imaging patterns on CXR images that are characteristic of COVID-19 might decrease or increase depending on the state of the severity of the patient and the effectiveness of the protocols applied [1–5].

Deep learning techniques have been widely adopted for COVID-19 classification from CXRs [6–8]. The main advantage of deep learning methods for CXR image classification is the capability to capture pixel-level information which human eyes cannot obviously notice. For example, in [9], Inception net was utilized for COVID-19 outbreak screening with CXRs. [10] proposed a patch-based convolutional neural network

A. Y. Rodríguez-González et al. (Eds.): MCPR 2023, LNCS 13902, pp. 211–220, 2023.
https://doi.org/10.1007/978-3-031-33783-3_20

(CNN) with a small number of trainable parameters for COVID-19 diagnosis. [11] leverage pre-trained CNN models as the backbone with further transfer learning to classify chest radiography images in 4 classes; the authors of [12] used CheXNet, DenseNet, VGG19, MobileNet, InceptionV3, ResNet18, ResNet101, and squeezeNet architectures to train a 3 class classification model using transfer learning and data augmentation techniques.

Apart from the above classification (COVID-19/non-COVID-19) schemes, several CXR severity scoring systems have been proposed to map a global or region-based qualitative judgment assessing the suspicion of pulmonary involvement of COVID-19 on a quantitative scale [5, 13]. Among such scoring systems is the "Radiographic Assessment of Pulmonary Edema" (RALE) [14]. To estimate RALE, the thorax is divided into four quadrants. Each quadrant was assigned the product of a consolidation score and a density score. The consolidation score (from 0–4) represents the percentage of the quadrant with opacification, and the density score (from 1–3) quantifies the density of ground glass opacities. The final RALE score is the sum of the quadrants' scores. The RALE score has been adopted by the Cuban Society of Imaging (SCI) [15] and used to develop machine-learning approaches [16, 17].

In [18], an end-to-end severity assessment architecture based on the Brixia score [5] has been proposed. The architecture consists of (1) a multi-task feature extraction backbone. Several backbones have been evaluated: ResNet, VGG, DenseNet, and Inception. (2) A state-of-the-art lung segmentation model (U-Net++). (3) A registration mechanism that acts as a "multi-resolution feature alignment," and (4) a scoring module that uses Feature Pyramid Networks for the combination of multi-scale feature maps, followed by a final Global Average Pooling layer and a SoftMax activation for classification.

Based on the RALE scoring [14], this paper proposes an end-to-end severity assessment method built on the recently proposed semantic genesis-based classification [19].

The remainder of the paper is structured as follows. Section 2 describes the proposed algorithm. In Sect. 3, we present the design of the experiment, the results achieved, and their discussion. Finally, conclusions are drawn in Sect. 4.

2 Proposed Method

Figure 1 presents the general scheme of the proposed method that consists of two main steps: 1) Image quality evaluation, enhancement, and lung segmentation; 2) Semantic classification for severity level evaluation.

After evaluating the quality of the input image, the algorithm establishes a conditional step that allows improving the quality of the input image if it is below an established threshold. For this, contrast-limited adaptive histogram equalization is used. This step allows the image improvement even in regions that are darker or lighter than most of the image [16]. The segmentation of the lung region is done using a trained UNet-CNN [16].

After lung region segmentation, a normalized image (rotated and scaled), standardized to a size of 180 X 180 pixels, is obtained. On the normalized image, we perform image cropping into 8 patches, corresponding to the 8 quadrants of the RALE system.

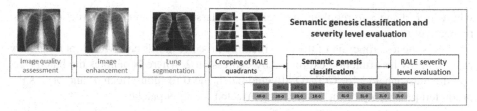

Fig. 1. General scheme of the proposed method for classification of RALE quadrants based on semantic genesis

2.1 Semantic Genesis Classification and Severity Level Evaluation

Once the patches corresponding to each RALE quadrant have been extracted, the binary classification (affected; unaffected) of each one is performed based on a classifier based on the semantic genesis approach [19]. For this, the training of the Unet2d model [19] was developed for the classification of the images (patches) obtained as a result of the division of the CXR image into patches according to the quadrants of the RALE classification. These patches were previously labeled according to the presence or absence of involvement in the lung region. Figure 2 shows the training scheme of the proposed classifier. Following the semantic genesis approach, this process is divided into two parts.

In this step, we apply the Semantic Genesis framework [19]. The model's objective is to learn different sets of semantics-enriched representations from multiple perspectives. The framework consists of three components: 1) self-discovery of anatomical patterns from similar patients, 2) self-classification of the patterns, and 3) self-restoration of the transformed patterns. In our implementation, we do not consider the first step, as the defined quadrants give the 'anatomical' structure. As illustrated in Fig. 2, the Semantic Genesis is conceptually simple: an encoder-decoder structure with skip connections between (Unet) and a classification head at the end of the encoder [19].

Anatomical Pattern Classification: As illustrated in Fig. 2, the classification branch encodes the input anatomical pattern in a latent space, followed by a sequence of fully connected (FC) layers, and predicts the label associated with the pattern. Previously, a series of transformations were made to the input image that allowed obtaining greater robustness in the extracted deep features while serving as a data augmentation method. In our case, we assume the series of transformations proposed in [19] that are linear, non-linear, local, local shutting, out-painting, and in-painting transformations.

Restoration of Anatomical Patterns: The objective of the restoration is for the model to learn different visual representations by recovering original anatomical patterns from the transformed ones. As shown in Fig. 2, the restoration branch encodes the input transformed anatomical pattern in a latent space and decodes it to the original resolution to recover the original anatomical pattern from the transformation.

For training the model, we follow [19] and define the following loss functions for the multi-task (Restoration & classification) (1):

$$L = \gamma cl * Lcl + \gamma rc * Lrc \tag{1}$$

where γcl cl and γrc regulate the weights of classification and reconstruction losses, respectively.

Lcl is the loss function of the classification process, in this case we adopt the binary cross entropy loss function expressed by expression 2, where $\mathbf{N}$ denotes the batch size; y is the class label (1 for COVID affected patch and 0 for non-affected) and $p(y)$ is the predicted probability of the patch being affected for all N patches.

$$Lcl = -\frac{1}{N} \sum_{i=1}^{N} (yi.\log(p(yi)) + (1-yi).\log(1-p(yi))) \qquad (2)$$

Lrc is the distance L2 between the original pattern and the reconstructed pattern expressed as a loss function through the expression 3, where N is the batch size, X is the ground truth (original anatomical pattern) and X' is the reconstructed prediction.

$$Lcl = -\frac{1}{N} \sum_{i=1}^{N} \|Xi - Xi'\|2 \qquad (3)$$

The adoption of Lcl based on [19] allows the model to learn a semantically enriched representation. Similarly, the use of the Lrc function encourages the model to learn from multiple perspectives by restoring original images from various image deformations. Once trained, in our proposal we then use the encoder for the task of classifying the RALE quadrants.

Once the classification process has been carried out, the degree of severity of the affectations is estimated. For this, the same scheme described in the RALE methodology [15] is followed. If the patch is classified as affected, it is assigned the value of 1. Otherwise, it is zero. The final score is obtained by summing the values assigned to each patch. A severity score is assigned to the image according to the values of Table 1.

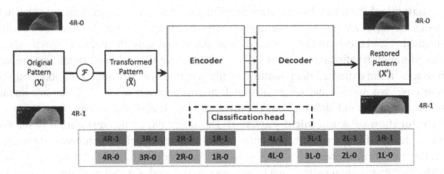

Fig. 2. Training scheme for the classification process through semantic genesis (modified from [19]).

Table 1. Severity categories and their scores according to RALE [15].

Score	RALE severity category
0–1	Normal
1–3	Mild
3–6	Moderate
6–8	Severe

3 Experimental Results and Discussion

3.1 Data Set

Training and validation of the proposed architecture (Fig. 2) take advantage of multiple datasets of CXR images from three Cuban hospitals. The images were taken from May 2020 to December 2021, including 500 images of patients diagnosed with COVID-19 and 154 images of healthy people. From them, a group of 335 images was selected (50 of healthy people and 285 of COVID-19 patients) that had been fully documented and evaluated by the radiologists of these hospitals. From them, 2680 labeled training samples were extracted.

This database was divided into three sets: training set (2144 samples), prediction set (268 samples), and test set (268 samples). The database was labeled according to the two classes corresponding to the affected quadrant (1), and unaffected quadrant (0).

3.2 Implementation and Training Details

For the implementation of the proposed model, the transformation from 3D to 2D of the Unet3D [19] model was performed. The original model was taken from the open source implementation on the official site of semantic genesis approach (https://github.com/fha ghighi/SemanticGenesis).

The implementation was carried out on the open source library Keras (with MIT license) written in Python. The objective of using this library was to facilitate the implementation of the proposed model because Keras does not work as an independent framework, but rather as an intuitive user interface (API) that allows access to various machine learning frameworks such as TensorFlow. All training sessions were carried out on a PC with an Intel Core i7-471HQ processor, 2.30 GHz, 16 GB RAM.

During the training process, we have balanced the training data by randomly sampling in each epoch the same number of patches for each class from all possible patches for that class.

In the training procedure, the input images and their corresponding labels are used to train the proposed model with stochastic gradient descent. We apply the Adaptive Moment Estimation (Adam) Method [20], which is a stochastic gradient descent method that calculates the adaptive learning rates for each parameter to minimize the loss function. The parameters of the Adam optimizer in the proposed architecture are set as learning rate = 0.0002 and the maximum number of epochs = 100.

3.3 Classifier Training

To compare the performance of the proposed model, we trained 3 backbone models for classification. Namely, Vgg16 [21], ResNet50 [22], Inception [23]. All models were trained with the same training set for 100 epochs using categorical cross entropy and the Adam optimizer as a loss function.

For the evaluation of the performance of the proposed model, the Accuracy measure was used. The results obtained are shown in Table 2. Two Accuracy values were measured. The first (*Pred_acc*) obtained on the training process (for which the maximum value obtained during the 100 training epochs was taken), and the second (*Test_acc*), on the test set using the trained model (the model that obtained the maximum value of *Pred_acc* during the 100 training epochs was taken). It can be seen that the proposed model and ResNet50 obtained the best results, with a similar performance in the test set.

Table 2. Results obtained in the training and evaluation process

Model	Pred_acc	Test_acc
Vgg16	0.87	0.87
ResNet50	0.97	**0.97**
Inception	0.87	0.87
Proposed model	**0.98**	**0.97**

3.4 Validation of the Obtained Classifier

To verify the robustness of the results obtained by the implemented classifier, we developed a process of evaluating it in a 10-fold cross-validation scheme. In order to compare the performance of the proposed model, this same cross-validation scheme was applied to the REsNet50 model which achieved results similar to ours in the first experiment.

Cross-validation is a method of resampling data to assess the generalizability of predictive models and to avoid overfitting. In k-fold cross-validation, the available learning set is divided into k disjoint subsets of approximately equal size. Here, "fold" refers to the number of resulting subsets. A random sampling of the training set does this partition. The model is trained using k − 1 subsets representing the training set together. The model is then applied to the remaining subset, called the validation set, and performance is measured. This procedure is repeated until each k subsets has served as a validation set. The average of the performance measurements on the k-validation sets is the cross-validation performance [24].

For our experiment, our database of 2680 samples was divided into 10 folds of 268 samples each, and the model was trained and tested using the 10-fold scheme.

Figure 3 shows the obtained results. It can be observed that although the average of the performance measurements of the proposed classifier is 0.968 with a standard deviation of 0.04, the classifier maintains its accuracy in all folds above 0.95. However, the ResNet50 model did not maintain the same performance in the 10 folds, obtaining a final average of 0.87 with a standard deviation of 0.05.

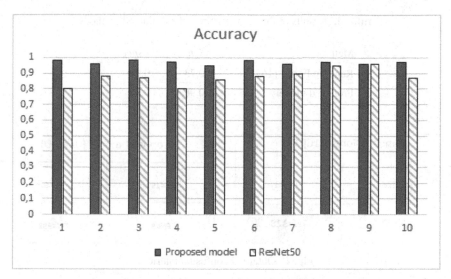

Fig. 3. Results of classifier validation using 10-fold cross-validation

3.5 Comparison to State-of-Art

To evaluate the effectiveness of the proposed method, we compared the performance of our proposal with the proposal of [16, 17]. To do this, we selected 75 CXR images, 20 of which correspond to healthy people and 55 to COVID-19 patients with different degrees of lung involvement. This set of images was not previously used in the training and testing of the classifier.

The set of images was processed according to the RALE classification [15] by a group of radiologists specializing in thorax from the Cuban Society of Imaging, obtaining 600 samples from labeled quadrants (affected, unaffected) as ground truth.

The classification method presented in [16, 17] was applied to this test set. The same was done with the method proposed in this work, and the results were compared.

For this, the Sensitivity and Specificity metrics were calculated, taking into account for each class the RALE quadrants correctly classified as affected (TP), those erroneously classified as affected (FP), those correctly classified as unaffected (TN), and those erroneously classified as unaffected (FN). The expressions in (4) calculated the metrics. Table 3 presents the results of these metrics obtained for the evaluated methods. Figure 4 shows the confusion matrices of both methods.

$$Sens = \frac{TP}{(TP + FN)} \quad Espec = \frac{TN}{(TN + FP)} \tag{4}$$

The results obtained demonstrate the superiority of the proposed method by obtaining better values of sensitivity and specificity in the binary classification process (affected, unaffected) of the RALE quadrants. Therefore this improvement will have an impact on a more reliable evaluation of the degree of severity of the affectations. However, we consider that we must continue investigating in the direction of improving the accuracy

Table 3. Results of the comparison of the evaluated methods.

Method	Sens	Espec
Random Forest [16, 17]	0.73	0.88
Proposed model	0.96	0.98

Random Forest [16][17]	
TP=166	FP=43
FN=62	TN=328

Proposed model (Unet2D)	
TP=194	FP=6
FN=8	TN=392

Fig. 4. Obtained confusion matrices.

in the calculation of the index of lung involvement proposed in [16, 17] to quantify the percentage of involvement of each RALE quadrant.

On the other hand, the proposed model presents a lower degree of complexity compared to other proposals of the state of the art such as [18]. This model [18], despite being an end to end model, is composed of several types of networks that perform different tasks in the processing pipeline. This characteristic favors the occurrence of residual errors that accumulate when passing the results from one network to another. In particular, since the task of segmenting lung involvement can be ambiguous and difficult to perform, even for the most experienced radiologists, this can lead to confusion in the results of the quantification of the degree of involvement. In our multitasking proposal, this difficulty is largely avoided by estimating the affectation from the direct classification of anatomical regions of the image. This task is performed from self-learned patterns by the same network that performs the classification. This characteristic favors that the influence of the possible residual errors obtained as a result of the process are lower as demonstrated in the comparison made with [16, 17].

4 Conclusions

In this work, we presented an algorithm that evaluates the degree of severity of the affectations caused by COVID-19 in the pulmonary region in CXR images. The results achieved in the experiments on images of healthy patients and those affected by COVID-19 showed high sensitivity and specificity values compared with the state-of-the-art method.

Acknowledgement. The VLIR-UOS has partially financed this research under the South Initiative: Toward Precision Medicine for the Prediction of Treatment Response to Covid-19 in Cuba (COVID-19 PROMPT).

References

1. Batista, J.A., Araujo-Filho, M., Sawamura, Y., et al.: COVID-19 pneumonia: what is the role of imaging in diagnosis? J. Bras. Pneumol. **46**(2), e20200114 (2020)
2. Ming-Yen, N., Lee, Y.P., Yang, J., et al.: Imaging profile of the COVID-19 infection: radiologic findings and literature review. Radiol. Cardiothogracic Imaging **2**(1), e200034 (2020)
3. Huang, C., Wang, Y., Li, X., et al.: Clinical features of patients infected with 2019 novel coronavirus in Wuhan China. Lancet **395**(10223), 497–506 (2020)
4. Borghesi, A., et al.: Radiographic severity index in COVID-19 pneumonia: relationship to age and sex in 783 Italian patients. Radiol. Med. (Torino) **125**(5), 461–464 (2020). https://doi.org/10.1007/s11547-020-01202-1
5. Monaco, C.G., et al.: Chest x-ray severity score in COVID-19 patients on emergency department admission: a two-centre study. Eur. Radiol. Exp. **4**(1), 1–7 (2020). https://doi.org/10.1186/s41747-020-00195-w
6. López-Cabrera, J.D., Portal Díaz, J.A., Orozco Morales, R., Pérez Díaz, M.: Revisión crítica sobre la identificación de COVID-19 a partir de imágenes de rayos x de tórax usando técnicas de inteligencia artificial. Revista Cubana De Transformación Digital **1**(3), 67–99 (2020)
7. Abbas, A., Abdelsamea, M.M., Gaber, M.M.: Classification of covid-19 in chest x-ray images using detrac deep convolutional neural network. Appl. Intell., 1–11 (2020)
8. Zhang, J., Xie, Y., Li, Y., Shen, C., Xia, Y.: Covid-19 screening on chest x-ray images using deep learning based anomaly detection. arXiv preprint arXiv:2003.12338 (2020)
9. Das, D., Santosh, K., Pal, U.: Truncated inception net: Covid-19 outbreak screening using chest x-rays. Phys. Eng. Sci. Med., 1–11 (2020)
10. Oh, Y., Park, S., Ye, J.C.: Deep learning covid-19 features on CXR using limited training data sets. IEEE Trans. Med. Imaging **39**(8), 2688–2700 (2020)
11. Lin, T.-C., Lee, H.-C.: Covid-19 chest radiography images analysis based on integration of image preprocess, guided grad-CAM, machine learning, and risk management. In: Proceedings ICMHI 2020, pp. 281–288 (2020). https://doi.org/10.1145/3418094.3418096
12. Li, Q., Guan, X., Wu, P., et al.: Early transmission dynamics in Wuhan, China, of novel coronavirus–infected pneumonia. New England J. Med., 1199–1207 (2020). https://doi.org/10.1056/NEJMoa2001316
13. Baratella, E., Crivelli, P., Marrocchio, C., et al.: Severity of lung involvement on chest X-rays in SARS-coronavirus-2 infected patients as a possible tool to predict clinical progression: an observational retrospective analysis of the relationship between radiological, clinical, and laboratory data. J. Bras. Pneumol. **46**(5), 20200226 (2020)
14. Warren, M.A., Zhao, Z., Koyama, T., et al.: Severity scoring of lung edema on the chest radiograph is associated with clinical outcomes in ARDS. Thorax **73**, 840–846 (2018)
15. ICS: Scale for the stratification of severity in relation to the chest X-ray. Cuban Society of Imaging. Internal document. Havana, Cuba (2020)
16. Garea-Llano, E., Castellanos-Loaces, H.A., Martinez-Montes, E., Gonzalez-Dalmau, E.: A machine learning based approach for estimation of the lung affectation degree in CXR images of COVID-19 patients. In: Hernández Heredia, Y., Milián Núñez, V., Ruiz Shulcloper, J. (eds.) IWAIPR 2021. LNCS, vol. 13055, pp. 13–23. Springer, Cham (2021). https://doi.org/10.1007/978-3-030-89691-1_2
17. Garea-Llano, E., Martinez-Montes, E., Gonzalez-Dalmaus, E.: Affectation index and severity degree by COVID-19 in Chest X-ray images using artificial intelligence. Int. Rob. Auto J. **8**(3), 103–107 (2022)
18. Savardi, M., Benini, S., Adami, N., et al.: BS-Net: learning COVID-19 pneumonia severity on a large chest X-ray dataset. Med. Image Anal. **71**, 102046 (2021)

19. Haghighi, F., Hosseinzadeh Taher, M.R., Zhou, Z., Gotway, M.B., Liang, J.: Learning semantics-enriched representation via self-discovery, self-classification, and self-restoration. In: Martel, A.L., et al. (eds.) MICCAI 2020. LNCS, vol. 12261, pp. 137–147. Springer, Cham (2020). https://doi.org/10.1007/978-3-030-59710-8_14
20. Sajjad, M., Khan, S., Muhammad, K., Wu, W., Ullah, A., Baik, S.W.: Multi-grade brain tumor classification using deep CNN with extensive data augmentation. J. Comput. Sci. **30**, 174–182 (2019)
21. Simonyan, K.A.: Very deep convolutional networks for large-scale image recognition (2015). arXiv:1409.1556
22. He, K., Zhang, X., Ren, S., Sun, J.: Deep residual learning for image recognition. In: Proceedings of the IEEE Conference on Computer Vision and Pattern Recognition, pp. 770–778 (2016)
23. Szegedy, C., Vanhoucke, V., Ioffe, S., Shlens, J., Wojna, Z.: Rethinking the inception architecture for computer vision. In: 2016 IEEE Conference on Computer Vision and Pattern Recognition (CVPR), pp. 2818–2826 (2016). https://doi.org/10.1109/CVPR.2016.308
24. Berrar, D.: Cross-validation. In: Encyclopedia of Bioinformatics and Computational Biology, vol. 1, pp. 542–545. Elsevier (2018)

Leukocyte Detection with Novel Fully Convolutional Network and a New Dataset of Blood Smear Complete Samples

Juan A. Ramirez-Quintana[1]([✉])(iD), Jesus H. Rios-Barrios[1],
Mario I. Chacon-Murguia[1](iD), Carlos Arzate-Quintana[2](iD),
and Alma D. Corral-Saenz[1]

[1] PVR Lab, Tecnologico Nacional de Mexico/I.T. Chihuahua, Chihuahua, Mexico
{juan.rq,m20061548,mario.cm,alma.cs}@chihuahua.tecnm.mx
[2] Universidad Autonoma de Chihuahua. FMCB, Chihuahua, Mexico
carzate@uach.com

Abstract. The analysis of leukocytes in blood smear sample images has been a successful tool for medical diagnosis, and there are machine-learning methods for segmenting and classifying leukocytes with these images. However, the datasets for designing these methods have images with different compositions than blood smear samples acquired with the standard protocols used in real clinical laboratories. Then, to contribute to the effort to improve the research related to the analysis of leukocytes, this paper presents a new dataset and a method for Leukocyte detection named Color Normalized UNet (CUNet). LeukoSet comprises 1497 images of blood smear complete samples using a protocol developed in a real clinical laboratory environment. The dataset has ground truths that classify the leukocytes into Lymphocytes, Monocytes, Neutrophils, Basophils, Eosinophils, and deformed leukocytes. CUNet is a Fully Convolutional Network (FCN) based on UNet for leukocyte detection designed with the images of LeukoSet. Experiments report that CUNet has an accuracy of 94.22% and an inference time of 27 ms. The results of CUNet are better than other leukocyte detection methods implemented in the literature.

Keywords: Fully Convolutional Network · Leukocite Segmentation · UNet · Blood Smear Image Dataset

1 Introduction

Leukocytes are immune system cells classified into Lymphocytes (Ly), Monocytes (Mc), Neutrophils (Np), Basophils (Bs), and Eosinophils (Ep). Analyzing the size, shape, and number of leukocytes in microscopic blood smear samples is crucial for diagnosing different diseases. This analysis is difficult for clinical technicians and hematologists due to the acquisition protocols and the wide variations in the shape and size of the different blood cells. For this reason, there are many types of research to analyze images of leukocyte cells, including color normalization, identification of nuclei and cytoplasm, and machine-learning methods

A. Y. Rodríguez-González et al. (Eds.): MCPR 2023, LNCS 13902, pp. 221–230, 2023.
https://doi.org/10.1007/978-3-031-33783-3_21

for the segmentation and classification of Leukocytes [1]. For example, Teng et al. propose in [2] a semisupervised leukocyte segmentation method based on a MobileNet v2. Dhalla et al. present in [3] an autoencoder with a convolutional block attention module and dilated convolutions to salient multiscale leukocyte segmentation. Roy et al. describe in [8] a method for leukocyte segmentation based on ResNet-50. Ashour et al. propose in [5] a method based on histogram analysis and third-degree polynomial Support Vector Machine (SVM) for segmenting and classifying basophils and eosinophils. Hussain et al. propose in [7] a fully automatic algorithm for the segmentation and classification of white blood cells, which suggests that the SVM and Artificial Neural Networks outclass other classifiers. Hemalatha et al. [4] categorize blood cells into normal and abnormal, using K Means to segment the blood cells and an Enhanced Convolution Neural Network (ECNN) to classify them. Barrera et al. develop a Generative Adversarial Network in [6] to generate Ly, Mc, Ep, Np, Bap, atypical promyelocytes, and abnormal cells. These machine-learning methods are developed with public or private datasets composed of cropped images with leukocytes, images with blood smear samples of animals, or the samples are depured with restrictions focused on having images with the same texture and color patterns. However, according to the experts in blood cell analysis, it is essential to design algorithms that segment and classify leukocytes from blood smear complete samples because the standard protocols used by technicians generate images with textures and color variations that are not considered in the datasets reported in literature [9,10,12]. Then, contributing to improving the leukocyte analysis, this research presents a dataset named LeukoSet and a novel method for Leukocyte detection named Color Normalization UNet (CUNet). LeukoSet is composed of 1497 images of blood smear complete samples acquired with a microscope using a protocol developed in a real clinical laboratory environment. CUNet is a Fully Convolutional Network (FCN) based on UNet for leukocyte detection, which was designed using the images of LeukoSet.

The rest of the paper is organized as follows: Sect. 2 describes LeukoSet, Sect. 3 presents the CUNet method, Sect. 4 reports the results, and Sect. 5 describes the conclusions.

2   Datasets

Few datasets are available in the literature. Most of them focused on leukocyte classification with cropped images. For example, Kouzehkanan et al. present Raabin-WBC [12], a public database of 4000 cropped images with leukocytes. The images were obtained from 72 blood smear samples with a microscope at a magnification of 100X. The ground truth (GTs) classify the leukocytes into Ly, Mc, Np, Bs, Eo, Bursts cells, and Artifacts. RoseAlipo-on et al. [13] describe a public database of 3457 leukocyte images labeled by the GTs into Ly, Mc, Np, Bs, and Eo. The images are obtained from blood smear samples of juvenile Visayan Warty Pigs. Paul Mooney published Blood Cell Images (BlCI) [14], a dataset with 12,500 images of blood cells divided into Ly, Mc, Np, Bs, and

Eo classes. Abdüssamet Aslan published Blood Cell Detection Dataset (BCDD) [15], a set of 119 images acquired for classifying leucocytes and erythrocytes from peripheral blood smear taken from a light microscope. Liyan published WBC images (WBC) [16], a dataset with 4427 images divided into Ly, Mc, Np, Bs, and Eo classes. Figure 1 presents an image example of each dataset.

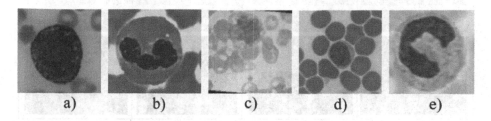

Fig. 1. Examples of images. a). Bs from [12] dataset. b). Eo from [13] dataset. c). Mc from [14] dataset. d). Ly from [15] dataset. e). Np from [16] dataset.

On the other hand, our proposed dataset, LeukoSet, has 1497 high-resolution images acquired with a microscope, where 689 have a magnification of 40X and 808 have a magnification of 100X. Each image is a complete sample of a blood smear with erythrocytes, leukocytes, and other blood objects. Each image has its ground truth (GTs) composed of leukocyte labels divided into the classes Ly, Mc, Np, Bs, Eo, and deformed leukocytes, as Table 1 shows. The blood smear sample images were acquired at Universidad Autónoma de Chihuahua (UACH) using a standard protocol of obtaining human blood with venipuncture and collecting it in tubes with EDTA anticoagulant. The samples are observed under a microscope using the Wright-Stain to color the leukocyte nucleus in purple [17]. The labels, GTs, dataset organization, and framework to use LeukoSet were developed in Tecnologico Nacional de Mexico/I.T. Chihuahua (ITCh). Figure 2 shows four image examples of blood smear samples obtained using the same protocol, anticoagulant, stain, microscope, and illumination. These samples have artifacts and significant color differences, common in samples obtained with the same protocol and restrictions in real clinical laboratories [9,10,12].

3   CUNet

The proposed method CUNet is developed to detect and count leukocytes in complete blood smear samples. Figure 3 presents the general scheme of the proposed method. The input is an RGB color image $I(x,y)^{RGB}$ where (x,y) is the pixel position. The next layer is a color normalization method to have samples with the same color patterns in the background, erythrocytes, and leukocytes. The next step is an autoencoder for leukocyte detection. This autoencoder is an UNet network [11] composed of three encoders, a convolutional bottleneck, three decoders, and two convolutional maps for leukocyte detection. The following subsections describe each part of the proposed method.

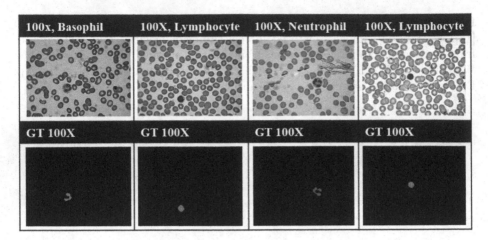

Fig. 2. Image examples with their GTs.

Table 1. Number of leukocytes in the dataset

Class	Number of cells	Label color	Pixel Resolution
Neutrophil	689	Red	
Eosinophil	153	Yellow	
Basophil	542	Green	1024x768 and
Lymphocyte	984	Blue	2560x1920 pixels
Monocyte	121	Gray	
Deformed	11	Violet	

3.1 Input and Preprocessing

LeukoSet has 1497 images, but we use data augmentation to have 2100 images, 1500 images for training, 300 for testing, and 300 for validation. We use linear transformations of translation, scaling, and rotation because these transformations generate more realistic samples than other data augmentation algorithms. Then, CUNet was trained with 1500 images, $I(x,y)^{RGB}$, of complete blood smear samples. The spatial resolution is MxN, where $x = 0, ..., M - 1$ and $x = 0, ..., N - 1$.

The preprocessing consists of a color normalization based on the method of Macenko [18], an algorithm for overcoming inconsistencies in the standard color staining process. The Macenko method uses a logarithmic function to transform

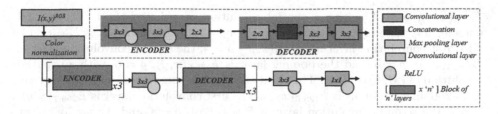

Fig. 3. General scheme of the proposed method.

the color concentration to have the background and the blood cells in the same color ranges. The result of the Macenko method is named $P(x, y)^{RGB}$, and Fig. 4 shows three blood smear image examples with magnification factors of 100X and 40X.

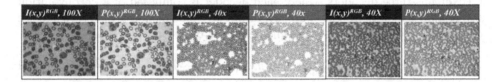

Fig. 4. Macenko normalization examples.

3.2 Encoder and Bottleneck

$P(x, y)^{RGB}$ is the input to three encoders of CUNet, where each encoder has two convolution layers with RELU activation functions and a max-pooling layer. The definition of convolution is:

$$E_{\tau_\rho,\rho}(x, y) = f[W_{\tau_\rho,\rho,l}(x, y) * F_{\tau_\rho-1,\rho-1}(x, y) + \beta_\rho], l = 3x3 \tag{1}$$

where $E_{\tau_\rho,\rho}(x, y)$ is the output of the convolution layer, $W_{\tau_\rho,\rho}(x, y)$ are the kernels, l is the kernel size, ρ is the layer index and τ_ρ is the depth of the layer ρ. All the kernels of the encoder convolutions have a size of $l = 3x3$ and a stride of one. $f(.)$ is a RELU activation function defined as $max[0, W(x, y) * E(x, y)]$. The max-pooling layer reduces the size of the features with the following definition:

$$F_{\tau_\rho,\rho+2}(x, y) = max[G_{\tau_\rho,\rho}(p, q, r)], p = 1, 2, q = 1, 2 \tag{2}$$

where $G_{\tau_\rho,\rho,l,r}(p, q)$ is a set of r windows $G_{\tau_\rho,\rho}(p, q) \subseteq F_{\tau_\rho,\rho,l}(x, y)$ with size $l = 2x2$ and $F_{\tau_\rho,\rho,l}(x, y) = \bigcup_r G_{\tau_\rho,\rho}(p, q)$.

The input to the first encoder is $F_{\tau_0,0}(x, y) = P(x, y)^{RGB}$, where $\tau_0 = 3$ because each input component is a color channel. This first encoder has three layers with 64 kernels, $\tau_\rho = 64$. The first convolution layer is $E_{64,1}(x, y)$, $\rho = 1$, the second convolution layer is $E_{64,2}(x, y)$, $\rho = 2$, and the pooling layer is

$F_{64,3}(x, y)$, $\rho = 3$, with an spatial resolution of $(M/2)x(M/2)$. The second encoder has three layers with 128 kernels, $\tau_\rho = 128$, and the input is $F_{64,3}(x, y)$. The first convolution layer is $E_{128,4}(x, y)$, $\rho = 4$, the second convolution layer is $E_{128,5}(x, y)$, $\rho = 5$, and the pooling layer is $F_{128,6}(x, y)$, $\rho = 6$, with an spatial resolution of $(M/4)x(M/4)$. The third encoder has three layers with 256 kernels, $\tau_\rho = 256$, and the input is $F_{128,6}(x, y)$. The first convolution layer is $E_{256,7}(x, y)$, $\rho = 7$, the second convolution layer is $E_{128,8}(x, y)$, $\rho = 8$, and the pooling layer is $F_{256,9}(x, y)$, $\rho = 9$, with an spatial resolution of $(M/8)x(M/8)$.

There is a 3x3 convolution layer after the encoder block, $E_{\tau_{10},10}(x, y)$, $\rho = 10$. This convolution layer has 512 kernels, $\tau_{10} = 512$, a RELU activation function, and a stride of one. This layer is a bottleneck that generates features that separate the leukocytes from the rest of the objects in the blood smear sample.

3.3   Decoder

CUNet has three decoders, where each decoder is composed of a deconvolution layer, a concatenation, and two convolution layers defined as Eq. (1) with a size of $l = 3x3$ and the stride is one. The definition of deconvolution is:

$$D_{\tau_{\rho+1},\rho+1}(x, y) = E_{\tau_\rho,\rho}(x, y) * Z_{\tau_\rho,\rho,l}(x, y) + \beta_{\rho+1}, l = 2x2 \qquad (3)$$

where $D_{\tau_{\rho+1},\rho+1,}(x, y)$ is the output of the deconvolution layer, $Z_{\tau_\rho,\rho}(x, y)$ are the transposed kernels with the size of $l = 2x2$ and the stride is two. In the case of these transposed convolutions, the stride increases the dimension of feature maps. This deconvolution is concatenated to reduce the depth of the features. The output of concatenation is called $H_{\tau_{\rho+1},\rho+1,}(x, y)$. The convolution layers of the decoder are defined as:

$$E_{\tau_\rho,\rho}(x, y) = W_{\tau_\rho,\rho,l}(x, y) * E_{\tau_{\rho-1},\rho-1}(x, y) + \beta_\rho, l = 3x3 \qquad (4)$$

The input of the first decoder is $E_{512,10}(x, y)$ with a resolution of $(M/8)x(M/8)$. The first decoder has a deconvolution layer $D_{512,11}(x, y)$ to resize the spatial resolution of features to $(M/4)x(N/4)$. The concatenation is $H_{256,11}(x, y)$ to have a depth of $\tau_{11} = 256$, $\rho = 11$. The next two layers are two convolutions defined by Eq. (4), generating the outputs $E_{256,12}(x, y)$ and $E_{256,13}(x, y)$ ($\rho = 12$ and $\rho = 13$). The input of the second decoder is $E_{256,13}(x, y)$, and the deconvolution is layer $D_{256,14}(x, y)$, which resizes the spatial resolution of features to $(M/2)x(N/2)$. The concatenation is $H_{128,14}(x, y)$ to have a depth of $\tau_{14} = 128$, $\rho = 14$. The next two layers are two convolutions defined by Eq. (4), generating the outputs $E_{128,15}(x, y)$ and $E_{128,16}(x, y)$ ($\rho = 15$ and $\rho = 16$). The input of the third decoder is $E_{128,16}(x, y)$, and the deconvolution is layer $D_{128,17}(x, y)$, which resizes the resolution of features to MxN. The concatenation is $H_{64,17}(x, y)$ to have a depth of $\tau_{17} = 64$, $\rho = 17$. The next two layers are two convolutions defined by Eq. (4), generating the outputs $E_{64,18}(x, y)$ and $E_{64,19}(x, y)$ ($\rho = 18$ and $\rho = 18$).

3.4   Final Convolution Layers

The final block of CUNet comprises two convolution layers where $\rho = 20$ and $\rho = 21$. The layer $\rho = 20$ is a convolution defined by Eq. (1) to reduce the depth to three channels. This convolution layer $E_{3,20}(x, y)$ has a RELU activation function $f(.)$, and $l = 3x3$. The next convolution $E_{1,21}(x, y)$ is to generate a binarized output of one channel with a RELU activation function $f(.)$, and $l = 3x3$. $E_{1,21}(x, y)$ is the output of CUNet, and Fig. 5 shows two examples (one is an image acquired at 40X image and the other is an image acquired at 100X).

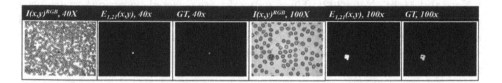

Fig. 5. Results of CUNet.

4   Results

This section presents information about the training and a comparative analysis of CUNet. The training and the experiments were developed on a computer with a 3 GHz Ryzen 5 processor, 16 GB RAM, and a GPU NVIDIA RTX 2060 SUPER.

4.1   Training and Performance of CUNet

We used the augmented set based on LeukoSet presented in Subsect. 3.1 to train, test, and validate CUNet. The training algorithm for the experiments is backpropagation with ADAM optimizer, a learning rate of 0.0001, a Batch of two, a loss function of cross-entropy, and six epochs. According to an ablation analysis of the Macenko method, CUNet learns irrelevant features that decrease the performance if we eliminate color normalization. However, if the Macenko method is included, CUNet learns abstract features during the training based on the morphology of leukocytes as follows:

1. The first encoder learns features that separate the background and artifacts from the blood cells.
2. The second encoder learns features that separate the erythrocytes from the leukocytes.
3. The third encoder learns features that inhibit the erythrocytes and preserve the leukocytes.
4. The bottleneck separates the leukocytes from the rest of the objects in the blood smear samples, generating pixel values higher than 0.8 in the pixels that belong to leukocytes ($Leukocyte = \{e_{\tau_{10},10}(x, y) > 0.8\}$) and generating pixel values lower than 0.2 in the rest of the pixels $e_{\tau_{10},10}(x, y) < 0.2$.

5. The three decoders increase the dimension of the features with the deconvolution layers. In addition, the convolution layers analyze the neighborhood of pixels with values higher than 0.8 to improve the morphology of the regions that represent the leukocytes.
6. The final convolution layers binarize the features to generate an image where the blobs represent the leukocytes.

4.2 Comparative Analysis of CUNet

The networks selected for the comparison are ResNet-50 v2 [8], Resnet-34 v2, UNet, and MobileNet v2 [2]. These networks are selected because they are used in literature to detect leukocyte cells. These networks were implemented and trained with the same hardware and training algorithm as CUNet. The metrics used to compare CUNet with the other networks are accuracy (Acc), time to train the network/method (TM), and inference time (TI). Table 2 shows the comparative results.

The UNet network has four encoders, one bottleneck, four decoders, and two convolutional layers. In this case, the fourth encoder inhibits the leukocyte features, generating problems in the correct detection in the decoder. The fourth decoder generates irrelevant morphology features in leukocyte detection. Also, the fourth encoder and the fourth decoder increase the computational cost. ResNet-34 v2 and ResNet-50 v2 have many layers that generate irrelevant features, confusing erythrocytes with leukocytes. MobileNet v2 generates many irrelevant features due to dilated convolutions confusing erythrocytes with similar colors to the leukocyte nucleus, and some Np cells are not detected.

We developed experiments to use the normalized images obtained with the Macenko method with UNet, ResNet-34 v2, Rresnet-50 v2, and MobileNet v2. However, the obtained accuracies were the same because many layers of these networks generate irrelevant features. On the other hand, CUNet has the necessary number of encoder and decoder layers to generate blobs that represent the leukocytes. Also, each encoder has two convolution layers that help to find features in two magnification levels which are 100X and 40X. However, CUNet needs to improve the correct morphology of Eo and Np cells because these blood cells have nuclei with a morphology more stochastic than the others blood cells.

Table 2. Comparative analysis

Network	Acc (%)	TM (h:min.)	TI (ms)
UNet	79.06	1:21 h	60 ms
ResNet-50 v2 [8]	63.79	1:33 h	60 ms
ResNet-34 v2	62.64	1:15 h	47 ms
MobileNet v2 [2]	42.03	0:24 min	46 ms
CUNet (ours)	94.22	0:45 min	27 ms

5   Conclusion

This paper presents two contributions to leukocyte analysis. The first contribution is a database named LeukoSet, a set of 1497 images of complete blood smear samples for leukocyte segmentation and classification. The other contribution is a method for leukocyte detection named Color Normalized UNet (CUNet). CUNet is an FCN with an architecture inspired by UNet composed of a color normalization layer, three encoders for feature extraction, a bottleneck, three decoders, and two convolution layer for leukocyte detection.

According to the results, CUNet has better inference time and accuracy than the other networks. These results are because CUNet has an appropriate architecture to segment the nucleus of leukocytes. The first encoder separates the background and blood cells, the second encoder separates erythrocytes from the leukocytes, and the third encoder preserves the leukocytes and inhibits the erythrocytes. The three decoders increase the size of the feature map to MxN, preserving the morphologic patterns of leukocytes as the decoder increases the resolution. The other analyzed networks have many layers that learn features irrelevant to leukocyte analysis.

The future work is to increase the number of images of LeuKoSet to generate better experiments of CUNet. Also, the next step is to design a method to classify the leukocytes.

Acknowledgement. The Tecnologico Nacional de Mexico supported this work under grants TecNM 14044.22-P.

References

1. Mukesh-Saraswat, E., Arya, K.V.: Automated microscopic image analysis for leukocytes identification: A survey. Micron **65**(1), 20–33 (2023)
2. Teng, S., Wu, J., Chen, Y., Fan, H., Cao, X., Li, Z.: Semi-Supervised Leukocyte Segmentation Based on Adversarial Learning With Reconstruction Enhancement. IEEE Trans. Instrum. Meas. **71**(5015511), 1–11 (2022)
3. Dhalla, S., Mittal, A., Gupta, S., Kaur, J., Kaur, H.II.: A combination of simple and dilated convolution with attention mechanism in a feature pyramid network to segment leukocytes from blood smear images. Biomed. Signal Process. Control **80**(2), 104344 (2023)
4. Hemalatha, B., Karthik, B., Krishna Reddy, C.V., Latha, A.: Deep learning approach for segmentation and classification of blood cells using enhanced CNN. Meas. Sensors **24**, 100582 (2022)
5. Ashour, A.S., Wahba, M.A., Ghannam, R.: A cascaded classification-segmentation reversible system for computer-aided detection and cells counting in microscopic peripheral blood smear basophils and eosinophils images. IEEE Access **9**, 78883–78901 (2021)
6. Barrera, K., Merino, A., Molina, A., Rodellar, J.: Automatic generation of artificial images of leukocytes and leukemic cells using generative adversarial networks (syntheticcellgan). Comput. Methods Programs Biomed. **229**, 107314 (2023)

7. Hussain, M.A., Ahmad, I., Shaukat, A., Islam, Z.U.: Leukocytes segmentation and classification in digital microscopic images. In: International Conference on Computing and Information Sciences. IEEE, Karachi, Pakistan (2021)
8. Roy Reena, M., Ameer, P.M.: Segmentation of leukocyte by semantic segmentation model: A deep learning approach. Biomed. Signal Process. Control 65, 102385 (2021)
9. Khan, S., Sajjad, M., Abbas, N., Rehman, A.: A review on machine learning-based wbcs analysis in blood smear images: key challenges, datasets, and future directions. In: Saba, T., Rehman, A., Roy, S., (eds.) Prognostic Models in Healthcare: AI and Statistical Approaches. Studies in Big Data, vol 109. Springer, Singapore (2022) https://doi.org/10.1007/978-981-19-2057-8_11
10. Aris, T.A., Nasir, A.S.A., Jaafar, H., Chin, L.C., Mohamed, Z.: Color constancy analysis approach for color standardization on malaria thick and thin blood smear images. In: Md. Zain, Z., et al. (eds.) Proceedings of the 11th National Technical Seminar on Unmanned System Technology 2019. LNEE, vol. 666, pp. 785–804. Springer, Singapore (2021). https://doi.org/10.1007/978-981-15-5281-6_57
11. Li, D., Yin, S., Lei, Y., Qian, J., Zhao, C., Zhang, L.: Segmentation of white blood cells based on CBAM-DC-UNet. IEEE Access 11, 1074–1082 (2023)
12. Mousavi-Kouzehkanan, Z.: A large dataset of white blood cells containing cell locations and types, along with segmented nuclei and cytoplasm. Sci. Rep. 12(1123), 1–14 (2022)
13. RoseAlipoon, J.: Dataset for Machine Learning-Based Classification of White Blood Cells of the Juvenile Visayan Warty Pig. IEEE Dataport (2022)
14. Blood Cell Images (2018). https://www.kaggle.com/datasets/paultimothymoon ey/blood-cells
15. Blood Cell Detection Dataset (2020). https://www.kaggle.com/datasets/draaslan/ blood-cell-detection-dataset
16. WBC images (2021). https://www.kaggle.com/datasets/liyan4321/wbc-images
17. Fang-Yue, Q., Xiong, B., Xin-Chen, W., Yue-Liu, X.: Comparative study of the efficacy of Wright-Giemsa stain and Liu's stain in the detection of Auer rods in acute promyelocytic leukemia. Acta Histochem. 116(6), 1113–1116 (2014)
18. Macenko, M.: A method for normalizing histology slides for quantitative analysis. In: IEEE Proceedings of International Symposium on Biomedical Imaging: From Nano to Macro, pp. 1107–1110 (2009). https://doi.org/10.1109/ISBI.2009.5193250

Comparison of Deep Learning Architectures in Classification of Microcalcifications Clusters in Digital Mammograms

Ricardo Salvador Luna Lozoya[1]([envelope]) [ID],
Humberto de Jesús Ochoa Domínguez[1] [ID], Juan Humberto Sossa Azuela[2] [ID],
Vianey Guadalupe Cruz Sánchez[1] [ID], and Osslan Osiris Vergara Villegas[1] [ID]

[1] Instituto de Ingeniería y Tecnología, Universidad Autónoma de Ciudad Juárez,
Ciudad Juárez, Mexico
al216618@alumnos.uacj.mx, {hochoa,vianey.cruz,overgara}@uacj.mx
[2] Laboratorio de Robótica y Mecatrónica, Centro de Investigación en Computación,
Instituto Politécnico Nacional, Mexico City, Mexico
hsossa@cic.ipn.mx

Abstract. Microcalcifications clusters (MCCs) are relevant breast cancer indirect evidence and early detection can prevent death. In this paper, we carry out a comparison of the deep learning architectures (DL) InceptionV3, DenseNet121, ResNet50, VGG-16, MobileNet V2, LeNet-5 and AlexNet in classification of MCCs in digital mammograms, with the aim to select the best configuration and building blocks that yield a reduced number of parameters. We used the INbreast database to extract patches of size 144×144 pixels corresponding to 1 cm^2. The networks were implemented and trained using four independent configurations that consisted of: training each architecture without any extra layer, by adding, after each convolutional and fully connected layer, a Batch Normalization layer, an L_2 regularization layer or a Dropout layer, respectively. The best overall accuracy was yielded by the MobileNetV2 with Dropout configuration. The network is built of residual blocks, depth separable convolutional blocks and 1×1 convolutional layers this allows a reduced number of parameters while yielding an accuracy of 0.99841. The comparison highlights the differences and similarities of the DL networks necessary to make the best decision possible to design and implement more optimal networks to classify MCCs. Furthermore, it demonstrates that for the classification of these lesions, the shallow architectures built with certain building blocks and trained with the right configuration, give similar results to their deeper and more complex counterparts.

Keywords: Microcalcifications clusters detection · Convolutional neural network · Deep learning

© The Author(s), under exclusive license to Springer Nature Switzerland AG 2023
A. Y. Rodríguez-González et al. (Eds.): MCPR 2023, LNCS 13902, pp. 231–241, 2023.
https://doi.org/10.1007/978-3-031-33783-3_22

1   Introduction

Microcalcifications (MCs) may represent an early sign of breast cancer. Breast radiographs are the most frequently acquired images as they are the most accurate method for detecting Microcalcifications

MCs are deposits of calcium with diameters from 0.1 to 1 mm, that vary in brightness and contrast, and they are scattered or clustered at different locations in the image [8,26]. A cluster consists of at least three MCs in a square centimeter. When they appear, a biopsy is recommended [21].

Microcalcifications clusters (MCCs) detection is challenging as they are impalpable by simple touch [2,18,25]. In the past, some classical detection methods reached maximum accuracies of 92.58% [7,13]. Recently, models based on Deep Learning (DL) have proven to be efficient in many areas [17]. Accordingly, Convolutional Neural Networks (CNN) can identify different objects on images making them useful for medical applications [2,10]. In this sense, Hsieh et al. [11] proposed a combination of pretrained networks based on the VGG-16 to detect MCCs, the Mask R-CNN to segment MCs in the cluster and the InceptionV3 to classify them into benign and malignant. The reported detection accuracy of VGG-16 was 93.3%.

According to the literature, the only architecture that has been used to detect MCCs is the VGG-16 [11]. However, the application of this model was straightforward without comparing the performance against other DL networks to support the use of the VGG-16. Moreover, networks like InceptionV3 and VGG-16 are pretrained with large color image data sets to classify 1,000 different categories [5,15]. This leads to more complex models when it is necessary to classify grayscale images such as MCCs [4].

In this article, we present a comparison of the state-of-the-art DL architectures InceptionV3, DenseNet121, ResNet50, VGG-16, MobileNetV2, LeNet-5 and AlexNet DL commonly used in classification tasks for classifying MCCs. We trained these networks using four different configurations to specifically classify MCCs. The aim of this work is to select the best configuration and building blocks that yield a reduced number of parameters, while maintaining the best accuracy. The main contributions of the paper are the following:

- We show that in a DL architecture used for MCCs classification, the building blocks connection and the configuration used train the models are two of the most important aspects which can lead to the design of shallow architectures.
- We propose the block structure to construct DL architectures to classify MCCs based on the compared networks.

The rest of the article is organized as follows: in Sect. 2, the material and methods are shown. The experiments and results are presented in Sect. 3. In Sect. 4, the discussion of the results is presented. Finally, the conclusions are presented in Sect. 5.

2   Materials and Methods

All software development was carried out through the online platform Google Colaboratory [3], which automatically assigns the necessary hardware according to the available resources when executing tasks. The implementation of the models was carried out using the TensorFlow 2.11 library [1]. The database utilized is the INbreast [19] because of the high resolution of the mammograms and the annotated of the MCCs by experts. INbreast, contains 410 images of size $2,560 \times 3,328$ and $3,328 \times 4,084$ pixels of different views in DICOM format. Each pixel is 70 microns. In the database, the MCCs are identified by their coordinates instead of binary labels indicating presence and absence.

2.1   Deep Learning Architectures

Most of the DL classification models are built from different building blocks such as convolutional layers, pooling layers, activation layers, flattening layers, and dense layers. Convolutional layers systematically apply n_f learnable filters on the input to capture features into the feature maps, which are passed to the next layer. The pooling layer reduces the size of the feature maps. The activation layer is built of perceptrons and is used to prevent linearity and represent the feature maps with complex functions. The flattening layer converts the input maps into a one-dimensional features array. Finally, the dense layer, used in classification tasks, is a one-dimensional layer of perceptrons whose outputs connect to each neuron in the next layer. During training, the learning process is carried out by minimizing a loss function that minimizes the classification or prediction error.

The main dissimilarities among the different DL architectures are the type of layer, the number of filters per layer, the type of neurons, the way the layers are connected, and the depth. In this work, we selected common DL architectures used for classification tasks due to their depths, the diversity of building blocks, and the way of connection among them. These architectures are described following:

LeNet-5 [16]. This architecture is a five layers network, two convolutional layers followed by two fully connected layers and a softmax layer at the output. The network detects freehand digits images of size 32×32 pixels. As the network gets deeper, the spatial dimension of the layers decreases, and the number of channels per layer increases.

AlexNet [15]. The network was designed to detect objects in color images. The input image or receptive field is $227 \times 227 \times 3$ pixels. AlexNet is made up of 8 layers, of which five are convolutional and three are fully connected.

VGG-16 [22]. This network is an update of the AlexNet [15]. The benefits are the use of a filter of size 3×3 and the 16 layers depth, of which 14 are convolutional and two are fully connected. The network operates on color images of $224 \times 224 \times 3$ pixels.

DenseNet121 [12]. This network is a 121 layer CNN. The outputs of each layer serve as inputs for the following layers. The use of DenseNet121 solves the vanishing gradient problem, reuses features and decreases the number of parameters. Two components are the foundations of the DenseNet: The Dense Block and the Transition Layer. The Dense Block consists of two convolutional layers of 1×1 and 3×3. The Transition Layer consists of a 1×1 convolutional layer and an average pooling layer with strides of 2.

ResNet50 [9]. This network is a 50 layer network built of 16 residual blocks of three layers each to solve the vanishing/exploding gradient problem. Each block uses a skip connection or shortcuts that connects activations of the input layer by skipping two layers in between. One max pooling and one average pooling layer with strides of 2 are connected at the output.

InceptionV3 [24]. The main feature of this network is the concatenation of its components in one step only, instead of adding sequential them one per one like the regular networks. The Inception is the main component of the network, it consists of a convolutional layer of 1×1, a convolutional layer of 3×3, a convolutional layer of 5×5 and a max pooling layer of with stride of 1. The concatenation achieves until a 90% computational complexity reduction without compromising the network performance.

MobileNetV2 [20]. This network allows building and deploying neural networks in environments with low computing power. It is built of 17 residual blocks to propagate the gradient more efficiently. Each block is made of three layers. The first layer is a 1×1 convolution with ReLU activation functions. The second layer is the depthwise separable convolution that applies a single filter to each input channel to reduce the computation. The third layer is a 1×1 convolution with linear activation functions to combine the outputs of the depthwise convolution. The output of the block is connected to a max pooling layer for downsizing.

2.2   Experimental Framework

Notice that in the TensorFlow library [1], Batch Normalization, L_2 regularization and Dropout are added as layers. Therefore, in this article, we treat them as layers with no parameters. Figure 1 shows the experimental framework. Here, the layers of each architecture are trained with the following configurations independently: (1) without any extra layer, using (2) Batch Normalization layers, (3) L2 regularization layers, or (4) Dropout layers.

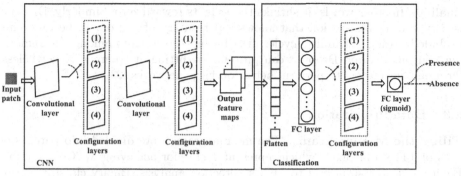

(1). No additional layer
(2). Batch Normalization layer
(3). L_2 regularization layer
(4). Dropout layer

Fig. 1. Experimental framework. Before training, to configure each architecture one of the four configuration layers is added after each convolutional and fully connected layer. Then, the training is run until the model is optimized. After training the resulting model is tested.

The feature maps at the output of the last configuration layer are concatenated to create a feature vector. A fully connected (FC) layer is fed with these features. Then, at the output a configuration layer is applied. Finally, a sigmoid function for binary classification into presence or absence of MCCs. The loss function used is the Binary Cross-Entropy of Eq. (1).

$$\mathcal{L}(y, \hat{y}) = -\frac{1}{m} \sum_{i=1}^{m} [y_i \cdot \log(\hat{y}_i) + (1 - y_i) \cdot \log(1 - \hat{y}_i)] + R(\omega) \qquad (1)$$

where m is the size of the training set used and it is an scaling factor, y_i is the target value that can take two possible values, 0 or 1 (presence or absence of MCCs), and $\hat{y}_i$ is the predicted value. $R(\omega)$ is a vector norm (regularizer) used to encourage smaller weights. We used the L_2 regularization of Eq. (2) to penalize the weights.

$$R(\omega) = \frac{\lambda}{2m} \sum_{l=1}^{L} \sum_{i=1}^{n^{[l]}} \sum_{j=1}^{n^{[l-1]}} \left(\omega^{[l]}\right)^2 \qquad (2)$$

where λ is the penalty factor, L is the number of layers, $n^{[l]}$ and $n^{[l-1]}$ are the number of neurons in layers l and $l-1$, respectively, and $\omega^{[l]}$ are the weight values in the lth layer.

The configurations were selected because the Batch Normalization generalizes the models for different data distributions by normalizing the current batch at the input of each layer. This prevents the distribution of the deep layers from changing concerning the input layer after the weights are updated and standardize the inputs, stabilizing the learning process and dramatically reducing the number of training epochs [14]. Regularization forces the model weights to be small [6]. In other words, it shrinks the weights toward zero. Similarly, Dropout is a type of regularization that allows a percentage of neurons to be randomly excluded during a training cycle, distributing the weights among the remaining neurons. L_2 and Dropout can prevent overfitting at training. Nevertheless, Dropout has proven to perform better on large networks [23].

2.3   Data Preparation

Tiling the Mammograms. The mammograms were divided into patches or tiles of 144 × 144 pixels which represent 1 cm^2 for achieving MCCs detection. Each patch was subjected to MCCs detection analysis. Binary classification is used to classify the patches into the presence or absence of MCCs. Figures 2a and 2b show patches with and without MCCs.

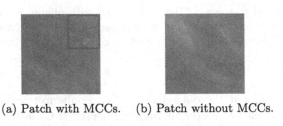

(a) Patch with MCCs.   (b) Patch without MCCs.

Fig. 2. Two patches of 1 cm^2 (a) with MCCs enclosed in a square, these show up as sets of large white dots, dashes and fine, white specks, similar to grains of salt; and (b) without MCCs.

Patches were obtained by sliding a 16 × 16 pixels window on the mammograms of the database: 1,576 patches with MCCs and 1,692 without MCCs. To ensure the correct data representation, an expert radiologist analyzed the integrity, trustability, and correct classification of the patches as the output of the models.

Data Augmentation. The number of patches was augmented using transformations reflection, 180° rotation, combination of both and 90° rotation. A total of 6,304 and 6,768 transformed patches with and without MCCs, respectively, were obtained. Hence, the database consists of 7,880 patches with MCCs and 8,460 patches without MCCs, for a total of 16,340 examples from which only 15,760 were used to have balanced classes. 64% (10,088) were used for training, 16% (2,520) for validation and 20% (3,152) for testing. Each set was made up of 50% patches with MCCs and 50% without MCCs.

3   Experiments and Results

The patches were normalized by dividing them by 255. All models were trained by using 100 epochs and the batch size was selected by the grid search method.

After hyperparameter tuning, the resulting penalty factor for the L_2 layer was $\lambda = 0.0001$ and the Dropout layer used a probability of 0.8. This means that 80% of the neurons were retained. The resulting optimal batch size is shown in Table 1. Table 2 shows the parameters of the architectures in each configuration. Tables 3 and 4 show the training accuracy and error. Tables 5 and 6 show the testing accuracy and error, respectively. It is essential to mention that an expert radiologist corroborated the testing results.

Table 1. Epochs and iterations for networks training.

CNN	Epochs	Iterations	Batch size
InceptionV3	100	631	16
DenseNet121	100	631	16
ResNet50	100	631	16
VGG-16	100	158	64
MobileNetV2	100	631	16
LeNet-5	100	158	64
AlexNet	100	158	64

Table 2. Parameters used in each configuration.

CNN	No additional layer	Batch Norm.	L_2 reg.	Dropout
InceptionV3	59,555,041	59,563,233	59,555,041	59,555,041
DenseNet121	40,589,761	40,597,953	40,589,761	40,589,761
ResNet50	128,443,137	128,451,329	128,443,137	128,443,137
VGG-16	65,057,473	65,107,137	65,057,473	65,057,473
MobileNetV2	67,797,505	67,805,697	67,797,505	67,797,505
LeNet-5	2,232,461	2,233,365	2,232,461	2,232,461
AlexNet	79,505,089	79,580,225	79,505,089	79,505,089

Table 3. Training accuracy.

CNN	No additional layer	Batch Norm.	L_2 reg.	Dropout
InceptionV3	0.99960	0.99980	0.99980	0.99791
DenseNet121	0.99980	0.99593	0.99980	0.99980
ResNet50	0.99980	0.99980	0.99910	0.99970
VGG-16	0.50138	0.99950	0.50118	0.50178
MobileNetV2	0.99827	**1.00000**	0.99990	0.99980
LeNet-5	**0.99990**	**1.00000**	**1.00000**	**0.99990**
AlexNet	0.50218	0.99950	0.99881	0.74643

Table 4. Training error.

CNN	No additional layer	Batch Norm.	L_2 reg.	Dropout
InceptionV3	0.00275	0.00263	0.00278	0.00715
DenseNet121	0.00224	0.01436	0.00301	0.00386
ResNet50	0.00207	0.00199	0.00589	0.00235
VGG-16	0.69315	0.00291	0.69316	0.69316
MobileNetV2	0.00735	0.00032	**0.00227**	0.00177
LeNet-5	**0.00156**	**0.00005**	0.01595	**0.00120**
AlexNet	0.69415	0.00191	0.01192	0.50968

Table 5. Testing accuracy.

CNN	No additional layer	Batch Norm.	L_2 reg.	Dropout
InceptionV3	0.99682	0.99714	0.99619	0.99270
DenseNet121	**0.99746**	0.99682	**0.99746**	0.99651
ResNet50	0.99714	0.99651	0.99555	0.99746
VGG-16	0.50000	**0.99746**	0.50000	0.50000
MobileNetV2	0.99555	**0.99746**	0.99714	**0.99841**
LeNet-5	0.98572	0.99302	0.98921	0.98953
AlexNet	0.50000	0.99460	0.70145	0.99206

Table 6. Testing error.

CNN	No additional layer	Batch Norm.	L_2 reg.	Dropout
InceptionV3	0.01522	0.01682	**0.01350**	0.01973
DenseNet121	0.01979	0.01903	0.01356	0.01891
ResNet50	**0.01292**	0.01385	0.01905	0.05738
VGG-16	0.69314	**0.01197**	0.69331	0.69314
MobileNetV2	0.02436	0.01927	0.01597	**0.00844**
LeNet-5	0.07174	0.02848	0.05329	0.04505
AlexNet	0.69317	0.01779	0.68587	0.03266

4   Discussion

Table 2 shows that Batch Normalization is the only configuration that changes the number of parameters. Table 5 shows that an accuracy greater than 0.98 is achieved in at least one configuration of the networks. DenseNet121 yielded the best accuracy without additional layer and surpassed the ResNet50 by approximately 0.03%. Notice that the ResNet is almost three times the number of parameters than the DenseNet121. When using a Batch Normalization layer, the VGG-16 and MobileNetV2 yield the same result with batches of 64 and 16 patches, respectively. However, the VGG-16 utilizes $2,698,560$ fewer parameters than the MobileNetV2 with L_2 regularization layer. Similarly, DenseNet121 yielded the highest accuracy followed by the MobileNetV2. In this case, the DenseNet121 has less parameters than the MobileNetV2. Finally, the MobileNetV2 yields the best overall performance if we train using a Dropout layer. Notice that MobileNetV2 uses approximately 52% less parameters as compared to ResNet50. Observe that, the tendency to implement deep models is not always the best choice. For example, using a Batch Normalization configuration, a network like the ResNet50 has 128,443,137 parameters yields a testing accuracy of only 0.35% higher than the LeNet-5, which has 2,232,461 parameters only. From the results, we can see that shorter networks with residual and depth separable convolutional blocks as well as 1×1 convolutional layers could increase the performance while reducing the number of parameters. Finally, we suggest to use global pooling layers, instead of flattening, at the output of the CNN to reduce the number of the total parameters.

5   Conclusion

In this article, we presented a comparison of the InceptionV3, the DenseNet121, the ResNet50, the VGG-16, the MobileNetV2, the LeNet-5 and the AlexNet architectures to classify MCCs using four different configurations to train each networks. The setups used were without using any additional layer, with Batch Normalization layer, with L_2 and Dropout regularization layers, respectively. The MobileNetV2 trained with Dropout layers and a batch size of 16 yielded the best accuracy during testing. Besides, the MobileNetV2 uses less parameters as compared to ResNet50. The comparison demonstrated that for MCCs classification, shallow networks produce results similar to their deeper and more complex counterparts. Based on these observations, we are developing a custom lightweight architecture for real-time analysis of digital mammograms, in collaboration with the Centro de Imagen e Investigación (Medimagen) of Chihuahua, México.

Acknowledgment. Ricardo Luna thanks the UACJ for the support provided and the CONACYT for the scholarship granted to pursue his doctoral studies.

We would like to express our gratitude to the radiologist Dra. Karina Núñez, from the Salud Digna Clinical and Imaging Laboratory, for her support in carrying out this work.

References

1. Abadi, M., Agarwal, A., Barham, P., Brevdo, E., Chen, Z., Citro, C., et al.: TensorFlow: large-scale machine learning on heterogeneous systems (2015). https://www.tensorflow.org/
2. Basile, T., Fanizzi, A., Losurdo, L., Bellotti, R., Bottigli, U., Dentamaro, R., et al.: Microcalcification detection in full-field digital mammograms: a fully automated computer-aided system. Physica Med. **64**, 1–9 (2019)

3. Bisong, E.: Building Machine Learning and Deep Learning Models on Google Cloud Platform: A Comprehensive Guide for Beginners, 1st edn. Apress, Berkeley (2019)
4. Bressem, K., Adams, L., Erxleben, C., Hamm, B., Niehues, S., Vahldiek, J.: Comparing different deep learning architectures for classification of chest radiographs. Sci. Rep. **10**, 13590 (2020)
5. Chollet, F., et al.: Keras (2015). https://github.com/fchollet/keras
6. Cortes, C., Mohri, M., Rostamizadeh, A.: L2 regularization for learning kernels. In: Proceedings of the Twenty-Fifth Conference on Uncertainty in Artificial Intelligence, pp. 109–116. AUAI Press, Arlington, Virginia, USA (2009)
7. Fanizzi, A., Basile, T., Losurdo, L., Bellotti, R., Bottigli, U., Campobasso, F., et al.: Ensemble discrete wavelet transform and gray-level co-occurrence matrix for microcalcification cluster classification in digital mammography. Appl. Sci. **9**(24), 5388 (2019)
8. Hadjidj, I., Feroui, A., Belgherbi, A., Bessaid, A.: Microcalcifications segmentation from mammograms for breast cancer detection. Int. J. Biomed. Eng. Technol. **29**, 1 (2019)
9. He, K., Zhang, X., Ren, S., Sun, J.: Deep residual learning for image recognition. In: 2016 IEEE Conference on Computer Vision and Pattern Recognition (CVPR), pp. 770–778. IEEE, Las Vegas, NV, USA (2016)
10. Henriksen, E., Carlsen, J., Vejborg, I., Nielsen, M., Lauridsen, C.: The efficacy of using computer-aided detection (CAD) for detection of breast cancer in mammography screening: a systematic review. PubMed **60**, 13–18 (2018)
11. Hsieh, Y., Chin, C., Wei, C., Chen, I., Yeh, P., Tseng, R.: Combining VGG16, mask R-CNN and Inception V3 to identify the benign and malignant of breast microcalcification clusters. In: 2020 IEEE International Conference on Fuzzy Theory and Its Applications (iFUZZY), pp. 1–4. IEEE, Hsinchu, Taiwan (2020)
12. Huang, G., Liu, Z., Van Der, M., Weinberger, K.: Densely connected convolutional networks. In: 2017 IEEE Conference on Computer Vision and Pattern Recognition (CVPR), pp. 2261–2269. IEEE, Honolulu, HI, USA (2017)
13. Illipse, M., Czene, K., Hall, P., Humphreys, K.: Association of microcalcification clusters with short-term invasive breast cancer risk and breast cancer risk factors. Sci. Rep. **9**, 14604 (2019)
14. Ioffe, S., Szegedy, C.: Batch normalization: accelerating deep network training by reducing internal covariate shift. In: Proceedings of the 32nd International Conference on International Conference on Machine Learning, pp. 448–456. JMLR.org, Lille, France (2015)
15. Krizhevsky, A., Sutskever, I., Hinton, G.: ImageNet classification with deep convolutional neural networks. In: Advances in Neural Information Processing Systems 25: 26th Annual Conference on Neural Information Processing Systems 2012, pp. 1106–1114. Curran Associates Inc, Lake Tahoe, Nevada, USA (2012)
16. Lecun, Y., Bottou, L., Bengio, Y., Haffner, P.: Gradient-based learning applied to document recognition. Proc. IEEE **86**, 2278–2324 (1998)
17. Miotto, R., Wang, F., Wang, S., Jiang, X., Dudley, J.: Deep learning for healthcare: review, opportunities and challenges. Brief. Bioinform. **19**, 1236–1246 (2018)
18. Mordang, J., Gubern-Mérida, A., Bria, A., Tortorella, F., Mann, R., Broeders, M., et al.: The importance of early detection of calcifications associated with breast cancer in screening. Breast Cancer Res. Treat. **167**, 451–458 (2018)
19. Moreira, I., Amaral, I., Domingues, I., Cardoso, A., Cardoso, M., Cardoso, J.: INbreast: toward a full-field digital mammographic database. Acad. Radiol. **19**, 236–48 (2011)

20. Sandler, M., Howard, A., Zhu, M., Zhmoginov, A., Chen, L.: MobileNetv 2: inverted residuals and linear bottlenecks. In: 2018 IEEE/CVF Conference on Computer Vision and Pattern Recognition, pp. 4510–4520. IEEE, Salt Lake City, UT, USA (2018)
21. Sickles, E., D'Orsi, C., Bassett, L., et al.: ACR BI-RADS®mammography. In: ACR BI-RADS®atlas, Breast Imaging Reporting and Data System. American College of Radiology, 5th edn. (2013)
22. Simonyan, K., Zisserman, A.: Very deep convolutional networks for large-scale image recognition. In: 2015 International Conference on Learning Representations (ICLR), pp. 1–14. Computational and Biological Learning Society, San Diego, CA, USA (2015)
23. Srivastava, N., Hinton, G., Krizhevsky, A., Sutskever, I., Salakhutdinov, R.: Dropout: a simple way to prevent neural networks from overfitting. J. Mach. Learn. Res. **15**, 1929–1958 (2014)
24. Szegedy, C., Liu, W., Jia, Y., Sermanet, P., Reed, S., Anguelov, D., et al.: Going deeper with convolutions. In: 2015 IEEE Conference on Computer Vision and Pattern Recognition (CVPR), pp. 1–9. IEEE, Boston, MA, USA (2015)
25. Yang, Z., Dong, M., Guo, Y.: A new method of micro-calcifications detection in digitized mammograms based on improved simplified PCNN. Neurocomputing **218**, 79–90 (2016)
26. Zhang, F., Luo, L., Sun, X., Zhou, Z., Li, X., Yu, Y., et al.: Cascaded generative and discriminative learning for microcalcification detection in breast mammograms. In: 2019 IEEE/CVF Conference on Computer Vision and Pattern Recognition (CVPR), pp. 12570–12578. IEEE, Long Beach, CA, USA (2019)

Retinal Artery and Vein Segmentation Using an Image-to-Image Conditional Adversarial Network

Jesús González Godoy[(⊠)] [iD] and Juan Humberto Sossa Azuela[iD]

Instituto Politécnico Nacional - CIC, Laboratorio de Robótica y Mecatrónica, CDMX, Mexico City, Mexico
contacto@jesusgonzalez.mx

Abstract. With the continuous increasing advances in hardware, there is a growing interest in the automation of clinical processes. In this sense, retinal blood vessels segmentation is a crucial step in the search of helping clinicians to get a better detection, diagnosis and treatment of many diseases. To solve this problem several solutions have been created, many of them using different deep learning architectures and with performances up to 95%. Some of these solutions need big datasets and they also use image preprocessing. In the present work we propose solving this problem with a cGAN on a small dataset and with color segmentation, making available distinguishing between arteries and veins, but more important we discuss how sometimes these high reported performances can be due to an improper use of the technic and this can lead to a not reliable model, bad reproducibility of results and non-sense comparatives with issues in the implementations and when used by clinicians.

Keywords: Retinal blood segmentation · cGan · Segmentation metrics

1 Introduction

Retinal blood vessels are a very important resource in detection, diagnosis and treatment of several diseases, the retinal vessel caliber and its changes under external impulses are related to the progression of retinopathy [1, 4] which is an important cause of visual loss. This retinal vasculature can be associated with hypertension [2, 9], even some biomarkers derived from the retinal vascular changes and degeneration have a relationship with the Alzheimer's disease [3], Imaging of retinal also is useful for understanding and treatment of tumors [11].

The improvement of medical service is closely related with the technological advances, and the early detection of diseases, furthermore the diagnosis requires the necessary specialized knowledge and experience to be reliable, this is time-consuming. Therefore, the automation of these processes is highly desirable, and a very common initial step on this automatization is the Retinal blood vessels segmentation [5, 7, 8] and is on this segmentation step and its metrics where this paper relies.

A. Y. Rodríguez-González et al. (Eds.): MCPR 2023, LNCS 13902, pp. 242–251, 2023.
https://doi.org/10.1007/978-3-031-33783-3_23

There are different approaches out there to achieve this segmentation task, for example, there is a moment-based approach able to cover thinner blood vessels [6], some advanced image processing algorithms [16] and combination of multiple detectors [17]. More recently taking advantage of the always-increase computational power, novel artificial intelligence approaches has appeared, these approaches get high performance on the dataset they were trained, turning into great candidates to substitute eye screening improving the medical system [12], among other algorithms used are convolutional neural networks [10], custom deep learning architectures [13, 14, 20] and [20], and combinations of classical image processing approaches with deep learning [15].

However, this is not an easy task, and a constant step is present in the previous works, and there is a necessity of image preprocessing also they need a big dataset and many learning iterations, here we show how we can use a generative adversarial network without this preprocessing step, a small dataset and few learning iterations. This is a challenging problem and the need special models and loos functions for a given problem is a must. We also generate a color segmentation dataset to be more helpful distinguishing Arteries and Veins, and last but not least we take advantage to discuss the common metrics used to compare these segmentation models and how even if they show highly performance compared with clinicians, in fact they are not reliable, even some studies show that several clinical research teams report issues when using this models [18] and [19].

2 Methodology

In this section we describe the deep learning architecture that is proposed to solve the retina vessels segmentation problem, reviewing the basics of a cGAN architecture and the configuration used for the experiments. Also, further in this section the dataset used for training and testing is described, emphasizing the novelty of this dataset and the reason it is a good fit for our goals.

2.1 Neatwork Architecture

For the retinal Arteries and Veins Segmentation we propose using a conditional generative neural network called Image-to-image [21]. This type of architecture has proven to be efficient in segmentation problems and was used before for Retinal Blood Vessel Segmentation [22] using the public databases: CHASE, DRIVE and STARE.

The goal of the Generative adversarial networks is to learn the probability distribution of a dataset that generates it [23], based on that, we can say that the Image-to-image cGAN is an ensemble of two networks one so called generative network that is trained to produce images indistinguishable from the real ones by the other network in the ensemble called discriminator, which is trained to do this discrimination job as best as possible (see Fig. 1).

Generator and Discriminator Architectures. These architectures are taken from [21], The generator is basically a U-Net with skip connections on every layer, with an encoder: C64-C128-C256-C512-C512-C512-C512-C512 and a decoder: CD512-CD512-CD512-C512-C256-C128-C64. The Discriminator is composed as C64-C128-C256-C512, where Ck is a Convolution (k filters)-BatchNorm-ReLU and D represents a 50% drop out.

Loss Functions. Given the cGan loss function.

$$L_{cGAN} = \mathbb{E}\big[logD(x, y)\big] + \mathbb{E}\big[\log(1 - D(x, G(x, z)))\big] \tag{1}$$

The main goal as we establish before is for G to minimize (generate the image as close as possible), and for D to maximize (the image needs to be distinguished as good as possible) this function.

$$L = \arg min_G max_D L_{cGAN} + \lambda L_1(G) \tag{2}$$

where L_1 is given by

$$L_1(G) = \mathbb{E}\big[y - G(x, z)\big] \tag{3}$$

And λ is a ponderation for the L_1 loss, it is 100 for this work.

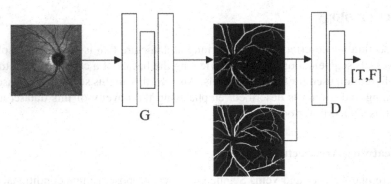

Fig. 1. Image-to-image cGAN architecture, G for Generator, D for discriminator and [T, F] True or False image as input.

2.2 Dataset

Some of the most common datasets for retina vessel segmentation are CHASE, DRIVE and STARE, but there is a very new and good dataset called RAVIR [24]. This dataset has 26 training images captured with an infrared laser of high quality and contrast that can be splinted to have some validation images. They are 768 × 768 png images. The authors of the dataset also show a novel segmentation method for this dataset based on convolutional networks with high accuracy and color differentiation of veins and arteries.

So, in the present work we use the RAVIR dataset because then we can use the original images for grayscale segmentation and one variant of this images, artificially colored with blue and red according to the grayscale of the image that aims to resemble a segmentation for the veins and arteries of the retina, as shown in Fig. 2.

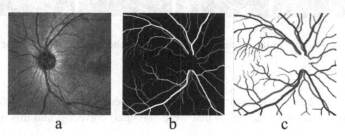

a   b   c

Fig. 2. Training images, (a) Original image, (b) Grayscale Arteries and Veins, (c) Artificially colored Arteries and Veins

Although the result for the artificially colored images is not what it could be if we had veins and arteries labeled by a human being, this method is quite close and most importantly allows us to have a realistic approach to know if the model can do the job.

3 Experiments and Results

In this section we show the successful use of the cGAN, then we have a detailed discussion of why we strongly discourage the use of some common metrics used to compare this segmentation models in the past and we proposed some other well-known metrics as a standard for this problem and extensible to other medical segmentation problems, then we focus on optimization using data augmentation and colored target images, finally a comparison between the different datasets mentioned above and using the proposed metrics as standard previously in this section is offered.

3.1 Understanding cGAN Predictions and Metrics

For this first experiment we use just the 23 images of the data set to train the neural model. This experiment far from just to help us understand how the architecture evolve their predictions on each iteration, it also helps us show how powerful is this approach facing a common challenge present in many biomedical datasets, that is the lack of information, because unlike other areas, in medicine it is incredibly difficult to get large volumes of data to work. In Fig. 3 we can see the evolution of the training.

Using just these 23 images and after just 30 epochs we can achieve an accuracy of 96%. We could think that this is good enough to compare with humans, however, let's go deeper into metrics. As we established before, the goal of the present work is to discuss this kind of metrics and see how it can lead to issues and misinterpretations.

First these metrics should be done on a validation test, which is different from the training one but is one dataset that is labeled also, so for all the experiments shown here we use 20 images for training and 3 for testing.

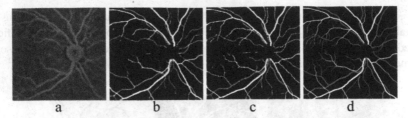

Fig. 3. (a, b, c) Insights of the cGan learning throughout the epochs (1,15,30) respectively, (d) target image.

Now let us focus on the example of Fig. 3. For accuracy, also called pixel accuracy we simply try to measure the pixels that were classified correctly, and this is given by

$$acc = \frac{TP + TN}{TP + TN + FN + FP} \tag{4}$$

where the positives are the blood vessel pixels and negatives represent the background. Accuracy metric is highly used, but we highly discouraged its use on this imbalanced problem where most of the pixels are black and even a really bad result can achieve high accuracy (see Fig. 4).

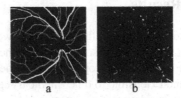

Fig. 4. Accuracy metric comparison for a good result (a) with 96% and bad result (b) with 92%

Table 1. Comparison metrics for experiments on Fig. 4.

Experiment	precision	recall	f1-score
Exp (a) background	0.98	0.97	0.98
Exp (a) blood vessels	0.76	0.85	0.80
Exp (b) background	0.92	1	0.96
Exp (b) blood vessels	0.77	0.12	0.21

Now for the other common metrics like precision, recall and f1-score they have a different result for the background and for the blood vessels (see Table 1). Here we can see that these results are more related with the reality, they are given by,

$$precision = \frac{TP}{TP + FP} \tag{5}$$

$$\text{recall} = \frac{TP}{TP + FN} \tag{6}$$

$$\text{f1} - \text{score} = \frac{2 \times TP}{2 \times TP + FN + FP} \tag{7}$$

Precision tells us how many of the blood vessels pixels we labeled as blood vessels are truly blood vessels so after this example, we also discourage the use of this metric because even if just a few blood vessels were predicted it can be all well predicted so to have a high precision.

Recall tells us of the blood vessels or background pixels how many of them were correctly predicted and F1 score could be seen as the equivalent for IoU metric that penalize false positives, a common occurrence in high imbalanced classes, so we think they are very appropriate metrics for this problem and medical images segmentation in general. Also, we suggest taking the average metrics as a more holistic metrics, i.e., calculate metrics for each label, and find their unweighted mean.

Finally, we want to introduce the Jaccard index [25], that is defined as the size of the intersection divided by the size of the union of two label sets.

$$J(P, N) = \frac{|P \cap N|}{|P \cup N|} \tag{8}$$

So, for example the Jaccard index for experiments a and b in Fig. 4 would be 0.67 and 0.12 respectively.

3.2 Using Data Augmentation

With this approach we do not need any preprocessing of the input image, the model itself can discover the hidden patterns to accomplish the segmentation goal, however this dataset is very small, so it is a real challenge for deep learning, due to that we propose here use common data augmentation techniques [26] such as rotation, with and height shift, shear, flip and zoom, after that we get about 1000 images to train the model.

In Fig. 5 we can see that visually the results are good, and some arteries are difficult for the model because they are too tight, also sometimes it is difficult for a human being differentiate them.

3.3 Colored Images

As was mentioned before we try to increase the value of this predictions by making a colored segmentation prediction, so the masks were artificially colored with respect to their grayscale value, after that the same data augmentation technique was applied the results are shown in Fig. 6.

3.4 Performance

Using the proposed metrics in the Sect. 3.1 we are able to evaluate and compare the three different models created from the different training datasets we have, the original

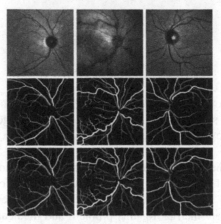

Fig. 5. Segmentation using data augmentation, first row up to down are the retina images, second row the targets, and last one the predictions. Table 2 shows the metrics performance for this model.

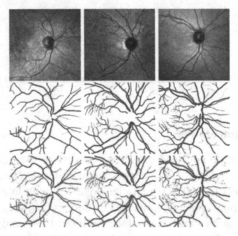

Fig. 6. Segmentation for colored images using data augmentation, first row up to down are the retina images, second row the targets, and last one the predictions. Table 2 shows the metrics performance for this model.

Table 2. Comparison metrics for different training datasets versions proposed here.

training dataset	Jaccard index	Avg recall	Avg f1-score
simple	0.67	91%	89%
gray	0.78	92%	91%
color	0.89	92%	92%

one with 23 images called "simple", the training with data augmentation with 1000 grayscale images called "gray" and the last one with 1000 augmented and artificially colored images called "color", the results are depicted in Table 2.

On Table 2 we can see that the difference in the performance using data augmentation is not so representative so we can say that the model it is going to perform well even with a small dataset, furthermore the performance with the colored images and the gray ones is almost the same so this model can be used for colored segmentation and help in differentiation for arteries and veins.

Also, we show here on Table 3 a comparative with other works using the common well-known metrics, we really hope that in the future the new ones proposed here can be used as a comparative method.

Table 3. Comparison of different models using the RAVIR dataset.

Model	Vein Accuracy	Vein Recall	Artery Accuracy	Artery Recall
U-Net	0.968	0.738	0.966	0.727
Dense U-Net	0.969	0.741	0.967	0.729
CE-Net	0.978	0.768	0.977	0.750
SegRAVIR	0.991	0.808	0.9815	0.777
cGAN	0.989	0.879	0.989	0.842

4 Conclusions and Future Work

In the present work we have successfully shown how to use an image-to-image cGAN for the blood vessel segmentation problem which is commonly carried out on binary (black and white) or grayscale images, here at this work we try to go further and also work with success on the differentiation for arteries and veins, both cases with an average performance up to 90%, this result was achieved without any previous preprocessing of the input images that was one of the proposed goals.

The best results were obtained using common data augmentation techniques, but we showed that this cGAN based model can achieve a superior performance even without data augmentation. For future works in this sense would be great to have the original images in color so the cGAN maybe would be able to get more hidden patterns that are impossible to solve from the gray scale images.

The second goal successfully achieved in this paper was to propose some standard and well-defined metrics to be used specifically on this problem, to avoid the misinterpretation of the results and be more effective in the model comparisons this metrics are also extensible to other segmentation problems for medical images, due to the common occurrence of high imbalance classes.

For future work it would be great to have some evolutions of this model to solve the problem, also it could be interesting to compare with binary images and propose now from the segmentations obtained with this architecture continue with some clinical process and try to help in the detection or diagnosis of a disease.

Acknowledgment. Authors would like to express their gratitude to the Instituto Politécnico Nacional and CONACYT for the economic support to undertake this research. We also thank the anonymous reviewers for their valuable comments that helped us to highly improve the quality of this paper.

References

1. Klein, R., Klein, B.E.K., Moss, S.E., et al.: The relation of retinal vessel caliber to the incidence and progression of diabetic retinopathy XIX: the Wisconsin epidemiologic study of diabetic retinopathy. Arch. Ophthalmol. **122**(1), 76–83 (2004). https://doi.org/10.1001/archopht.122. 1.76
2. Cheung, C.Y., Ikram, M.K., Sabanayagam, C., Wong, T.Y.: Retinal microvasculature as a model to study the manifestations of hypertension. Hypertension **60**(5), 1094–1103 (2012). https://doi.org/10.1161/HYPERTENSIONAHA.111.189142. Epub 2012 Oct 8. PMID: 23045470
3. Frost, S., Kanagasingam, Y., Sohrabi, H., et al.: Retinal vascular biomarkers for early detection and monitoring of Alzheimer's disease. Transl. Psychiatry **3**, e233 (2013). https://doi.org/10. 1038/tp.2012.150
4. Mandecka, A., et al.: Influence of flickering light on the retinal vessels in diabetic patients. Diabetes Care **30**(12), 3048–3052 (2007)
5. Akram, U.M., Khan, S.A.: Automated detection of dark and bright lesions in retinal images for early detection of diabetic retinopathy. J. Med. Syst. **36**, 3151–3162 (2012)
6. Adapa, D., Joseph Raj, A.N., Alisetti, S.N., Zhuang, Z., Ganesh, K., Naik, G.: A supervised blood vessel segmentation technique for digital Fundus images using Zernike Moment based features. PLoS One **15**(3), e0229831 (2020). https://doi.org/10.1371/journal.pone.0229831. PMID: 32142540; PMCID: PMC7059933
7. Jamal, A., et al.: Retinal imaging analysis based on vessel detection. Microscopy Res. Tech. **80**(7), 799–811 (2017)
8. Dougherty, G., Johnson, M.J., Wiers, M.D.: Measurement of retinal vascular tortuosity and its application to retinal pathologies. Med. Biol. Eng. Compu. **48**, 87–95 (2010)
9. Cuspidi, C., et al.: High prevalence of retinal vascular changes in never-treated essential hypertensives: an inter-and intra-observer reproducibility study with non-mydriatic retinography. Blood Pressure **13**(1), 25–30 (2004)
10. Uysal, E., Güraksin, G.E.: Computer-aided retinal vessel segmentation in retinal images: convolutional neural networks. Multimedia Tools Appl. **80**(3), 3505–3528 (2020). https:// doi.org/10.1007/s11042-020-09372-w
11. Heimann, H., Jmor, F., Damato, B.: Imaging of retinal and choroidal vascular tumours. Eye **27**(2), 208–216 (2013)
12. Islam, Md.M., et al.: Artificial intelligence in ophthalmology: a meta-analysis of deep learning models for retinal vessels segmentation. J. Clin. Med. **9**(4), 1018 (2020)
13. Tajbakhsh, N., et al.: ErrorNet: learning error representations from limited data to improve vascular segmentation. In: 2020 IEEE 17th International Symposium on Biomedical Imaging (ISBI). IEEE (2020)
14. Guo, C., et al.: SD-UNet: a structured dropout U-Net for retinal vessel segmentation. In: 2019 IEEE 19th International Conference on Bioinformatics and Bioengineering (BIBE). IEEE (2019)
15. Tchinda, B.S., et al.: Retinal blood vessels segmentation using classical edge detection filters and the neural network. Inform. Med. Unlocked **23**, 100521 (2021)

16. Karn, P.K., Biswal, B., Samantaray, S.R.: Robust retinal blood vessel segmentation using hybrid active contour model. IET Image Process. **13**(3), 440–450 (2019)
17. Biswal, B., Pooja, T., Bala Subrahmanyam, N.: Robust retinal blood vessel segmentation using line detectors with multiple masks. IET Image Process. **12**(3), 389–399 (2018)
18. Müller, D., Soto-Rey, I., Kramer, F.: Towards a guideline for evaluation metrics in medical image segmentation. BMC. Res. Notes **15**(1), 1–8 (2022)
19. Parikh, R.B., Teeple, S., Navathe, A.S.: Addressing bias in artificial intelligence in health care [Internet]. JAMA – J. Am. Med. Assoc. (2019)
20. Kamran, S.A., Hossain, K.F., Tavakkoli, A., Zuckerbrod, S.L., Sanders, K.M., Baker, S.A.: RV-GAN: segmenting retinal vascular structure in fundus photographs using a novel multi-scale generative adversarial network. In: de Bruijne, M., et al. (eds.) MICCAI 2021. LNCS, vol. 12908, pp. 34–44. Springer, Cham (2021). https://doi.org/10.1007/978-3-030-87237-3_4
21. Isola, P., et al.: Image-to-image translation with conditional adversarial networks. In: Proceedings of the IEEE Conference on Computer Vision and Pattern Recognition (2017)
22. Popescu, D., et al.: Retinal blood vessel segmentation using pix2pix GAN. In: 2021 29th Mediterranean Conference on Control and Automation (MED). IEEE (2021)
23. Goodfellow, I., et al.: Generative adversarial networks. Commun. ACM **63**(11), 139–144 (2020)
24. Hatamizadeh, A., et al.: RAVIR: a dataset and methodology for the semantic segmentation and quantitative analysis of retinal arteries and veins in infrared reflectance imaging. IEEE J. Biomed. Health Inform. **26**(7), 3272–3283 (2022)
25. da Fontoura Costa, L.: Further generalizations of the Jaccard index. arXiv preprint arXiv: 2110.09619 (2021)
26. Yang, S., et al.: Image data augmentation for deep learning: a survey. arXiv preprint arXiv: 2204.08610 (2022)

Evaluation of Heatmaps as an Explicative Method for Classifying Acute Lymphoblastic Leukemia Cells

José de J. Velázquez-Arreola[1] (ID), Oliver A. Zarraga-Vargas[2] (ID),
Raquel Díaz-Hernández[1(✉)] (ID), and Leopoldo Altamirano-Robles[1] (ID)

[1] Instituto Nacional de Astrofísica Óptica y Electrónica, Puebla, Mexico
raqueld@inaoep.mx
[2] Universidad Politécnica de Morelos, Morelos, Mexico

Abstract. Explainable artificial intelligence (XAI) is a field of research that has captured researchers' interest in recent years. These algorithms seek to bring transparency to artificial intelligence (AI) models, which are often highly complex and opaque algorithms. Implementing explanatory methods like heat maps to pathological diagnosis systems opens the door to using AI in potentially life-saving applications, generating new tools as auxiliaries in the corroboration of predictions made by an AI. In the present work, retraining four CNN models (VGG16, VGG19, ResNet50, and MobileNet V1) was performed, performing a fine tuning to classify segmented images without a background of Acute Lymphoblastic Leukemia (ALL) cells. Heat maps were generated using the iNNvestigate library, selecting the LRP, Deep Taylor, and Input*Gradient methods for this end. With the help of five hematologists and experts in morphological cell classification, the 120 generated heat maps were evaluated. The evaluation focused on the amount of information provided by the heat maps and how they relate to morphological characteristics present in the classified cells. Results of the best heatmaps and hematologist evaluations are presented in this work. The central outcome is that the heatmaps must include morphological information to be a valuable tool for medical diagnosis systems.

Keywords: Explainable Artificial Intelligence (XAI) · Acute Leukemia Lymphoblastic (ALL) · Heatmaps

1 Introduction

Explainable artificial intelligence (XAI) is an emerging field of research that seeks to bring transparency to machine learning (ML) and deep learning (DL) models. Convolutional neural networks (CNNs) used in deep learning are often highly complex and opaque algorithms referred to as black boxes. Despite the development of many methods to explain the decisions of black-box classifiers, these tools are rarely used beyond visualization. Researchers have recently begun to employ visual explanations, such as heat maps, to improve classification models.

A. Y. Rodríguez-González et al. (Eds.): MCPR 2023, LNCS 13902, pp. 252–260, 2023.
https://doi.org/10.1007/978-3-031-33783-3_24

Besides that, the increasing prevalence of digitized workflows in diagnostic pathology opens the door to life-saving artificial intelligence (AI) applications. One option for adding these explanatory methods to the diagnosis systems is to employ heat maps as an additional tool in the corroboration of predictions made by a neural network.

1.1 Explanatory Methods

This work uses methods that generate heat maps; these are considered a way to explain the functioning of a neural network. But what is meant by Explainable Artificial Intelligence (XAI)? Barredo et al. [1] define three concepts that are usually misused and interchanged. As a result of their research, they arrive at the following definitions:

- Interpretability is the ability to explain or provide meaning in terms understandable to a human being.
- Explainability is associated with the notion of explanation as an interface between humans and decision-makers. At the same time, it accurately represents the decision-maker and is understandable to humans.
- Transparency: A model is considered transparent if it is understandable. Since a model can have different degrees of comprehensibility, transparent models are divided into three categories: simulatable, decomposable, and algorithmically transparent.

Explainability is critical for the safety, approval, and acceptance of AI systems for clinical use. The work of Weber et al. [2] is a comprehensive overview of techniques that practically apply XAI to improve various properties of ML models and systematically classifies these approaches, comparing their respective strengths and weaknesses.

2 Related Work

The work presented by Jiang et al. [3] proposes a method for Acute Lymphoblastic Leukemia (ALL) diagnosis using a ViT-CNN model for classifying lymphoblastic cell images. This type of model combines visual and convolutional transformation models, allowing it to extract in two ways features to achieve better classification results than an architecture such as Resnet50, DenseNet121, and VGG16. In work presented by Abir et al. [4], trained CNN models with the InceptionV3, Res-Net101V2, InceptionRes-NetV2, and VGG19 architectures are used to classify ALL images to compare which architecture presents better results in terms of accuracy and visual explanation generated by the LIME method.

Addressing the issue of explanatory methods for generating heat maps, Mamalakis et al. [5] conducted research in which they compared explanatory methods applied to a CNN model focused on predicting the number of atmospheric rivers in daily snapshots of climate simulations. This work compares the explanatory methods: Gradient, Smooth Gradient, PatterNet, Input*Gradient, Integrated Gradient, PatterAttribution, Deep Taylor, LRP methods, and Deep SHAP, which obtain their heat maps using the iNNvestigate library.

3 Methodology

3.1 iNNvestigate Library

Neural networks broaden state-of-the-art in many domains, such as object detection and speech recognition. Despite their success, neural networks are often still treated as black boxes. Their inner workings are not fully understood, and the basis for their predictions is unclear. Several methods were proposed to understand better neural networks, e.g., Saliency, Deconvnet, GuidedBackprop, SmoothGrad, Integrated-Gradients, LRP, PatternNet, and PatternAttribution. Due to the lack of reference implementations, comparing them is a significant effort. Maximilian et al. in [6] made available the library iNNvestigate, which addresses this problem by providing a standard interface and implementing some heat map generation methods, facilitating the analysis of neural network predictions by generating heat maps.

3.2 Evaluation of Heat Maps by Expert Hematologists

With libraries as the iNNvestigate mentioned in the last section, generating and comparing Heat Maps is possible. Nonetheless, they are oriented to explain the results of the classification process, for example, to an artificial intelligence specialist. For the use of Heat maps as a tool to leverage diagnostic pathology, it was necessary to consider the opinion of medical personnel about the usefulness of such explanatory tools. To this end, five hematologists with expertise in cell morphology evaluated heat maps. Each of them assessed a total of 120 heat maps. They assigned a score to each heat map, according to the amount of information provided corresponding to the cell morphology, to corroborate the cell classification generated by the convolutional neural network. That is, medical experts in the field evaluated the results of the network. Figures 1, 2, and 3 show examples of the maps assessed for the VGG19, ResNet50, and MobileNet V1 models.

The medical experts compared the morphological features present in the cell (original image), according to their own experience, and the information provided in the heat maps generated from the same image. They then assigned an evaluation to this comparison. The evaluation scale consists of values from one to five. One equals an information percentage of 0% to 20%, up to a maximum of five, which equals 81% to 100%. The results of this evaluation are presented in the following section.

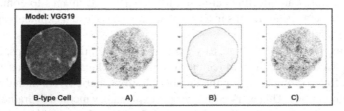

Fig. 1. Example of heat maps obtained from VGG19 v1 architecture. Cell type B and heat maps: A) LRP, B) Deep Taylor, and C) Input*Gradient.

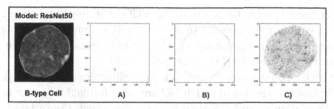

Fig. 2. Example of heat maps obtained from Resnet50 architecture. Cell type B and heat maps: A) LRP, B) Deep Taylor, and C) Input*Gradient.

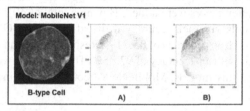

Fig. 3. Example of the heat maps obtained from the MobileNet v1 architecture. Cell type B and heat maps: A) Input*Gradient, B) Deep Taylor

4 Experiments and Results

This section presents the experiments and results of applying the methodology explained in the previous paragraph. Firstly, the results obtained from the retraining of the CNN models are presented. Secondly, the results of the generated heat maps are shown. Finally, the results and analysis of the evaluation of the heat maps carried out by a group of expert hematologists who supported the validation of the methodology are presented.

4.1 Retrained Architectures

The database [7] used consisted of 363 images of segmented cells with the background removed. The image set was distributed into three categories: 135 images for the B-cell category (ALL-B), 135 for the T-cell class (ALL-T), and 93 for the healthy cell category.

Since the set of images was considered to be small because the trained models did not present satisfactory results at the time of classification, an algorithm was run to generate an increase in data, applying 90°, 180°, and 270° rotation transformations, and the mirror effect to the original image. After this data augmentation step, the database now consisted of 1545 images. This new database was divided into three groups, training, test, and validation, with the percentages 80, 10, and 10, respectively.

In this phase of the work, Visual Geometry Group 2016 and 2019 (VGG16, VGG19), MobileNetv1 and Residual Neural Network 50 (Resnet50) neural network architectures are retrained and fine tuned using the transfer learning technique.

As the first architecture to be used, models were trained with VGG16 using 16 layers, 13 of which are convolutional layers for normalization and batch, 3 Dense layers and Flatten layers were added. Having a total of 18,942,531 parameters.

In addition, models were trained with the VGG19 architecture using 20 layers, of which 16 are convolutional layers for 16 are convolutional layers for normalization and batch, 4 Dense layers and Flatten layers were added. Dense and Flatten layers were added. Having a total of 24,268,739 parameters.

Models were trained with the MobileNet V1 architecture using 130 layers, of which 142 are convolutional layers for of which 142 are convolutional layers for normalization and batch, 4 Dense layers and 4 Flatten layers were added. Dense layers and Flatten layers were added. Having a total of 11,667,523 parameters.

For this research, the Resnet50 architecture was used, employing 141 layers, of which 42 are activation layers, 46 convolutional layers for normalization and batch, 4 Dense layers and Flatten layers were added. Having a total of 40,414,979 parameters.

The retrained models with their accuracy are listed hereafter: VGG16, got an accuracy of 99.35%; VGG19, with an accuracy of 85.71%; ResNet50, with an accuracy of 65.58%; finally MobileNet V1, with an accuracy of 92.85%. These models were typical examples of large, medium, and tiny models. MobileNetV1 could be used in mobile devices.

4.2 Heat Map Generation

The iNNvestigate library, described in Sect. 3.2, was used to generate heat maps. The available algorithms generated heat maps using a cell image for each category. Figure 4 shows an example of heat maps generated from a photo with the BCELL label, entering the same input image into the selected four models. For all cases with the MobileNetv1 model, it was impossible to obtain the heat map by applying the LRP method due to the characteristics of the architecture. Regarding the VGG16 and VGG19 architectures, both maps show similar results despite their different accuracy scores, with the VGG19 maps standing out more.

Based on the results visualized in the heat maps generated with the different methods and models, the models to be evaluated were VGG19, ResNet50, and MobileNet V1, as well as the heat map generation methods: LRP [8], Deep Taylor [9] and Input*Gradient [10]. The results of the evaluation are described in the next section.

4.3 Results of Heat Map Evaluation by Expert Hematologists

Our work evaluates and identifies the best neural network model and heat map generation method, measuring the morphological information they provide to the medical expert. The evaluation methodology is described in Sect. 3.2.

Table 1 shows the results of the heat maps generated with the LRP, Deep Taylor, and Input*Gradient methods for the VGG19 model, using T-cells as the input image. According to the evaluation, the Input*Gradient process obtained the best result with an average score of 2.79 points, 56% of information according to observed morphology, obtaining a total of 10.5 maps with the highest score out of a total of 15 images evaluated.

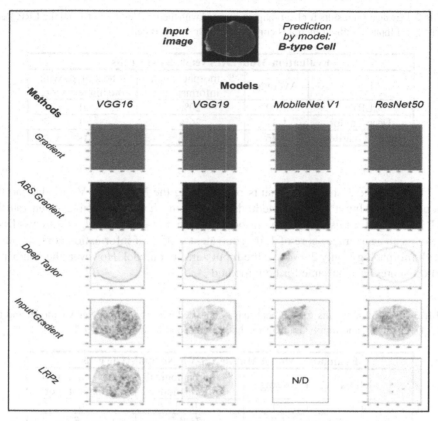

Fig. 4. Maps obtained from the different methods applied to the trained models for a B-cell image. The heat map is not determined for the LRP method with MobileNet V1

Table 1. Evaluation results for heat maps generated with the VGG19 model and the LRP, Deep Taylor, and Input*Gradient methods corresponding to a T-type cell.

Evaluation Model VGG19. T-type cells			
Method	Average	% morphological information	# heat maps with the highest score
LRP	2.56	51%	4
Deep Taylor	2.01	40%	0.5
Input*Gradient	2.79	56%	10.5

As shown in Table 2, the Input*Gradient model has the best score. On this occasion, the heat maps generated with the ResNet50 model and the LRP, Deep Taylor, and Input*Gradient methods were evaluated to classify B-cell images. A score of 2.45 was obtained, equivalent to 49% of the information corresponding to cell morphology. In addition, this method received the highest scores in all cases.

Table 2. Evaluation results for heat maps generated with the ResNet50 model and the LRP, Deep Taylor, and Input*Gradient methods corresponding to a type B cell.

Evaluation Model ResNet50. B-type cells			
Method	Average	% morphological information	# heat maps with the highest score
LRP	1.00	20%	0
Deep Taylor	1.31	26%	0
Input*Gradient	**2.45**	**49%**	**14**

Finally, Table 3 shows the results of evaluating the MobileNet V1 model and the Deep Taylor and Input*Gradient methods, recalling that it was impossible to generate the LRP heat maps for this model. On this occasion, the best-evaluated algorithm was Deep Taylor, with an average score of 1.76, equivalent to 35% of information corresponding to cell morphology, only 2% above the Input*Gradient model. However, the number of highest scores was the same for both methods.

Table 3. Evaluation results for the heat maps generated with the MobileNet V1 model and the LRP, Deep Taylor, and Input*Gradient methods corresponding to a type B cell.

Evaluation Model MobileNet-V1. Normal-type cells			
Method	Average	% morphological information	# heat maps with the highest score
LRP	0	0%	0
Deep Taylor	**1.76**	**35%**	**7.5**
Input*Gradient	1.67	33%	7.5

According to Table 4, the Input*Gradient method is the best qualified considering the three neural network models, obtaining an average score of 2.30 points, equivalent to 46% of the information corresponding to the morphology of the cells. Likewise, the method received the highest number of best-qualified maps, making a total of 25 maps generated with this method with the highest qualification.

Table 4. Overall evaluation results for the heat maps generated with the VGG19, ResNet50, and MobileNet V1 models and the LRP, Deep Taylor, and Input*Gradient methods corresponding to the three cell categories.

General Evaluation of the three models and cells types			
Method	Average	% morphological information	# heat maps with the highest score
LRP	1.19	24%	4
Deep Taylor	1.69	34%	8
Input*Gradient	**2.30**	**46%**	**25**

Finally, another step was taken: replicating one of the evaluations, corresponding to the MobileNet V1 model with the input image of cell 3. This action aimed to measure the consistency of the evaluation performed by expert hematologists. From the results obtained, see Table 5, it is corroborated that the scores obtained in both evaluations are consistent for the five experts who performed the activity.

Table 5. Results of measuring the consistency of the evaluation performed by expert hematologists

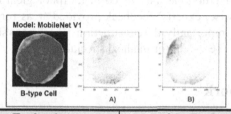

	1st Evaluation		2dn Evaluation	
	C-type Cell #3 Input*Gradient (A)	C-type Cell #3 Deep Taylor (B)	C-type Cell #3 Input*Gradient (A)	C-type Cell #3 Deep Taylor (B)
Hematologist 1	1	3	2	3
Hematologist 2	1	1	1	1
Hematologist 3	2	4	2	3
Hematologist 4	1	1	1	2
Hematologist 5	1	1	1	1
Average	1.2	2	1.4	2
% morphological information	24%	40%	28%	40%

5 Discussion

According to the results, the Deep Taylor and Input*Gradient methods produced the best heat maps that allowed us to highlight and identify the pixels of interest that were of greater importance for the classification process. In addition, they provide more information that could be related to morphological features present in the cells compared to the other heat map generation methods.

According to the evaluation made by the experts, the heat maps with the selected methods and models do not provide the ideal information corresponding to the classified cells' morphological characteristics. Some of the comments made by the physicians emphasize that to perform a morphological classification of leukemia cells, it is often necessary to identify more than one feature in the cell. This need for more morphological features should lead to improving the methods of generating heat maps for applications like assessing cell diseases.

6 Conclusions

When making a prediction, the purpose of implementing heat maps in a neural network is to identify the region or pixels most important for the neural network classification process. In this work, we generated heat maps with five different methods applied to four convolutional neural networks.

The three most significant models and three most significant heat map generation methods were evaluated by hematology specialists. This evaluation concludes that the Input*Gradient method can be related to morphological characteristics used for cell diagnosis. Likewise, experts' feedback provided areas for improvement in generating heat maps. Most importantly, the construction of heat maps should include morphological characteristics to be useful for medical specialists.

7 Future Work

In future work, we propose testing other heat map generation methods, including evaluating the generated heat maps with automatic feature extraction tools, to compare and contrast the differences and similarities between the newly obtained heat maps and those presented here. It also is essential to improve the methods of heat map generation, aiming to relate more regions of interest with morphological features present in the cells.

References

1. Arrieta, A.B., et al.: Explainable Artificial Intelligence (XAI): concepts, taxonomies, opportunities and challenges toward responsible AI. Inf. Fusion **58**, 82–115 (2020)
2. Weber, L., et al.: Beyond explaining: opportunities and challenges of XAI-based model improvement. Inf. Fusion **92**, 154–176 (2023)
3. Jiang, Z.D.: Method for diagnosis of Acute Lymphoblastic Leukemia based on ViT-CNN ensemble model. Comput. Intell. Neurosci. **2021**, 1–12 (2021)
4. Abir, W.H.: Explainable AI in diagnosing and Anticipating Leukemia using transfer learning method. Comput. Intell. Neurosci. **2022**, 1–14 (2022)
5. Mamalakis, A.B.-U.: Investigating the fidelity of explainable artificial intelligence methods for applications of convolutional neural networks in geoscience (2022)
6. Alber, M., et al.: iNNvestigate neural networks! J. Mach. Learn. Res. **20**(93), 1–8 (2019)
7. Gupta, A., Gupta, R.: ALL Challenge dataset of ISBI 2019 Data set. The Cancer Imaging Archive (2019)
8. Bach, S., et al.: On pixel-wise explanations for non-linear classifier decisions by layer-wise relevance propagation, July 2015
9. Montavon, G., et al.: Explaining nonlinear classification decisions with deep Taylor decomposition. Pattern Recogn. **65**, 211–222 (2017)
10. Shrikumar, A., Greenside, P., Shcherbina, A., Kundaje, A.: Not Just a Black Box: Learning Important Features Through Propagating Activation Differences, vol. 6 (2016). https://doi.org/10.48550/arXiv.1605.01713

Language Processing and Recognition

Machine Learning Models Applied in Sign Language Recognition

Esteban Gustavo Novillo Quinde$^{(\boxtimes)}$ (ID), Juan Pablo Saldaña Torres (ID),
Michael Andres Alvarez Valdez (ID), John Santiago Llivicota León (ID),
and Remigio Ismael Hurtado Ortiz (ID)

Universidad Politécnica Salesiana, Cuenca, Ecuador
estebannovilioq@gmail.com
https://www.ups.edu.ec/

Abstract. One of the most relevant worldwide problems is the inclusion
of people with disabilities. In this research we want to help focusing in
the people with hearing disabilities, being able to translate sign language
into words that we could read. It is a common worldwide problem to be
able to accurately predict the gestures of non-hearing people in order
to be able to communicate efficiently with them and not have a barrier
when they want to perform their daily activities. In order to that we
propose a three phase method combining Data preparation(The dataset
used for this is the "Australian Sign Language sings", which is public
and free to use) and cleaning phase, modeling using Random Forest
Vector Support Machine and Neural Networks, able to optimize and
qualify these models using the measures of accuracy, precision, recall
and f1-score. Therefore, in this work we try to offer the highest possible
quality measures to the prediction of signs in the Australian language
with the mentioned dataset. This also opens the way for future research
where more advanced supervised modeling techniques can be applied to
improve the values obtained.

Keywords: Data science · Machine Learning · Sign Language · Neural
Network · Vector Support Machine · Random Forest

1 Introduction

The inclusion of people with hearing - linguistic disabilities has been a matter
of attention by various governments and private institutions over several years.
Their way of communication is based on the strict interpretation of the visual
field. Historically, sign language has been interpreted as a complement to oral
language, precisely to give greater relevance and provide content that is visually
much easier to explain while phonemes are being formed [2]. Nevertheless there
is a part of society that can only communicate in this way, also known as deaf-
mute. Since they have never heard the sound associated with a word, they can

---

The original version of this chapter was revised: The last names order has been reversed
for all authors. The correction to this chapter is available at
https://doi.org/10.1007/978-3-031-33783-3_31

not replicate it either, being sign language their only way of communication. However, sing language has been adapted to every language, such as English, Spanish, Japanese, etc. This means that there's only a minority sector of society that is able to understand it properly. This is why there are many experiments dedicated to detect sign language movements and the translation of these to written language and code language as well.

In this case, we will be using Machine Learning (ML) Models to recognize sing language. ML has been defined as the study that gives computers the ability to learn without being explicitly programmed to what they have to do [1]. Therefore, we are using different processes to make a computer able to recognize sign language. These methods are known also as models; and specifically, we will focus on the application of Neural Networks (NN), Support Vector Machines(SVM) and Random Forests. NN are a series of algorithms designed to recognize underlying relationships in a set of data through a process that tries to replicate the way the human brain operates [5]. SVM is an technique that proposes to create the best possible differentiation in n dimensions to classify the input data and associate them to sets, Random Forest is a model that processes several decision trees to generate a result by voting against each other and last the K-means algorithm is an iterative one that tries to partition the dataset into K-defined distinct non-overlapping subgroups (clusters) where each data point belongs to only one group. So, the highlights of this research are those described below:

- A Data Science based architecture for preparation, learning process, optimization and reporting results.
- An analysis using K-means to classify the interpreters and their movements.
- Three different machine learning models incorporating optimization and cross-validation techniques.
- A phase of optimization which gives the best accuracy on each model proposed.

The rest of the document is structured as follows: Section 2 Related work: where the most significant papers pertaining to the issue and the methods employed in them are mentioned Section 3. Proposed method: where the proposed method's procedure is fully described. Section 4 Design of experiments: the dataset characteristics, optimization parameters, and quality measures to assess and contrast the methods described. Section 5 Results and Discussion: The final parameters of each technique, the most important conclusions, and a discussion of the outcomes Section 6 Conclusions: at the end, on the basis of this research, the key findings and upcoming work that could be done.

2   Related Work

In this section we present the most relevant works. The most successful and popular techniques have been the approaches based on Neural Networks, Support Vector Machines (SVM) and Random Forest. First of all, focusing on the work related to sign language in general, we have in [1] a research on the task of language translation, since this task aims to achieve a breakthrough towards barrier-free communication. Their purpose is to present background on sign language and to provide survey results, which list the challenges that are addressed within the language translation task and the adoption of language translation technologies. Now focusing on Machine Learning we have that in [2] the recognition of signs using a classification system with neural networks is proposed. The main idea is to recognize sign language and convert it to text in real time, first the hand image is passed through a filter, then it goes through a classifier that predicts the class of hand gestures. In [3] several methods are provided to detect hand spelling in sign language, using gloves with appropriately placed sensors, the most relevant methods they propose are Neural Networks, KNN and Random Forest. The main goal is for the system to be able to accurately detect static and dynamic symbols in alphabets.

Therefore, in this research we propose a method that follows a data science process and handless standard data structures. Our method incorporates a transformer capable of generating predictions that can be justified and understood from the new calculated variables, in addition to providing high prediction quality.

3   Proposed Method

Our proposed method is based on the public dataset donated by Mohammed Kadous on [7]. This dataset contains the variables described in Table 1, where all variables are numeric except Signal, which is a string. In addition, the variables that most condition the results of our models are marked with an asterisk in the Relevant box. The description of the parameters and measurements of the proposed method is presented in Table 2. This method could be subdivided in a total of three main phases which are shown in the Fig. 1. On this figure we can notice that there are a lot of train and tests phases, that is because we wanted to test which one was the best combination at all.

Phase 1. Data preparation: During this phase, first of all we ignore all signs with less than 20 movements registered, then we get a sample of ten movements per sign and put them together in one row. After that, we normalise the data getting an output between 0 to 1 for each movement. We save both datasets, the one with normalization and the other one without it. Finally, apply PCA and LDA techniques to reduce the dimensions of the dataset without normalization, saving them too. We divide all our saved datasets into train and test in a proportion of 70 - 30.

Phase 2. Modeling: The chosen models used to analyse and predict the output signs are the SVM, Random Forest and Neural Network. During this phase the models are trained and fine tuned to get the highest accuracy of them.

Phase 3. Prediction and Evaluation: In this phase we evaluated the models with and without the normalization to get the best one. These three models will produce a multi-class classification according to which sign are trying to predict.

Table 1. Original columns of the dataset.

Attribute	Description	Relevant
x	Position on x axis	*
y	Position on y axis	*
z	Position on z axis	*
roll	Palm rotation	*
pitch	No description	
yaw	No description	
thumb	Thumb finger position	*
fore	Fore finger position	*
index	Index finger position	*
ring	Ring finger position	*
little	Little finger position	
keycode	Key on the globe pressed	
gs1	First state of the glove	
gs2	Second state of the glove	
Sign	Signal read	

4   Design of Experiments

The proposed method is applied to a dataset with a total of 394710 rows and 16 columns, as we can see on Table 3. Each sample contains the measurements of a sign of sign language , generated by an expert translator for a total of 95 possible symbols. It has been decided to discriminate samples with a total less than 20 recorded movements. With the remaining set, a random sampling of 10 movements has been established to represent each sign. With this, we get a dataset shape shown in Table 4. Sadly there are not too many samples to train our models.

The quality measures for the analysis of the results of the various models are given by the following parameters.

$$\text{Precision} = \frac{TP}{TP + FP} \tag{1}$$

$$\text{Recall} = \frac{TP}{TP + FN} \tag{2}$$

$$\text{F1-Score} = 2 \cdot \frac{Precision \cdot Recall}{Precision + Recall} \tag{3}$$

$$\text{Accuracy} = \frac{TP + TN}{TP + TN + FP + FN} \tag{4}$$

where TP, TN, FP and FN are the number of True Positives, True Negatives, False Positives and False Negatives, respectively.

Table 2. Description of parameters of the proposed method

Neural Network (NN)	
Parameter	**Description**
epochs	An epoch is an iteration over the entire x and y data provided.
batch size	Number of samples per gradient update.
optimizer	It involves randomly initializing and manipulating the value of weights for every epoch to increase the model network's accuracy potential.
density	The layer that contains all the neurons that are deeply connected within themselves.
dropout	It is a technique where randomly selected neurons are ignored during training.
Random Forest (RF)	
Parameter	Description
criterion	The function to measure the quality of a split.
n_estimators	The number of trees in the forest.
random_state	Controls both the randomness of the bootstrapping of the samples used when building trees and the sampling of the features.
max_depth	The maximum depth of the tree.
Supported Vector Machine (SVM)	
Parameter	Description
gamma	Kernel coefficient for 'rbf', 'poly' and 'sigmoid'.
kernel	Specifies the kernel type to be used in the algorithm.
Clustering	
PCA	Dimensionality reduction (unsupervised).
LDA	Dimensionality reduction (supervised)

Table 3. Original data shape of the dataset

Dataset	Number of attributes	Number of samples
Australian Sign Language sings [10]	15	394710

Table 4. Shape of the data in the preprocessed dataset

Dataset	Number of attributes	Number of samples
Australian Sign Language sings	81	6746

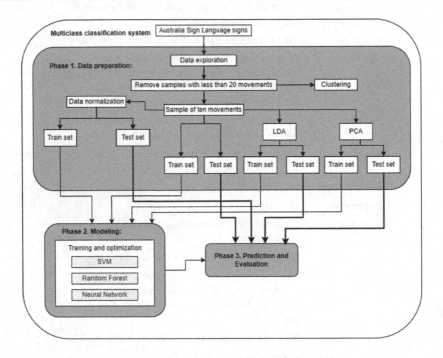

Fig. 1. Proposed method of multiclass classification

On the Table 5 we notice the optimization parameters for each model used.

We apply two techniques for Dimensionality Reduction, Principal Component Analysis or PCA and Linear Discriminant Analysis or LDA. The number of chosen components is being decided based on the accumulated variance of the sample, when the sample is bigger than 0.98 it gets chosen. The Fig. 2 shows that with 45 principal components the variance gets flatten in a value higher than the specified. The same amount of components will be used in both algorithms. As LDA is focused on supervised learning datasets we expect that its predictions will be better. After we execute our Machine Learning models, we could ensemble the Table 6 using the several combinations that could be generated.

Table 5. Optimization parameters of predictive methods

Method	Parameters (Normalized)	Parameters (No Normalized)
NN	epochs: 1000, 500, 250, 125, 65, **60**, 30 batch size: 6746, 4000, 2000, 1000, 500, **250**, 100, 50 optimizers: Adaptative Gradient, Adadelta, Adamax, RMSprop, **Adaptative Moment (Adam)**. density: L1: **80**, 100, 120, 150, 200; L2: 100, 130, **160**, 190, 250; L3: 200, 240, 280, **320**, 360, 400; L4: 460, 520, 580, **640**, 700, 760 dropout: in layer 1: **0**, 0.05, 0.1; in layer 2: **0**, 0.05, 0.1; in layer 3: **0**, 0.05, 0.1; in layer 4: **0**, 0.05, 0.1	epochs: 1000, 500, 250, 125, 65, **50**, 40, 30 batch size: 6746, 4000, 2000, 1000, 500, **250**, 100, 50 optimizers: Adaptative Gradient, Adadelta, Adamax, RMSprop, **Adaptative Moment (Adam)**. density: L1: **45**, 90, 135, 180, 225; L2: 70, 80, **90**, 100, 110; L3: 90, 105, 120, **135**, 150, 155; L4: 160, **180**, 200, 220 dropout: in layer 1: **0**, 0.05, 0.1; in layer 2: **0**, 0.05, 0.1; in layer 3: **0**, 0.05, 0.1; in layer 4: **0**, 0.05, 0.1
RF	criterion: **gini**, entropy, log_loss n_estimators: 300, 500, 600, **700**, 750, 800, 900, 1000 random_state: 300, 400, **450**, 500, 600 max_depth: **none**, 10, 50, 100	criterion: **gini**, entropy, log_loss n_estimators: 300, 500, 600, 700, 750, **800**, 900, 1000 random_state: 300, 400, **450**, 500, 600 max_depth: **none**, 10, 50, 100
SVM	gamma: **scale**, 0.0025, 0.002 kernel: linear, poly, **rbf**, sigmoid	gamma: **scale**, 0.0025, 0.002 kernel: linear, poly, **rbf**, sigmoid

5 Results and Discussion

In this section, the most relevant results are presented following the phases of the proposed method. We have proceeded with the calculation of singular values and measures with the Train set. The Fig. 2 shows the variance explained.

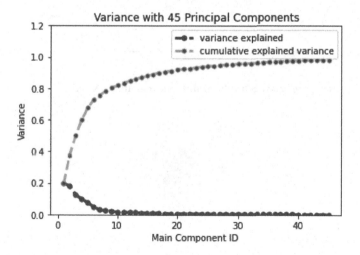

Fig. 2. Variance according to number of components

Applying k-means to classify the five interpreters we extracted an assortment of a sample of movements in the x axis in Figs. 3, 4 and 5. We notice that in all movements the values of the position in x are too near from each other, which will difficult to differentiate the characteristic movements of each sign at the time of learning phase.

The Table 6 provides us with a general statement, that all models do a better job at the accuracy level when normalization is not included as the data is measured with the parameters and technology previously described. The same happens when we use dimensional reduction techniques, in the same Table we have the results using PCA and LDA algorithms giving us the same results. When we apply this analysis of components to reduce the dimension we sacrifice our grade of accuracy in a range of 5% to 10% but we get a better efficiency during the learning and testing phase. This is because we have less columns to process and, that makes that the algorithm runs faster and with lower resource consumption. According to the Table 5 the best model in accuracy and precision is the Random Forest. We can attribute this learning capability to its decision tree architecture, which makes it suitable for problems where data generalization

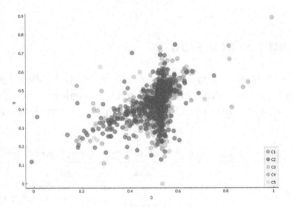

Fig. 3. Sample of first movement in X axis.

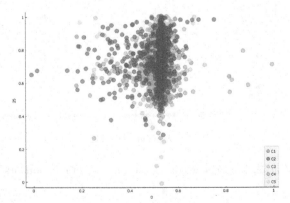

Fig. 4. Sample of second movement in X axis.

is applied. The number of trees needed to obtain the best result is 700 with a random state of 450 and with the default maximum depth. The learning model does not work properly because the sample is insufficient to generate a consistent specimen. In addition, the random selection of the motion sample confuses the system by not maintaining an order in the selection of the parameters, the motion data on the axes are continuous numbers and their representations in the position corresponding to the fingers of the subjects in question is affected by the same.

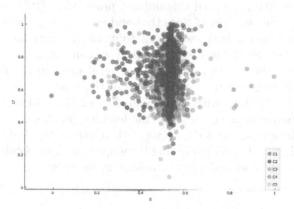

Fig. 5. Sample of third movement in X axis.

Table 6. Results with higher accuracy on each model

Method	Variant	Accuracy	Precision	Recall	F1-Score
NN	Normalization	0.3644	0.3707	0.3677	0.3599
	Original (without normalization)	**0.3807**	**0.3875**	**0.3979**	**0.3777**
	PCA	0.3170	0.3254	0.32	0.3126
	LDA	0.2829	0.2916	0.2858	0.2791
RF	Normalization	0.4607	0.5016	0.4797	0.4598
	Original (without normalization)	**0.4756**	**0.4992**	**0.4801**	**0.4662**
	PCA	0.2533	0.2631	0.2610	0.2366
	LDA	0.3504	0.3635	0.3594	0.3337
SVM	Normalization	0.2992	0.3203	0.3171	0.3026
	Original (without normalization)	**0.3214**	**0.3402**	**0.3228**	**0.3167**
	PCA	0.2548	0.2896	0.2653	0.2588
	LDA	0.3044	0.34	0.3189	0.3077

6   Conclusions

Finally, in this research we have given a deeper approach one of great relevance, to the problem related to hearing impaired people. Since our work aims to help and improve the quality of life of this minoritary group, such as to help people who do not have this impairment but are able to understand them perfectly. We are able to achieve all of this with the help of Machine Learning algorithms, specifically with: Neural Networks, Random Forest and Support Vector Machines. We have used this dataset provided in [10]. To carry out this big task we did a big amount of tests that and noticed that the "Random Fores" algorithm was giving the best results due to its architecture based on tress with a certain degree of depth, on the other hand we can say that an analysis, with other kind of elements, with a higher precision degree, in the measurement of movement would improve the classification of the model. The results with the best quality were obtained without normalizing our data. Stating that this pre-processing technique does not improve the learning process of all models, it will depend on each problem and the value of their attributes. For future work we suggest an analysis using deep learning techniques; and, to obtain more samples measured with the most updated technology in the area.

References

1. Núñez-Marcos, Adrián, Olatz Perez-de-Viñaspre, and Gorka Labaka. "A survey on Sign Language machine translation". Expert Systems with Applications (2022): 118993
2. Obi, Y., Claudio, K.S., Budiman, V.M., Achmad, S., Kurniawan, A.: Sign language recognition system for communicating to people with disabilities. Procedia Comput. Sci. **216**, 13–20 (2023). https://doi.org/10.1016/j.procs.2022.12.106
3. Saquib, N., Rahman, A.: Application of machine learning techniques for real-time sign language detection using wearable sensors. In: Proceedings of the 11th ACM Multimedia Systems Conference (2020)
4. Prognostics and Health Management of Electronics : Fundamentals, Machine Learning, and the Internet of Things, edited by Michael G. Pecht, and Myeongsu Kang, John Wiley & Sons, Incorporated, 2018. ProQuest Ebook Central
5. Raul, R.: Neural Networks : A Systematic Introduction, Springer, Berlin / Heidelberg (1996). ProQuest Ebook Central
6. Sign Language Acquisition, edited by Anne Baker, and Bencie Woll, John Benjamins Publishing Company (2008). ProQuest Ebook Central
7. Kadous, M.W.: Learning Comprehensible Descriptions of Multivariate Time Series. ICML, vol. 454 (1999)
8. Adeyanju, I.A., Bello, O.O., Adegboye, M.A.: Machine learning methods for sign language recognition: a critical review and analysis. Intelligent Systems with Applications **12**, 200056 (2021). https://doi.org/10.1016/j.iswa.2021.200056
9. Chong, T.-W., Lee, Boon-Giin.: American Sign Language Recognition Using Leap Motion Controller with Machine Learning Approach. Sensors **18**(10), 3554 (2018). https://doi.org/10.3390/s18103554
10. Kadous, M. L. Australian Sign Language signs Data Set. UCI. https://archive.ics.uci.edu/ml/datasets/australian+sign+language+signs

Urdu Semantic Parsing: An Improved SEMPRE Framework for Conversion of Urdu Language Web Queries to Logical Forms

Nafees Ahmad[1]([✉]), Muhammad Aslam[1], Sana Shams[1],
and Ana Maria Martinez-Enriquez[2]

[1] University of Engineering and Technology Lahore, Lahore, Pakistan
nafeesahmad361@yahoo.com, maslam@uet.edu.pk,
sana.shams@kics.edu.pk
[2] Department of CS, CINVESTAV-IPN, Mexico, D.F., Mexico
ammartin@cinvestav.mx

Abstract. The paper presents a semantic parser for Urdu language web queries about the journal's dataset. It is built on the Sempre framework and trained using natural language paraphrases of logical queries from the Tehqeeqat domain. The parser uses linguistic information, including part of speech (POS), skip-bigrams, word alignment, and paraphrases. Sempre can be used on a new domain with zero training examples. In this methodology, First, we used domain-specific and domain-general grammars to generate canonical utterances paired with logical forms. The canonical utterances are meant to capture the meaning of logical forms, and logical forms cover the meaning of the set of compositional operators. These queries are then paraphrased carefully, keeping the semantics of the original query. The result data set containing utterances, paraphrases, and logical forms was used to train the semantic parser. Our semantic parser performs well on domain-specific queries and can be easily trained on a new domain.

Keywords: Semantic Parsing · Web Queries · Natural Language
Understanding · Natural Language Processing · Logical Forms

1 Introduction

Semantic parsing is the conversion of natural language sentences into a complete, formal, symbolic meaning representation that can be executed against the real-world environment, e.g., knowledge base or relational databases [1]. Recent natural language understanding research has focused on shallow semantic analysis, such as word-sense disambiguation [2] and semantic role labeling [3]. On the other hand, semantic parsing comprises deep semantic analysis that combines the word senses, semantic roles, and other components to produce symbolic meaning representations for a particular domain. The last decade has developed several techniques for learning semantic parsers that map a natural language (NL) to a meaning representation language (MRL). These algorithms aim to develop an accurate semantic parser that maps novel NL into the target MRL

A. Y. Rodríguez-González et al. (Eds.): MCPR 2023, LNCS 13902, pp. 273–282, 2023.
https://doi.org/10.1007/978-3-031-33783-3_26

using a training corpus of NL sentences and the correct semantic interpretation in a specific representation of meaning [4]. In recent years, neural sequence-to-sequence models have had a lot of success in this task, but they normally require a lot of labeled data (i.e., utterance, logical form pairs) for training and testing [5, 6]. However, annotating utterances to MRL is expensive and requires expert knowledge of MRL language and the environment against which they are executed. An alternative to annotations is to collect denotations rather than programs [7].

Some real-world applications that use semantic parsing techniques are web search engines, question-answering systems, personal assistants, mobile applications, and social media analysis, where complex NL is translated into MRL or database queries [8]. With the increasing use of search engines, the importance of a better understanding of user queries is also increasing. Human languages allow the representation of queries with different structures and words with the same semantic meaning. One example of this type of user query is shown in Fig. 1. Each set of queries has the same semantics and should be mapped to the logical form, covering the desired set of compositional operators. Semantic understanding of the user queries significantly improves the user experience for the information retrieval systems. There are several techniques used for different languages, including English [8, 9], Arabic [10, 11], and Persian [12]. Semantic parsing techniques used across different languages require large data sets for training. Rule-based models train semantic parsers on small datasets and within specific domains. These models can be easily trained on new domains and achieve good results within specific domains [6]. Urdu is a widely spoken language in several countries, including Pakistan, India, and Bangladesh. It is among the top five most spoken languages in the world. Urdu has an estimated more than 163 million speakers worldwide [13]. The majority of the vocabulary in Urdu is taken from Persian and Arabic.

Urdu is a free word-order language, having different morphological orders and grammar [14]. Research studies performed for the Urdu language's syntactic and semi-semantic parsing techniques are lexicon-based sentiment analysis, opinion mining, adjective phrases-based sentimental analysis, and named entity recognition [15]. Some articles discuss shallow semantic analysis techniques [16]. Urdu is a low-resource language with very few domain-specific data sets available. There is no semantic parsing framework available for the Urdu language, and also, there is no annotated dataset available for semantic parsing. So, a semantic framework for the Urdu language needs to be developed. The following sections are organized; Sect. 2 explains related work. Our proposed approach is presented in Sect. 3. Section 4 presents the results and discussion. Finally, Sect. 5 presents the conclusion and future work.

مجلہ جس کی قسم سائنس ہے اور جو لمز چھاپتا ہے

(Journal whose type is science and which is published by LUMS)

مجلہ جو لمز میں چھپتا ہے اور جس کی قسم سائنس ہے

(Journal which is published by LUMS and whose type is science)

مجلہ جس کی ناشر لمز ہے اور قسم سائنس ہے

(Journal whose publisher is LUMS and type is Science)

Fig. 1. Paraphrases

2 Related Work

We have analyzed the existing semantic parsing techniques used for different languages. There are several techniques for semantic analysis, including Semantic role labeling (SRL) [3, 9, 17], Abstract meaning representation (AMR) [18], Universal Conceptual Cognitive Annotation (UCCA) [19], Uniform meaning representation (UMR) [18] and context-free grammar (CFG) based schemes [4]. Semantic parsing is the conversion of natural language queries into query language or logical forms. Across logical formalisms, there have been several proposals for multilingual semantic parsing which employ multiple natural languages in parallel. In recent years, natural language semantic parsing has gained significant research interest. Several existing models exist for English, Arabic, Persian, and other languages. Manshadi and Li [20] proposed a rule-based semantic tagging model for web search queries. One of the drawbacks of this approach is that it ignores the query's order and treats the sentence as a bag of words. Kollar et al. [21] introduced the Alexa meaning representation language (AMRL), representing natural language utterances in a graph linked with a large ontology. The proposed system shows 78% parsing accuracy. Cc et al. [9] presented a deep learning model for natural language sentence semantic parsing. This approach uses BILSTM architecture with 8 layers used on the CoNLL 2005 and coNLL 2012 datasets achieving an F1 score of 83.2 and 83.4, respectively. The proposed research shows there is still needed to use syntactic parsing to improve the results of semantic parsing. Gardner et al. [3] proposed a deep learning-based semantic labeling platform using different pre-trained models. Embeddings from the language model are used for semantic parsing. They have used Additional models of semantic parsing and reading multi-paragraph comprehension. They achieved an accuracy of 86.4% using the dataset of SNLI 1.0. The Urdu language has many words from the languages like Arabic, Persian, English, Hindi, and Turkish. The majority of the vocabulary in Urdu is taken from Persian and Arabic [22]. Etaiwi et al. [10] designed a graph-based semantic representation of Arabic language sentences. Although the model gives better results for semantic graph generation, this model generates different graphs for sentences having the same meaning. Nasri et al. [11] describe a semantic analysis technique using linguistic resources WordNet and Arabic VerbNet. They build an Arabic ontology and NLP tools from Stanford syntactic parser to generate the semantics of Arabic sentences. It's a conceptual graph-based representation technique used for the semantic analysis of sentences, and although it shows better results after integration with the semantic analysis of Arabic text. Sughra et al. [12] presented a semantic role labeling-based model for the Persian language. A classification approach is used to assign the appropriate role labels for each word. They achieved an F1 score of 74.87 on the Persian dataset.

Ali et al. [23] presented an Urdu text summarization model by computing co-occurrences of words and sentences. Depending on the sensitivity of the word in different sentences, local weights and global weights for each word and sentence are calculated. They achieved an F1 score of 80%. Kamran et al. [15] presented name entity recognition to identify and classify entities into person, location, and organization names. There are research articles on name entity recognition, part of speech tagging, and sentimental analysis of the Urdu language [15]. Few articles mention semantic parsing, but no datasets are available for semantic parsing of web queries, and semantic parsing requires annotated datasets. Various techniques used for different languages require large annotated datasets for training and testing. Urdu is a low-resource language, and generating a large annotated dataset is challenging. These techniques require a large annotated dataset for training on specific domains. Large language models lack the domain specific knowledge and require significant computational power as compared to sempre [19]. Developing a baseline semantic parser that requires minimum data set for training and achieves good accuracy is necessary. Domain general grammar in our parser includes a set of compositional operators that generate the numeric queries in the data sets, improving the results of the numeric questions. We need extra effort to design the domain-specific grammar to improve the system's scalability. Our approach uses the paraphrase model, which is cheaper and faster to obtain better results in a specific domain.

3 Semantic Parser for Urdu Web Queries

We have used the sempre framework for parsing Urdu language queries. Sempre converts natural language sentences to logical forms, which can be used to generate database queries. Parser consists of the domain generalizable grammar having many relationships between the arbitrary entities. The domain-general grammar (DGG) uses dependency-based compositional semantics, a limited lambda calculus form, more concisely representing the relationship between the database entities [24]. The first step in the sempre framework is to provide the builder the domain-specific grammar (DSG) containing entities and relationships. DGG defines the rules for the relationships between arbitrary entities. Rules are written in lambda dependency-based compositional semantics [24]. This grammar specifies all the general rules for query generation used to generate the possible utterance, logical forms pair for a domain-specific grammar entity, and relationships. The DGG builds noun phrases (NP), verb phrases (VP), and complementizer phrases (CP), which form denote unary logical forms. The rules R1 to R4 and C1 to C4 combine binary phrases and noun phrases (optionally through comparatives, counting, and negation) to form complementizer phrases. Rule G3 combines these complementizer phrases with a noun phrase. In addition, superlatives (argmin and argmax are included) are handled by rules S0 to S4, which take an NP and return the extremum-attaining subset. We also support join and disjunction transformations using rules T1 and T4, respectively. Finally, rules A1 and A2 support aggregation. DGG rules are shown in Table 2. The builder uses GGG rules, DSG entities, and relationships to generate almost all possible utterances. All types (e.g., مجلہ) have the syntactic TYPENP; Verb phrases or noun phrases (VP/NP) (e.g., چھاپتا) are used to express unary predicates. The builder can represent binaries as relational noun phrases (RELNP) or generalized transitive verbs (VP/NP). RELNPs are used to combine functional properties like (قسم, نوعیت) while VP/NPs are used for the transitive verbs (چھاپتا). DSG is shown in Table 1. The major difference between the two languages is word order. English grammar structure has the word order of SVO (subject-verb-object), while Urdu has SOV (subject-object-verb). In Urdu, Comparative and superlative modifiers are also placed before the verb (subject + object + comparative/superlative + verb). In English, these are places after the verb (subject + verb + comparative/superlative + object). Besides these structural changes, we have translated adjectives, nouns, pronouns, and constants from English to proper Urdu words.

The parser can convert the answer to the queries based on the relationships described in domain-specific grammar. It produces a pair of utterances and corresponding logical forms by applying rules and their combinations. These derived logical forms are constructed by lexicon mapping with the database predicates and composition rules from domain-general grammar. In the second step, each canonical utterance is paraphrased through crowdsourcing. These paraphrases give small depth to learning the different contexts of the query. We have noticed the basic changes in using words after that sentence

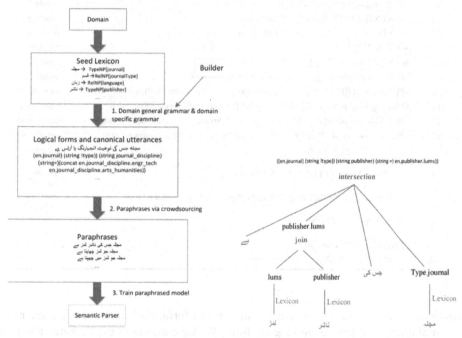

Fig. 2. Urdu Semantic parsing framework   **Fig. 3.** Query parse tree

Table 1. Domain-Specific Grammar

Entity	Type	Database Representation
مجلہ (Journal)	TypeNP	en.journal
قسم (Type)	RelNP	en.journal_type
نوعیت (Discipline)	RelNP	en.journal_discipline
جلد (Volume)	RelNP	en.volume
زبان (Language)	RelNP	en.language
ناشر (Publisher)	TypeNP	en.publisher
چھاپتا (published by)	VP/NP	published_by

Table 2. Domain General Grammar

Rule	Definition	Type
G1	ENTITYNP[x] → NP[x]	glue
G2	TYPENP[x] → NP [type.x]	glue
G3	NP[x] CP[f] (اور) CP[g]) * → NP [x u f u g]	glue
R0	جو VP[x] → CP[x]	simple
R1	جس کی/کا RELNP[r] CMP[c] NP[y] ہے → CP[r.c.y]	simple
	CMP[= | != | < | > | ≤ | ≥] → سب سے زیادہ | سب سے کم | سے زیادہ ہے | سے کم ہے | نہیں ہے | ہے	
R2	جو NP[y] (نہیں)? VP/NP[r] ہے → CP [(¬) y.r]	simple
R3	جو RELNP[r] کی NP[y] (نہیں)? ہے → CP[R(r).(¬).y]	simple
R4	جو NP[y] (نہیں)? VP/NP[r] ہے → CP [(y. (¬). R(r))]	simple
C1	جس کی CNT[c] RELNP[r] ہیں → CP[R(λx.count(R(r).x)).c]	counting
C2	جو CNT[c] NP[y] VP/NP[r] ہے → CP[R(λy.count(x u R(r).x)).c]	counting
C3	جو CNT[c] NP[y] کی RELNP[r] → CP[R(λx.count(y u x r)).c]	counting
C4	جو CNT[c] NP[y] VP/NP[r] → CP[R(λx.count(y u r.x)).c]	counting
S0	NP[x] جس کا RELNP[r] سب سے زیادہ ہے → NP [arg max (x, r)]	superlatives
S1	NP[x] جس کی of RELNP[r] سب سے زیادہ کی تعداد → NP [arg max (x, R(λy.count(R(r).y)))]	superlatives
S2	NP[x] جو سب سے کم NP[y] VP/NP[r] ہے → NP [arg max (x, R(λr.count(R(x).y)))]	superlatives
S3	NP[x] جو سب سے کم NP[y] کی RELNP[r] ہے → NP [arg max (x, R (λz.count(y u r.z)))]	superlatives
S4	NP[x] جو سب سے زیادہ NP[y] VP/NP[r] ہے → NP [arg max (x, R (λz.count(y u r.z)))]	superlatives
T1	NP[y] کے RELNP[r] → NP[R(r). y]	transformation
T2	RELNP0[h]CP[f] (اور) CP[g]) * → NP[R(h). (f u g)]	transformation
T3	RELNP[r] کی RELNP0[h] NP[x] CP[f] (اور) CP[g]) * → NP[R(r). (h.x u f u g)]	transformation
T4	NP[x] یا NP[y] → NP [x t y]	transformation
A1	کی تعداد NP[x] → NP [count(x)]	aggregation
A2	اوسط RELNP[r] کی NP[x] → NP[sum|average(x, r)]	aggregation

structure. Users can put the same query in a shorter form. Each dataset entry contains an original query, paraphrase, and logical form. We have also used the Berkeley aligner's calculated word alignments [25]. Finally, the semantic parser is trained on this dataset. The domain-specific grammar contains entities and relationships between entities, and domain-general grammar and domain-specific grammar rules are shown in Table 2 and Table 1. Berant and Liang [30] introduced the paraphrase model to handle these queries. The model generates the set of canonical utterances and the corresponding probability scores. We convert the lexicon to simple logical forms, e.g., "where" to "Type. Location". Then the intersection, aggregation, join, and enclosing span rules are applied. After the generation of derivations log-linear model is used to generate the feature vector for each candidate utterance and optimize the likelihood of correct prediction. For testing the dataset, we have used query logical form pairs. Figure 2 shows the details to generate the dataset required for the sempre parser. Each dataset entry contains an original query, paraphrase, and logical form. We have parsed the training set to obtain the lexical features, and it computes the conditional probability between the two types of original queries and paraphrases. These linguistic features are helpful for the paraphrase model to learn, along with the standard features of annotations and logical forms. The complexity of the paraphrase is measured by the number of nodes in the parse tree shown in Fig. 3.

4   Results and Discussion

The semantic parser is evaluated on the Tehqeeqat domain dataset with 900 examples. We have used 80% of the dataset for training and 20% for testing. Accuracy is calculated by dividing the examples for which it predicts correct logical forms and total examples. It achieved 75.2% accuracy on the training set and 77.2% on the testing set. We have also calculated the Oracle accuracy of 80% for training and 85.1% for the testing dataset. To better understand the importance of each feature, we conducted experiments by leaving one feature in each experiment and compared the results with full features. We have used part of speech, skip bigram, PPDB, tokens, word alignment, and database relationships. During these experiments, Oracle's accuracy remains almost static across all experiments. It suggests that marginal improvement in accuracy is from using additional features due to improved ranking of candidate parses. Figure 4 shows that removing the word alignment feature causes a significant drop in inaccuracy. We have also analyzed that POS tags and skip bigrams did not affect the accuracy of the parser. One of the benefits of using a paraphrasing model with domain-specific grammar is that it requires less training dataset. We trained our model with 4 dataset sizes using full features. In each dataset, we have unique queries along with their paraphrases. There is also a quiet spread between different samples, which shows the impact of the specific composition of the sample. Accuracy varies depending on the sample data. If the dataset is taken uniformly, which means generated from all the rules. Taking the training dataset examples, which do not represent all the rules, will reduce the results. Figure 4 shows the detailed comparison. We performed experiments on one, two, or three paraphrases. We find a significant difference in results on different paraphrases, showing that each additional paraphrase has relatively little new linguistic information. We have also tested with varying sets of paraphrases and observed that it shows poorly on paraphrases with less information or extra information. Figure 4 shows the detailed comparison.

Paraphrases and word alignments are essential for the semantic parser in learning the necessary linguistic features from queries. Testing the parser on different paraphrases for each query improves the system's accuracy with carefully designed paraphrases. There are some examples in which the parser fails to parse correctly. After error analysis, we realized that most errors were due to problems with the paraphrasing model. Sometimes, the paraphrases are missing something or have extra material or incorrect paraphrases. So, to achieve better results, paraphrases should be written carefully to maintain the same semantics as the original query. We have tested the system on different feature sets. Most linguistic features are learned from paraphrases, lexicons, and word alignments. We find that the parser has difficulty with numerical relationships. For some specific numerical relationships, we can attribute these mistakes to the fact that no similar relationships were modeled in the training data. For example, due to our particular random train/validation/test split, no single training example demonstrated relationships. This illustrates that model is pretty good at parsing any paraphrase of queries it has seen

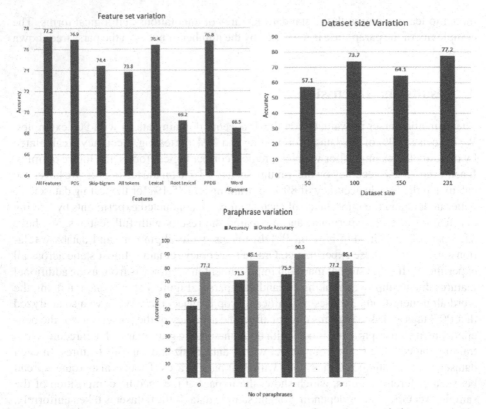

Fig. 4. Results: feature set, dataset size, number of paraphrase variations

before but very bad at understanding types of queries it has not seen. Our error analysis thus confirms this common characterization of paraphrase models with domain-specific grammar.

5   Conclusion and Future Work

The semantic parser achieves 75.2% accuracy on the training dataset and 77.2% on the testing dataset. We found that the linguistic feature word alignment, POS tags, tokens, bigram, and trigram improve the semantic parser's performance. Our system performs well in a specific domain but does not perform well on queries outside it. For this, we need more datasets from different domains. There remains room for further improvements so it can be trained on a limited dataset and learns to flexibly parse a wide range of queries. We can also use it along with syntactic parsers to enhance its performance.

References

1. Zettlemoyer, L.S., Michael, C.: Learning to map sentences to logical form: structured clas-sification with probabilistic categorial grammars. In: Proceedings of 21st Conference on Uncertainty in Artificial Intelligence, UAI 2005, pp. 658–666 (2005)

2. Abid, M., Habib, A., Ashraf, J., Shahid, A.: Urdu word sense disambiguation using machine learning approach. Clust. Comput. **21**, 515–522 (2017). https://doi.org/10.1007/s10586-017-0918-0
3. Gardner, M., et al.: AllenNLP: a deep semantic natural language processing platform, pp. 1–6. arXiv Prepr. arXiv1803.07640 (2019)
4. Wong, Y.W., Mooney, R.J.: Learning synchronous grammars for semantic parsing with lambda calculus. In: ACL 2007 – Proceedings of 45th Annual Meeting, pp. 960–967. Association for Computational Linguistics (2007)
5. Dong, L., Lapata, M.: Language to logical form with neural attention. In: 54th Annual Meeting of the Association for Computational Linguistics. ACL 2016 - Long Paper, vol. 1, pp. 33–43 (2016)
6. Jia, R., Liang, P.: Data recombination for neural semantic parsing. In: 54th Annual Meeting of the Association for Computational Linguistics, ACL 2016 - Long Papers, pp. 12–22. Association for Computational Linguistics (ACL) (2016)
7. Yi, S., Li, H., Wang, X.: Understanding pedestrian behaviors from stationary crowd groups. In: Proceedings of IEEE Computer Society Conference on Computer Vision Pattern Recognition, pp. 3488–3496, 07–12 June 2015. https://doi.org/10.1109/CVPR.2015.7298971
8. Mirzaei, A., Sedghi, F., Safari, P.: Semantic role labeling system for Persian language. ACM Trans. Asian Low-Resource Lang. Inf. Process. **19**, 1–12 (2020)
9. He, L., Lee, K., Lewis, M., Zettlemoyer, L., Allen, P.G.: Deep semantic role labeling: what works and what's next. In: Proceedings of 55th Annual Meeting Association Computing Linguistics, vol. 1, pp. 473–483 (2017). https://doi.org/10.18653/v1/P17-1044
10. Etaiwi, W., Awajan, A.: Graph-based Arabic text semantic representation. Inf. Process. Manag. **57**, 102183 (2020). https://doi.org/10.1016/j.ipm.2019.102183
11. Nasri, M., Jaafar, Y., Bouzoubaa, K.: Semantic analysis of Arabic texts within SAFAR framework. Colloq. Inf. Sci. Technol. CiSt, 194–199 (2018)
12. Lazemi, S., Ebrahimpour-Komleh, H., Noroozi, N.: Persian semantic role labeling based on dependency tree. Int. J. Inf. Sci. Manag. **18**, 93–108 (2020)
13. Weber, G.: The World's 10 most influential languages. Lang. Today **3** (2008)
14. Ali, A., Habib, A., Ashraf, J., Javed, M.: A review on Urdu language parsing. Int. J. Adv. Comput. Sci. Appl. **8**, 93–97 (2017). https://doi.org/10.14569/ijacsa.2017.080413
15. Kamran Malik, M., Mansoor Sarwar, S.: Named entity recognition system for postpositional languages: Urdu as a case study. IJACSA Int. J. Adv. Comput. Sci. Appl. **7** (2016)
16. Munir, S., Abbas, Q., Jamil, B.: Dependency parsing using the URDU.KON-TB treebank. Int. J. Comput. Appl. **167**, 25–31 (2017)
17. Foland, W.R., Martin, J.H.: Abstract meaning representation parsing using LSTM recurrent neural networks. In: ACL 2017 - 55th Annual Meeting, vol. 1, pp. 463–472. ACL (2017)
18. Van Gysel, J.E.L., et al.: Designing a uniform meaning representation for natural language processing. KI - Künstliche Intelligenz **35**(3–4), 343–360 (2021). https://doi.org/10.1007/s13218-021-00722-w
19. Abend, O., Rappoport, A.: The state of the art in semantic representation. In: ACL 2017 - 55th Annual Meeting of the Association for Computational Linguistics Proceedings Conference (Long Paper), vol. 1, pp. 77–89 (2017)
20. Manshadi, M., Li, X.: Semantic tagging of web search queries. In: Proceedings of the Joint Conference of the 47th Annual Meeting of the ACL (2009)
21. Kollar, T., et al.: The Alexa meaning representation language. In: Proceedings of 2018 Conference North American Chapter of the Association for Computational Linguistics: Human Language Technologies, pp. 177–184 (2018)
22. Hardie, A.: Developing a tagset for automated part-of-speech tagging in Urdu Andrew Hardie Department of Linguistics, LU (2003)

23. Nawaz, A., Bakhtyar, M., Baber, J., Ullah, I., Noor, W., Basit, A.: Extractive text summarization models for Urdu language. Inf. Process. Manag. **57**, 102383 (2020)
24. Liang, P.: Lambda Dependency-Based Compositional Semantics (2013)
25. Liang, P., Ben, T., Klein, D.: Alignment by agreement. In: HLT-NAACL 2006, pp. 104–111 (2006)

Improving the Identification of Abusive Language Through Careful Design of Pre-training Tasks

Horacio Jarquín-Vásquez[✉], Hugo Jair Escalante,
and Manuel Montes-y-Gómez

Instituto Nacional de Astrofísica, Óptica y Electrónica (INAOE), Puebla, Mexico
{horacio.jarquin,hugojair,mmontesg}@inaoep.mx

Abstract. The use of Deep Learning-based solutions has become popular in Natural Language Processing due to their remarkable performance in a wide variety of tasks. Specifically, Transformer-based models (e.g. BERT) have become popular in recent years due to their outstanding performance and their ease of adaptation (fine-tuning) in a large number of domains. Despite their outstanding results, the fine-tuning of these models under the presence of informal language writing, especially the one that contains offensive words and expressions, remains a challenging task, due to the lack of vocabulary coverage and proper task contextual information. To overcome this issue, we proposed the domain adaptation of the BERT language model to the abusive language detection task. In order to achieve this, we constrain the language model with the adaptation of two default pre-trained tasks, through the retraining of the model parameters. The obtained configurations were evaluated in six abusive language datasets, showing encouraging results; a remarkable improvement was achieved with the use of the proposed approaches in comparison with its base model. In addition to this, competitive results were obtained with respect to state-of-the-art approaches, thus obtaining a robust and easy-to-train model for the identification of abusive language.

Keywords: Abusive language · Transformer models · Pretraining tasks

1 Introduction

The integration of social media platforms into the everyday lives of billions of users has increased the number of online social interactions, encouraging the exchange of different opinions and points of view that would otherwise be ignored by traditional media [1]. The use of these social media platforms has revolutionized the way people communicate and share information. Unfortunately, not all of these interactions are constructive, as the presence of Abusive Language (AL) has spread to these media. AL is characterized by the presence of insults, teasing, criticism and intimidation [4]. It mainly includes epithets directed at an

A. Y. Rodríguez-González et al. (Eds.): MCPR 2023, LNCS 13902, pp. 283–292, 2023.
doi.org/10.1007/978-3-031-33783-3_27

individual's characteristic, which are personally offensive, degrading and insulting. Because of its negative social impact [8], the automatic identification of AL has stimulated the interest of social media companies and governments. Derived from this, multiple efforts have been made to combat the proliferation of AL, ranging from the establishment of codes of conduct, norms and regulations in the content publication on social media, to the use of Natural Language Processing (NLP) for its computational analysis [17].

Concerning the several efforts and approximations made by the NLP community, a wide variety of them have focused on the use of Deep Learning (DL), due to its outstanding classification performance in a large number of NLP tasks [1]. Among the proposed DL approaches, the use of pre-trained Transformer-based language models has excelled in recent years, due to its great performance in different natural language understanding tasks and its ease of adaptation (via fine-tuning) [16]. Despite this encouraging results, the adaptation of these language models remains challenging for specific language domains, such as the AL identification task, due to the lack of vocabulary coverage and the lack of proper task contextual information [2]. Aiming to overcome these issues, different approaches has focused on the creation of a wide variety of pre-trained models for specific language domains [10], this has been accomplished through the training of the language model with large volumes of data from the referred domain, with the use of default pre-training tasks, designed for general language understanding. Since the natural language is usually expressed differently between specific contexts and domains, the use of these default pre-training tasks may restrict the language model in the recognition of stylistic language patterns and the interpretation of certain words in specific language domains.

In this research, we hypothesize that the adaptation of the default pre-training tasks into the target domain may improve the domain language understanding and therefore the classification performance. In this research we will focus on the domain adaptation of Transformer language models into the AL detection task. Specifically, we will focus on the adaptation of the default BERT pre-training tasks [7]. The main contributions in this paper are: 1) The adaptation of the default BERT pre-training tasks into the AL detection tasks, 2) the design and creation of two specialized datasets for the adapted pre-training tasks, and 3) the creation of a robust pre-trained model that is especially suited for the AL detection task.

2   Related Work

Considering the well-acknowledged increase of AL on social media platforms, several datasets [6,14,19] and evaluation campaigns [8] have been proposed in order to mitigate the impact of such a kind of messages. The detection of AL in text has been mainly addressed from a supervised perspective [1], considering a great variety of features, ranging from the use of hand-crafted features such as bag-of-words representations, as well as, syntactical and linguistical features [17], to the use of word embeddings, and Transformer-based pre-trained models, such as GPT-2 and BERT [5,11,15].

Among all the aforementioned approaches, the Transformer-based ones constitute the current state-of-the-art on the AL detection task [1]. Since the use of these models has focused on the general language understanding, in recent research the NLP community has focused on pre-training these models in specific language domains, aiming to capture domain-specific patterns, which lead to improve the performance classification on specific tasks [2]. These approaches have been extended to the AL detection task, specifically, in [3] was proposed the HateBERT model, which was trained with the default BERT pre-trained tasks [7], and a large-scale dataset of Reddit comments in English from communities banned for being offensive, abusive, or hateful; despite its great performance in the identification of AL, this model requires from large volumes of data and high computational cost. Unlike the HateBERT model, in this research we propose the domain adaptation of the BERT model, through the re-training of a pre-trained model with two especially suited pre-training tasks for the AL detection task, with the use of limited data of different AL types.

3   Adaptation of Pretraining Tasks

This section presents the proposed methodology to re-training the BERT model, through the adaptation of two default pre-training tasks into the AL detection task. The section is divided in three subsections, in the first subsection we present the data collection approach for the construction of the training datasets for the adapted pre-training tasks. In the second subsection we present in detail the adapted pre-training tasks for the detection of AL. Finally, in the third subsection we present our evaluation framework for the detection of AL.

Before introducing the following subsections, we briefly present the BERT default pre-training tasks definitions. The first one is the Masked Language Model (MLM) task, it masks some of the tokens from the input, and its main objective is to predict the original vocabulary token of the masked word, based on its context (the input sequence). The second one is the Next Sentence Prediction (NSP) task, which is based on text-pair representations (sentences A and B), its main objective is to predict whether B is a continuation of A or not. For more details on the description of these pre-training tasks, we refer the reader to the following paper [7].

3.1   Data Collection Approach

Since our main contribution is based on the retraining of the BERT model for its adaptation into the AL detection task, two different datasets were designed to adapt the default MLM and NSP pre-trained tasks, respectively. The first dataset which we will refer to as: $Dataset_{MLM}$ (DS_{MLM}) is designed to contain AL instances in order to constraint the model in the prediction of potentially offensive words/expressions. In order for the language model to capture the writing style of the different types of AL in the evaluation datasets, the DS_{MLM} dataset was built from the union of all the AL instances of the training datasets (refer to Sect. 4.1); in addition, this dataset was extended with the integration of extracted toxic comments from the *Toxic Comment Classification Challenge*[1] dataset, generating a final dataset with total of 75k AL instances.

Regarding the second dataset which we will refer to as: DS_{NSP}, it contains pairs of AL and non-AL instances and is designed to constraint the model in the prediction of whether two sentences have the same label or not. This dataset was generated with four partitions (PT_1, PT_2, PT_3, and PT_4) of 25k instances per partition, where PT_1 and PT_2 were generated with 50k random samples taken from the DS_{MLM} dataset. On the other hand, PT_3 and PT_4 were created with the union of all the non-AL instances from the training datasets, and completed with the integration of non-toxic comments from the *Toxic Comment Classification Challenge*. With these partitions, we generate the following combinations: $\{(PT_1, PT_2, label : 1), (PT_3, PT_4, label : 1), (PT_1, PT_4, label : 0), (PT_2, PT_3, label : 0)\}$, where we assign the label 1 in all the pairs of sentences which share either an AL context or a non-AL one; otherwise we assign the label 0, this results in a dataset with total of 100k instance pairs. The details of all the evaluation datasets will be presented in the next section.

3.2   Adapted Pre-training Tasks

In order to constraint the model in the identification of AL patterns, we proposed the retraining of the BERT model through the adaptation of its default pre-training tasks, aiming to improve the detection of AL. Figure 1 presents the general architecture of the adapted pre-trained tasks. The input of the architecture contains two different sentences conformed with the use of 3 special tokens ([CLS], [SEP] and [MASK]), as presented in [7] the [CLS] token is used for the classification of whether the two sentences share the same label or not, the [SEP] token is used to delimit both sentences and to indicate the end of the second sentence, the [MASK] token is used to indicate the masked tokens which will be used in the MLM task. As illustrated in our architecture, both pre-training tasks were trained in a joint perspective. Below, we present in detail the adaptation of the pre-training tasks.

Regarding the adaptation of the MLM task, unlike [7] we assigned a masking probability of 15% to each token, with the limitation of not masking consecutive tokens. In addition to this, in order to constraint the model in the recognition of AL, we assigned a masking probability of 50% to potentially offensive words/expressions, we consider a word/expression as potentially offensive if it is contained in the *HATE-BASE*[2] database labeled as mildly, highly and extremely offensive. Concerning the adaptation of the NSP task, unlike [7], we decided to change the approach, by constraining the model to distinguish between instances with the same label, we hypothesize that this will help the language model in distinguishing between AL and non-AL instances. Since we changed the focus of

---

[1] https://www.kaggle.com/c/jigsaw-toxic-comment-classification-challenge.
[2] https://hatebase.org/.

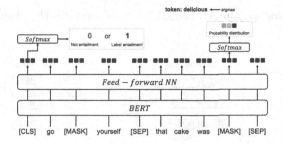

Fig. 1. General architecture of our adapted pre-trained tasks for the detection of AL.

this pre-training task, from now on we will refer to this proposed adaptation as: Following Label Prediction (FLP) task.

Since both tasks are jointly learned during the training process, we proposed a weighted training loss function ($WLoss$) based on the number of correctly predicted offensive mask tokens, we designed this loss function with the intention of providing more focus on the MLM task, while fewer offensive words the model is capable of predicting, on the other hand, while more offensive words the model is capable of predicting, it should focus more on the FLP task, this could prevent the model from overfitting. The proposed loss function is presented in Eq. 1, where α is defined as the quotient of the correctly predicted offensive mask tokens and the total number of offensive masked tokens, L_{MLM} and L_{FLP} are the cross-entropy loss on predicting the masked tokens and label prediction, respectively. As baseline, we considered the addition of the L_{MLM} and L_{FLP} loss functions, as shown in Eq. 2.

$$WLoss = (1 - \alpha)L_{MLM} + \alpha L_{FLP} \tag{1}$$

$$SLoss = L_{MLM} + L_{FLP} \tag{2}$$

For sake of clarity, in this subsection we presented the explanation of the specially suited MLM and FLP pre-training tasks, this configuration was trained with the use of the DS_{NSP} dataset. For our evaluation, we additionally used the MLM and FLP task separately, in the case of the MLM task, we trained on the $DS_{M}LM$ dataset and did not performed any classification with the [CLS] token, on the other hand, for the FLP task we trained on the DS_{NSP} dataset and did not mask any token.

3.3 Generation of Robust Language Models for the Detection of AL

Since we aim to generate robust BERT language models for the detection of AL, our evaluation framework comprises two main phases: 1) the retraining phase, where we adapt de BERT model into the AL domain through the specially suited pre-training tasks, and 2) the fine-tuning phase, where we adjust the retrained model for specific AL tasks. Figure 2 illustrates the proposed evaluation framework.

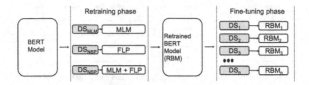

Fig. 2. Proposed framework for the detection of AL.

As shown in the above Figure, the first phase utilizes a pre-trained BERT model as starting point for the model retraining with our specially suited pre-training tasks (MLM and/or FLP). The produced Retrained BERT Model (RBM) is then used in the second phase, were we independently fine-tuned each RBM with the evaluation datasets, in order to adapt the retrained model in specific AL tasks. As suggested in [7], the fine-tuning was achieved with the stacking of a fully-connected softmax layer on top of the last [CLS] encoding vector, to obtain the class probabilities and get the final classification.

4   Experimental Settings

4.1   Datasets for the Detection of Abusive Language

AL can be of different types, its main divisions are distinguished by the target and severity of the insults [13]. Accordingly, different collections and evaluation campaigns have considered different kinds of AL for its study [12,17]. Below we present a brief description of the six English evaluation datasets we used in our experiments.

The first three datasets: *Waseem* [19], *Davidson* [6] and *Golbeck* [9] were some of the first large-scale datasets for abusive tweet detection. Specifically, the *Davidson* dataset focuses on identifying offensive language and hate speech in tweets, the *Waseem* dataset focuses on the identification of racist and sexist tweets; whereas the *Golbeck* dataset focuses on the detection of harassment in tweets. On the other hand, the *SE 2019 T 6* [14] and *AMI 2018* [8] datasets were presented at the *SemEval-2019 Task 6*, and at the *Evalita 2018* Task on Automatic Misogyny Identification (AMI) respectively. The *SE 2019 T 6* dataset focuses on identifying offensive tweets, whereas the *AMI 2018* dataset focuses on identifying misogyny in tweets. Finally, the *HASOC 2019* [13] dataset was presented at the *11th Forum for Information Retrieval Evaluation (FIRE)*, in the Hate Speech and Offensive Content Identification (HASOC) shared-task, where the main goal was the classification of Hate Speech and non-offensive online content in Indo-European Languages. Even though the aforementioned shared tasks consider different subtasks to perform the evaluation at different levels of granularity, in our experiments we only focused on their respective cases of binary classification.

4.2 Implementation Details

Regarding the text preprocessing phase, different operations were applied in both, the re-training and fine-tuning phases: in order to avoid biases, user mentions and links were replaced by the default tokens: $<user>$ and $<url>$; in order to enrich the vocabulary, all hashtags were segmented by words (*e.g.* #BuildThe-Wall - build the wall) with the use of the ekphrasis library[3]; in addition to this, all emojis were converted into words using the demoji[4] library. All text was lowercased and non-alphabetical characters as well as consecutive repeated words were removed.

All the models from the retraining, as well as, the fine-tuning phases were trained using the Adam optimizer, with a learning rate of 5e–5, as suggested in [7]. Specifically, the retraining models were trained for a total of 2 epochs and a batch size of 32, while the fine-tuning models were trained for a total of 3 epochs and a 32 batch size. For evaluation purposes we used two variants of the BERT model: 1) the BERT base uncased[5] model, and 2) the HateBERT[6] model.

5   Experimental Results

5.1   Effectiveness of the Specially Suited Pre-training Tasks

Table 1 shows the evaluation results of the proposed model configurations. For sake of comparison of our obtained results against SOTA approaches, we use different evaluation metrics, specifically: the *Waseem, Davidson* and *Golbeck* datasets were evaluated with the weighted-average F_1 score, the *SemEval 2019 task 6* and *HASOC 2019* datasets were evaluated using the macro-average F_1 score, finally, the *AMI 2018* dataset was evaluated using the accuracy.

Centering the analysis of results on the pre-trained BERT and HateBERT models (rows 2 and 3), the results indicate that the use of HateBERT outperforms the use of BERT in all the evaluation datasets. This can be attributed to the fact that HateBERT was trained on data from the AL detection domain. Regarding the independent retraining with our especially suited FLP and MLM tasks, it can be observed an improvement in performance in all datasets in comparison with the original pre-trained models (rows 4–7 vs. rows 2 and 3), furthermore, the best performance is obtained with the retraining of HateBERT with our MLM and FLP tasks (row 4 vs. row 5 and row 6 vs. row 7). Concerning the joint retraining results of our proposed pre-training tasks, it can be noticed an improvement in performance in comparison with the single FLP and MLM retraining (rows 8–11 vs. rows 4–7), which indicates that our especially suited tasks are complementary to each other. When comparing the use of our proposed loss function (*WLoss*) coupled in the joint model retraining, better results are

---

[3] https://github.com/cbaziotis/ekphrasis.
[4] https://pypi.org/project/demoji/.
[5] https://huggingface.co/bert-base-uncased.
[6] https://huggingface.co/GroNLP/hateBERT.

Table 1. Comparison results from our proposed model configurations in six datasets for the AL detection task. PT stands for Pre-training task, the (+) and (*) symbols after the MLM+FLP indicates the use of the *SLoss* and *WLoss*, respectively.

BERT Model	PT	Waseem	Davidson	Golbeck	SE 2019 T 6	AMI 2018	HASOC 2019
BERT-BASE	–	0.864	0.932	0.718	0.786	0.709	0.765
HateBERT	–	0.872	0.938	0.724	0.791	0.721	0.773
BERT-BASE	FLP	0.874	0.935	0.725	0.792	0.720	0.768
HateBERT	FLP	0.881	0.940	0.733	0.801	0.727	0.775
BERT-BASE	MLM	0.870	0.938	0.723	0.794	0.718	0.772
HateBERT	MLM	0.879	0.946	0.731	0.803	0.732	0.778
BERT-BASE	MLM+FLP(+)	0.877	0.940	0.729	0.801	0.725	0.779
HateBERT	MLM+FLP(+)	0.884	0.951	0.739	0.813	0.742	0.783
BERT-BASE	MLM+FLP(*)	0.881	0.948	0.732	0.809	0.735	0.782
HateBERT	MLM+FLP(*)	**0.889**	**0.957**	**0.742**	0.815	**0.747**	0.786
SOTA	–	0.880	0.920	0.727	**0.829**	0.704	**0.788**
Reference	–	[15]	[15]	[5]	[11]	[8]	[18]

obtained compared to the unweighted loss function (rows 10 and 11 vs. rows 8 and 9).

Overall, the best results were obtained with the joint retraining of the Hate-BERT model, with the use of our proposed weighted loss function. When comparing our best results against the state-of-the-art approaches (row 10 vs. row 11), we get better results in 4 of the 6 evaluation datasets. It is important to notice that these approaches are conformed by a variety of DL architectures, data pre-processing, and data augmentation techniques [5,11,15], whereas our approach is solely based on a fine-tuning approach with a retrained BERT model.

5.2 Qualitative Analysis

NOTE: This section contains examples of language that may be offensive to some readers, these do not represent the perspectives of the authors.

Table 2. Examples of inference over masked words (represented by the [MASK] token), comparing the BERT model vs. the BERT model retrained with the especially suited pre-training tasks.

Sentence	BERT	BERT (MLM + FLP)
all politicians are [MASK]	good (0.0771), important (0.0291), different (0.0285), bad (0.0267)	corrupt (0.0980), stupid (0.0618), unhappy (0.0366), popular (0.0268)
show me your [MASK]	body (0.0600), face (0.0510), hand (0.0460), name (0.0346)	pussy (0.3407), tits (0.0706), penis (0.0411), dick (0.0356)
feminism is very [MASK]	important (0.1361), strong (0.0937), popular (0.0387), powerful (0.0227)	stupid (0.0667), serious (0.0474), real (0.0423), oppressive (0.0368)
women can [MASK] very well	work (0.0601), fight (0.0572), dress (0.0563), communicate (0.0532)	cook (0.2604), dress (0.1219), wash (0.0515), wipe (0.0329)
you are a [MASK]	. (0.6704), ! (0.1137), ? (0.0408), ; (0.0323)	bitch (0.2884), pussy (0.1202), dick (0.0685), loser (0.0540)

In order to analyze the captured patterns in the retraining phase, we performed an inference comparison between the predictions of masked tokens with the BERT model (without retraining) and the BERT model retrained with the MLM and FLP pre-training tasks. Table 2 presents the inference comparison from 5 baseline sentences, when comparing the predictions of the BERT vs retrained BERT. From these examples, a big difference can be observed, on the one hand, the BERT model produces positive, as well as, neutral words given the inference sentence, even predicting the use of punctuation marks. On the other hand, the BERT (MLM + FLP) model generates potentially offensive words with sexual and negative connotations. This evidences the outstanding performance of the retrained models in the identification of AL.

6   Conclusions and Future Work

In this paper we proposed the domain adaptation of the BERT model into the AL identification domain, through the proposal of two especially suited pre-trained tasks. The evaluation results in 6 different datasets for the identification of AL showed a great improvement with the use of our adapted pre-training tasks, in comparison to the pre-trained BERT and HateBERT models. Furthermore, when comparing our best model against state-of-the-art approaches encouraging results were obtained, as our proposal outperformed their results in 4 out of 6 datasets. This allow us concluding that performance in the AL detection task could be improved with the careful design of the pre-training tasks. As future work we plan to extend our pre-training tasks into multilingual Transformers, and evaluate their performance in the identification of AL in other languages.

Acknowledgements. We thank CONACyT-Mexico for partially supporting this work under project grant CB-S-26314 and scholarship 925996.

References

1. Alkomah, F., Ma, X.: A literature review of textual hate speech detection methods and datasets. Information **13**(6), 273 (2022)
2. Beltagy, I., Lo, K., Cohan, A.: SciBERT: a pretrained language model for scientific text. In: Proceedings of the 2019 Conference on Empirical Methods in Natural Language Processing, pp. 3615–3620. Association for Computational Linguistics (2019)
3. Caselli, T., Basile, V., Mitrović, J., Granitzer, M.: HateBERT: retraining BERT for abusive language detection in English. In: Proceedings of the 5th Workshop on Online Abuse and Harms (WOAH 2021), pp. 17–25. Association for Computational Linguistics, Online, August 2021
4. Cecillon, N., Labatut, V., Dufour, R., Linarès, G.: Abusive language detection in online conversations by combining content- and graph-based features. Front. Big Data **2** (2019)
5. Chakrabarty, T., Gupta, K., Muresan, S.: Pay "attention" to your context when classifying abusive language. In: Proceedings of the Third Workshop on Abusive Language Online, pp. 70–79. Association for Computational Linguistics (2019)

6. Davidson, T., Warmsley, D., Macy, M., Weber, I.: Automated hate speech detection and the problem of offensive language. In: Proceedings of the Eleventh International Conference on Web and Social Media, pp. 512–515. AAAI Press (2017)
7. Devlin, J., Chang, M.W., Lee, K., Toutanova, K.: BERT: pre-training of deep bidirectional transformers for language understanding. In: Proceedings of the 2019 Conference of the North American Chapter of the Association for Computational Linguistics: Human Language Technologies, pp. 4171–4186. Association for Computational Linguistics (2019)
8. Fersini, E., Nozza, D., Rosso, P.: Overview of the Evalita 2018 task on automatic misogyny identification (AMI). In: Proceedings of the Sixth Evaluation Campaign of Natural Language Processing and Speech Tools for Italian, vol. 2263, pp. 107–114. CEUR-WS.org (2018)
9. Golbeck, J., et al.: A large labeled corpus for online harassment research. In: Proceedings of the 2017 ACM on Web Science Conference, pp. 229–233. Association for Computing Machinery (2017)
10. Kamath, R., Ghoshal, A., Eswaran, S., Honnavalli, P.: An enhanced context-based emotion detection model using roberta. In: 2022 IEEE International Conference on Electronics, Computing and Communication Technologies, pp. 1–6 (2022)
11. Liu, P., Li, W., Zou, L.: NULI at SemEval-2019 task 6: transfer learning for offensive language detection using bidirectional transformers. In: Proceedings of the 13th International Workshop on Semantic Evaluation, pp. 87–91. Association for Computational Linguistics (2019)
12. MacAvaney, S., Yao, H.R., Yang, E., Russell, K., Goharian, N., Frieder, O.: Hate speech detection: challenges and solutions. PLOS ONE 14(8), 1–16 (2019)
13. Mandl, T., et al.: Overview of the HASOC track at fire 2019: hate speech and offensive content identification in Indo-European languages. In: Proceedings of the 11th Forum for Information Retrieval Evaluation, pp. 14–17. Association for Computing Machinery (2019)
14. Marcos, Z., Shervin, M., Preslav, N., Sara, R., Farra, N., Kumar, R.: SemEval-2019 task 6: identifying and categorizing offensive language in social media (OffensEval). In: Proceedings of the 13th International Workshop on Semantic Evaluation, pp. 75–86. Association for Computational Linguistics (2019)
15. Mozafari, M., Farahbakhsh, R., Crespi, N.: A BERT-based transfer learning approach for hate speech detection in online social media. In: Cherifi, H., Gaito, S., Mendes, J.F., Moro, E., Rocha, L.M. (eds.) COMPLEX NETWORKS 2019. SCI, vol. 881, pp. 928–940. Springer, Cham (2020). https://doi.org/10.1007/978-3-030-36687-2_77
16. Ramprasath, M., Dhanasekaran, K., Karthick, T., Velumani, R., Sudhakaran, P.: An extensive study on pretrained models for natural language processing based on transformers. In: 2022 International Conference on Electronics and Renewable Systems (ICEARS), pp. 382–389 (2022)
17. Schmidt, A., Wiegand, M.: A survey on hate speech detection using natural language processing. In: Proceedings of the Fifth International Workshop on Natural Language Processing for Social Media, pp. 1–10. Association for Computational Linguistics, Valencia, Spain (2017)
18. Wang, B., Ding, Y., Liu, S., Zhou, X.: YNU_Wb at HASOC 2019: ordered neurons LSTM with attention for identifying hate speech and offensive language. In: Forum for Information Retrieval Evaluation, vol. 2517, pp. 191–198 (2019)
19. Zeerak, W., Dirk, H.: Hateful symbols or hateful people? Predictive features for hate speech detection on Twitter. In: Proceedings of the NAACL Student Research Workshop, pp. 88–93. Association for Computational Linguistics (2016)

Industrial Applications of Pattern Recognition

TOPSIS Method for Multiple-Criteria Decision-Making Applied to Trajectory Selection for Autonomous Driving

Andrés Antonio Arenas Muñiz⬤, Dante Mújica Vargas(✉)⬤,
Arturo Rendon Castro⬤, and Antonio Luna Álvarez⬤

Centro Nacional de Investigación y Desarrollo Tecnologico - CENIDET,
62594 Cuernavaca, Morelos, Mexico
{m22ce03,dante.mv}@cenidet.tecnm.mx

Abstract. An autonomous driving system performs various tasks, including perception, vehicle control, and trajectory planning. In the process of generating the various trajectories that the vehicle can take, a situation arises in which one of them must be selected. The *Decision-Making* task is complex because multiple options often have different criteria; each solution may have its own set of pros and cons. The system needs to weigh these factors and select the option that best fits the specific needs and goals of the situation. This task is carried out by constraint-driven methods, or by deep learning in conjunction with other machine learning techniques. To manage this complexity, Multiple-Criteria Decision-Making (MCDM) methods, such as the Technique for Order of Preference by Similarity to the Ideal Solution (TOPSIS), can be used to evaluate each candidate trajectory toward an ideal solution. This ensures that the selected trajectory is well-rounded and meets the system's needs. By providing decision making capability, performance can be improved to more natural and safe driving. The proposed approach has been tested in a Matlab simulation environment under a variety of conditions. Experiments showed that the proposed approach generates an average increase of 30% in speed, with 16.44% fewer maneuvers compared to other methods.

Keywords: Decision-Making · TOPSIS · MCDM · Autonomous-Driving

1 Introduction

Autonomous driving systems aim to improve the safety of passengers and other drivers through enhanced perception and trajectory planning by selecting an appropriate trajectory to avoid a collision. The trajectory selection decision process is a critical component of autonomous driving systems. To ensure the safety of passengers and other road users, the trajectory selection module must select the optimal path for the vehicle. This process involves the evaluation of multiple factors such as vehicle speed, road conditions, the presence of other vehicles,

A. Y. Rodríguez-González et al. (Eds.): MCPR 2023, LNCS 13902, pp. 295–307, 2023.
https://doi.org/10.1007/978-3-031-33783-3_28

pedestrians and obstacles, and compliance with traffic rules and regulations. The trajectory selection module must also take into account the predicted behavior of other vehicles. This ensures that the autonomous vehicle operates predictably and safely. Trajectory selection must also consider passenger comfort and convenience, as well as the vehicle's ability to perform the selected maneuvers, such as turning or changing lanes. By integrating all of these factors, the trajectory selection module is able to make informed decisions to select the optimal path that will achieve the vehicle's goal of reaching its destination in a safe and efficient manner.

Therefore, it is of great interest to develop a method for these systems that can make decisions robust enough to deal with the uncertainty inherent in the environmental conditions and select the most appropriate trajectory in accordance with the situation. Various approaches have been proposed to address this challenge. These include constraint driven algorithms, finite state machines (FSM), long-short term memory (LSTM) networks, probabilistic models, fuzzy inference systems, reinforcement learning (RL), and deep learning methods. The more classical approaches, as described in [2,3], determine the optimal trajectory by evaluating the generated trajectories on the basis of a weighted loss function and by measuring the error with respect to a reference path. FSMs perform decision tasks by categorizing scenarios, assessing risks, and selecting actions, such as the tree-layer FSM described in [6]. LSTM networks, such as the improved LSTM network with support vector machine (SVM) proposed in [7], extract relevant features from the environment. The SVM uses a grasshopper optimization algorithm to make decisions. Probabilistic models, such as those proposed in [8,9], consider human behavior and driving styles to make decisions based on non-cooperative game theory methods and Markov Decision Process (MDP). In [10], MDP is used to generate turn policies for a polynomial path generator. FIS, as used in [11], to simulate the cognitive process of drivers. LSTM recurrent neural networks are used to predict lane-changing behavior. Reinforcement Learning (RL) based methods combine planning and learning to make tactical decisions, such as the Monte Carlo Tree Search and Deep RL frameworks proposed in [14]. In [15], RL is used to learn the parameters of rule-based controllers, while in [16] a DRL training program is used to train the car-following behavior.

In order to integrate decision-making methods into autonomous driving systems, researchers have used various approaches. Deep learning techniques have been widely used because of their ability to work with uncertainty in conjunction with machine learning. However, these approaches have the disadvantage of large data requirements and high implementation complexity. More straightforward methods use loss functions to estimate the error between the reference and the trajectories, but they produce less smooth driving and can run out of trajectories as the complexity of the scenario increases. Fuzzy techniques have been implemented to convey the driver's experience to autonomous systems on the basis of rule sets, but these proposals have been limited to lane-change maneuvers only. Some proposals have focused on solutions that implement finite state machines, but they can easily fall into scenarios that have not yet been considered in the design of these systems. Since autonomous vehicles primarily interact with human drivers who may not strictly follow driving rules, other attempts have been made to mimic human driving.

The TOPSIS trajectory selection algorithm does not require large amounts of data or training. It does not use complex operations that increase computational cost. Without the need for rules, it can easily transfer the experience of a human driver. Fuzzy properties make them resistant to measurement errors or adverse conditions and also more versatile than other techniques because it does not depend on a specific perception or trajectory generation method. The trajectories were generated using a planner that uses fifth and fourth order polynomials in conjunction with the Stanly model [17], which generates a set of trajectories that are then evaluated using the TOPSIS method to decide which trajectory to use based on the experience of an experienced human driver. The ability of the decision making process to take into account multiple criteria allows for easy scalability to take into account other factors without the need for significant modifications. This decision-making method is ideal for implementation in embedded systems because it does not require of large computational power.

This paper is structured as follows. The first section presents a detailed explanation of the proposed method. It combines a trajectory planner using the Frenet reference system with TOPSIS. The next section is the experimental section, where the experimental design, the execution of the experiments, and the preliminary results are described in detail. Finally, the results are discussed and conclusions are drawn, emphasizing the contribution of this research and outlining future work to be done.

2   Proposed Method

The proposed solution combines a path planner algorithm with a TOPSIS decision making method that selects a trajectory among the candidate trajectories, taking into account user-defined parameters that mimic human experience. A diagram is shown in Fig. 1 for better understanding. These trajectories connect the initial states with the final states defined by the path planner, which draws the path from point a to point b based on specific parameters as described in [1]. The resulting score of each trajectory is used to determine the vehicle's path. The path planner algorithm generates trajectories from the environment data collected by the perception module by first creating the Frenet frame on a parametric curve $\gamma(t)$ describing the path as given by the expression 1; formulated by [2]:

$$\gamma(t) = (f(t)x + g(t)y + h(t)z) \tag{1}$$

where $f(t)x$ represents the change of position at x with respect to time t, $g(t)y$ represents the change of position at y with respect to time t, and $h(t)z$ is the function expressing the change of position at z with respect to time t. The vectors tangent and normal work as axes for the new reference system and come from $\gamma(t)$ as shown in the next expressions:

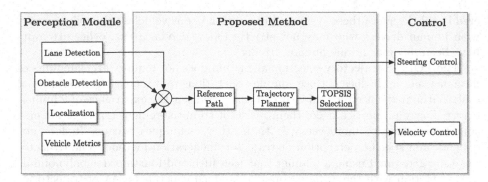

Fig. 1. General diagram of the proposed method.

$$T = \frac{\gamma'(t)}{||\gamma'(t)||_2} \qquad N = \frac{T'(t)}{||T'(t)||_2} \tag{2}$$

$\gamma'(t)$ is the first derivative and $||\gamma'(t)||_2$ is the Euclidean norm. The vector T is the axis for the longitudinal motion and N is the axis for the lateral motion. The fifth order polynomial generates the trajectory that connects the initial states $\mathbf{S}_i = [\psi_0^1, \psi_0^2, ..., \psi_0^n]$; with the target states $\mathbf{S}_t = [\psi_f^1, \psi_f^2, ..., \psi_f^n]$; of the global path. The trajectory conjuncts a certain number of motions in lateral $d(t)$ and longitudinal $s(t)$ and is defined by the following expressions:

$$d(t) = d_0 + d_1t + d_2t^2 + d_3t^3 + d_4t^4 + d_5t^5 \tag{3}$$

$$s(t) = s_0 + s_1t + s_2t^2 + s_3t^3 + s_4t^4 + s_5t^5 \tag{4}$$

where the coefficients $[d_0, ..., d_5]$ and $[s_0, ..., s_5]$ are determined by the geometry of the road. The velocity in d and s comes from the first derivative and the acceleration from the second derivative of the expressions 3 and 4. The coefficients d_n and s_n are calculated with the initial and final states. With different sets of $\mathbf{S}_i$ and $\mathbf{S}_t$, the polynomial algorithm generates different candidate trajectories. In the case of the steering angle, it is computed as shown in [17], and it is assumed that the velocity is constant to perform the calculations. Where ρ is the angle of the vehicle's actual path, σ is the angle the vehicle should have, V_f is the angle of the direction, e is the distance from the front axle to the path, and L is the distance between the vehicle's axles. The first step is to eliminate the error between the current path and the desired path using the following expression:

$$\sigma(t) = \rho(t) \tag{5}$$

Then, the lane crossing error is eliminated by finding the closest point between the traced trajectory and the center of the vehicle's front axle, denoted by $e(t)$ in the subsequent expression:

$$\sigma(t) = tan^{-1}(\frac{Ke(t)}{V_f(t)}) \tag{6}$$

where K is the gain and σ is the corrected angle of the vehicle, but this angle must be restricted to the maximum turning angles, i.e. $\sigma(t) \in [\sigma_{min}, \sigma_{max}]$. This leads us to the following expression:

$$\sigma(t) = \rho(t) + tan^{-1}(\frac{Ke(t)}{V_f(t)}), \ \sigma(t) \in [\sigma_{min}, \sigma_{max}] \tag{7}$$

Another gain k_s can be added to smooth the control and ensure that the denominator is not zero, as shown in the following expression:

$$\sigma(t) = \rho(t) + tan^{-1}(\frac{Ke(t)}{k_s + V_f(t)}) \tag{8}$$

The trajectory planner generates an array δ with columns $[d, s, \alpha, v, a]$, where d contains the points in the lateral axis, s the points in the longitudinal axis, α the steering angle at each point calculated in relation to the initial states, the target state, and the lateral deviation, v the velocity, and a the acceleration at each point that is a row of δ. The process described above is illustrated by the following pseudocode:

Algorithm 1. Trajectory generator with Frenet frame.

Require: $\gamma(t)$, $[\psi_0^1, \psi_0^2, ..., \psi_0^n]$, $[\psi_f^1, \psi_f^2, ..., \psi_f^n]$ $\triangleright$ $\gamma(t)$ Parametric curve of the road,
$\quad \psi_0^n$ and ψ_f^n initial and target states.
Ensure: $\delta = [d, s, \alpha, v, a]$ $\triangleright$ Array of the way-points of the generated trajectory.
$\quad T \leftarrow \frac{\gamma'(t)}{||\gamma'(t)||_2}$ $\triangleright$ Vector T as longitudinal axis for the reference frame.
$\quad N \leftarrow \frac{T'(t)}{||T'(t)||_2}$ $\triangleright$ Vector N as lateral axis for the reference frame.
$\quad d(t) = d_0 + d_1 t + d_2 t^2 + d_3 t^3 + d_4 t^4 + d_5 t^5$ $\triangleright$ Lateral displacement points.
$\quad s(t) = s_0 + s_1 t + s_2 t^2 + s_3 t^3 + s_4 t^4 + s_5 t^5$ $\triangleright$ Longitudinal points.
$\quad \alpha \leftarrow \sigma(t)$ $\triangleright$ The steering angle comes from Eq. 5 to 8.
$\quad v \leftarrow s'(t)$ $\triangleright$ Velocity comes from the first derivative of the Eq. 3.
$\quad a \leftarrow s''(t)$ $\triangleright$ Acceleration comes from the second derivative of the Eq. 3.
$\quad \delta = [d, s, \alpha, v, a]$

The next step is to condense the information of the trajectory array δ into a vector $\mathbf{T}_n$. Each vector has the values of $[\alpha, v, a]$ that are taken into account and shows the significant values for each column. Then the TOPSIS method is used, taking as input the $\mathbf{T}_n$ as a matrix of candidates. The Technique for Order of Preference by Similarity to Ideal Solution proposed by Alaoui in [1] is a multi-criteria decision making method that evaluates the similarity of the candidates to an ideal solution determined by an ideal worst and ideal best of each criterion considered for evaluation. The TOPSIS algorithm requires an array of candidates Γ, the weight vector W and the influence vector I, the vector $W = [w_1, ..., w_n]$; contains the weight for each column of the array Γ, which can be any value from $[1, \infty]$, and the vector $I = [i_1, ..., i_n]$; contains the effect that is an indicator of the human preference to stimulate the increase or decrease of the values of the respective columns in the TOPSIS algorithm. For a better understanding of the TOPSIS algorithm, the pseudocode 2 explains in detail the steps to be taken to obtain the *Score* for each candidate.

Algorithm 2. TOPSIS applied to evaluate trajectories.

Require: Γ_{ij},   ▷ Trajectories array Γ.
   $W_j = [w_1, ..., w_n]$ ▷ Weight vector W.
   $I_j = [i_1, ..., i_n]$ ▷ Impact vector I.
Ensure: *Score*   ▷ A number between $[0,1]$.
   $\mathbf{N\Gamma_{ij}} = \|\Gamma_{ij}\|_2 = \sqrt{\sum_{i=1}^{n}\sum_{j=1}^{n}(x_{ij})^2}$ ▷ Normalization of the array.
   for i in $\mathbf{N\Gamma}_i$ **do**
      for j in W_j **do**
         $\mathbf{W\Gamma}_{ij} \leftarrow \mathbf{N\Gamma}_{ij} * W_j$ ▷ Applied weight to the normalized array.
      end for
   end for
   if $i_j ==\ '+'$ **then**   ▷ For wanted increase in one parameter.
      $\mathbf{I}_{B_j} = max(\mathbf{N\Gamma}_j)$ ▷ $\mathbf{I}_{B_j}$ Ideal best.
      $\mathbf{I}_{W_j} = min(\mathbf{N\Gamma}_j)$ ▷ $\mathbf{I}_{W_j}$ Ideal worst.
   else   ▷ For wanted decrease in one parameter.
      $\mathbf{I}_{B_j} = min(\mathbf{N\Gamma}_j)$
      $\mathbf{I}_{W_j} = max(\mathbf{N\Gamma}_j)$
   end if
   $\mathbf{p}_d \leftarrow \sqrt{\sum_{i=1}^{n}(\mathbf{I}_{B_j} - \mathbf{N\Gamma}_{ij})^2}$ ▷ Find the positive euclidean distance between $\mathbf{I}_{B_j}$
   and the values on $\mathbf{N\Gamma}_{ij}$.
   $\mathbf{n}_d \leftarrow \sqrt{\sum_{i=1}^{n}(\mathbf{I}_{W_j} - \mathbf{N\Gamma}_{ij})^2}$ ▷ Find the negative euclidean distance between $\mathbf{I}_{W_j}$
   and the values on $\mathbf{N\Gamma}_{ij}$.
   Score $\leftarrow \mathbf{n}_d/(\mathbf{n}_d + \mathbf{p}_d)$ ▷ Resulting *Score* for each Γ_i rows.

The trajectory with the highest score is selected as the one that best fits the situation on the road and avoids collisions. As can be seen in Fig. 1, once the appropriate trajectory has been selected, it is passed to the control module as a reference, which allows the execution of actions to keep the vehicle on course within the planned route.

2.1   Experimentation

The experiments were done in Matlab R2021a with the Automated Driving Toolbox, in a computer with the following specs: CPU *Ryzen 5* 3600 3.6 GHz, 12 threads; GPU *RX*590 8 GB VRAM and 16 GB of RAM, 1 TB SSD. The dynamic scenarios consist of two simulations of a road with fourth lanes without ambient phenomena such as rain, fog, or others, as the perception was not needed to be considered for the scope of this research, and no detailed dynamic model of the vehicle. The simulation had four non-controllable vehicles of the exact dimensions as the controlled vehicle that followed a determinate path that included lane changing and lane keeping maneuvers. The vehicle that was controlled, or the ego vehicle, traveled around the path from a start point to a target point and had the following characteristics: *Car lenght* = 4.7 m *Car width* = 1.8 m *Car rear axle ratio* = 0.25. The scenario designed for the first experiment is shown in Fig. 2. In this scenario, the controlled or ego vehicle follows a route along a straight road in the company of non-controlled vehicles. The ego vehicle must travel without colliding with the actor vehicles performing the various maneuvers mentioned above (Fig. 3).

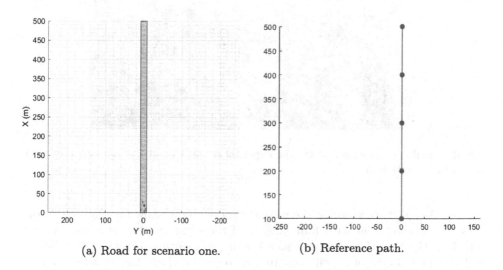

(a) Road for scenario one.   (b) Reference path.

Fig. 2. Driving scenario for the first experiment.

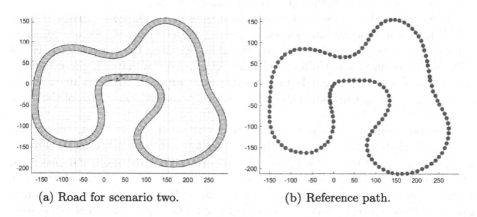

(a) Road for scenario two.   (b) Reference path.

Fig. 3. Driving scenario for the second experiment.

A reference path is created, as shown in Fig. 2b, which the vehicle is expected to follow as it determines the target states for the trajectory planner algorithm to work with, as seen in the pseudocode 1. The simulation starts by planning the trajectories for the ego vehicle to avoid collisions, as shown in Fig. 4. Then the TOPSIS algorithm is called to evaluate the generated trajectories.

Fig. 4. Simulated environment for the experiments on Unreal Engine with the Automated Driving Toolbox.

The designed scenario for the second experiment is shown in Fig. 2 and consists of a curved road with four lanes and the same number of actor and ego vehicles. The lane-changing and lane-keeping maneuvers increase the difficulty and the probability of a collision. In this scenario, the actor vehicles follow a route along the road in the company of non-controlled vehicles. The ego vehicle needs to drive without colliding with the actor vehicles.

The other methods used for comparison were, the Constrain Driven Method (CDM), this method evaluates each trajectory with constraints for acceleration, velocity and steering angles, if a constraint its violated the trajectory it is not taken into account. The Collision Checker (CC) only evaluates if the generated trajectory put the ego vehicle in the same position of an actor vehicle, this is done by comparing the final states of the trajectories with the states of the actor vehicles.

The test consists of adjusting the weight W_j and impact I_j vectors in the same scenario to determine the optimal values for each one and measure the performance of the TOPSIS, trough an intuitive process, prioritizing the increment of top speed and reduced steering angles whit the less changes of acceleration to maintain comfort, as an experienced driver would behave in this type of scenarios. This shows the simplicity of the experience transfer process. Since the system does not require datasets or training that would denote some prior knowledge of the environment, there was no need for any type of ground truth, which limits the application of conventional metrics. It was decided to quantify the performance in terms more related to driving, such as the number of collisions, the number of times the vehicle left the road, the number of lane changing maneuvers and the top speed reached along the route.

For the first two tests, the scenario in which the simulation takes place is number one, shown in Fig. 2; two versions of TOPSIS are compared, one with the initial weight set to 1 for all columns in the data array; the influence was adjusted to reduce the values $I_j = ['-',' -',' -']$, the unadjusted TOPSIS (TnA); and other with more realistic values $W_j = [17, 30, 25]$ and $I_j = ['-',' +',' -']$, which will be called the adjusted TOPSIS (TA). For the first test, the speed limit was set to 10 m/s, and for the second test, the speed limit was set to 25 m/s.

In the subsequent two tests, the scenario in was the simulation takes place is the number two shown in Fig. 2; the identical two versions of TOPSIS are compared, one with the initial weight assigned as 1 for all columns in the data array; the impact was adjusted to reduce values $I_j = ['-',' -',' -']$, and other with more real values $W_j = [36, 20, 25]$ and $I_j = ['-',' +',' -']$. For the first test, the speed limit was set to 10 m/s, and for the second one, the speed limit was set to 25 m/s.

2.2   Results and Discussion

A comparison of the variations of the proposed method, the CDM, and the CC included in the toolbox was made in the above mentioned experiments with ten iterations for each model in each test. The comparison shows a reduction in the number of lane change maneuvers as shown in Fig. 5a. In some cases where there is no adjustment of the experience through the impact and weight vector, an impact on performance in terms of increased number of maneuvers made.

Figure 5b shows the top speed results. An increase in speed was observed with the CC, as it has no restrictions on speed, but with erroneous lane keeping and reckless driving that generated loss of feasible trajectories. The CDM stays close to the constraint. However, it runs out of trajectories in some iterations. The TnA method shows erratic behavior that cannot maintain the reference path; the TA shows an increase in speed in the first scenarios, and for the scenarios with more curved segments, keeps the speed below the limit.

Figure 6a shows the iterations with collisions for each test. For each trial, the collision terminates the simulation. The results show that the TOPSIS with adjusted values stays below the media, and the unadjusted model made the worst performance. For the Constraint Driven, the number of collisions increases for the more curved path. The CC maintains good performance up to the most extreme of scenarios where collisions appear since it does not take into account steering angles or maximum speed. The number of times the vehicle left the road is shown in Fig. 6b, as the results show that all models have cases. In the case of the method that evaluates constraints, the number of times the vehicle leaves the road increases with speed and the number of curves on the road. The collision checker always presented cases where it had to leave the track to avoid collisions. The TnA method showed the highest number of cases where the vehicle left the track, while the best performance was obtained by the adjusted TOPSIS method, although it was not exempt from leaving the track.

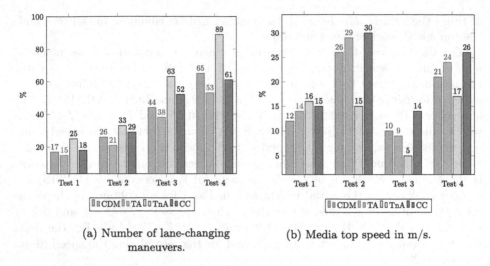

(a) Number of lane-changing maneuvers.

(b) Media top speed in m/s.

Fig. 5. Results of the experimentation.

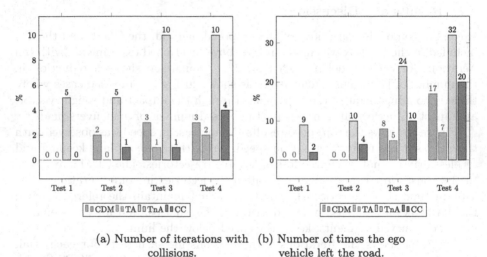

(a) Number of iterations with collisions.

(b) Number of times the ego vehicle left the road.

Fig. 6. Results of the experimentation.

The results show that the proposed method performs better than other methods, although it could be better since it tends to exceed the speed limit in some scenarios and to leave the lane when faced with aggressive behavior from other vehicles; collisions cannot be avoided entirely. The fact that the unadjusted model performs so poorly in every condition reinforces what was stated in [4], where the data showed that a human driver does not take a trajectory into account, so not reflecting any bias for trajectory parameters results in the *SCORE* assignment being almost random.

It was expected that the TOPSIS with adjusted values behavior would be in the direction that the results show; however, it should be noted that compared to other methods, the adjustment of the impact and weight vectors for a reduced number of features loses definition, so increasing the number of parameters considered could be an option to consider the lane maintenance of the vehicle and a more dynamic range of speed. The difference between the proposed model and others lies in the enhanced decision capabilities over the standard methods with an improvement in execution times. The proposed method can consider more parameters for decision making compared to other methods for trajectory selection. Moreover, it is independent of the method used to generate the trajectories. This is an absolute advantage in the implementation, because the input from different sensors or data generated by the trajectory planner can be submitted to the TOPSIS method for consideration without affecting the computational cost. This decision-making method ensures a more human-like behavior, complemented by the enhanced perception capabilities of autonomous systems.

3   Conclusions and Future Work

The trajectories were generated using a planner that uses fifth and fourth order polynomials in conjunction with the Stanly control model, which generates a set of trajectories that were subsequently evaluated using the TOPSIS MCDM method to decide which trajectory to use based on the experience of a human experienced driver by means of a weight and impact vectors as well as certain parameters that reflect the properties of individual trajectories. The experiments for this study were conducted using the Automated Driving Toolbox in Matlab R2021a. The dynamic scenarios simulated a four-lane road and did not include any environmental phenomena, as perception was not a focus of the research. The simulation included a fourth non-controllable vehicle that followed a predetermined path consisting of lane changes and lane keeping maneuvers. The ego vehicle traveled along a path from a starting point to a destination. The experiments varied the weight and impact vectors to determine the optimal values for each scenario and to evaluate the performance of the TOPSIS algorithm. The simulations did not include a detailed dynamic model of the vehicle, and the study aimed to determine the best parameter values for optimal performance without considering external factors that affect driving conditions.

The results show that for lane change maneuvers, TA reduces the number of maneuvers by 16.44% compared to CDM and by 39.52% compared to TnA. For the media top speed, TA keeps the speed 15% above the limit for straight roads and 6% above for the curved road, the other methods in order CDM, TnA and CC show 10%, 5%, 45% for the first scenario and −6%, −36%, 12% for the second. In the case of iterations with collisions, TA shows 7.5% of 40 total iterations for each method, a reduction of 77.5% compared to TnA and 12.5% and 7.5% compared to CDM and CC respectively, other methods show the following iterations with collisions 20%, 85%, 15%. In the number of times the vehicle left the road, the method with more occurrences was TnA with 75, the CC method with 36 followed by the CDM with 25, TA had 12 occurrences showing a reduction of 52% with respect to TnA.

The TOPSIS has several advantages over other decision making techniques. It does not require data sets or training and is computationally inexpensive. It can incorporate human experience without rule-based systems, making it more flexible. It is also robust to measurement error and adaptable to different scenarios. It can be applied to different situations and is scalable without significant modifications. It can also consider a large number of criteria; for this work, only three characteristics were considered for the decision. As future work is contemplated the inclusion of more specific criteria for evaluating the candidate for improved behavior in scenarios with numerous curves, in addition to optimizing the calculation of the *Score* in the TOPSIS method and better compression of the data generated by the trajectory planner to ensure that the data is compressed into a single vector without loss of information. The implementation of the model in an embedded system for testing in a scaled environment is also under consideration.

Acknowledgements. The authors thank CONACYT, as well as TecNM- CENIDET for their financial support.

References

1. Alaoui, E.M.: Fuzzy TOPSIS: Logic, Approaches, and Case Studies, 1st edn. CRC Press, Boca Raton (2021)
2. Ji, J., Wang, H., Ren, Y.: Path Planning and Tracking for Vehicle Collision Avoidance in Lateral and Longitudinal Motion directions (Synthesis Lectures on Advances in Automotive Technology), 12th edn. Morgan & Claypool Publishers (2021)
3. Yoneda, K., Iida, T., Kim, T.H., Yanase, R., Aldibaja, M., Suganuma, N.: Trajectory optimization and state selection for urban automated driving. Artifi. Life Robot. **23**(4), 474–480 (2018). https://doi.org/10.1007/s10015-018-0484-4
4. Li, A., Jiang, H., Li, Z., Zhou, X.: Human-like trajectory planning on curved road: learning from human drivers. IEEE Trans. Intell. Trans. Syst. **21**(8) (2020)
5. Wang, W., Jiang, L., Lin, S., et al.: Imitation learning based decision-making for autonomous vehicle control at traffic roundabouts. Multimed Tools Appl. **81**, 39873–39889 (2022). https://doi.org/10.1007/s11042-022-12300-9
6. Wang, X., Qi, X., Wang, P., Yang, J.: Decision making framework for autonomous vehicles driving behavior in complex scenarios via hierarchical state machine. Autonomous Intell. Syst. **1**(1), 1–12 (2021). https://doi.org/10.1007/s43684-021-00015-x
7. Shi, Y., Li, Y., Fan, J., Wang, T., Yin, T.: A novel network architecture of decision-making for self-driving vehicles based on long short-term memory and grasshopper optimization algorithm. IEEE Access **8**, 155429–155440 (2020). https://doi.org/10.1109/ACCESS.2020.3019048
8. Hang, P., Lv, C., Huang, C., Cai, J., Hu, Z., Xing, Y.: An integrated framework of decision making and motion planning for autonomous vehicles considering social behaviors. IEEE Trans. Vehicular Technol. textbf69(12), 14458–14469 (2020). https://doi.org/10.1109/TVT.2020.3040398

9. Hang, P., Lv, C., Xing, Y., Huang, C., Hu, Z.: Human-Like decision making for autonomous driving: a noncooperative game theoretic approach. IEEE Trans. Intell. Transp. Syst. **22**(4), 2076–2087 (2021). https://doi.org/10.1109/TITS.2020.3036984

10. Shu, K., Yu, H., Chen, X., Li, S., Chen, L., Wang, Q., Li, L., Cao, D.: Autonomous driving at intersections: A behavior-oriented critical-turning-point approach for decision making. IEEE/ASME Trans. Mechatron. **27**(1), 234–244 (2021). https://doi.org/10.1109/TMECH.2021.3061772

11. Wang, W., Qie, T., Yang, C., Liu, W., Xiang, C., Huang, K.: An intelligent lane-changing behavior prediction and decision-making strategy for an autonomous vehicle. IEEE Trans. Industr. Electron. **69**(3), 2927–37 (2021). https://doi.org/10.1109/TIE.2021.3066943

12. Duan, J., Eben Li, S., Guan, Y., Sun, Q., Cheng, B.: Hierarchical reinforcement learning for self-driving decision-making without reliance on labelled driving data. IET Intel. Transport Syst. **14**(5), 297–305 (2020). https://doi.org/10.1049/iet-its.2019.0317

13. Huang, C., Lv, C., Hang, P., Xing, Y.: Toward safe and personalized autonomous driving: Decision-making and motion control with DPF and CDT techniques. IEEE/ASME Trans. Mechatron. **26**(2), 611–20 (2021). https://doi.org/10.1109/TMECH.2021.3053248

14. Hoel, C.J., Driggs-Campbell, K., Wolff, K., Laine, L., Kochenderfer, M.J.: Combining planning and deep reinforcement learning in tactical decision making for autonomous driving. IEEE Trans. Intell. Veh. **5**(2), 294–305 (2019). https://doi.org/10.1109/TIV.2019.2955905

15. Likmeta, A., Metelli, A.M., Tirinzoni, A., Giol, R., Restelli, M., Romano, D.: Combining reinforcement learning with rule-based controllers for transparent and general decision-making in autonomous driving. Robot. Auton. Syst. **131**, 103568 (2021). https://doi.org/10.1016/j.robot.2020.103568

16. Ye, Y., Zhang, X., Sun, J.: Automated vehicle's behavior decision making using deep reinforcement learning and high-fidelity simulation environment. Trans. Res. Part C: Emerging Technol. **107**, 155–170 (2019). https://doi.org/10.1016/j.trc.2019.08.011

17. Sorniotti, A., Barber, P., De Pinto, S.: Path tracking for automated driving: A tutorial on control system formulations and ongoing research. Automated driving: Safer and More Efficient Future Driving **71**(140) (2017). https://doi.org/10.1007/978-3-319-31895-0_5

Machine-Learning Based Estimation of the Bending Magnitude Sensed by a Fiber Optic Device

Luis M. Valentín-Coronado[1,2]($\boxtimes$) ⓘ, Rodolfo Martínez-Manuel[1] ⓘ,
Jonathan Esquivel-Hernández[1] ⓘ, and Sophie LaRochelle[3] ⓘ

[1] Centro de Investigaciones en Óptica, Ags., 20200 Aguascalientes, Mexican, Mexico
{luismvc,rodolfom,jesquivelh}@cio.mx
[2] Consejo Nacional de Ciencia y Tecnología, Ciudad de México 03940, Mexico
[3] Center for Optics, Photonics and Lasers (COPL), ECE Department,
Université Laval, Québec, QC G1V 0A6, Canada
sophie.larochelle@gel.ulaval

Abstract. Bending estimation is an important property that must be assessed in several engineering applications including structural health monitoring, aerospace, robotics, geophysics, etc. While strain gauges and accelerometers are used to estimate bending behavior based on Machine-Learning (ML), few works in the literature have focused on the estimation of the magnitude of bending by combining ML techniques and fiber optic sensors. In this work, an ML-based method for estimating bending magnitude using the signal generated by an optical fiber sensor is presented. The sensor is formed by splicing a single-mode fiber with a multimode fiber. The interferogram generated from the sensor is processed to create a set of signal feature vectors (FVs). Thus, for estimating the bending magnitude, these FVs are used to train Machine-learning algorithms including Support Vector Machine, K-Nearest Neighbors, Naive Bayes, and Random Forest. To evaluate how each ML model performs, the accuracy, precision, recall, and F_1-score metrics are used. The best performance is obtained by the Random Forest algorithm with a classification accuracy of 100%.

Keywords: Bending · Machine learning · Optical fiber sensors

1 Introduction

Bending measurement is a highly relevant issue for many engineering applications. Bending measurement may be interpreted as the amount of deformation that occurs when an external force is applied to an element. Therefore, measuring this phenomenon in mechanical structures, such as airplane wings, beams/columns of buildings, for earthquake detection, or even to determine the position of a robotic arm, is highly relevant. Usually, to measure deformation, devices like strain gauges and accelerometers have been used [1]. Nevertheless,

A. Y. Rodríguez-González et al. (Eds.): MCPR 2023, LNCS 13902, pp. 308–316, 2023.
https://doi.org/10.1007/978-3-031-33783-3_29

in recent years, optical fiber sensors have been introduced to perform this task. Using optical fiber sensors has many advantages including its light weight, high sensitivity, good repeatability, electromagnetic interference immunity, electrical insulation, and robustness in hazardous environments [2–4], to name a few. To measure the magnitude of bending, the most commonly used fiber optic sensor is based on a fiber interferometer. However, bending monitoring implies accurate interference signal detection in order to track the shift in wavelength at a peak/dip of the interferogram. Although this may seem simple, peak/dip tracking has a small linear response, limiting the range of bending monitoring; also, the direction of bending can become difficult to identify. Nevertheless, given the nature of the interference signal, it is feasible to use a machine learning-based approach to infer the magnitude of the bending. Machine learning (ML) has proven to be a powerful tool for solving a wide variety of problems, e.g., image recognition, natural language processing, speech recognition, or autonomous driving [5–7]. Moreover, machine learning algorithms have also been used for solving optical research problems, for instance, optical imaging [8,9], optical communications [10], and microscopy resolution enhancement [11,12].

In this work, in contrast to the classical approach reported in the literature to infer the magnitude of the bending from a set of data acquired with an optical fiber sensor, we propose a machine learning-based method such as Support Vector Machine, K-Nearest Neighbors, Naive Bayes, and Random Forest. These classifiers have been selected because they are easy to implement, such as KNN and Naive Bayes. Furthermore, it has also been reported that these classifiers have achieved the highest performance rates, as is the case with SVM and Random Forest. In addition, we have made a performance comparison of the four ML models by means of the accuracy, precision, recall, and F_1-score metrics. Obtained results demonstrate that ML can be implemented in fiber sensor systems, especially in fiber interferometric sensors, generating excellent results.

2   Methods

The proposed method for recognizing the magnitude of the bending is shown in Fig. 1. As you may see, this method follows the classical supervised learning algorithm for classification.

To implement this approach, three elements need to be defined; i) the database construction, ii) the signal features to be extracted, and iii) the model to be implemented. Database construction is detailed in Sect. 2.1. Once the signal database has been built, a set of relevant features are extracted from these signals. Hence, a ML model can be trained to infer the bending magnitude. These two last steps are described in Sect. 2.2.

2.1   Setup

The implemented optical fiber sensor as well as a representative interference signal are shown in Fig. 2.

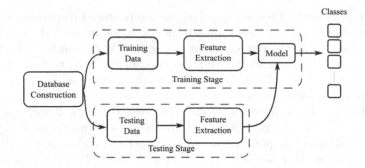

Fig. 1. Supervised learning method for classification.

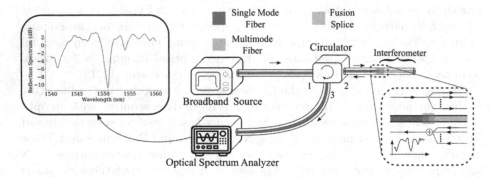

Fig. 2. Implemented optical fiber sensor setup and its resulting interferogram.

The implemented sensor works as follows. A broadband source (BBS) emits light over a 40 nm spectral range, centered at 1,545 nm. The emitted light propagates through the circulator from port one to port two until it reaches the multimode fiber, exciting some of its modes. The light then is reflected at the tip of the fiber and travels back through the multimode fiber until it is recoupled to the core of the single-mode fiber. At this point, the interference signal is generated. The blue dotted border box shows a schematic overview of the interference signal generation. Finally, the light reflected from the fiber goes through the circulator again, but now from port two to port three, until it is detected by an optical spectrum analyzer (OSA). It is worth mentioning that the multimode fiber used is an elliptical-core fiber whose design and characterization can be found in [13].

The optical fiber sensor has been placed around a fixed-free flexible rod (see Fig. 3a). From this configuration, three different bending measurements have been taken. It is worth mentioning that each time a bend is performed, a projection of radial movement can be identified on the plane which is perpendicular to the rest position of the rod. Figure 3 shows the bending phenomenon. Starting from the rest state (Fig. 3a), the flexible rod is bent due to some applied force

F (Fig. 3b), causing the projection of the flexible rod tip to move radially from p_0 to p_i (Fig. 3c).

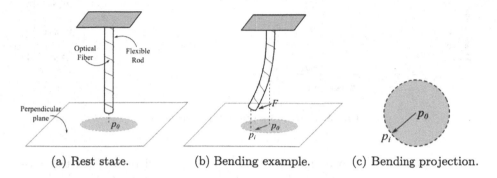

(a) Rest state.   (b) Bending example.   (c) Bending projection.

Fig. 3. Bending process scheme.

Once the bending movement is performed, the optical fiber sensor generates an interference signal which is detected by the OSA. Let $\zeta : \mathbb{R} \to \mathbb{R}$ be the function that represents the interferogram. As mentioned, the flexible rod is bent reaching three different positions, i.e., a set of three different projections are produced, $\{p_i \mid i = 1, 2, 3\}$. Furthermore, the generated projection can be defined as the polar point given by $p_i = (r_i, \theta_i)$. Moreover, to make the system invariant to the direction, r_i is fixed and the angle (θ_i) at which this position is reached is changed, specifically, to carry out the proof of concept, eight different equidistant angles for each r_i have been selected. Hence, p_i can be redefined as the polar point $p_i = (r_i, \theta_{ij})$ where $i = 1, 2, 3$ and $j = 1, \ldots, 8$. Hence, 80 data for each p_i are generated.

2.2   Bending Classification

To classify the bending movements, a supervised classification approach has been implemented. It is well known that to train a supervised machine learning model, a set of descriptive features have to be extracted from the signal, in this case ζ. All these features are used to build a feature vector $X \in \mathbb{R}^m$, $m \in \mathbb{N}$. Let $\varphi : \zeta(\mathbb{R}) \to \mathbb{R}^m$ be the operator that maps the signal ζ into the feature vector X. To build X, 26 features have been used. It is worth mentioning that the selected features include common statistical values (mean, standard deviation, etc.), as well as the "characteristic" values of any arbitrary signal (maximum, minimum, number of peaks, etc.). However, other more "complex" features can be used; nevertheless, given the nature of the analyzed signal, standard and easy-to-calculate features are just enough.

Figure 4 shows some of the extracted features as well as the generated feature vector. Once the feature vector is defined, a dataset denoted by D and defined as $D = \{(X_s, y_s) \mid X_s \in X, y_s \in \{p_1, p_2, p_3\}\}$, can be built. As a last step, the dataset is used for building a bending classifier.

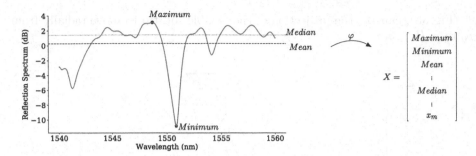

Fig. 4. Feature mapping representation.

Four classical inference algorithms have been selected to perform the classification task. Support Vector Machines (SVM) algorithm that classifies information by constructing a decision boundary (high-dimensional hyperplanes) to separate feature vectors of different classes [14]. K-Nearest Neighbors (KNN), a non-parametric algorithm that does not need any explicit training phase for the classification process [15]. Naive Bayes (NB) classifier, a probabilistic algorithm founded on the Bayes rule that is based on estimating conditional probabilities [16]. Random Forest (RF) classifier that performs the classification task based on the generation of a set of random decision trees [17].

The pseudo-code of the overall workflow is shown in Algorithm 1. As you can see, in lines 1 to 3 the feature extraction process and the training/test sets generation are performed. As the next steps, each of the four classifiers is trained and used to infer the bending measurement (lines 4 to 6). Finally, the performance of each model is calculated (line 7).

Algorithm 1: Overall workflow strategy.
___

Input: $\{\zeta_1, \zeta_2 \ldots, \zeta_m\}$

1 $X_s \leftarrow \varphi(\zeta_s) \ \forall \ s = 1, \cdots, m$ // Features extraction
2 $y_s \leftarrow \text{Label}(X_s) \ \forall \ s = 1, \cdots, m$
3 $(X^{trn}, y^{trn}), (X^{tst}, y^{tst}) \leftarrow \text{TrainTestSplit}(X, y)$
4 **for** Classifier $\in \{SVM, KNN, NB, RF\}$ **do**
5 $\quad$ clf$\leftarrow$Classifier.fit(X^{trn}, y^{trn}) // Train step
6 $\quad$ predicted$\leftarrow$Classifier.predict(X^{tst}) // Classification step
7 $\quad$ PerformanceEvaluation$(predicted, y^{tst})$

Note that $X^{trn}, X^{tst} \subset X$ such that $X = X^{trn} \cup X^{tst}$. In the same way $y^{trn}, y^{tst} \subset y$ where $y = y^{trn} \cup y^{tst}$.

3 Results and Discussion

The results of our experiments are presented and discussed in this section. The metrics used to evaluate the performance of each classification model are the most often used measures for multi-class classification. Hence, for each class C_i the performance metrics are defined in terms of *true positive* (tp_i), *true negative* (tn_i), *false positive* (fp_i), *false negative* (fn_i), *Accuracy*, *Precision*, and *Recall*. In particular, in this work the macro-averaging metrics given by Eqs. 1–4 are used [18].

$$Accuracy = \frac{\sum_{i=1}^{l} \frac{tp_i+tn_i}{tp_i+fn_i+fp_i+tn_i}}{l} \tag{1}$$

$$Precision_M = \frac{\sum_{i=1}^{l} \frac{tp_i}{tp_i+fp_i}}{l} \tag{2}$$

$$Recall_M = \frac{\sum_{i=1}^{l} \frac{tp_i}{tp_i+fn_i}}{l} \tag{3}$$

$$F_\beta-score_M = \frac{(\beta^2+1)Precision_M\ Recall_M}{\beta^2\ Precision_M + Recall_M} \tag{4}$$

It is worth mentioning that in the case of $F_\beta-score_M$, $\beta = 1$, resulting in the "classical" F_1-score. The reason for selecting these metrics is to know the overall performance of the different implemented classifiers.

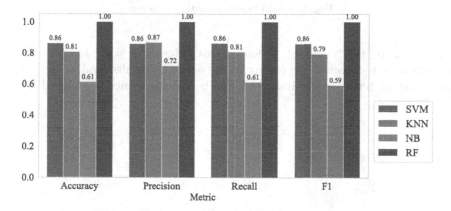

Fig. 5. Performance of classification models. The implemented algorithms were Support Vector Machines (SVM), K-Nearest Neighbors (KNN), Naive Bayes (NB), and Random Forest (RF).

The performance achieved by each of the implemented classifiers according to the aforementioned metrics is presented in Fig. 5. As it may be seen, the best classification result was achieved with the RF model, followed by the SVM model, as indicated by all metrics. The worst performance was obtained using the NB model. In addition, it may be observed that the RF model achieves an error-free classification, i.e., all the tested instances have been correctly classified. This may be attributed to the fact that the model is correctly learning the characteristics of the different classes. However, in order to achieve a more statistically reliable estimate of the performance of each model, than the one achieved with a single training/test set split, k-fold cross-validation has been implemented [19]. In Fig. 6 the k-fold cross-validation flowchart is shown. As can be appreciated, first the dataset is randomly divided into k disjoint folds. Then, every fold in turn is used to test the model whereas the rest of $(k-1)$ folds are used for training. Finally, overall performance is calculated.

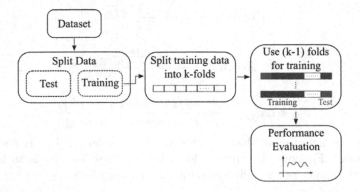

Fig. 6. k-fold cross-validation scheme.

In this work, the "classical" 10-fold cross-validation ($k = 10$) has been implemented for each classifier. According to the obtained results, and as the performance metrics have already indicated, the best performance is achieved by RF

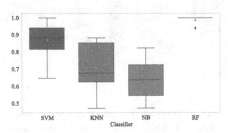
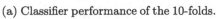

(a) Classifier performance of the 10-folds.

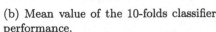

(b) Mean value of the 10-folds classifier performance.

Fig. 7. Comparison of the 10-fold cross-validation result achieved by each classifier.

model, followed by the SVM model, whereas, the NB model scores the lowest results. These behaviors can be confirmed in the box-plot shown in Fig. 7.

In summary, the best classification results have been achieved by the RF model. Nevertheless, although the SVM model has a slightly lower performance, is still a very good alternative for this application. Actually, the SVM model could even be the best alternative if you want to scale the number of bending movements to be identified, since the training time of the SVM model is considerably less (around eight times lower) than the training time of the RF model, as can be confirmed in the graph shown in Fig. 8.

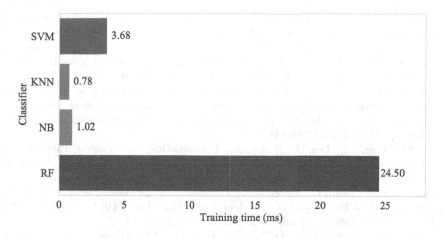

Fig. 8. Training time of each classifier.

4   Conclusions

In this work, machine-learning methods for estimating bending magnitude have been proposed based on the use of an interferogram obtained from an optical fiber sensor. In the proposed methods, different bending positions have been encoded. Furthermore, to achieve an invariant-direction system, measurements in diverse directions have been taken. Here, the performance and prediction accuracy of four "classical" machine learning models (SVM, KNN, NB, and RF) have been evaluated.

The results obtained in this work show that the proposed approach performs highly well with two of the machine learning models (SVM and RF). In particular, obtained results evince that the RF model presents the highest prediction accuracy for estimating the bending magnitude. Nevertheless, the SVM model is also a suitable alternative due to its faster training time (around eight times lower than the RF training time). Thus, in summary, the proposed approach is an effective alternative to be used for estimating bending magnitude.

References

1. Ogundare, J.O.: Precision surveying: the principles and geomatics practice. John Wiley & Sons (2015)
2. Kersey, A., et al.: Fiber grating sensors. J. Lightwave Technol. **15**(8), 1442–1463 (1997)
3. Lee, B.H.: Interferometric fiber optic sensors. Sensors **12**(3), 2467–2486 (2012). https://www.mdpi.com/1424-8220/12/3/2467
4. Cięszczyk, S., Kisała, P.: Inverse problem of determining periodic surface profile oscillation defects of steel materials with a fiber bragg grating sensor. Appl. Opt. **55**(6), 1412–1420 (2016). https://opg.optica.org/ao/abstract.cfm?URI=ao-55-6-1412
5. Voulodimos, A., Doulamis, N., Bebis, G., Stathaki, T.: Recent developments in deep learning for engineering applications. Computational Intell. Neurosc. (2018)
6. Pasupa, K., Sunhem, W.: A comparison between shallow and deep architecture classifiers on small dataset. In: 2016 8th International Conference on Information Technology and Electrical Engineering (ICITEE), pp. 1–6 (2016)
7. Pham, C.C., Jeon, J.W.: Robust object proposals re-ranking for object detection in autonomous driving using convolutional neural networks. Signal Proces. Image Commun. **53**, 110–122, (2017). https://www.sciencedirect.com/science/article/pii/S0923596517300231
8. Li, S., Deng, M., Lee, J., Sinha, A., Barbastathis, G.: Imaging through glass diffusers using densely connected convolutional networks. Optica, 5(7), 803–813 (2018). https://opg.optica.org/optica/abstract.cfm?URI=optica-5-7-803
9. Aisawa, S., Noguchi, K., Matsumoto, T.: Remote image classification through multimode optical fiber using a neural network. Opt. Lett. **16**(9), 645–647 (1991). https://opg.optica.org/ol/abstract.cfm?URI=ol-16-9-645
10. Lohani, S., Knutson, E.M., O'Donnell, M., Huver, S.D., Glasser, R.T.: On the use of deep neural networks in optical communications. Appl. Opt. **57**(15), 4180–4190 (2018). https://opg.optica.org/ao/abstract.cfm?URI=ao-57-15-4180
11. Rivenson, Y., et al.: Deep learning microscopy. Optica **4**(11), 1437–1443 (2017). https://opg.optica.org/optica/abstract.cfm?URI=optica-4-11-1437
12. Nehme, E., Weiss, L.E., Michaeli, T., Shechtman, Y.: Deep-storm: super-resolution single-molecule microscopy by deep learning. Optica **5**(4), 458–464 (2018). https://opg.optica.org/optica/abstract.cfm?URI=optica-5-4-458
13. Corsi, A., Chang, J.H., Wang, R., Wang, L., Rusch, L.A., LaRochelle, S.: Highly elliptical core fiber with stress-induced birefringence for mode multiplexing. Opt. Lett. **45**(10), 2822–2825 (2020). https://opg.optica.org/ol/abstract.cfm?URI=ol-45-10-2822
14. Jakkula, V.: Tutorial on support vector machine (svm), School of EECS, vol. 37(2.5), p. 3. Washington State University (2006)
15. Sun, S., Huang, R.: An adaptive k-nearest neighbor algorithm. In: 2010 Seventh International Conference on Fuzzy Systems and Knowledge Discovery, vol. 1, pp. 91–94 IEEE (2010)
16. Nir Friedman, M.G., Geiger, D.: Bayesian network classifiers. Mach. Learn. **29**, 131–163 (1997)
17. Leo, B.: Random forests. Mach. Learn. **45**, 5–32 (2001)
18. Sokolova, M., Lapalme, G.: A systematic analysis of performance measures for classification tasks. Information Process. Manag. **45**(4), 427–437 (2009)
19. Wong, T.-T., Yeh, P.-Y.: Reliable accuracy estimates from k-fold cross validation. IEEE Trans. Knowl. Data Eng. **32**(8), 1586–1594 (2019)

Graph-Based Semi-supervised Learning Using Riemannian Geometry Distance for Motor Imagery Classification

Eric Smrkovsky[ID] and Hubert Cecotti[✉][ID]

Department of Computer Science, California State University, Fresno, CA, USA
hcecotti@csufresno.edu

Abstract. A great challenge for brain-computer interface (BCI) systems is their deployment in clinical settings or at home, where a BCI system can be used with limited calibration sessions. BCI should be ideally self-trained and take advantage of unlabeled data. When performing a task, the EEG signals change over time, hence the recorded signals have non-stationary properties. It is necessary to provide machine-learning approaches that can deal with self-training and/or use semi-supervised learning methods for signal classification. A key problem in graph-based semi-supervised learning is determining the characteristics of the affinity matrix that defines the relationships between examples, including the size of the neighborhood of each example. In this paper, we propose two approaches for building the affinity matrix using the distance between examples and the number of neighbors, with a limited number of hyper-parameters, making it easy to reuse. We also compare the Euclidean distance and Riemannian geometry distances to construct the affinity matrix. We assess the classification performance with motor imagery data with two classes from a publicly available dataset of 14 participants. The results show the interest of the proposed semi-supervised approaches with the use of distances to define the neighborhood using Riemannian geometry-based distances with an average accuracy of 73.75%.

Keywords: Semi-supervised learning · Brain-Computer Interface

1 Introduction

Electroencephalography (EEG) based brain-computer interfaces (BCIs) that are spontaneous in nature typically do not require external stimulation on the user. One example of this spontaneous BCI approach uses a process known as motor imagery (MI), where the user imagines a specific controlled activity, such as moving a limb [8–10]. When this movement is imagined, the BCI can collect information on brain activity non-invasively by using EEG signal acquisition through sensors applied to the user's scalp [7]. These signals correspond to the brain activity that would occur when the user physically performs the controlled movement.

This study was supported by the NIH-R15 NS118581 project.

Motor imagery tasks have been widely used in non-invasive EEG-based BCI systems, which would give people with severe disabilities the ability to communicate with their surroundings through a computer or prosthetic device [4].

Typical EEG signals are viewed as a time series that are non-stationary, considering that the signal's source and the signal's statistical characteristics change over time [5]. These changes in the signal occur for various reasons, over time and across sessions. Examples of these effects include when a person sneezes, a person is startled, or even when a person has a seizure [1]. In addition, as the user gets more comfortable with motor imagery, the task to perform, then the characteristics of the brain-evoked responses change accordingly. For all these reasons, the system must adapt over time. The MI EEG signal classification algorithms must be able to process and evaluate the signal data while there is noise from abnormal states present in the data.

An important area of BCI research is determining machine learning methods that can accurately classify the signal data collected when running tests on BCI systems regardless of the noise. Graph-based semi-supervised learning (GSSL) uses labeled and unlabeled data to construct a similarity graph. It can then use different methods of label inference to propagate label information to the unlabeled nodes within the graph, thus classifying the data [2,11]. Certain assumptions must hold for SSL to work, including the semi-supervised smoothness assumption, the cluster assumption, the manifold assumption, and the decision boundary that separates the classes must lie in a low-density region on the similarity graph [3]. An example of applying GSSL to a toy dataset with a decision boundary that meets these assumptions is shown in Fig. 1 and 2 with an accuracy of 100% and 98.995 respectively.

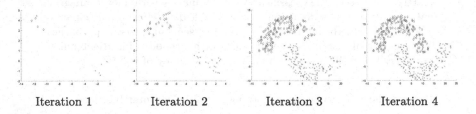

| Iteration 1 | Iteration 2 | Iteration 3 | Iteration 4 |

Fig. 1. Toy example with the double moon dataset using GSSL: Neighbors Euclidean

The performance of GSSL algorithms relates to the different hyper-parameters given to the algorithm. These inputs determine how the labeled and unlabeled data is used within the algorithm, such as the percentage of training data, how the similarity between two examples is defined, and the distance used to create the similarity graph. The toy example shows this well as Fig. 1 uses more iterations of the main process producing a higher accuracy while Fig. 2 uses less iterations but accuracy is effected.

In this study, we compare three different distance calculation methods used to construct the affinity matrix W that is used in the GSSL algorithms. The

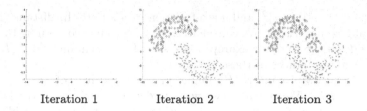

Iteration 1   Iteration 2   Iteration 3

Fig. 2. Toy example with the double moon dataset using GSSL: Distances Euclidean

typical standard distance often used when constructing a similarity graph in a linear vector space is Euclidean distance [6]. We compare and analyze the increase in accuracy that occurs when introducing Riemannian distance to the classification algorithm. The second focus is to compare two different ways to compute the affinity matrix used to make inferences during the label propagation step of the GSSL algorithm. We will compare propagating from labeled data to unlabeled data using two approaches based on how the affinity matrix is created, i.e., how the neighborhood of an example is defined: in relation to the number of neighbors or the distance between the example and its neighbors.

The contributions of this paper are 1) two SSL approaches with a limited number of hyper-parameters, with an evaluation across different splits for training and testing, 2) using the split that provides the highest accuracy, we analyze the number of iterations and accuracy of each GSSL algorithm at its peak performance. The remainder of the paper is organized as follows. The semi-supervised methods and the datasets are described in Sect. 2. The evaluation of results are given in Sect. 3. Finally, the impact of the results are discussed in Sect. 4.

2   Methods

2.1   Semi-supervised Methods

The problem includes labeled data and unlabeled data. Let X be the matrix of size $n_{total} \times n_{features}$, with n_{total} examples, each having $n_{features}$ data points. Let Y be a vector of size n_{total} containing the different labels for each example in a two-class problem. Each label has a value of 1 and -1, for classes 1 and 2, respectively. We split the data into two parts corresponding to labeled and unlabeled examples: X_l and X_u of size n_{total}^l and n_{total}^u, respectively ($n_{total}^l + n_{total}^u = n_{total}$). The label of the examples Y are split as Y_l and Y_u where $Y_l(i) \in \{-1; 1\}$, $1 \le i \le n_{total}^l$ and $Y_u(i) = 0$, with $1 \le i \le n_{total}^u$, where 0 represents the unlabeled class.

Let $G = (V, E)$ be the undirected graph representing all the distances between all the n_{total} examples, with V being the set of vertices $V = \{v_1, \ldots, v_{n_{total}}\}$ corresponding to the examples (each vertex v_i in the graph represents a data point x_i), and E the set of edges represented by an adjacency matrix:

$$E(i, j) = d(x(i), x(j)) \tag{1}$$

where $(i, j) \in \{1 \ldots n_{total}\}^2$, and d is a function to compute the distance between the examples $x(i)$ and $x(j)$. We consider (E_s, I_s) the couple containing the matrix where the distances to other examples are sorted in ascending order (E_s), with the corresponding indices of these examples (I_s).

We define the affinity matrix W, being symmetric positive of size $n_{total} \times n_{total}$ $(W(i, j) = W(j, i))$. We consider two ways to define the values in W: 1) by considering the number of neighbors for a given example and 2) by considering the maximum distance embedding neighbors. For the first case, it corresponds to the creation of the ϵ-neighborhood graph where we connect all examples whose pairwise distances are smaller than ϵ. As the distances between all connected points are about the same scale, weighting the edges would not incorporate additional information about the relationships between examples to the graph. The ϵ-neighborhood graph can be therefore considered as an unweighted graph. For the second case, it corresponds to the creation of the k-nearest neighbor graphs, we connect vertex v_i with vertex v_j if v_j is among the k-nearest neighbors of v_i. With this definition, it leads to a directed graph because the neighborhood relationship is not symmetric. It is possible to transform the graph as undirected by ignoring the directions of the edges (i.e., we connect v_i and v_j with an undirected edge if v_i belongs to the k-nearest neighborhood of v_j or if v_j is part of the k-nearest neighborhood of v_i). The second possibility for obtaining an undirected graph is to connect vertices v_i and v_j only if v_i is part of the k-nearest neighbors of v_j and likewise v_j is part of the k-nearest neighbors of v_i. Such a graph is the mutual k-nearest neighbor graph.

In both approaches, the problem is to determine the value ϵ or k. If the value is too small, many examples will not be connected and there will be many islands. If the value is too large, too many examples will be connected together, propagating labels to wrong examples, such as through unwanted bridges due to outliers. In order to avoid this problem, we repeat the label propagation procedure by increasing the values of ϵ or k until all the examples in the graph are labelled.

The affinity matrix based on the number of neighbors is defined by:

$$W(i, j) = \begin{cases} 1 \text{ if } j \in \{I_s(i, 2), \ldots, I_s(i, N_s - 1)\} \\ 0 \text{ otherwise} \end{cases} \tag{2}$$

where $N_s - 1$ is the size of the neighborhood, $2 \leq N_s \leq N_s^{max}$.

The affinity matrix based on the distances is defined by:

$$W(i, j) \quad = \quad \begin{cases} 1 \text{ if } E(i, j) \leq V_s \\ 0 \text{ otherwise} \end{cases} \tag{3}$$

$$\min(E(i, j)) \leq V_s \leq \max(E(i, j)) \tag{4}$$

where V_s is the maximum distance between the example i and its neighbors in the graph.

The main algorithm is presented in Algorithm 1. It runs label propagation with the given state of the affinity matrix W, with the affinity matrix W depending on the number of neighbors that are selected for all the examples (each example has the same number of neighbors), or the distance from an example to its neighbors (the number of neighbors depends on the example).

Algorithm 1. GSSL: Main Algorithm

Input: Data (X, Y) partially-labelled
Output: Data (X, Y) fully-labelled
    ▷ Initialization
1: $k \leftarrow 1$
2: $k_{total} \leftarrow 1$
3: allLabelled $\leftarrow FALSE$
4: $n_u \leftarrow 0$
5: **while** $k < n + 1$ & ¬allLabelled **do**
6:     $W = \text{SetAffinity}(X, k)$
7:     $[Y_{test}, Y_{label}, t] = LabelPropagation(W, Y)$
8:     $n_u(k) = \sum_{i=1}^{N} \begin{cases} 1 \text{ if } (Y_{label} == 0) \\ 0 \text{ otherwise} \end{cases}$
9:     **if** $n_u(k) == 0$ **then**
10:         allLabelled $\leftarrow TRUE$
11:     **end if**
12:     $k_{total} \leftarrow k_{total} + t$
13:     $k \leftarrow k + 1$
14: **end while**
15: **return** $Y_{test}, Y_{label}, k_{total}$

Algorithm 2. Label Propagation

1: **function** LABELPROP(W, Y)
2:     $t_{max} \leftarrow 150$
3:     $\epsilon \leftarrow 1 \times 10^{-4}$ ▷ Handles Convergence
4:     N: size of W
5:     $t \leftarrow 1$
6:     $D_{ii} = \sum_{j=1}^{N} W_{ij}$
7:     **while** $(t < t_{max})$ & $(\Delta Y_t > \epsilon)$ **do**
8:         $Y^{t+1} \leftarrow D_{ii}^{-1} \times W \times Y^t$
9:         $Y_l^{t+1} \leftarrow Y_{all}$
10:         $\Delta Y_t \leftarrow \sum_{j=1}^{N}(Y^t - Y_l^{t+1})^2$
11:         $t \leftarrow t + 1$
12:     **end while**
13:     label Y_{label} by the sign of Y
14:     **return** Y, Y_{label}, t
15: **end function**

2.2 Distances

Each trial is defined by a segment of signals of length N_t time points across N_c channels. We use the covariance matrix of the signal of each trial as input features. The structure of the covariance matrices is symmetric and positive definite (SPD), easily manipulated by Riemannian geometry and working in the differentiable Riemannian manifold M. To calculate the minimum length curve that connects two points A and B on the Riemannian manifold we define the geodesic distance to be:

$$d_{Riem} = \left[\sum_{i=1}^{N_c} log^2 \lambda_i \right]^{1/2} \tag{5}$$

where λ_i, $1 \leq i \leq N_c$ are the real eigenvalues of W stored as a matrix whose columns are the generalized left eigenvectors that satisfy $W^T A = \lambda W^T B$. λ contains the generalized eigenvalues of the pair, (A, B), along the main diagonal.

We define the standard Euclidean metric to be used as our baseline below:

$$d_{L2} = \left[\sum_{i=1}^{N_c} \sum_{i=1}^{N_t} (A(i,j) - B(i,j))^2 \right]^{1/2} \tag{6}$$

We then apply geodesic filtering on X_l and X_u, concatenating to create X_{all} to be used as input to both distance calculation methods. It is also necessary to concatenate Y_l and Y_u to create Y_{all} to be used within the main algorithm.

2.3   Performance Evaluation

The GSSL is tested with the four following cases: 1) the Riemannian distance with affinity matrix based on k-nearest neighbors in the graph; 2) Riemannian distance with affinity matrix based on distances; 3) Euclidean distance with affinity matrix based on k-nearest neighbors; 4) Euclidean distance with affinity matrix based on distances. We test the GSSL algorithms across methods on ten different percentage splits for the labeled/unlabelled examples to find the best split to evaluate. The percentage splits that we consider are: 90/10, 80/20, 70/30, 60/40, 50/50, 40/60, 30/70, 20/80, and 10/90. 10/90 means that 10% is used with labeled examples and the remaining 90% is used for the test with unlabeled examples. The initialization steps for these GSSL algorithms are the same across methods. First, the loaded dataset (X, Y) has a size of N labeled data examples to be represented as nodes in the similarity graph. After the initialization steps, the GSSL Main Algorithm computes the distances for the adjacency matrix used to produce the similarity graph G with indexes G_{ix} via the specified distance metric d. This similarity graph is sorted in ascending order and used as input for the specified label propagation method.

2.4   Database

The dataset used for testing contains EEG signals from 14 participants using 15 sensors including C3, Cz, and C4, with a sampling rate 512 Hz. The time segment is $3s$, after $3s$ post-trial onset. The participants were asked to perform a kinesthetic MI task of the right hand and the feet when asked. The training database used has 5 runs of 20 trials. The testing database has 3 runs of 20 trials. These databases lead to a total of 160 examples. Therefore, we have $N_c = 17$ and $N_t = 3 \cdot f_s = 750$. We bandpass the signal in the following four frequency bands: 8-12, 12-16, 16-20, 20-24 Hz. This dataset can be found on the BNCI Horizon 2020 project website [12].

3   Results

The accuracy and iterations across the different data splits between labeled and unlabeled examples for each GSSL algorithm are presented in Figs. 3 and 4 in the first row and second row, respectively. The envelope in the figures is based on the standard error. We observe a steady accuracy from 90/10 to 20/80, and then the performance drops substantially when only 10% of the data is used with labeled examples (16 examples for training, 144 examples for the test). It drops from 72.32% with 90% with labeled examples to 64.08% with 10% of labeled examples for training, with the GSSL algorithm using distances and the Riemannian distance.

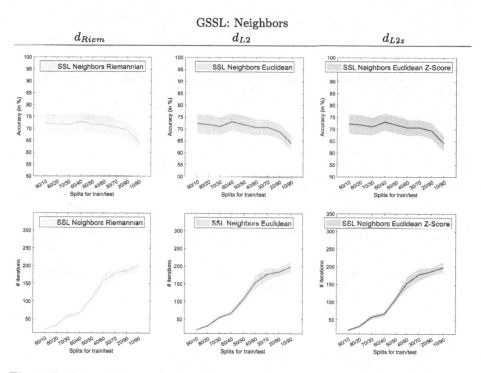

Fig. 3. Evolution of the accuracy and the number of iterations in relation to the ratio between labeled and unlabeled examples.

Focusing now on the 50/50 split, we give the detailed results for each GSSL algorithm in Table 1. showing the accuracy and number of iterations that directly denotes the complexity of the algorithm. The average accuracy using GSSL based on the number of neighbors is 71.88 ± 13.62 for the three distances, suggesting that the neighborhoods grow the same way for each distance. However, the average accuracy using GSSL based on the distances is 73.75 ± 13.96, 72.77 ± 14.21, and 72.86 ± 13.4 for the Riemannian distance, the Euclidean distance, and the Euclidean distance after the data being z-score normalized. The best average accuracy is obtained with GSSL based on the distances, suggesting that the neighborhood of each example should grow in an adaptive manner individually, based on the distance to the examples, and not by increasing the size of all neighborhoods the same way.

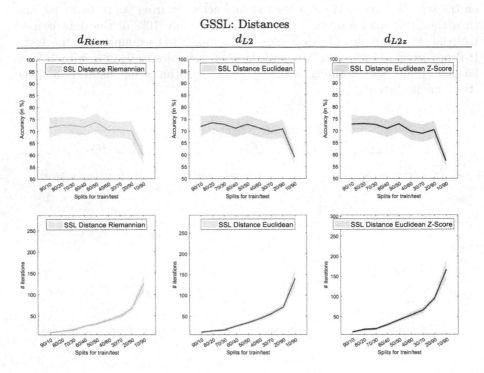

Fig. 4. Evolution of the accuracy and the number of iterations in relation to the ratio between labeled and unlabeled examples.

Table 1. Accuracy and the number of iterations for the GSSL algorithm with the 50/50 data split.

	GSSL: Neighbors						GSSL: Distances					
	Riemannian		Euclidean		Euclidean+Z		Riemannian		Euclidean		Euclidean+Z	
Sub.	Acc.	Ite.	Acc.	Ite.	Acc.	Ite.	Acc.	Ite.	Acc.	Ite.	Acc.	Ite.
1	62.5	181	62.5	181	62.5	181	62.5	20	62.50	20	62.5	31
2	71.25	64	71.25	64	71.25	64	71.25	27	63.75	36	67.5	55
3	95	46	95	46	95	73	100	41	100	41	100	44
4	90	138	90	138	90	138	88.75	35	85	45	82.5	48
5	61.25	114	61.25	114	61.25	114	70	26	70	25	71.25	25
6	71.25	83	71.25	83	71.25	83	71.25	43	73.75	45	73.75	55
7	82.5	176	82.5	157	82.5	157	82.5	33	81.25	43	80	59
8	85	128	85	128	85	132	91.25	50	87.5	44	87.50	73.00
9	85	92	85	92	85	92	86.25	45	87.5	45	85	63.00
10	58.75	81	58.75	81	58.75	81	58.75	13	58.75	13	58.75	13
11	65	124	65	124	65	124	67.5	32	72.5	39	75	37
12	71.25	118	71.25	118	71.25	118	71.25	43	71.25	44	68.75	48
13	56.25	89	56.25	89	56.25	89	55	13	55	13	55	14
14	51.25	76	51.25	76	51.25	76	56.25	19	50	29	52.5	29
Mean	71.88	107.86	71.88	106.5	71.88	108.71	73.75	31.43	72.77	34.43	72.86	42.43
SD	13.62	39.63	13.62	37.38	13.62	34.8	13.96	12.14	14.21	12.1	13.4	18.25

4 Discussion and Conclusion

Brain-Computer Interface should be able to adapt over time and acquire new knowledge based on upcoming as well as past test trials without prior knowledge of the labels in order to be deployed outside of the laboratory. Knowledge is power, and unlabeled data, e.g., test data, can provide key insights for building a classifier with the current data distribution.

In this paper, we have proposed a semi-supervised learning approach that considers graphs with an adjacency matrix based on Riemannian geometry. The affinity matrix changes across multiple iterations, with the neighborhood of each example changing based on 1) the number of neighbors or 2) the distance to the examples in the neighborhood. This approach allows us to not need to make prior choices in relation to the affinity matrix. Label propagation is applied multiple times until convergence, with the neighborhood of each iteration increasing. Such an approach reduces the number of manually chosen input parameters, hence the approach can be applied in different applications that have an appropriate distance.

Many algorithms require to set multiple parameters through cross-validation for obtaining a good performance [13]. With the proposed approach, we limit the number of parameters to be chosen through cross-validation, which would require a substantial amount of labeled data before the method can be used. In the present case, we have considered the test data as unlabeled examples that are present in the semi-supervised algorithms. Therefore, the different trials are not processed one by one, but they are analyzed in batch mode; which is not appropriate for some types of online BCI. Future works include the evaluation of the approach with other BCI paradigms.

We have presented two graph-based semi-supervised learning approaches that require a limited number of hyper-parameters, i.e., maximum number of iterations, for the classification of motor imagery data with EEG signals. We have highlighted the change in performance occurring in relation to the number of labeled training examples being used.

References

1. Boashash, B., Azemi, G., Ali Khan, N.: Principles of time-frequency feature extraction for change detection in non-stationary signals: Applications to newborn eeg abnormality detection. Pattern Recogn. **48**(3), 616–627 (2015)
2. Cecotti, H.: Active graph based semi-supervised learning using image matching: Application to handwritten digit recognition. Pattern Recogn. Lett. **73**, 76–82 (2016)
3. Chapelle, O., Schölkopf, B., Zien, A. (eds.): Adaptive computation and machine learning series. MIT Press, Cambridge, Massachusetts (2010)
4. Cincotti, F., et al.: Non-invasive brain-computer interface system: Towards its application as assistive technology. Brain Res. Bull. **75**(6), 796–803 (2008)
5. Klonowski, W.: From conformons to human brains: an informal overview of nonlinear dynamics and its applications in biomedicine. Nonlinear Biomed. Phys. **1**(1), 5–5 (2007)
6. Li, Y., Wong, K.M., deBruin, H.: Eeg signal classification based on a riemannian distance measure. In: 2009 IEEE Toronto International Conference Science and Technology for Humanity (TIC-STH), pp. 268–273 (2009). https://doi.org/10.1109/TIC-STH.2009.5444491
7. Nicolas-Alonso, L.F., Gomez-Gil, J.: Brain computer interfaces, a review. Sensors **12**(2), 1211–1279 (2012). https://doi.org/10.3390/s120201211, https://www.mdpi.com/1424-8220/12/2/1211
8. Padfield, N., Zabalza, J., Zhao, H., Masero, V., Ren, J.: Eeg-based brain-computer interfaces using motor-imagery: Techniques and challenges. Sensors **19**, 1423 (2019). https://doi.org/10.3390/s19061423
9. Raza, H., Cecotti, H., Li, Y., Prasad, G.: Adaptive learning with covariate shift-detection for motor imagery based brain-computer interface. Soft. Comput. **20**(8), 3085–3096 (2016)
10. Raza, H., Rathee, D., Zhou, S.M., Cecotti, H., Prasad, G.: Covariate shift estimation based adaptive ensemble learning for handling non-stationarity in motor imagery related EEG-based brain-computer interface. Neurocomputing (2018)
11. Song, Z., Yang, X., Xu, Z., King, I.: Graph-based semi-supervised learning: A comprehensive review. IEEE Trans. Neural Netw. Learn. Syst., 1–21 (2022)
12. Steyrl, D.: Two class motor imagery (002–2014) (2020). http://bnci-horizon-2020.eu/database/data-sets
13. Varoquaux, G., Raamana, P.R., Engemann, D.A., Hoyos-Idrobo, A., Schwartz, Y., Thirion, B.: Assessing and tuning brain decoders: Cross-validation, caveats, and guidelines. NeuroImage (Orlando, Fla.) **145**(Pt B), 166–179 (2017)

Correction to: Machine Learning Models Applied in Sign Language Recognition

Esteban Gustavo Novillo Quinde , Juan Pablo Saldaña Torres ,
Michael Andres Alvarez Valdez , John Santiago Llivicota León ,
and Remigio Ismael Hurtado Ortiz

Correction to:
Chapter "Machine Learning Models Applied in Sign
Language Recognition" in: A. Y. Rodríguez-González et al.
(Eds.): *Pattern Recognition*, LNCS 13902,
https://doi.org/10.1007/978-3-031-33783-3_25

In the originally published chapter "Machine Learning Models Applied in Sign Language Recognition" the last names order of all authors were reversed erroneously. This has been corrected.

The updated original version of this chapter can be found at
https://doi.org/10.1007/978-3-031-33783-3_25

Author Index

A. Y. Rodríguez-González et al. (Eds.): MCPR 2023, LNCS 13902, pp. 327–328, 2023.
https://doi.org/10.1007/978-3-031-33783-3

Printed in the United States
by Baker & Taylor Publisher Services